MILITARY CRYPTANALYTICS
PART I — VOLUME 1

by
William F. Friedman
and
Lambros D. Callimahos

ISBN: 0-89412-073-5

AEGEAN PARK PRESS
P.O. Box 2837
Laguna Hills, California 92654
(714) 586-8811

Manufactured in the United States of America

Foreword

"MILITARY CRYPTANALTICS, PART I", was originally published in 1956 as a classified text by the U.S. Government. Recently declassified and expanded with computer programs written by Wayne G. Barker, we are proud to add this book to our Cryptographic Series. The book is probably the most comprehensive and one of the best books ever written concerning the introductory phase of military cryptanalytics.

—AEGEAN PARK PRESS

The Golden Guess
Is Morning-Star to the full round of Truth.
—Tennyson.

Preface

This text represents an extensive expansion and revision, both in scope and content, of the earlier work entitled "Military Cryptanalysis, Part I" by William F. Friedman. This expansion and revision was necessitated by the considerable advancement made in the art since the publication of the previous text.

I wish to express grateful acknowledgment for Mr. Friedman's generous assistance and invaluable collaboration in the preparation of this volume. I also extend particular appreciation to my colleague Robert E. Cefail for his numerous valuable comments and assistance in writing the new material which is contained herein.

—L.D.C.

TABLE OF CONTENTS

Military Cryptanalytics, Part I

Volume 1

Chapter	Page
I. Introductory remarks	**1**

1. Scope of this text. 2. Mental equipment necessary for cryptanalytic work. 3. Validity of results of cryptanalysis.

II. Basic cryptologic considerations	**9**

4. Cryptology, communication intelligence, and communication security. 5. Secret communication. 6. Plain text and encrypted text. 7. Cryptography, encrypting, and decrypting. 8. Codes, ciphers, and enciphered code. 9. General system, specific key, and cryptosystem. 10. Cryptanalytics and cryptanalysis. 11. Transposition and substitution. 12. Nature of alphabets. 13. Types of alphabets.

III. Fundamental cryptanalytic operations	**17**

14. The role of cryptanalysis in communication intelligence operations. 15. The four basic operations in cryptanalysis. 16. The determination of the language employed. 17. The determination of the general system. 18. The reconstruction of the specific key. 19. The reconstruction of the plain text. 20. The utilization of traffic intercepts.

IV. Frequency distributions and their fundamental uses	**25**

21. The simple or uniliteral frequency distribution. 22. Important features of the normal uniliteral frequency distribution. 23. Constancy of the standard or normal uniliteral frequency distribution. 24. The three facts which can be determined from a study of the uniliteral frequency distribution for a cryptogram. 25. Determining the class to which a cipher belongs. 26. Determining whether a substitution cipher is monoalphabetic or nonmonoalphabetic. 27. The ϕ (phi) test for determining monoalphabeticity. 28. Determining whether a cipher alphabet is standard or mixed.

V. Uniliteral substitution with standard cipher alphabets	**45**

29. Types of standard cipher alphabets. 30. Procedure in encipherment and decipherment by means of uniliteral substitution. 31. Principles of solution by contruction and analysis of the unilitieral frequency distribution. 32. Theoretical example of solution. 33. Practical example of solution by the frequency method. 34. Solution by completing the plain-component sequence. 35. Special remarks on the method of solution by completing the plain-component sequence. 36. Value of mechanical solution as a short cut. 37. Basic reason for the low degree of cryptosecurity afforded by monoalphabetic cryptograms involving standard cipher alphabets.

VI. Uniliteral substitution with mixed cipher alphabets	**61**

38. Literal keys and numerical keys. 39. Types of mixed cipher alphabets. 40. Additional remarks on cipher alphabets. 41. Preliminary steps in the analysis of a monoalphabetic, mixed-alphabet cryptogram. 42. Preparation of the work sheet. 43. Triliteral frequency distributions. 44. Classifying the cipher letters into vowels and consonants. 45. Further anaysis of the letters representing vowels and consonants. 46. Substituting deduced values in the cryptogram. 47. Completing the solution. 48. General remarks on the foregoing solution. 49. The "probable-word" method; its value and applicability. 50. Solution of additional cryptograms produced by the same components. 51. Recovery of key words.

VII. Multiliteral substitution with single-equivalent cipher alphabets **91**

52. General types of multiliteral cipher alphabets. 53. The Baconian and Tritheminan ciphers. 54. Analysis of multiliteral, monoalphabetic substitution ciphers. 55. Historically interesting examples. 56. The international (Baudot) teleprinter code.

VIII. Multiliteral substitution with variants **103**

57. Purpose of providing variants in monoalphabetic substitution. 58. Simple types of cipher alphabets with variants. 60. Analysis of simple examples. 61. Analysis of more complicated examples. 62. Analysis involving the use of isologs. 63. Further remarks on variant systems.

IX. Polygraphic substitution systems **129**

64. General remarks on polygraphic substitution. 65. Polygraphic substitution methods employing large tables. 66. Polygraphic substitution methods employing small matrices. 67. Methods for recognizing polygraphic substitution. 68. General procedure in the identification and analysis of polygraphic substitution ciphers. 69. Analysis of four-square matrix systems. 70. Analysis of two-square matrix systems. 71. Analysis of Playfair cipher systems. 72. Analysis of polygraphic systems involving large tables. 73. Further remarks on polygraphic substitution systems.

X. Cryptosystems employing irregular-length ciphertext units **189**

74. Preliminary observations. 75. Monome-dinome alphabets and other alphabets with irregular-length ciphertext units. 76. General remarks on analysis. 77. Analysis of simple examples. 78. Analysis of more complicated examples. 79. Further remarks on cryptosystems employing irregular-length ciphertext units.

XI. Miscellaneous monoalphabetic systems; concluding remarks **209**

80. Cryptosystems employing syllabary squares and code charts. 81. Cryptosystems employing characters other than letters or figures. 82. Special remarks concerning the initial classficiation of cryptograms. 83. Disguised secret communications. 84. Concluding remarks.

CHAPTER I

INTRODUCTORY REMARKS

                                                            Paragraph

Scope of this text_____ 1

Mental equipment necessary for cryptanalytic work_____ 2

Validity of results of cryptanalysis_____ 3

1. **Scope of this text.**—*a.* This text constitutes the first of a series of six basic texts [1] on the science of *cryptanalytics* and the art of *cryptanalysis*. Although most of the information contained herein is applicable to cryptograms of various types and sources, special emphasis will be laid upon the principles and methods of solving military [2] cryptograms. Except for an introductory discussion of fundamental principles underlying the science of cryptanalytics, this first text in the series will deal solely with the principles and methods for the analysis of *monoalphabetic substitution ciphers*. Even with this limitation it will be possible to discuss only a few of the many variations of this type that are met in practice; but with a firm grasp upon the general principles few difficulties should be experienced with any modifications or variations that may be encountered.

b. This and the succeeding texts will deal with, among others, some basic types of cryptosystems not because they may be encountered unmodified in military operations but because their study is essential to an understanding of the principles underlying the solution of the modern, very much more complex types of codes, ciphers, and certain encrypted transmission systems that are likely to be employed by the larger governments of today in the conduct of their military affairs in time of war.

c. It is presupposed that the student has no prior background in the field of cryptology; therefore cryptography is presented concurrently with cryptanalysis. It is also presupposed that the reader has had but a minimal mathematical background; a student who has had elementary algebra should encounter no difficulty with the mathematical treatment in the body of the text, and he will be progressively guided into augmenting his mathematical background to fit the needs of cryptanalytics. Basic terminology and preliminary cryptologic considerations are treated in Chapter II; other terms are usually defined upon their first occurrence, or they may be found in the Glossary (Appendix 1). Footnotes, besides amplifying general information, include occasional treatment of mathematical principles that may be beyond a beginner in the field; the student therefore should not spend too much time trying to assimilate all the information contained therein.

d. The cryptograms presented in the examples embrace messages from hypothetical air, ground, and naval traffic; thus, the student will have the opportunity to familiarize himself with the language and phraseology of all three military Services.

---

[1] Each text has its accompanying course in cryptanalysis, so that the student may test his learning and develop his skill in the solution of the types of cryptograms treated in the respective texts. The problems which pertain to this text constitute Appendix 9.

[2] The word "military" is here used in its broadest sense. In this connection see subpar. *d*, below.

2. **Mental equipment necessary for cryptanalytic work.**—*a.* Captain Parker Hitt, in the first United States Army manual[3] dealing with cryptology, opens the first chapter of his valuable treatise with the following sentence:

"Success in dealing with unknown ciphers is measured by these four things in the order named: perseverance, careful methods of analysis, intuition, luck."

These words are as true today as they were then. There is no royal road to success in the solution of cryptograms. Hitt goes on to say:

"Cipher work will have little permanent attraction for one who expects results at once, without labor, for there is a vast amount of purely routine labor in the preparation of frequency tables, the rearrangement of ciphers for examination, and the trial and fitting of letter to letter before the message begins to appear."

The author deems it advisable to add that the kind of work involved in solving cryptograms is not at all similar to that involved in solving crossword puzzles, for example. The wide vogue the latter have had and continue to have is due to the appeal they make to the quite common interest in mysteries of one sort or another; but in solving a crossword puzzle there is usually no necessity for performing any preliminary labor, and palpable results become evident after the first minute or two of attention. This successful start spurs the crossword "addict" on to complete the solution, which rarely requires more than an hour's time. Furthermore, crossword puzzles are all alike in basic principles and once understood, there is no more to learn. Skill comes largely from the embellishment of one's vocabulary, though, to be sure, constant practice and exercise of the imagination contribute to the ease and rapidity with which solutions are generally reached. In solving cryptograms, however, many principles must be learned, for there are many different systems of varying degrees of complexity. Even some of the simpler varieties require the preparation of tabulations of one sort or another which many people find irksome; moreover, it is only toward the very close of the solution that results in the form of intelligible text become evident. Often, indeed, the student will not even know whether he is on the right track until he has performed a large amount of preliminary "spade work" involving many hours of labor. Thus, without at least a willingness to pursue a fair amount of theoretical study, and a *more than average amount of patience and perseverance*, little skill and experience can be gained in the rather difficult art of cryptanalysis. General Givierge, the author of an excellent treatise on cryptanalysis, remarks in this connection:[4]

"The cryptanalyst's attitude must be that of William the Silent: 'No need to hope in order to undertake, nor to succeed in order to persevere'."

b. As regards Hitt's reference to careful methods of analysis, before one can be said to be a cryptanalyst worthy of the name it is necessary that one should have, firstly, a sound knowledge of the basic principles of cryptanalysis, and secondly, a long, varied, and active *practical* experience in the successful application of those principles. It is not sufficient to have read treatises on this subject. One month's actual practice in solution is worth a whole year's mere reading of theoretical principles. An exceedingly important element of success in solving the more intricate cryptosystems is the possession of the rather unusual mental faculty designated in general terms as the power of inductive and deductive reasoning. Probably this is an inherited rather than an acquired faculty; the best sort of training for its emergence, if latent in the individual, and for its development is the study of the natural sciences, such as chemistry,

---

[3] Hitt, Capt. Parker, *Manual for the Solution of Military Ciphers.* Army Service Schools Press, Fort Leavenworth, Kansas, 1916. 2d Edition, 1918. (Both out of print.)

[4] Givierge, Général Marcel, *Cours de Cryptographie*, Paris, 1925, p. 301.

physics, biology, geology, and the like. Other sciences such as linguistics, archaeology, and philology are also excellent.

c. Aptitude in mathematics is quite important, more especially in the solution of ciphers and enciphered codes than in codebook reconstruction, which latter is purely and simply a linguistic problem. Although in the early days of the emergence of the science of cryptanalytics little thought was given to the applications of mathematics in this field, many branches of mathematics and, in particular, probability and statistics, have now found cryptologic applications. Those portions of mathematics and those mathematical methods which have cryptologic applications [5] are known collectively as *cryptomathematics.*

d. An active imagination, or perhaps what Hitt and other writers call *intuition,* is essential, but mere imagination uncontrolled by a judicious spirit will be more often a hindrance than a help. In practical cryptanalysis the imaginative or intuitive faculties must, in other words, be guided by good judgment, by practical experience, and by as thorough a knowledge of the general situation or extraneous circumstances that led to the sending of the cryptogram as is possible to obtain. In this respect the many cryptograms exchanged between correspondents whose identities and general affairs, commercial, social, or political, are known are far more readily solved [6] than are isolated cryptograms exchanged between unknown correspondents, dealing with unknown subjects. It is obvious that in the former case there are good data upon which the intuitive powers of the cryptanalyst can be brought to bear, whereas in the latter case no such data are available. Consequently, in the absence of such data, no matter how good the imagination and intuition of the cryptanalyst, these powers are of no particular service to him. Some writers, however, regard the intuitive spirit as valuable from still another viewpoint, as may be noted in the following: [7]

"Intuition, like a flash of lightning, lasts only for a second. It generally comes when one is tormented by a difficult decipherment and when one reviews in his mind the fruitless experiments already tried. Suddenly the light breaks through and one finds after a few minutes what previous days of labor were unable to reveal."

---

[5] It is quite important to stress at this point that in professional cryptologic work the *science* of cryptanalytics is subordinated to the *art* of cryptanalysis, just as in the world of music the technical virtuosity of a great violinist is adjuvant to the expression of music, that is, the virtuosity is a "tool" for the recovery of the complete musical "plain text" conceived by the composer. Since the practice of cryptanalysis *is* an art, mathematical approaches cannot always be expected to yield a solution in cryptology, because art can and must transcend the cold logic of scientific method. By way of example, an experienced Indian guide can usually find his way out of a dense forest more readily than a surveyor equipped with all the refined apparatus and techniques of his profession. Likewise, an experienced cryptanalyst can generally find his way through a cryptosystem more readily than a pure mathematician equipped merely with the techniques of his field no matter how abstruse or refined they may be. A cryptomathematician of repute once stated that "the only effect of [refined mathematical techniques] is frequently to discourage one so much that one does nothing at all and some unmathematical ignoramus then gets the problem out in some very unethical way. This is intensely irritating." See also in this connection the remarks made in subpar. 27*e* in reference to the validity of statistical tests in cryptanalysis.

[6] The application in practical, operational cryptanalysis of "probable words" or "cribs", i. e., plain text assumed or known to be present in a cryptogram, is developed in time of war into a refinement the extent and usefulness of which cannot be appreciated by the uninitiated. Even as great a thinker as Voltaire found the subject of cryptanalysis stretching his credulity to the point that he said:

"Those who boast that they can decipher a letter without knowing its subject matter, and without preliminary aid, are greater charlatans than those who would boast of understanding a language which they have never learned."—*Dictionnaire Philosophique,* under the article "Poste".

[7] Lange et Soudart, *Traité de Cryptographie,* Libraire Félix Alcan, Paris, 1925, p. 104.

This, too, is true, but unfortunately there is no way in which the intuition may be summoned at will, when it is most needed.[8] There are certain authors who regard as indispensable the possession of a somewhat rare, rather mysterious faculty that they designate by the word "flair", or by the expression "cipher brains". Even so excellent an authority as General Givierge,[9] in referring to this mental faculty, uses the following words:

"Over and above perseverance and this aptitude of mind which some authors consider a special gift, and which they call intuition, or even, in its highest manifestation, clairvoyance, cryptographic studies will continue more and more to demand the qualities of orderliness and memory."

Although the author believes a special aptitude for the work is essential to cryptanalytic success, he is sure there is nothing mysterious about the matter at all. Special aptitude is prerequisite to success in all fields of endeavor. There are, for example, thousands of physicists, hundreds of excellent ones, but only a handful of world-wide fame. Should it be said, then, that a physicist who has achieved very notable success in his field, has done so because he is the fortunate possessor of a *mysterious* faculty? That he is fortunate in possessing a special aptitude for his subject is granted, but that there is anything mysterious about it, partaking of the nature of clairvoyance (if, indeed, the latter is a *reality*) is not granted. While the ultimate nature of any mental process seems to be as complete a mystery today as it has ever been, the author would like to see the superficial veil of mystery removed from a subject that has been shrouded in mystery from even before the Middle Ages down to our own times. (The principal and readily understandable reason for this is that governments have always closely guarded

----

[8] The following extracts are of interest in this connection:

"The fact that the scientific investigator works 50 per cent of his time by non-rational means is, it seems, quite insufficiently recognized. There is without the least doubt an instinct for research, and often the most successful investigators of nature are quite unable to give an account of their reasons for doing such and such an experiment, or for placing side by side two apparently unrelated facts. Again, one of the most salient traits in the character of the successful scientific worker is the capacity for knowing that a point is proved when it would not appear to be proved to an outside intelligence functioning in a purely rational manner; thus the investigator feels that some proposition is true, and proceeds at once to the next set of experiments without waiting and wasting time in the elaboration of the formal proof of the point which heavier minds would need. Questionless such a scientific intuition may and does sometimes lead investigators astray, but it is quite certain that if they did not widely make use of it, they would not get a quarter as far as they do. Experiments confirm each other, and a false step is usually soon discovered. And not only by this partial replacement of reason by intuition does the work of science go on, but also to the born scientific worker—and emphatically they cannot be made—the structure of the method of research is as it were given, he cannot explain it to you, though he may be brought to agree *a posteriori* to a formal logical presentation of the way the method works".—Excerpt from Needham, Joseph, *The Sceptical Biologist*, London, 1929, p. 79.

"The essence of scientific method, quite simply, is to try to see how data arrange themselves into causal configurations. Scientific problems are solved by collecting data and by "thinking about them all the time." We need to look at strange things until, by the appearance of known configurations, they seem familiar, and to look at familiar things until we see novel configurations which make them appear strange. We must look at events until they become luminous. That is scientific method . . . Insight is the touchstone . . . The application of insight as the touchstone of method enables us to evaluate properly the role of imagination in scientific method. The scientific process is akin to the artistic process: it is a process of selecting out those elements of experience which fit together and recombining them in the mind. Much of this kind of research is simply a ceaseless mulling over, and even the physical scientist has considerable need of an armchair . . . Our view of scientific method as a struggle to obtain insight forces the admission that science is half art . . . Insight is the unknown quantity which has eluded students of scientific method".—Excerpts from an article entitled *Insight and Scientific Method*, by Willard Waller, in *The American Journal of Sociology*, Vol. XL, 1934.

[9] *Op cit.*, p. 302.

cryptographic secrets and anything so guarded soon becomes "mysterious".) He would, rather, have the student approach the subject as he might approach any other science that can stand on its own merits with other sciences, because cryptanalytics, like other sciences, has a practical importance in human affairs. It presents to the inquiring mind an interest in its own right as a branch of knowledge; it, too, holds forth many difficulties and disappointments, and these are all the more keenly felt when the nature of these difficulties is not understood by those unfamiliar with the special circumstances that very often are the real factors that led to success in other cases. Finally, just as in the other sciences wherein many men labor long and earnestly for the true satisfaction and pleasure that comes from work well done, so the mental pleasure that the successful cryptanalyst derives from his accomplishments is very often the only reward for much of the drudgery that he must do in his daily work. General Givierge's words in this connection are well worth quoting:[10]

"Some studies will last for years before bearing fruit. In the case of others, cryptanalysts undertaking them never get any result. But, for a cryptanalyst who likes the work, the joy of discoveries effaces the memory of his hours of doubt and impatience."

e. With his usual deft touch, Hitt says of the element of luck, as regards the role it plays in analysis:

"As to luck, there is the old miners' proverb: 'Gold is where you find it.'"

The cryptanalyst is lucky when one of the correspondents whose cryptograms he is studying makes a blunder that gives the necessary clue; or when he finds two cryptograms identical in text but in different keys in the same system; or when he finds two cryptograms identical in text but in different systems, and so on. The element of luck is there, to be sure, *but the crypt-analyst must be on the alert* if he is to profit by these lucky "breaks".

f. If the author were asked to state, in view of the progress in the field since 1916, what elements might be added to the four ingredients Hitt thought essential to cryptanalytic success, he would be inclined to mention the following:

(1) A broad, general education, embodying interests covering as many fields of practical knowledge as possible. This is useful because the cryptanalyst is often called upon to solve messages dealing with the most varied of human activities, and the more he knows about these activities, the easier his task.

(2) Access to a large library of current literature, and wide and direct contacts with sources of collateral information. These often afford clues as to the contents of specific messages. For example, to be able instantly to have at his disposal a newspaper report or a personal report of events described or referred to in a message under investigation goes a long way toward simplifying or facilitating solution. Government cryptanalysts are sometimes fortunately situated in this respect, especially where various agencies work in harmony.

(3) Proper coordination of effort. This includes the organization of cryptanalytic personnel into harmonious, efficient teams of cooperating individuals.

(4) Under mental equipment he would also include the faculty of being able to concentrate on a problem for rather long periods of time, without distraction, nervous irritability, and impatience. The strain under which cryptanalytic studies are necessarily conducted, is quite severe and too long-continued application has the effect of draining nervous energy to an unwholesome degree, so that a word or two of caution may not here be out of place. One should continue at work only so long as a peaceful, calm spirit prevails, whether the work is fruitful or not. But just as soon as the mind becomes wearied with the exertion, or just as soon as a feeling

---

[10] *Op. cit.*, p. 301.

of hopelessness or mental fatigue intervenes, it is better to stop completely and turn to other activities, rest, or play. It is essential to remark that systematization and orderliness of work are aids in reducing nervous tension and irritability. On this account it is better to take the time to prepare the data carefully, rewrite the text if necessary, and so on, rather than work with slipshod, incomplete, or improperly arranged material.

(5) A retentive memory is an important asset to cryptanalytic skill, especially in the solution of codes. The ability to remember individual groups, their approximate locations in other messages, the associations they form with other groups, their peculiarities and similarities, saves much wear and tear of the mental machinery, as well as much time in looking up these groups in indexes.

(6) The assistance of machine aids in cryptanalysis. The importance and value of these aids cannot be overemphasized in their bearing on practical, operational cryptanalysis, especially in the large-scale effort that would be made in time of war on complex, high-grade cryptosystems at a theater headquarters or in the zone of the interior. These aids, under the general category of rapid analytical machines, comprise both punched-card tabulating machinery and certain other general- and special-purpose high-speed electrical and electronic devices. Some of the more compact equipment may be employed by lower echelons within a theater of operations to facilitate the cryptanalysis of medium-grade cryptosystems found in tactical communications.

g. It may be advisable to add a word or two at this point to prepare the student to expect slight mental jars and tensions which will almost inevitably come to him in the conscientious study of this and the subsequent texts. The author is well aware of the complaint of students that authors of texts on cryptanalysis base much of their explanation upon their foreknowledge of the "answer"—which the student does not know while he is attempting to follow the solution with an unbiased mind. They complain, too, that these authors use such expressions as "it is obvious that", "naturally", "of course", "it is evident that", and so on, when the circumstances seem not at all to warrant their use. There is no question that this sort of treatment is apt to discourage the student, especially when the point elucidated becomes clear to *him* only after many hours' labor, whereas, according to the book, the author noted the weak spot at the first moment's inspection. The author can only promise to try to avoid making the steps appear to be much more simple than they really are, and to suppress glaring instances of unjustifiable "jumping at conclusions". At the same time he must indicate that for pedagogical reasons in many cases a message has been consciously "manipulated" so as to allow certain principles to become more obvious in the illustrative examples than they ever are in practical work. During the course of some of the explanations attention will even be directed to cases of unjustified inferences. Furthermore, of the student who is quick in observation and deduction, the author will only ask that he bear in mind that if the elucidation of certain principles seems prolix and occupies more space than necessary, this is occasioned by the author's desire to carry the explanation forward in very short, easily-comprehended, and plainly-described steps, for the benefit of students who are perhaps a bit slower to grasp but who, once they understand, are able to retain and apply principles slowly learned just as well, if not better than the students who learn more quickly.[11]

---

[11] In connection with the use of the word "obvious", the following extract is of interest:

"Now the word 'obvious' is a rather dangerous one. There is an incident, which has become something of a legend in mathematical circles, that illustrates this danger. A certain famous mathematician was lecturing to a group of students and had occasion to use a formula which he wrote down with the remark, 'This statement is obvious.' Then he paused and looked rather hesitantly at the formula. 'Wait a moment,' he said. 'Is it

3. Validity of results of cryptanalysis.—Valid or authentic cryptanalytic solutions cannot and do not represent "opinions" of the cryptanalyst. They are valid only so far as they are wholly objective, and are susceptible of demonstration and proof, employing authentic, objective methods. It should hardly be necessary (but an attitude frequently encountered among laymen makes it advisable) to indicate that the results achieved by any serious cryptanalytic studies on authentic material rest upon the same sure foundations and of necessity are reached by the same general steps as the results achieved by any other scientific studies, *viz.*, observation, hypothesis, deduction and induction, and confirmatory experiment. Implied in the latter is the possibility that two or more qualified investigators, each working independently upon the same material, will achieve identical (or practically identical) results—there is one and only one (valid) solution to a cryptogram. Occasionally a "would-be" or pseudo-cryptanalyst offers "solutions" which cannot withstand such tests; a second, unbiased, investigator working independently either cannot *consistently* apply the methods alleged to have been applied by the pseudo-cryptanalyst, or else, if he can apply them at all, the results (plaintext translations) are far different in the two cases. The reason for this is that in such cases it is generally found that the "methods" are not clear-cut, straightforward or mathematical in character. Instead, they often involve the making of judgments on matters too tenuous to measure, weigh, or otherwise subject to careful scrutiny. Often, too, they involve the "correction" of an inordinate number of "errors" which the pseudo-crypt-analyst assumes to be present and which he "corrects" in order to make his "solution" intelligible. And sometimes the pseudo-cryptanalyst offers as a "solution" plain text which is intelligible only to him or which he makes intelligible by expanding what he alleges to be abbreviations, and so on. In all such cases, the conclusion to which the unprejudiced observer is forced to come is that the alleged "solution" obtained by the pseudo-cryptanalyst is purely subjective.[12] In nearly all cases where this has happened (and they occur from time to time) there has been uncovered nothing which can in any way be used to impugn the integrity of the

obvious? I think it's obvious.' More hesitation, and then, 'Pardon me, gentlemen, I shall return.' Then he left the room. Thirty-five minutes later he returned; in his hands was a sheaf of papers covered with calculations, on his face a look of quiet satisfaction. 'I was right, gentlemen. It is obvious,' he said, and proceeded with his lecture."—Excerpt from *The Anatomy of Mathematics* by Kershner and Wilcox. New York, 1950.

[12] A mathematician is often unable to grasp the concept behind the expression "subjective solution" as used in the cryptanalytic field, since the idea is foreign to the basic philosophy of mathematics and thus the expression appears to him to represent a contradiction in terms. As an illustration, let us consider a situation in which a would-be cryptanalyst offers a solution to a cryptogram he alleges to be a simple monoalphabetic substitution cipher. His so-called solution, however, requires that he assume the presence of, let us say, approximately 50% garbles (which he claims to have been introduced by cipher clerks' errors, faulty radio reception because of adverse weather conditions, etc.). That is, the "plain text" he offers as the "solution" involves his making helter-skelter many "corrections and emendations", which, one may be sure, will be based on what his subconscious mind expects or desires to find in the cleartext message. Unfortunately, another would-be cryptanalyst working upon the same cryptogram and hypothesis independently might conceivably "degarble" the cryptogram in different spots and produce an entirely dissimilar "plain text" as his "solution". Both "solutions" would be invalid because they are based upon an erroneous hypothesis—the cryptogram actually happens to be a polyalphabetic substitution cipher which when correctly analyzed requires on the part of unbiased observers no assumption of garbles to a degree that strains their credulity. The last phrase is added here because in professional cryptanalytic work it is very often necessary to make a few corrections for errors; but it is rarely the case that the garble rate exceeds more than a few percent of the characters of the cryptogram, say 5 to 10% at the outside. It is to be noted, however, that occasionally the solution to a cryptogram may involve the correction of more than this percentage of errors, but the solution would be regarded as valid only if the errors can be shown to be *systematic* in some significant respect, or can otherwise be explained by *objective* rationalization.

pseudo-cryptanalyst. The worst that can be said of him is that he has become a victim of a special or peculiar form of self-delusion, and that his desire to solve the problem, usually in accord with some previously-formed opinion, or notion, has over-balanced, or undermined, his judgment and good sense.[13]

[13] Specific reference can be made to the following typical "case histories":
Donnelly, Ignatius, *The Great Cryptogram*. Chicago, 1888.
Owen, Orville W., *Sir Francis Bacon's Cipher Story*. Detroit, 1895.
Gallup, Elizabeth Wells, *Francis Bacon's Biliteral Cipher*. Detroit, 1900.
Arensberg, Walter Conrad, *The Cryptography of Shakespeare*. Los Angeles, 1922.
   The Shakespearean Mystery. Pittsburgh, 1928.
   The Baconian Keys. Pittsburgh, 1928.
Margoliouth, D. S., *The Homer of Aristotle*. Oxford, 1923.
Newbold, William Romaine, *The Cipher of Roger Bacon*. Philadelphia, 1928. (For a scholarly and complete demolition of Professor Newbold's work, see an article entitled *Roger Bacon and the Voynich MS*, by John M. Manly, in *Speculum*, Vol. *VI*, No. 3, July 1931.)
Feely, Joseph Martin, *The Shakespearean Cypher*. Rochester, N. Y., 1931.
   Deciphering Shakespeare. Rochester, N. Y., 1934.
   Roger Bacon's Cypher: the right key found. Rochester, N. Y., 1943.
Wolff, Werner, *Déchiffrement de l'Ecriture Maya*. Paris, 1938.
Strong, Leonell C., *Anthony Askham, the author of the Voynich manuscript*, in *Science*, Vol. 101, June 15, 1945, pp. 608–9.

Chapter II

BASIC CRYPTOLOGIC CONSIDERATIONS

Paragraph

Cryptology, communication intelligence, and communication security _____ 4
Secret communication _____ 5
Plain text and encrypted text _____ 6
Cryptography, encrypting, and decrypting _____ 7
Codes, ciphers, and enciphered code _____ 8
General system, specific key, and cryptosystem _____ 9
Cryptanalytics and cryptanalysis _____ 10
Transposition and substitution _____ 11
Nature of alphabets _____ 12
Types of alphabets _____ 13

4. **Cryptology, communication intelligence, and communication security.**—The need for secrecy in the conduct of important affairs has been recognized from time immemorial. In the case of diplomacy and organized warfare this need is especially important in regard to communications. However, when such communications are transmitted by electrical means, they can be heard and copied by unauthorized persons. The protection resulting from all measures designed to deny to unauthorized persons information of value which may be derived from such communications is called *communication security*. The evaluated information concerning the enemy, derived principally from a study of his electrical communications, is called *communication intelligence*. The collective term including all phases of communication intelligence and communication security is *cryptology*.[1] Or, stated in broad terms, cryptology is that branch of knowledge which treats of hidden, disguised, or secret [2] communications.

5. **Secret communication.**—*a.* Communication may be conducted by any means susceptible of ultimate interpretation by one of the five senses, but those most commonly used are sight and hearing. Aside from the use of simple visual and auditory signals for communication over relatively short distances, the usual method of communication between or among individuals separated from one another by relatively long distances involves, at one stage or another, the act of writing or of speaking over a telephone.

b. Privacy or secrecy in communication by telephone can be obtained by using equipment which affects the electrical currents involved in telephony so that the conversations can be understood only by persons provided with suitable equipment properly arranged for the purpose. The same thing is true in the case of facsimile transmission (i. e., the electrical transmission of pictures, drawings, maps) and television transmission. However, this text will not treat of these aspects [3] of cryptology.

---

[1] From the Greek *kryptos* (hidden)+*logos* (discourse). The prefix "crypto-" in compound words pertains to "cryptologic", "cryptographic", or "cryptanalytic", depending upon the use of the particular word as defined.

[2] In this text the term "secret" will be used in its ordinary sense as given in the dictionary. Whenever the designation is used in the more restricted sense of the security classification as defined in official regulations, it will be capitalized. There are in current use the three classifications CONFIDENTIAL, SECRET, and TOP SECRET, listed in ascending order of degree.

[3] These aspects of cryptology are now known as *ciphony* (from *ci*pher+tele*phony*); *cifax* (from *ci*pher+*fac*simile); and *civision* (from *ci*pher+tele*vision*).

9

c. Writing may be either *visible* or *invisible*. In the former, the characters are inscribed with ordinary writing materials and can be seen with the naked eye; in the latter, the characters are inscribed by means or methods which make the writing invisible to the naked eye. Invisible writing can be prepared with certain chemicals called *invisible, sympathetic,* or *secret inks,* and in order to "develop" such writing, that is, make it visible, special processes must usually be applied. There are also methods of producing writing which is invisible to the naked eye because the characters are of microscopic size, thus requiring special photographic or microscopic apparatus to make such writing visible to the naked eye.

d. Invisible writing and unintelligible visible writing constitute *secret writing.*

6. Plain text and encrypted text.—*a.* Visible writing which is intelligible, that is, conveys a more or less understandable or sensible meaning (in the language in which written) and which is not intended to convey a hidden meaning, is said to be in *plain text.*[4] A message in plain text is termed a *plaintext message,* a *cleartext message,* or a *message in clear.*

b. Visible writing which conveys no intelligible meaning in any recognized language [5] is said to be in *encrypted text* and such writing is termed a *cryptogram.*[6]

7. Cryptography, encrypting, and decrypting.—*a. Cryptography* is that branch of cryptology which treats of various means, methods, and apparatus for converting or transforming plaintext messages into cryptograms and for reconverting the cryptograms into their original plaintext forms by a simple reversal of the steps used in their transformation.

b. To *encrypt* is to convert or transform a plaintext message into a cryptogram by following certain rules, steps, or processes constituting the *key* or *keys* and agreed upon in advance by correspondents, or furnished them by higher authority.

c. To *decrypt* is to reconvert or to transform a cryptogram into the original equivalent plaintext message *by a direct reversal of the encrypting process,* that is, by applying to the cryptogram the key or keys (usually in a reverse order) used in producing the cryptogram.

d. A person skilled in the art of encrypting and decrypting, or one who has a part in devising a cryptographic system is called a *cryptographer;* a clerk who encrypts and decrypts, or who assists in such work, is called a *cryptographic clerk.*

8. Codes, ciphers, and enciphered code.—*a.* Encrypting and decrypting are accomplished by means collectively designated as *codes* and *ciphers.* Such means are used for either or both of two purposes: (1) secrecy, and (2) economy or brevity. Secrecy usually is far more important in military cryptography than economy or brevity. In ciphers or *cipher systems,* cryptograms are produced by applying the cryptographic treatment to *individual letters* of the plaintext messages, whereas, in codes or *code systems,* cryptograms are produced by applying the cryptographic treatment to entire *words, phrases, and sentences* of the plaintext messages. The specialized meanings of the terms *code* and *cipher* are explained in detail later (subpar. 11*d*).

b. A cryptogram produced by means of a cipher system is said to be *in cipher* and is called

---

[4] Visible writing may be intelligible but the meaning it obviously conveys may not be its real meaning, that is, the meaning intended to be conveyed. To quote a simple example of an apparently innocent message containing a secret or hidden meaning, prepared with the intention of escaping censorship, the sentence "Son born today" may mean "Three transports left today." Secret communication methods or artifices of this sort are impractical for field military use but are often encountered in espionage and counter-espionage activities.

[5] There is a certain type of writing which is considered by its authors to be intelligible, but which is either completely unintelligible to the wide variety of readers or else requires considerable mental struggle on their part to make it intelligible. Reference is here made to so-called "modern literature" and "modern verse", products of such writers as E. E. Cummings, Gertrude Stein, James Joyce, et al.

[6] From *kryptos+gramma* (that which is written).

10

a *cipher message*, or sometimes simply a *cipher*. The act or operation of encrypting a cipher message is called *enciphering*, and the enciphered version of the plain text, as well as the act or process itself, is often referred to as the *encipherment*. The cryptographic clerk who performs the process serves as an *encipherer*. The corresponding terms applicable to the decrypting of cipher messages are *deciphering*, *decipherment*, and *decipherer*. A clerk who serves as both an encipherer and decipherer of messages is called a *cipher clerk*.

c. A *cipher device* is a relatively simple mechanical contrivance for encipherment and decipherment, usually "hand-operated" or manipulated by the fingers, as for example a device with concentric rings of alphabets, manually powered; a *cipher machine* is a relatively complex apparatus or mechanism for encipherment and decipherment, usually equipped with a typewriter keyboard and often requiring an external power source.

d. A cryptogram produced by means of a code system is said to be *in code* and is called a *code message*. The text of the cryptogram is referred to as *code text*. This act or operation of encrypting is called *encoding*, and the encoded version of the plain text, as well as the act or process itself, is referred to as the *encodement*. The clerk who performs the process serves as an *encoder*. The corresponding terms applicable to the decrypting of code messages are *decoding*, *decodement*, and *decoder*. A cryptographic clerk who serves as both an encoder and decoder of messages is called a *code clerk*.

e. Sometimes, for special purposes (usually increased security), the code text of a cryptogram undergoes a further step in concealment involving *superencryption*, that is, encipherment of the characters comprising the code text, thus producing what is called an *enciphered-code message*, or *enciphered code*. *Encoded cipher*, that is, the case where the final cryptogram is produced by enciphering the plain text and then encoding the cipher text obtained from the first operation, is also possible, but rare.

9. **General system, specific key, and cryptosystem.**—*a.* There are a great many different methods of encrypting messages, so that correspondents must first of all be in complete agreement as to which of them will be used in their secret communications, or in different types or classes of such communications. Furthermore, it is to be understood that all the detailed rules, processes, or steps comprising the cryptography agreed upon will be *invariant*, that is, constant or unvarying in their use in a given set of communications. The totality of these basic, invariable rules, processes, or steps to be followed in encrypting a message according to the agreed method constitutes the general cryptographic system or, more briefly, the *general system*.

b. It is usually the case that the general system operates in connection with or under the control of a number, a group of letters, a word, a phrase, or sentence which is used as a *key*, that is, the element which specifically governs the manner in which the general system will be applied in a specific message, or the exact *setting* of a cipher device or a cipher machine at the initial point of encipherment or decipherment of a specific message. This element—usually of a variable nature or changeable at the will of the correspondents, or prearranged for them by higher authority—is called the *specific key*. The specific key may also involve the use of a set of specially prepared tables, a special document, or even a book.

c. The term *cryptosystem*[7] is used when it is desired to designate or refer to all the crypto-material (device, machine, instructions for use, key lists, etc.) as a unit to provide a single, complete system and means for secret communication.

---

[7] The term *cryptosystem* is used in preference to *cryptographic system* so as to permit its use in designating secret communication systems involving means other than *writing*, such as ciphony and cifax.

10. **Cryptanalytics and cryptanalysis.**—*a.* In theory any cryptosystem (except one [8]) can be "broken", i. e., solved, if enough time, labor, and skill are devoted to it, and if the volume of traffic in that system is large enough. This can be done even if the general system and the specific key are unknown at the start. In military operations theoretical rules must usually give way to practical considerations. How the theoretical rule in this case is affected by practical considerations will be discussed in Appendix 8, "Principles of cryptosecurity."

b. That branch of cryptology which deals with the principles, methods, and means employed in the solution or *analysis* of cryptosystems is called *cryptanalytics.*

c. The steps and operations performed in applying the principles of cryptanalytics constitute *cryptanalysis.* To *cryptanalyze* a cryptogram is to *solve* it by cryptanalysis.

d. A person skilled in the art of cryptanalysis is called a *cryptanalyst,* and a clerk who assists in such work is called a *cryptanalytic clerk.*

11. **Transposition and substitution.**—*a.* Technically there are only two distinct types of treatment which may be applied to written plain text to convert it into secret text, yielding two different *classes* of cryptograms. In the first, called *transposition,* the *elements* or *units* of the plain text retain their original identities and merely undergo some change in their relative positions, with the result that the original text becomes unintelligible. In the second, called *substitution,* the elements of the plain text retain their original relative positions but are replaced by other elements with different values or meanings, with the result that the original text becomes unintelligible. Thus, in the case of transposition ciphers, the unintelligibility is brought about merely by a change in the original sequence of the elements or units of the plain text; in the case of substitution ciphers, the unintelligibility is brought about by a change in the elements or units themselves, without a change in their relative order.

b. It is possible to encrypt a message by a substitution method and then to apply a transposition method to the substitution text, or vice versa. Such *combined transposition-substitution* methods do not form a third class of methods. They are occasionally encountered in military cryptography, but the types of combinations that are sufficiently simple to be practicable for field use are very limited.[9]

c. Under each of the two principal classes of cryptograms as outlined above, a further classification can be made based upon the number of characters composing the *textual elements* or *units* undergoing cryptographic treatment. These textual units are composed of (1) individual letters, (2) combinations of letters in regular groupings, (3) combinations of letters in irregular, more or less euphonious groupings called syllables, and (4) complete words, phrases, and sentences. Methods which deal with the first type of units are called *monographic* methods; those which deal with the second type are called *polygraphic* (digraphic, trigraphic, etc.); those which deal with the third type, or syllables, are called *syllabic;* and, finally, those which deal with the fourth type are called *lexical* (of or pertaining to words).

d. It is necessary to indicate that the foregoing classification of cryptographic methods is more or less artificial in nature, and is established for purpose of convenience only. No sharp line of demarcation can be drawn in every case, for occasionally a given system may combine methods of treating single letters, regular or irregular-length groupings of letters, syllables, words, phrases, and complete sentences. When in a single system the cryptographic treatment

---

[8] The exception is the "one-time" system in which the specific key has no systematic construction and is used only once.

[9] One notable exception is the *ADFGVX system,* used extensively by the Germans in World War I.

is applied to textual units of regular length, usually monographic or digraphic (and seldom longer, or intermixed monographic and digraphic), the system is called a *cipher system*. Likewise, when in a single system the cryptographic treatment is applied to textual units of irregular length, usually syllables, whole words, phrases, and sentences, and is only exceptionally applied to single letters or regular groupings of letters, the system is called a *code system* and generally involves the use of a *code book*.[10]

12. **Nature of alphabets.**—*a*. One of the simplest kinds of substitution ciphers is that which is known in cryptologic literature as Julius Caesar's Cipher, but which, as a matter of fact, was a favorite long before his day. In this cipher each letter of the text of a message is replaced by the letter standing the third to the right of it in the ordinary alphabet; the letter A is replaced by D, the letter B by E, and so on. The word *cab* becomes converted into FDE, which is cipher.

b. The English language is written by means of 26 simple characters called *letters* which, taken together and considered as a *sequence of symbols*, constitute the alphabet of the language. Not all systems of writing are of this nature. Chinese writing is composed of about 44,000 complex characters, each representing one sense of a word. Whereas English words are composite or polysyllabic and may consist of one to eight or more syllables, Chinese words are all monosyllables and each monosyllable is a word. Written languages of the majority of other civilized peoples of today are, however, alphabetic and polysyllabic in construction, so that the principles discussed here apply to all of them.

c. The letters comprising the English alphabet used today are the results of a long period of evolution, the complete history of which may never fully be known.[11] They are conventional symbols representing *elementary sounds*, and any other simple symbols, so long as the sounds which they represent are agreed upon by those concerned, will serve the purpose equally well. If taught from early childhood that the symbols $, *, and @ represent the sounds "Ay", "Bee", and "See" respectively, the combination @$* would still be pronounced *cab*, and would, of course, have exactly the same meaning as before. Again, let us suppose that two persons have agreed to change the sound values of the letters F, G, and H, and after long practice have become accustomed to pronouncing them as we pronounce the letters A, B, and C, respectively; they would then write the "word" HFG, pronounce it *cab*, and see nothing strange whatever in the matter. But to others no party to their arrangements, HFG constitutes cipher. The combination of sounds called for by this combination of symbols is perfectly intelligible to the two who have adopted the new sound values for those symbols and therefore pronounce HFG as *cab;* but HFG is utterly unpronounceable and wholly unintelligible to others who are reading it according to their own long-established system of sound and symbol equivalents. It would be stated that there is no such word as HFG which would mean merely that the particular combination of sounds represented by this combination of letters has not been adopted by convention to represent a thing or an idea in the English language. Thus, it is seen that, in order for the written words of a language to be pronounceable and intelligible to all who speak that language, it is necessary, first, that the sound values of the letters or symbols be universally understood and agreed upon and, secondly, that the particular combination of sounds denoted by the letters should have been adopted to represent a thing or an idea.

---

[10] A list of single letters, frequent digraphs, trigraphs, syllables, and words is often called a *syllabary;* cryptographic treatment of the units of such syllabaries places them in the category of code systems.

[11] An excellent and most authoritative book on this subject is *The Alphabet: a Key to the History of Mankind* by David Diringer. London, 1949.

d. It is clear also that in order to write a polysyllabic language with facility it is necessary to establish and to maintain by common agreement or convention, equivalency between *two* sets of elements, first, a set of elementary sounds and, second, a set of elementary symbols to represent the sounds. When this is done the result is what is called an *alphabet*, a word derived from the names of the first two letters of the Greek alphabet, "alpha" and "beta".

e. Theoretically, in an ideal alphabet each symbol or letter would represent only one elementary sound, and each elementary sound would invariably be represented by the same symbol. But such an alphabet would be far too difficult for the average person to use. It has been conservatively estimated that a minimum of 100 characters would be necessary for English alone. Attempts toward producing and introducing into usage a practical, scientific alphabet have been made, one being that of the Simplified Spelling Board in 1928, which advocated a revised alphabet of 42 characters. Were such an alphabet adopted into current usage, in books, letters, telegrams, etc., the flexibility of cryptographic systems would be considerably extended and the difficulties set in the path of the enemy cryptanalysts greatly increased. The chances for its adoption in the near future are, however, quite small. Because of the continually changing nature of every living language, it is doubtful whether an initially "perfect alphabet" could, over any long period of time, remain so and serve to indicate with great precision the exact sounds which it was originally designed to represent.

13. Types of alphabets.—*a.* In the study of cryptography the dual nature of the alphabet becomes apparent. It consists of two parts or components, (1) an arbitrarily-arranged sequence of sounds, and (2) an arbitrarily-arranged sequence of symbols.

b. The *normal alphabet* for any language is one in which these two components are the ordinary sequences that have been definitely fixed by long usage or convention. The dual nature of our normal or everyday alphabet is often lost sight of. When we write A, B, C, . . . we really mean:

Sequence of sounds: "Ay"   "Bee"   "See"   . . . . .

Sequence of symbols: A   B   C   . . . . . .

Normal alphabets of different languages vary considerably in the number of characters composing them and the arrangement or sequence of the characters. The English, Dutch, and German alphabets each have 26; the French, 25; the Italian, 21; the Spanish, 27 (including the digraphs CH and LL); and the Russian, 31.[12] The Japanese language has a syllabary consisting of 72 syllabic sounds which require 48 characters for their representation.

c. A *cipher alphabet*, or *substitution alphabet* as it is sometimes called, is one in which the elementary speech-sounds are represented by characters other than those representing them in the normal alphabet. These characters may be letters, figures, signs, symbols, or combinations of these.

d. When the plain text of a message is converted into encrypted text by the use of one or more cipher alphabets, the resultant cryptogram constitutes a *substitution cipher.* If only one cipher alphabet is involved, it is called a *monoalphabetic substitution cipher;* if two or more cipher alphabets are involved, it is called a *polyalphabetic substitution cipher.*

e. It is convenient to designate that component of a cipher alphabet constituting the sequence of speech-sounds as the *plain component* and the component constituting the sequence of symbols as the *cipher component.* If omitted in a cipher alphabet, the plain component is understood to be the normal sequence. For brevity and clarity, a letter of the plain text, or of the

---

[12] In contrast to the foregoing alphabets, it is of interest to note that in the Hawaiian language the alphabet consists of only 12 letters, *viz.*, the five vowels A, E, I, O, U, and the seven consonants H, K, L, M, N, P, W.

plain component of a cipher alphabet, is designated by suffixing a small letter "p" to it: A_p means A of the plain text, or of the plain component of a cipher alphabet. Similarly, a letter of the cipher text, or of the cipher component of a cipher alphabet, will be designated by suffixing a small letter "c" to it: X_c means X of the cipher text, or of the cipher component of a cipher alphabet. The expression $A_p = X_c$ means that A of the plain text, or A of the plain component of a cipher alphabet, is represented by X in the cipher text, or by X in the cipher component of a cipher alphabet.

f. With reference to the arrangement or sequence of letters forming their components, cipher alphabets are of two types:

(1) *Standard cipher alphabets,* in which the sequence of letters in the plain component is the normal, and in the cipher component is the same as the normal, but reversed in direction or shifted from its normal point of coincidence with the plain component.

(2) *Mixed cipher alphabets,* in which the sequence of letters or characters in one or both of the components is no longer the same as the normal in its entirety.

g. Although the basic considerations of the preceding paragraphs place the student in a position to undertake the study of certain fundamental principles of cryptanalysis, this may be a good point at which to pause and to make a few remarks with regard to the role that cryptanalysis plays in the whole chain of more or less complex operations involved in deriving communication intelligence, after which these fundamental cryptanalytic principles will be treated.

CHAPTER III

FUNDAMENTAL CRYPTANALYTIC OPERATIONS

	Paragraph
The role of cryptanalysis in communication intelligence operations	14
The four basic operations in cryptanalysis	15
The determination of the language employed	16
The determination of the general system	17
The reconstruction of the specific key	18
The reconstruction of the plain text	19
The utilization of traffic intercepts	20

14. The role of cryptanalysis in communication intelligence operations.—*a.* Through the medium of communication intelligence an attempt is made to answer three questions concerning enemy communications: "Who?" "Where?" "What?"—*Who* are their originators and addressees? *Where* are these originators and addressees located? *What* do the messages say?

b. All of the foregoing questions are very important in the military application of communication intelligence. Hence, even though this text deals almost exclusively with the principles and operations involved in deriving the answer to the third question—"What do the messages say?"—a few words on the importance of the first and second questions may be useful. It is a serious mistake to think that one can necessarily and always correctly interpret the mere text of a message without identifying and locating the originator and the addressee or, on many occasions, without having a background against which to interpret the message in order to appreciate its real import or significance.

c. The very first step in the series of activities involved in deriving communication intelligence is the collection of the raw material, that is, the *interception* [1] and copying of the transmissions constituting the messages to be studied and analyzed.

d. Then, with the raw material in hand, studies are made in order to answer the first two questions—"Who?" and "Where?" The answers to these questions are not always obvious in modern military communications, especially in the case of messages exchanged by units in the combat zone, since messages of this sort rarely indicate in plain language *who* the originator and the addressee are or *where* they are located. Consequently, certain apparatus and techniques specifically developed for finding the answers to these questions must be employed. These apparatus and techniques are embraced by that part of communication intelligence theory and practice which is known as *traffic analysis*. This latter subject and interception are treated briefly in Appendix 7, "Communication intelligence operations". (The serious student will derive much practical benefit from a careful reading of this appendix.)

e. The foregoing operations, interception and traffic analysis, along with *cryptanalysis* constitute the first three operations of communication intelligence. But generally there must follow at least one additional operation. If the plain texts recovered through cryptanalysis are

---

[1] To *intercept* means, in its cryptologic sense, to gain possession of communications which are intended for other recipients, without obtaining the consent of these addressees and without preventing or (ordinarily) delaying the transmission of the communications to them.

in a foreign language, they must usually be translated, and *translation* constitutes this fourth operation. In the course of translating, it may be found that, because of errors in transmission or reception, corrections and emendations must be made in these plain texts; however, although this often requires skill and experience of a high order, it does not constitute another communication intelligence operation, since it is but an auxiliary step to the process of translation.

f. In a large-scale communication intelligence effort these four steps, interception, traffic analysis, cryptanalysis, and translation, must be properly organized and coordinated in order to gain the most benefit from the potentialities of communication intelligence, that is, the production of the maximum quantity of information from the raw traffic. This information must then be *evaluated* by properly trained intelligence specialists, *collated* with intelligence derived from other sources, and, finally, *disseminated* to the commanders who need the intelligence in time to be of *operational* use to them, rather than of mere historical interest. The foregoing operations and especially the first three—interception, traffic analysis, and cryptanalysis—usually complement one another. This, however, is not the place for elaboration on the interrelationships which exist and which when properly integrated make the operations as a whole an efficient, unified complex geared to the fulfillment of its principal goal, namely, the production of timely communication intelligence.

g. With the foregoing general background, the student is prepared to proceed to the technical considerations and principles of cryptanalysis.

15. The four basic operations in cryptanalysis.—*a.* The solution of practically every cryptogram involves four fundamental operations or steps:

(1) The determination of the language employed in the plaintext version.
(2) The determination of the general system of cryptography employed.
(3) The reconstruction of the specific key in the case of a cipher system, or the reconstruction, partial or complete, of the code book, in the case of a code system; or both, in the case of an enciphered code system.
(4) The reconstruction or establishment of the plain text.

b. These operations will be taken up in the order in which they are given above and in which they usually are performed in the solution of cryptograms, although occasionally the second step may precede the first.[2]

---

[2] Although the foregoing four steps represent the classical or ideal approach to cryptanalysis, the art may be reduced to the following:

Procedures in cryptanalysis	*Requirements*
1. Arrangement and rearrangement of data to disclose nonrandom characteristics or manifestations (i. e., in frequency counts, repetitions, patterns, symmetrical phenomena, etc.).	Experience or ingenuity, and time (which latter may be appreciably lowered by the use of machine aids in cryptanalysis).
2. Recognition of the nonrandom characteristics or manifestations when disclosed.	Experience or statistics.
3. Explanation of the nonrandom characteristics when recognized.	Experience or imagination, *and* intelligence.

In all of the foregoing, the element of luck plays a very important part, as it is possible to side-step a large amount of labor and effort, in many cases, if "hunches" or intuition lead the analyst forthwith to the right path. Therefore, the phrase "or luck" should be added to each of the requirements above.

In fact, it all boils down to the simple statement: "Find something significant, and attach some significance thereto."

16. The determination of the language employed.—*a.* There is not much that need be said with respect to this operation except that the determination of the language employed seldom comes into question in the case of studies made of the cryptograms of an organized enemy. By this is meant that during wartime the enemy is of course known, and it follows, therefore, that the language he employs in his messages will almost certainly be his native or mother tongue. Only occasionally nowadays is this rule broken. Formerly it often happened, or it might have indeed been the general rule, that the language used in diplomatic correspondence was not the mother tongue, but French. In isolated instances during World War I the Germans used English when their own language could for one reason or another not be employed. For example, for a year or two before the entry of the United States into that war, during the time America was neutral and the German Government maintained its embassy in Washington, some of the messages exchanged between the Foreign Office in Berlin and the Embassy in Washington were encrypted in English, and a copy of the code used was deposited with the Department of State and our censor. Another instance is found in the case of certain Hindu conspirators who were associated with and partially financed by the German Government in 1915 and 1916; they employed English as the language of their cryptographic messages. Occasionally the cryptograms of enemy agents may be in a language different from that of the enemy. But in general these are, as has been said, isolated instances; as a rule, the language used in cryptograms exchanged between members of large organizations is the mother tongue of the correspondents. Where this is not the case, that is, when cryptograms of unknown origin must be studied, the cryptanalyst looks for any indications on the cryptograms themselves which may lead to a conclusion as to the language employed. Address, signature, and other data, *if in plain text* in the preamble, in the body, or at the end of the cryptogram, all come under careful scrutiny, as well as all extraneous circumstances connected with the manner in which the cryptograms were obtained, the person on whom they were found, or the locale of their origin and destination.

b. In special cases, or under special circumstances a clue to the language employed is found in the nature and composition of the cryptographic text itself. For example, if the letters K and W are entirely absent or appear very rarely in messages, it may indicate that the language is Spanish or Portuguese for these letters are absent in the alphabets of these languages and are used only to spell foreign words or names. The presence of accented letters or letters marked with special signs of one sort or another, peculiar to certain languages, will sometimes indicate the language used. The Japanese Morse telegraph alphabet contains combinations of dots and dashes which are peculiar to that alphabet and thus the interception of messages containing these special Morse combinations at once indicates the language involved. Finally, there are certain peculiarities of alphabetic languages which, in certain types of cryptograms, *viz.*, pure transposition, give clues as to the language used. For example, the frequent digraph CH, in German, leads to the presence, in cryptograms of the type mentioned, of many isolated C's and H's; if this is noted, the cryptogram may be assumed to be in German.

c. In some cases it is perfectly possible to perform certain steps in cryptanalysis *before* the language of the cryptogram has been definitely determined. Frequency studies, for example, may be made and analytic processes performed without this knowledge, and by a cryptanalyst wholly unfamiliar with the language even if it has been identified, or who knows only enough about the language to enable him to recognize valid combinations of letters, syllables, or a few common words in that language. He may, after this, call to his assistance a translator who may not be a cryptanalyst but who can materially aid in making necessary assumptions based upon his special knowledge of the characteristics of the language in question. Thus, cooperation between cryptanalyst and translator results in solution.[3]

17. The determination of the general system.—*a.* Except in the case of the more simple types of cryptograms, the step often referred to as *diagnosis,* that is, ascertaining the general system according to which a given cryptogram has been produced is usually a difficult, if not the most difficult, step in its solution. The reason for this is not hard to find.

b. As will become apparent to the student as he proceeds with his study, *in the final analysis, the solution of every cryptogram involving a form of substitution depends upon its reduction to monoalphabetic terms, if it is not originally in those terms.* This is true not only of ordinary substitution ciphers, but also of combined substitution-transposition ciphers, and of enciphered code. If the cryptogram must be reduced to monoalphabetic terms, the manner of its accomplishment is usually indicated by the cryptogram itself, by external or internal phenomena which become apparent to the cryptanalyst as he studies the cryptogram. If this is impossible, or too difficult, the cryptanalyst must, by one means or another, discover how to accomplish this reduction, by bringing to bear all the special or collateral information he can get from all the sources at his command. If both these possibilities fail him, there is little left but the long, tedious, and often fruitless process of elimination. In the case of transposition ciphers of the more complex type, the discovery of the basic method is often simply a matter of long and tedious elimination of possibilities. For cryptanalysis has unfortunately not yet attained, and may indeed never attain, the precision found today in qualitative analysis in chemistry, for example, where the analytic process is absolutely clear-cut and exact in its dichotomy. A few words in explanation of what is meant may not be amiss. When a chemist seeks to determine the identity of an unknown substance, he applies certain specific reagents to the substance and in a specific sequence. The first reagent tells him definitely into which of two primary classes the unknown substance falls. He then applies a second test with another specific reagent, which tells him again quite definitely into which of two secondary classes the unknown substance falls, and so on, until finally he has reduced the unknown substance to its simplest terms and has found out what it is. In striking contrast to this situation, cryptanalysis affords exceedingly few "reagents" or tests that may be applied to determine positively that a given cipher belongs to one or the other of two systems yielding externally similar results. And this is what makes the analysis of an isolated, complex cryptogram so difficult. Note the limiting adjective "isolated" in the foregoing sentence, for it is used advisedly. It is not often that the general system fails to disclose itself or cannot be discovered by painstaking investigation when there is a great volume of text accumulating from a regular traffic between numerous correspondents in a large organization. *Sooner or later* the system becomes known, either because of blunders and carelessness on the part of the personnel entrusted with the encrypting of the messages, or because the accumulation of text itself makes possible the determination of the general sys-

---

[3] The writer has seen in print statements that "during the World War . . . . decoded messages in Japanese and Russian without knowing a word of either language." The extent to which such statements are exaggerated will soon become obvious to the student. Of course, there are occasional instances in which a mere clerk with quite limited experience may be able to "solve" a message in an extremely simple system in a language of which he has no knowledge at all; but such a "solution" calls for nothing more arduous than the ability to recognize pronounceable combinations of vowels and consonants—an ability that hardly deserves to be rated as "cryptanalytic" in any real sense. To say that it is possible to solve a cryptogram in a foreign language "without knowing a word of that language" is not quite the same as to say that it is possible to do so with only a slight knowledge of the language; and it may be stated without cavil that the better the cryptanalyst's knowledge of the language, the greater are the chances for his success and, in any case, the easier is his work.

tem by cryptanalytic, including statistical, studies. But in the case of a single or even a few isolated cryptograms concerning which little or no information can be gained by the cryptanalyst, he is often unable, without a knowledge of, or a shrewd guess as to the general system employed, to decompose the heterogeneous text of the cryptogram into homogeneous, monoalphabetic text, which is the ultimate and essential step in analysis. The only knowledge that the cryptanalyst can bring to his aid in this most difficult step is that gained by long experience and practice in the analysis of many different types of systems. In this respect the practice of cryptanalysis is analogous to the practice of medicine: correct diagnosis is the most important and often the most difficult first step toward success.

c. On account of the complexities surrounding this particular phase of cryptanalysis, and because in any scheme of analysis based upon successive eliminations of alternatives the cryptanalyst can only progress as far as the extent of his own knowledge of *all* the possible alternatives will permit, it is necessary that detailed discussion of the eliminative process be postponed until the student has covered most of the field. For example, the student will perhaps want to know at once how he can distinguish between a cryptogram that is in code or enciphered code from one that is in cipher. It is at this stage of his studies impracticable to give him any helpful indications on his question. In return it may be asked of him why he should expect to be able to do this in the early stages of his studies when often the experienced expert cryptanalyst is baffled on the same score!

d. Much of the labor involved in cryptanalytic work, as referred to in par. 2, is connected with this determination of the general system. The preparation of the text, its rewriting in different forms, sometimes being rewritten in dozens of ways, the recording of letters, the establishment of frequencies of occurrences of letters, comparisons and experiments made with known material of similar character, and so on, constitute much labor that is most often indispensable, but which sometimes turns out to have been wholly unnecessary, or in vain. In one treatise [4] it is stated quite boldly that "this work once done, the determination of the system is often relatively easy." This statement can certainly apply only to the simpler types of cryptosystems; it is entirely misleading as regards the much more frequently encountered complex cryptograms of modern times.

18. The reconstruction of the specific key.—*a.* Nearly all practical cryptographic methods require the use of a specific key to guide, control, or modify the various steps under the general system. Once the latter has been disclosed, discovered, or has otherwise come into the possession of the cryptanalyst, the next step in solution is to determine, if necessary and if possible, the specific key that was employed to encrypt the message or messages under examination. This determination may not be in complete detail; it may go only so far as to lead to a knowledge of the number of alphabets involved in a substitution cipher, or the number of columns involved in a transposition cipher, or that a one-part code has been used, in the case of a code system. But it is often desirable to determine the specific key in as complete a form and with as much detail as possible, for this information will very frequently be useful in the solution of subsequent cryptograms exchanged between the same correspondents, since the nature or source of the specific key in a solved case may be expected to give clues to the specific key in an unsolved case.

b. Frequently, however, the reconstruction of the key is not a prerequisite to, and does not constitute an absolutely necessary preliminary step in, the fourth basic operation, *viz.*, the reconstruction or establishment of the plain text. In many cases, indeed, the two processes are carried along simultaneously, the one assisting the other, until in the final stages both have been com-

---

[4] Lange et Soudart, *op. cit.*, p. 106.

21

pleted in their entireties. In still other cases the reconstruction of the specific key may follow the reconstruction of the plain text instead of preceding it and is accomplished purely as a matter of academic interest; or the specific key may, in unusual cases, never be reconstructed.

19. The reconstruction of the plain text.—*a.* Little need be said at this point on this phase of cryptanalysis. The process usually consists, in the case of substitution ciphers, in the establishment of equivalency between specific letters of the cipher text and the plain text, letter by letter, pair by pair, and so on, depending upon the particular type of substitution system involved. In the case of transposition ciphers, the process consists in rearranging the elements of the cipher text, letter by letter, pair by pair, or occasionally word by word, depending upon the particular type of transposition system involved, until the letters or words have been returned to their original plaintext order. In the case of code, the process consists in determining the meaning of each code group and inserting this meaning in the code text to reestablish the original plain text.

b. The foregoing processes do not, as a rule, begin at the beginning of a message and continue letter by letter, or group by group in sequence up to the very end of the message. The establishment of values of cipher letters in substitution methods, or of the positions to which cipher letters should be transferred to form the plain text in the case of transposition methods, comes at very irregular intervals in the process. At first only one or two values scattered here and there throughout the text may appear; these then form the "skeletons" of words, upon which further work, by a continuation of the reconstruction process, is made possible; in the end the complete or nearly complete [5] text is established.

c. In the case of cryptograms in a foreign language, the translation of the solved messages is a final and necessary step, but is not to be considered as a cryptanalytic process. However, it is commonly the case that the translation process will be carried on simultaneously with the cryptanalytic, and will aid the latter, especially when there are lacunae which may be filled in from the context. (See also subpar. 16*c* in this connection.)

20. The utilization of traffic intercepts.[6]—*a.* There are, of course, other operations which are not as basic in nature as those just outlined but which must generally be performed as preliminary steps in *practical* cryptanalytic work (as distinguished from *academic* cryptanalysis). Before a military cryptanalyst can begin the analysis of an enemy cryptosystem, it is necessary for him to study the intercept material that is available to him, isolate the messages that have been encrypted by means of the cryptosystem to be examined, and to arrange the latter in a systematic order for analysis. This work, although apparently very simple, may require a great deal of time and effort.

b. Since, whenever practicable, two or more intercept stations are assigned to copy traffic [7] emanating from the stations of one enemy radio net, it is natural that there should be a certain amount of duplication in the work of these several intercept stations. This is desirable since it provides the cryptanalysts with two or more sets of the same messages, so that when one intercept station fails to receive all the messages completely and correctly, because of radio diffi-

---

[5] Sometimes in the case of code, the meaning of a small percentage of the code groups occurring in the traffic may be lacking, because there is insufficient text to establish their meaning.

[6] A *traffic intercept* is a copy of a communication gained through interception.

[7] In manual transmission systems, traffic is usually sent in Morse code, consisting of combinations of short signals ("dots") and long signals ("dashes") to make up an "alphabet" for the transmission of the letters, digits, and punctuation symbols of a particular language. It is interesting to note that Samuel F. B. Morse constructed his alphabet in such a manner that, generally speaking, the shorter signals applied to the highest frequency letters in English, while the longer signals were used to represent the lowest frequency letters.

22

culties, local static, or poor operation, it is possible by studying the other sets to reconstruct accurately the entire traffic of the enemy net.

 c. In all intercept activities where operators are used for copying the traffic, one of the most likely errors to be found is caused by the human element in reception. For this reason cryptanalysts and their assistants should be familiar with the international Morse alphabet and the

Ltrs. and Figs.	Morse equivalent	Frequent Errors	Ltrs. and Figs.	Morse equivalent	Frequent Errors
A	.—	i, m, t, et	S	...	h, d, i, r, u
B	—...	d, ts	T	—	a, e, n
C	—.—.	f, k, r, nn	U	..—	a, s, v, it
D	—..	b, s, l, ti	V	...—	h, u, x, st
E	.	t, i	W	.——	a, m, o, r, u, at
F	..—.	r, in	X	—..—	v, k, y, tu
G	——.	m, o, z, me	Y	—.——	x, c, nm
H	....	s, v, b, ii, se	Z	——..	b, g, q, mi
I	..	a, n, s	1	.————	Ø, 2
J	.———	w, o, am, eo	2	..———	1, 3
K	—.—	d, o, ta	3	...——	2, 4
L	.—..	r, d, ed	4	....—	3, 5
M	——	a, n, tt	5	.....	4, 6
N	—.	i, m, t, te	6	—....	5, 7
O	———	g, k, w, mt	7	——...	6, 8
P	.——.	j, g, l, w, an	8	———..	7, 9
Q	——.—	o, x, z, ma	9	————.	8, Ø
R	.—.	a, f, g, l, n, s, w	Ø	—————	9, 1

CHART 1. Most common errors in telegraphic transmission.

most common errors in wire and radio transmission methods so as to be able to correct garbled groups when they occur. In this connection, Chart 1, above, will be found useful.

 d. Besides the message texts themselves, the intercept operator also copies the *call signs* (together with the frequencies on which heard) and the elements of the *preamble* of the messages as transmitted by the enemy. The preamble may have great flexibility among various users, but usually includes a *station serial number* (abbr. "NR") assigned by the radio operator for referencing transmitted traffic, and a *group count* (abbr. "GR") as a check on the number of groups transmitted. In addition, there may also be preamble elements that signify precedence, routing or addressee instructions, the date and time of file, and other items that might facilitate the handling or processing of the traffic.

CHAPTER IV

FREQUENCY DISTRIBUTIONS AND THEIR FUNDAMENTAL USES

	Paragraph
The simple or uniliteral frequency distribution	21
Important features of the normal uniliteral frequency distribution	22
Constancy of the standard or normal uniliteral frequency distribution	23
The three facts which can be determined from a study of the uniliteral frequency distribution for a cryptogram	24
Determining the class to which a cipher belongs	25
Determining whether a substitution cipher is monoalphabetic or nonmonoalphabetic	26
The ϕ (phi) test for determining monoalphabeticity	27
Determining whether a cipher alphabet is standard or mixed	28

21. The simple or uniliteral frequency distribution.—*a.* It has long been known to cryptographers and typographers that the letters composing the words of any intelligible written text composed in any language which is alphabetic in construction are employed with greatly varying frequencies. For example, if on cross-section paper a simple tabulation, shown in Fig. 1, called a *uniliteral frequency distribution*, is made of the letters composing the words of the preceding sentence, the variation in frequency is strikingly demonstrated. It is seen that whereas certain letters, such as A, E, I, N, O, R, and T, are employed very frequently, other letters, such as C, G, H, L, P, and S are employed not nearly so frequently, while still other letters, such as F, J, K, Q, V, X, and Z are employed either seldom or not at all.

A	B	C	D	E	F	G	H	I	J	K	L	M	N	O	P	Q	R	S	T	U	V	W	X	Y	Z
14	3	8	4	22	2	9	10	15	0	1	9	3	17	14	8	1	13	10	20	3	1	5	1	7	0

(Total = 200 letters)

FIGURE 1.

b. If a similar tabulation is now made of the letters comprising the words of the second sentence in the preceding subparagraph, the distribution shown in Fig. 2 is obtained. Both sentences have exactly the same number of letters (200).

A	B	C	D	E	F	G	H	I	J	K	L	M	N	O	P	Q	R	S	T	U	V	W	X	Y	Z
12	2	8	7	25	7	4	5	20	0	1	9	5	17	14	6	2	13	14	17	5	1	2	1	3	0

(Total = 200 letters)

FIGURE 2.

c. Although each of these two distributions exhibits great variation in the relative frequencies with which *different* letters are employed in the respective sentences to which they apply, no marked differences are exhibited between the frequencies of the *same* letter in the two distributions. Compare, for example, the frequencies of A, B, C . . . Z in Fig. 1 with those of A, B, C . . . Z in Fig. 2. Aside from one or two exceptions, as in the case of the letter F, these two distributions agree rather strikingly.

d. This agreement, or *similarity*, would be practically complete if the two texts were much longer, for example, five times as long. In fact, when two texts of similar character, each containing more than 1,000 letters, are compared, it would be found that the respective frequencies of the 26 letters composing the two distributions show only very slight differences. This means, in other words, that in normal plain text each letter of the alphabet occurs with a rather *constant* or *characteristic frequency* which it tends to approximate, depending upon the length of the text analyzed. The longer the text (within certain limits), the closer will be the approximation to the characteristic frequencies of letters in the language involved. However, when the amount of text being analyzed has reached a substantial volume (roughly, 1,000 letters), the practical gain in accuracy does not warrant further increase in the amount of text.[1]

e. An experiment along these lines will be convincing. A series of 260 official telegrams [2] passing through the Department of the Army Message Center was examined statistically. The

TABLE 1–A.—*Absolute frequencies of letters appearing in the five sets of Governmental plaintext telegrams, each set containing 10,000 letters, arranged alphabetically*

Set No. 1		Set No. 2		Set No. 3		Set No. 4		Set No. 5	
Letter	Absolute Frequency	Letter	Absolute Frequency	Letter	Absolute Frequency	Letter	Absolute Frequency	Letter	Absolute Frequency
A	738	A	783	A	681	A	740	A	741
B	104	B	103	B	98	B	83	B	99
C	319	C	300	C	288	C	326	C	301
D	387	D	413	D	423	D	451	D	448
E	1,367	E	1,294	E	1,292	E	1,270	E	1,275
F	253	F	287	F	308	F	287	F	281
G	166	G	175	G	161	G	167	G	150
H	310	H	351	H	335	H	349	H	349
I	742	I	750	I	787	I	700	I	697
J	18	J	17	J	10	J	21	J	16
K	36	K	38	K	22	K	21	K	31
L	365	L	393	L	333	L	386	L	344
M	242	M	240	M	238	M	249	M	268
N	786	N	794	N	815	N	800	N	780
O	685	O	770	O	791	O	756	O	762
P	241	P	272	P	317	P	245	P	260
Q	40	Q	22	Q	45	Q	38	Q	30
R	760	R	745	R	762	R	735	R	786
S	658	S	583	S	585	S	628	S	604
T	936	T	879	T	894	T	958	T	928
U	270	U	233	U	312	U	247	U	238
V	163	V	173	V	142	V	133	V	155
W	166	W	163	W	136	W	133	W	182
X	43	X	50	X	44	X	53	X	41
Y	191	Y	155	Y	179	Y	213	Y	229
Z	14	Z	17	Z	2	Z	11	Z	5
Total	10,000		10,000		10,000		10,000		10,000

[1] See footnote 5, p. 30.

[2] These comprised messages from several official sources in addition to the Department of the Army and were all of an administrative character.

messages were divided into five sets, each totaling 10,000 letters, and the five distributions shown in Table 1–A were obtained.

f. If the five distributions in Table 1–A are summed, the results are as shown in Table 2–A.

TABLE 2–A.—*Absolute frequencies of letters appearing in the combined five sets of messages totaling 50,000 letters, arranged alphabetically*

A	3,683	G	819	L	1,821	Q	175	V	766
B	487	H	1,694	M	1,237	R	3,788	W	780
C	1,534	I	3,676	N	3,975	S	3,058	X	231
D	2,122	J	82	O	3,764	T	4,595	Y	967
E	6,498	K	148	P	1,335	U	1,300	Z	49
F	1,416								

g. The frequencies noted in Table 2–A above, when reduced to a base of 1,000 letters and then used as a basis for constructing a simple chart that will exhibit the variations in frequency in a striking manner, yield the following distribution which is hereafter designated as the *normal* or *standard uniliteral frequency distribution* for English telegraphic plain text:

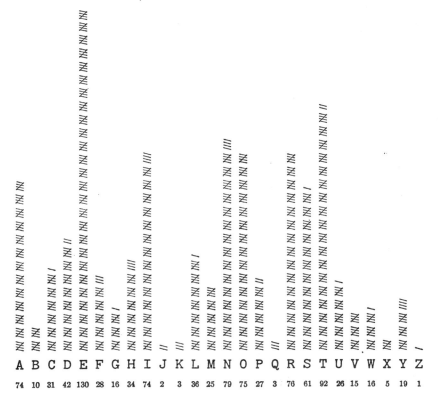

	A	B	C	D	E	F	G	H	I	J	K	L	M	N	O	P	Q	R	S	T	U	V	W	X	Y	Z
	74	10	31	42	130	28	16	34	74	2	3	36	25	79	75	27	3	76	61	92	26	15	16	5	19	1

FIGURE 3.

27

22. Important features of the normal uniliteral frequency distribution.—a. When the distribution shown in Fig. 3 is studied in detail, the following features are apparent:

(1) It is quite irregular in appearance. This is because the letters are used with greatly varying frequencies, as discussed in the preceding paragraph. This irregular appearance is often described by saying that the distribution shows marked *crests and troughs*, that is, points of high frequency and low frequency.

(2) The relative positions in which the crests and troughs fall within the distribution, that is, the *spatial relations* of the crests and troughs, are rather definitely fixed and are determined by circumstances which have been explained in subpar. 13*b*.

(3) The relative heights and depths of the crests and troughs within the distribution, that is, the *linear extensions* of the lines marking the respective frequencies, are also rather definitely fixed, as would be found if an equal volume of similar text were analyzed.

(4) The most prominent crests are marked by the vowels A, E, I, O, and the consonants N, R, S, T; the most prominent troughs are marked by the consonants J, K, Q, X, and Z,

(5) The important data are summarized in tabular form in Table 3.

TABLE 3

	Frequency	Percent of total	Percent of total in round numbers
6 Vowels: A E I O U Y	398	39. 8	40
20 Consonants:			
5 High Frequency (D N R S T)	350	35. 0	35
10 Medium Frequency (B C F G H L M P V W)	238	23. 8	24
5 Low Frequency (J K Q X Z)	14	1. 4	1
Total	1, 000	100. 0	100

(6) The frequencies of the letters of the alphabet, reduced to a base of 1,000, are as follows:

A	74	G	16	L	36	Q	3	V	15
B	10	H	34	M	25	R	76	W	16
C	31	I	74	N	79	S	61	X	5
D	42	J	2	O	75	T	92	Y	19
E	130	K	3	P	27	U	26	Z	1
F	28								

(7) The relative order of frequency of the letters is as follows:

E	130	I	74	C	31	Y	19	X	5
T	92	S	61	F	28	G	16	Q	3
N	79	D	42	P	27	W	16	K	3
R	76	L	36	U	26	V	15	J	2
O	75	H	34	M	25	B	10	Z	1
A	74								

28

(8) The four vowels A, E, I, O (combined frequency 353) and the four consonants N, R, S, T (combined frequency 308) form 661 out of every 1,000 letters of plain text; in other words, *less than one-third of the alphabet is employed in writing two-thirds of normal plain text.*

b. The data given in Fig. 3 and Table 3 represent the relative frequencies found in a large volume of English telegraphic text of a governmental, administrative character.[3] These frequencies will vary somewhat with the nature of the text analyzed. For example, if an equal number of telegrams dealing solely with *commercial* transactions in the *leather industry* were studied statistically, the frequencies would be slightly different because of the repeated occurrence of words peculiar to that industry. Again, if an equal number of telegrams dealing solely with *military* messages of a *tactical* character were studied statistically, the frequencies would differ slightly from those found above for general governmental messages of an administrative character.

c. If ordinary English literary text (such as may be found in any book, newspaper, or printed document) were analyzed, the frequencies of certain letters would be changed to an appreciable degree. This is because, in telegraphic text, words which are not strictly essential for intelligibility (such as the definite and indefinite articles, certain prepositions, conjunctions, and pronouns) are omitted. In addition, certain essential words, such as "stop", "period", "comma", and the like, which are usually indicated in written or printed matter by symbols not easy to transmit telegraphically and which must, therefore, be spelled out in telegrams, occur very frequently. Furthermore, telegraphic text often employs longer and more uncommon words than does ordinary newspaper or book text.

d. As a matter of fact, other tables compiled from Army sources gave slightly different results, depending upon the source of the text. For example, three tables based upon 75,000, 100,000, and 136,257 letters taken from various sources (telegrams, newspapers, magazine articles, books of fiction) gave as the relative order of frequency for the first 10 letters the following:

For 75,000 letters_____ E T R N I O A S D L
For 100,000 letters_____ E T R I N O A S D L
For 136,257 letters_____ E T R N A O I S L D

e. Frequency data applicable purely to English military text were compiled by Hitt,[4] from a study of 10,000 letters taken from orders and reports; these data are given in Table 4, on the next page. Hitt also compiled data for telegraphic text (but does not state what kind of messages); these data are given in Table 5.

---

[3] Just as the individual letters constituting a large volume of plain text have more or less characteristic or fixed frequencies, so it is found that *digraphs* and *trigraphs* (two- and three-letter combinations, respectively) have characteristic frequencies, when a large volume of text is studied statistically. In Table 6 of Appendix 2, "Letter frequency data—English", are shown the relative frequencies of all digraphs appearing in the 260 telegrams referred to in subpar. 21e. This appendix also includes several other kinds of tables and lists of frequency data which will be useful to the student in his work. It is suggested that the student refer to this appendix now, to gain an idea of the data available for his future reference.

Other languages, of course, each have their own individual characteristic plaintext frequencies of single letters, digraphs, trigraphs, etc. A brief summary of the letter frequency data for German, French, Italian, Spanish, Portuguese, and Russian constitutes Appendix 5, "Letter frequency data—foreign languages".

[4] Op. cit., pp. 6–7.

TABLE 4.—*Frequency table for 10,000 letters of nontelegraphic English military text, as compiled by Hitt*

ALPHABETICALLY ARRANGED

A	778	G	174	L	372	Q	8	V	112
B	141	H	595	M	288	R	651	W	176
C	296	I	667	N	686	S	622	X	27
D	402	J	51	O	807	T	855	Y	196
E	1,277	K	74	P	223	U	308	Z	17
F	197								

ARRANGED ACCORDING TO FREQUENCY

E	1,277	R	651	U	308	Y	196	K	74
T	855	S	622	C	296	W	176	J	51
O	807	H	595	M	288	G	174	X	27
A	778	D	402	P	223	B	141	Z	17
N	686	L	372	F	197	V	112	Q	8
I	667								

TABLE 5.—*Frequency table for 10,000 letters of telegraphic English military text, as compiled by Hitt*

ALPHABETICALLY ARRANGED

A	813	G	201	L	392	Q	38	V	136
B	149	H	386	M	273	R	677	W	166
C	306	I	711	N	718	S	656	X	51
D	417	J	42	O	844	T	634	Y	208
E	1,319	K	88	P	243	U	321	Z	6
F	205								

ARRANGED ACCORDING TO FREQUENCY

E	1,319	S	656	U	321	F	205	K	88
O	844	T	634	C	306	G	201	X	51
A	813	D	417	M	273	W	166	J	42
N	718	L	392	P	243	B	149	Q	38
I	711	H	386	Y	208	V	136	Z	6
R	677								

23. Constancy of the standard or normal uniliteral frequency distribution.—*a.* The relative frequencies disclosed by the statistical study of large volumes of text may be considered to be the standard or *normal* frequencies of the letters of written English. Counts made of smaller volumes of text will tend to approximate these normal frequencies, and, within certain limits,[5]

[5] It is useless to go beyond a certain limit in establishing the normal-frequency distribution for a given language. As a striking instance of this fact, witness the frequency study made by an indefatigable German, Kaeding, who in 1898 made a count of the letters in about 11,000,000 words, totaling about 62,000,000 letters in German text. When reduced to a percentage basis, and when the relative order of frequency was determined, the results he obtained differed very little from the results obtained by Kasiski, a German cryptographer, from a count of only 1,060 letters. See Kaeding, *Haeufigkeitswoerterbuch*, Steglitz, 1898; Kasiski, *Die Geheimschriften und die Dechiffrir-Kunst*, Berlin, 1863.

the smaller the volume, the lower will be the degree of approximation to the normal, until, in the case of a very short message, the normal proportions may not manifest themselves at all. It is advisable that the student fix this fact firmly in mind, for the sooner he realizes the true nature of any data relative to the frequency of occurrence of letters in text, the less often will his labors toward the solution of specific ciphers be thwarted and retarded by too strict an adherence to these generalized principles of frequency.[6] He should constantly bear in mind that such data are merely statistical generalizations, that they will be found to hold strictly true only in large volumes of text, and that they may not even be approximated in short messages.

b. Nevertheless the normal frequency distribution or the "normal expectation" for any alphabetic language is, in the last analysis, the best guide to, and the usual basis for, the solution of cryptograms of a certain type. It is useful, therefore, to reduce the normal, uniliteral frequency distribution to a basis that more or less closely approximates the volume of text which the cryptanalyst most often encounters in individual cryptograms. As regards length of messages, counting only the letters in the body, and excluding address and signature, a study of the 260 telegrams referred to in par. 21 shows that the arithmetical average is 217 letters; the statistical mean, or weighted average,[7] however, is 191 letters. These two results are, however, close enough together to warrant the statement that the *average* length of telegrams is approximately 200 letters. The frequencies given in par. 21 have therefore been reduced to a basis of 200 letters, and the following uniliteral frequency distribution may be taken as showing the most typical distribution to be expected in 200 letters of English telegraphic text:

FIGURE 4.

c. The student should take careful note of the appearance of the distribution [8] shown in Fig. 4, for it will be of much assistance to him in the early stages of his study. The manner of setting down the tallies should be followed by him in making his own distributions, indicating every fifth occurrence of a letter by an oblique tally. This procedure almost automatically shows the total number of occurrences for each letter, and yet does not destroy the graphical appearance

[6] A curiosity in this connection is the book "GADSBY" by Ernest Vincent Wright published in Los Angeles, 1939. Written as a tour de force, in this novel of about 50,000 words there is not a single occurrence of the letter "E"!

[7] The arithmetical average is obtained by adding each different length and dividing by the number of different-length messages; the mean is obtained by multiplying each different length by the number of messages of that length, adding all products, and dividing by the total number of messages.

[8] The use of the terms "distribution" and "frequency distribution", instead of "table" and "frequency table," respectively, is considered advisable from the point of view of consistency with the usual statistical nomenclature. When data are given in tabular form, with frequencies indicated by numbers, then they may properly be said to be set out in the form of a *table*. When, however, the same data are distributed in a chart which partakes of the nature of a graph, with the data indicated by horizontal or vertical linear extensions, or by a curve connecting points corresponding to quantities, then it is more proper to call such a graphic representation of the data a *distribution*.

of the distribution, especially if care is taken to use approximately the same amount of space for each set of five tallies. Cross-section paper is very useful for this purpose, since when one is making a frequency distribution on it, he may place each set of five tallies in an individual cell. In making a frequency distribution, each consecutive letter of the sample under study should be recorded as a tally mark; only with this procedure can errors in making a distribution be kept at a minimum. For instance, if the first group of a message is O W Q W Z, the first tally mark would be recorded over the "O" in the base of the distribution; the second tally mark, recorded over the "W"; the third tally, over the "Q"; the fourth, over the "W"; and so forth.

d. The word "uniliteral" in the designation "uniliteral frequency distribution" means "single letter," and it is to be inferred that other types of frequency distributions may be encountered. For example, a distribution of pairs of letters, constituting a biliteral frequency distribution, is very often used in the study of certain cryptograms in which it is desired that pairs made by combining successive letters be listed. A biliteral distribution of A B C D E F would take these pairs: AB, BC, CD, DE, EF. The distribution could be made in the form of a large square divided up into 676 cells. When distributions beyond biliteral are required (triliteral, quadriliteral, etc.) they can only be made by listing them in some order, for example, alphabetically based on the 1st, 2d, 3d, . . . letter.

24. The three facts which can be determined from a study of the uniliteral frequency distribution for a cryptogram.—*a*. The following three facts (to be explained subsequently) can usually be determined from an inspection of the uniliteral frequency distribution for a given cipher message of average length, composed of letters:

(1) Whether the cipher belongs to the substitution or the transposition class;

(2) If to the former, whether it is monoalphabetic [9] or nonmonoalphabetic [10] in character;

(3) If monoalphabetic, whether the cipher alphabet is standard (direct or reversed) or mixed.

b. For immediate purposes the first two of the foregoing determinations are quite important and will be discussed in detail in the next two paragraphs; the other determination will be touched upon very briefly, leaving its detailed discussion for subsequent sections of the text.

25. Determining the class to which a cipher belongs.—*a*. The determination of the class to which a cipher belongs is usually a relatively easy matter because of the fundamental difference between transposition and substitution as cryptographic processes. In a transposition cipher the original letters of the plain text have merely been rearranged, without any change whatsoever in their identities, that is, in the conventional values they have in the normal alphabet. Hence, the numbers of vowels (A, E, I, O, U, Y), high-frequency consonants (D, N, R, S, T), medium-frequency consonants (B, C, F, G, H, L, M, P, V, W), and low-frequency consonants (J, K, Q, X, Z) are exactly the same in the cryptogram as they are in the plaintext message. Therefore, the percentages of vowels, high-, medium-, and low-frequency consonants are the same in the transposed text as in the equivalent plain text. In a substitution cipher, on the other hand, the identities of the original letters of the plain text have been changed, that is, the conventional values they have in the normal alphabet have been altered. Consequently, if a count is made

---

[9] In connection with uniliteral frequency distributions, the term monoalphabetic is considered to embrace the concept of monoalphabetic-monographic-uniliteral systems only, thus excluding *polygraphic* and *multiliteral* systems, both of which, however, usually fall into the monoalphabetic category.

[10] The term nonmonoalphabetic as applied in this instance is considered to embrace all deviations from the characteristic appearance of monoalphabetic distributions. These deviations include the phenomena inherent in polyalphabetic, polygraphic, and multiliteral cryptograms, as well as in *random* text, i. e., text which appears to have been produced by chance or accident, having no discernible patterns or limitations.

of the various letters present in such a cryptogram, it will be found that the number of vowels, high-, medium-, and low-frequency consonants will usually be quite different in the cryptogram from what they are in the original plaintext message. Therefore, the percentages of vowels, high-, medium-, and low-frequency consonants are usually quite different in the substitution text from what they are in the equivalent plain text. From these considerations it follows that if in a specific cryptogram the percentages of vowels, high-, medium-, and low-frequency consonants are approximately the same as would be expected in normal plain text, the cryptogram *probably* belongs to the transposition class; if these percentages are quite different from those to be expected in normal plain text the cryptogram *probably* belongs to the substitution class.

b. In the preceding subparagraph the word "probably" was emphasized by italicizing it, for there can be no certainty in every case of this determination. *Usually* these percentages in a transposition cipher are close to the normal percentages for plain text; *usually*, in a substitution cipher, they are far different from the normal percentages for plain text. But occasionally a cipher message is encountered which is difficult to classify with a reasonable degree of certainty because the message is too short for the general principles of frequency to manifest themselves. It is clear that if in actual messages there were no variation whatever from the normal vowel and consonant percentages given in Table 3, the determination of the class to which a specific cryptogram belongs would be an extremely simple matter. But unfortunately there is always some variation or deviation from the normal. Intuition suggests that as messages decrease in length there may be a greater and greater departure from the normal proportions of vowels, high-, medium-, and low-frequency consonants, until in very short messages the normal proportions may not hold at all. Similarly, as messages increase in length there may be a lesser and lesser departure from the normal proportions, until in messages totalling a thousand or more letters there may be no difference at all between the actual and the theoretical proportions. But intuition is not enough, for in dealing with specific messages of the length of those commonly encountered in practical work the question sometimes arises as to exactly how much deviation (from the normal proportions) may be allowed for in a cryptogram which shows a considerable amount of deviation from the normal and which might still belong to the transposition rather than to the substitution class.

c. Statistical studies have been made on this matter and some graphs have been constructed thereon. These are shown in Charts 2–5 in the form of simple curves, the use of which will now be explained. Each chart contains two curves marking the lower and upper limits, respectively, of the theoretical amount of deviation (from the normal percentages) of vowels or consonants which may be allowable in a cipher believed to belong to the transposition class.

d. In Chart 2, curve V_1 marks the lower limit of the theoretical amount of deviation [11] from the number of vowels theoretically expected to appear [12] in a message of given length; curve V_2 marks the upper limit of the same statistic. Thus, for example, in a message of 100 letters in plain English there should be between 33 and 47 vowels (A E I O U Y). Likewise, in Chart 3, curves H_1 and H_2 mark the lower and upper limits as regards the high-frequency consonants. In a message of 100 letters there should be between 28 and 42 high-frequency consonants (D N R S T). In Chart 4, curves M_1 and M_2 mark the lower and upper limits as regards the medium-frequency consonants. In a message of 100 letters there should be between 17 and 31 medium-frequency

---

[11] In Charts 2–5, inclusive, the limits of the upper and lower curves have been calculated to include approximately 70 per cent of messages of the various lengths.

[12] The expression "the number of . . . theoretically expected to appear" is often condensed to "the theoretical expectation of . . ." or "the normal expectation of . . ."

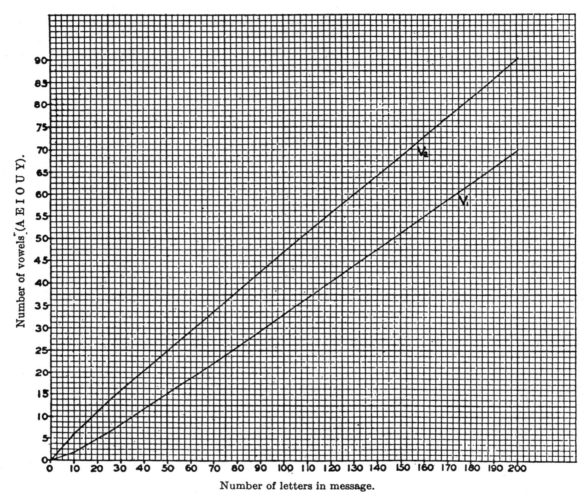

CHART 2. Curves making the lower and upper limits of the theoretical amount of deviation from the number of vowels theoretically expected in messages of various lengths.   (See subpar. 25*d*.)

consonants (B C F G H L M P V W).   Finally, in Chart 5, curves L_1 and L_2 mark the lower and upper limits as regards the low-frequency consonants.   In a message of 100 letters there should be between 0 and 3 low-frequency consonants (J K Q X Z).   In using the charts, therefore, one finds the point of intersection of the coordinate (below the chart) corresponding to the length of the message, with the coordinate (to the left of the chart) corresponding to (1) the number of vowels, (2) the number of high-frequency consonants, (3) the number of medium-frequency consonants, and (4) the number of low-frequency consonants actually counted in the message.   If all four points of intersection fall within the area delimited by the respective curves, then the numbers of vowels and high-, medium-, and low-frequency consonants correspond with the numbers theoretically expected in a normal plaintext message of the same length; since the message under investigation is not plain text, it follows that the cryptogram may certainly be

34

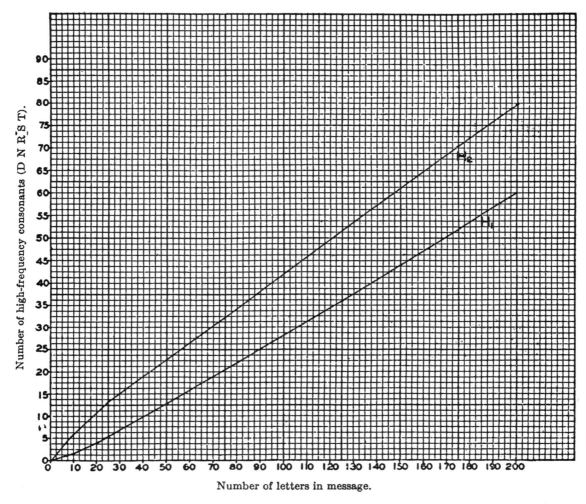

CHART 3. Curves making the lower and upper limits of the theoretical amount of deviation from the number of high-frequency consonants theoretically expected in messages of various lengths. (See subpar. 25d.)

classified as a transposition cipher. On the other hand, if one or more of these points of intersection fall outside the area delimited by the respective curves, it follows that the cryptogram is probably a substitution cipher. The distance that the point of intersection falls outside the area delimited by these curves is a more or less rough measure of the improbability of the cryptogram's being a transposition cipher.

e. Sometimes a cryptogram is encountered which is hard to classify with certainty even with the foregoing aids, because it has been consciously prepared with a view to making the classification difficult. This can be done either by selecting peculiar words (as in "trick cryptograms") or by employing a cipher alphabet in which letters of *approximately similar normal frequencies* have been interchanged. For example, E may be replaced by O, T by R, and so on,

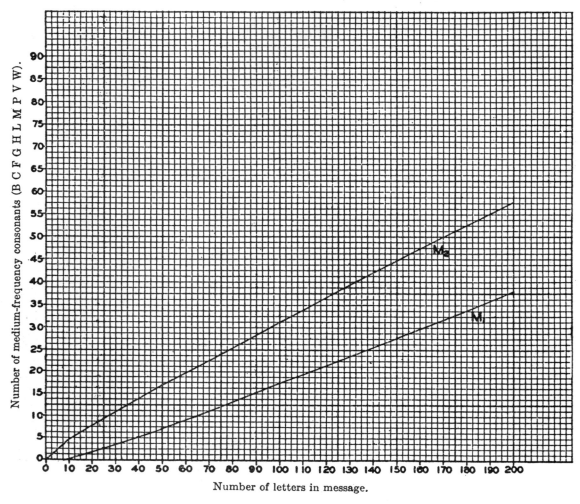

CHART 4. Curves marking the lower and upper limits of the theoretical amount of deviation from the number of medium-frequency consonants theoretically expected in messages of various lengths. (See subpar. 25d.)

thus yielding a cryptogram giving external indications of being a transposition cipher but which is really a substitution cipher. If the cryptogram is not too short, a close study will usually disclose what has been done, as well as the futility of so simple a subterfuge.

f. In the majority of cases, in practical work, the determination of the class to which a cipher of average length belongs can be made from a mere inspection of the message, after the cryptanalyst has acquired a familiarity with the normal appearance of transposition and of substitution ciphers. In the former case, his eyes very speedily note many high-frequency letters, such as E, T, N, R, O, A, and I, with the absence of low-frequency letters, such as J, K, Q, X, and Z; in the latter case, his eyes just as quickly note the presence of many low-frequency letters, and a corresponding absence of some of the high-frequency letters.

36

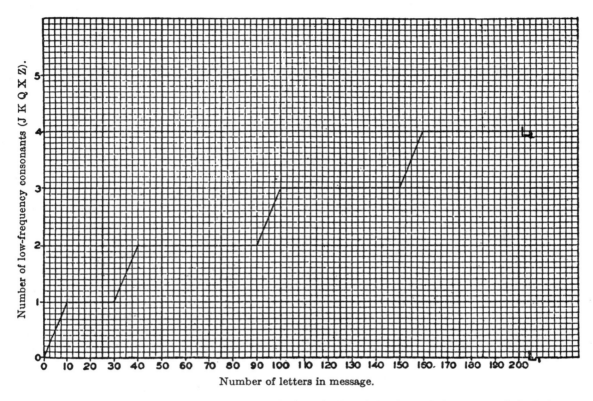

CHART 5. Curves marking the lower and upper limits of the theoretical amount of deviation from the number of low-frequency consonants theoretically expected in messages of various lengths. (See subpar. 25*d*.)

g. Another rather quickly completed test, in the case of the simpler varieties of ciphers, is to look for *repetitions of groups of letters*. As will become apparent very soon, recurrences of syllables, entire words and short phrases constitute a characteristic of all normal plain text. Since a transposition cipher involves a change in the *sequence* of the letters composing a plaintext message, such recurrences are broken up so that the cipher text no longer will show repetitions of more or less lengthy sequences of letters. But if a cipher message does show many repetitions and these are of several letters in length, say over four or five, the conclusion is at once warranted that the cryptogram is most probably a substitution and not a transposition cipher. However, for the beginner in cryptanalysis, it will be advisable to make the uniliteral frequency distribution, and note the frequencies of the vowels and of the high-, medium-, and low-frequency consonants. Then, referring to Charts 2 to 5, he should carefully note whether or not the observed frequencies for these categories of letters fall within the limits of the theoretical frequencies for a normal plaintext message of the same length, and be guided accordingly.

h. It is obvious that the foregoing rule applies only to ciphers composed wholly of letters. If a message is composed entirely of figures, or of arbitrary signs and symbols, or of intermixtures of letters, figures and other symbols, it is immediately apparent that the cryptogram is a substitution cipher.

37

i. Finally, it should be mentioned that there are certain kinds of cryptograms whose class cannot be determined by the method set forth in subpar. *d* above. These exceptions will be discussed in a subsequent chapter of this text.[13]

26. **Determining whether a substitution cipher is monoalphabetic or nonmonoalphabetic.—** *a.* It will be remembered that a monoalphabetic substitution cipher is one in which a single cipher alphabet is employed throughout the whole message; that is, a given ciphertext unit invariably represents one and only one particular plaintext unit, this relationship holding throughout the message. On the other hand, a polyalphabetic substitution cipher is one in which two or more cipher alphabets are employed within the same message; that is, a given ciphertext unit may represent two or more different elements in the plain text, according to some rule governing the selection of the equivalent to be used in each case.

b. It is easy to see why and how the appearance of the uniliteral frequency distribution for a substitution cipher may be used to determine whether the cryptogram is monoalphabetic or nonmonoalphabetic in character. The normal distribution presents marked crests and troughs by virtue of two circumstances. First, the elementary sounds which the symbols represent are used with greatly varying frequencies, it being one of the striking characteristics of every alphabetic language that its elementary sounds are used with greatly varying frequencies.[14] In the second place, except for orthographic aberrations peculiar to certain languages (conspicuously, English and French), each such sound is represented by the same symbol. It follows, therefore, that since in a monoalphabetic substitution cipher each different cipher letter (=elementary symbol) represents one and only one plaintext letter (=elementary sound), the uniliteral frequency distribution for such a cipher message must also exhibit the irregular crest-and-trough appearance of the normal distribution, but with this important modification—*the absolute positions of the crests and troughs will not be the same as in the normal.* That is, the letters accompanying the crests and the troughs in the distribution for the cryptogram will be different from those accompanying the crests and the troughs in the normal distribution. But the marked irregularity or "roughness" of the distribution, that is, the presence of accentuated crests and troughs, is in itself an indication that each symbol or cipher letter always represents the same plaintext letter in the cryptogram. Hence the general rule: *A marked crest-and-trough appearance in the uniliteral frequency distribution for a given cryptogram indicates that a single cipher alphabet is involved and constitutes one of the tests for a monoalphabetic substitution cipher.*

c. On the other hand, suppose that in a cryptogram each cipher letter represents several different plaintext letters. Some of them are of high frequency, others of low frequency. The net result of such a situation, so far as the uniliteral frequency distribution for the cryptogram is concerned, is to prevent the appearance of any marked crests and troughs and to tend to reduce the elements of the distribution to a more or less common level. This imparts a "flattened out" appearance to the distribution. For example, in a certain cryptogram of polyalphabetic construction, $K_c = E_p$, G_p and J_p; $R_c = A_p$, D_p, and B_p; $X_c = O_p$, L_p, and F_p. The frequencies of K_c, R_c, and X_c will be approximately equal because the summations of the frequencies of the several plaintext letters which each of these cipher letters represents at different times will be about equal. If this same phenomenon were true of all the letters of the cryptogram, it is clear that the frequencies of the 26 letters, when shown by means of the ordinary uniliteral frequency distribution, would show

[13] Chapter XI.

[14] The student who is interested in this phase of the subject may find the following reference of value: *Zipf, G. K., Selected Studies of the Principle of Relative Frequency in Language,* Cambridge, Mass., 1932.

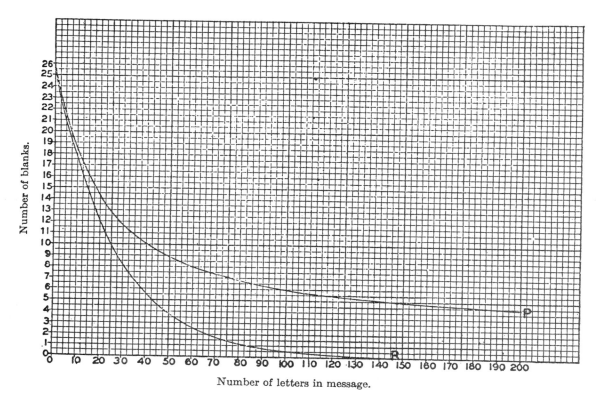

Number of blanks.

Number of letters in message.

CHART 6. Curves showing the average number of blanks theoretically expected in distributions for plain text (P) and for random text (R) for messages of various lengths. (See subpar. 26f.)

no striking differences and the distribution would have the flat appearance of a typical polyalphabetic substitution cipher. Hence, the general rule: *The absence of marked crests and troughs in the uniliteral frequency distribution indicates that a complex form of substitution is involved. The flattened-out appearance of the distribution, then, is one of the criteria for the rejection of a hypothesis of monoalphabetic [15] substitution.*

d. The foregoing test based upon the appearance of the frequency distribution is only one of several means of determining whether a substitution cipher is monoalphabetic or nonmonoalphabetic in composition. It can be employed in cases yielding frequency distributions from which definite conclusions can be drawn with more or less certainty by mere ocular examination. In those cases in which the frequency distributions contain insufficient data to permit drawing definite conclusions by such examination, certain statistical tests can be applied. One of these tests, called the ϕ (phi) test, warrants detailed treatment and is discussed in par. 27, below.

e. At this point, however, one additional test will be given because of its simplicity of application. This test, the Λ (lambda) or *blank-expectation test*, may be employed in testing messages up to 200 letters in length, it being assumed that in messages of greater length ocular examination of the frequency distribution offers little or no difficulty. This test concerns the

———
[15] Cf. footnote 9 on p. 32.

number of blanks in the frequency distribution, that is, the number of letters of the alphabet which are entirely absent from the message. It has been found from statistical studies that rather definite "laws" govern the theoretically expected number of blanks in normal plaintext messages and in frequency distributions for cryptograms of different natures and of various sizes. The results of certain of these studies have been embodied in Chart 6.

f. This chart contains two curves. The one labeled P applies to the average number of blanks theoretically expected in frequency distributions based upon normal plaintext messages of the indicated lengths. The other curve, labeled R, applies to the average number of blanks theoretically expected in frequency distributions based upon *random* assortments of letters; that is, assortments such as would be found by random selection of letters out of a hat containing thousands of letters, all of the 26 letters of the alphabet being present in equal proportions, each letter being replaced after a record of its selection has been made. Such random assortments correspond to polyalphabetic cipher messages in which the number of cipher alphabets is so large that if uniliteral frequency distributions are made of the letters, the distributions are practically identical with those which are obtained by random selections of letters out of a hat.

g. In using this chart, one finds the point of intersection of the vertical line corresponding to the length of the message, with the horizontal line corresponding to the observed number of blanks in the distribution for the message. If this point of intersection falls closer to curve P than it does to curve R, the number of blanks in the message approximates or corresponds more closely to the number theoretically expected in a plaintext message (or a simple substitution thereof) than it does to a sample of equal length of a more or less "random" assortment of letters (for example, the cipher text of a complex polyalphabetic cipher); therefore, this is evidence that the cryptogram is monoalphabetic. Conversely, if the point of intersection falls closer to curve R than to curve P, the number of blanks in the message approximates or corresponds more closely to the number theoretically expected in a random text than it does to a plaintext message of the same length; therefore, this is evidence that the cryptogram is nonmonoalphabetic.

27. The ϕ (phi) test for determining monoalphabeticity.—*a.* The student has seen in the preceding paragraph how it is possible to determine by ocular examination whether or not a substitution cipher is monoalphabetic. This tentative determination is based on the presence of a marked crest-and-trough appearance in the uniliteral frequency distribution, and also on the number of blanks in the distribution. However, when the distribution contains a small number of elements, ocular examination and evaluation becomes increasingly difficult and uncertain. In such cases, recourse may be had to a mathematical test, known as the ϕ test, to determine the relative monoalphabeticity or nonmonoalphabeticity of a distribution.

b. Without going into the theory of probability at this time, or into the derivation of the formulas involved, let it suffice for the present to state that with this test the "observed value of ϕ" (symbolized by ϕ_o) for the distribution being tested is compared with the "expected value of ϕ random" (ϕ_r) and the "expected value of ϕ plain" (ϕ_p). The formulas are $\phi_r = .0385N(N-1)$ and, for English military text, $\phi_p = .0667N(N-1)$, where N is the total number of elements in the distribution.[16] The use of these formulas is best illustrated by an example.

---

[16] The constant .0385 is the decimal equivalent of 1/26, i. e., the reciprocal of the number of elements in the alphabet. The constant .0667 is the sum of the squares of the probabilities of occurrence of the individual letters in English plain text. These constants are treated in detail in *Military Cryptanalytics, Part III.*

c. The following short cryptogram with its accompanying uniliteral frequency distribution is at hand:

```
O W Q W Z   A E D T D   Q H H O B   A W F T Z   W O D E Q

T U W R Q   B D Q R O   X H Q D A   G T B D H   P Z R D K
```

A B C D E F G H I J K L M N O P Q R S T U V W X Y Z

ϕ_o for the distribution is calculated by applying the formula $f(f-1)$ to the frequency (f) of each letter and totaling the result; or, expressed in mathematical notation,[17] $\phi_o = \Sigma f(f-1)$. Thus,

```
3 3   7 2 1 1 4       1       4 1 6 3   4 1   5 1     3
A B C D E F G H I J K L M N O P Q R S T U V W X Y Z
6 6   42 2 0 0 12     0       12 0 30 6   12 0   20 0   6
```

$N = \Sigma f = 50$

$\phi_o = \Sigma f(f-1) = 154$

For this distribution, $\phi_r = .0385 N(N-1) = .0385 \times 50 \times 49 = 94$, and
$\phi_p = .0667 N(N-1) = .0667 \times 50 \times 49 = 163$.

Now since ϕ_o, 154, more closely approximates ϕ_p than it does ϕ_r, we have a mathematical corroboration of the hypothesis that the cryptogram is a monoalphabetic substitution cipher. If ϕ_o were nearer to ϕ_r than to ϕ_p, then the assumption would be that the cryptogram is not a monoalphabetic cipher. If ϕ_o were just half way between ϕ_r and ϕ_p, then decision would have to be suspended, since no further statistical proof in the matter is possible with this particular test.[18]

d. Two further examples may be illustrated:

```
(1) A B C D E F G H I J K L M N O P Q R S T U V W X Y Z
    0     0 2 6 12 2     0       12 2   0           0   6
```

$N = 25$

$\Sigma f(f-1) = 42$

---

[17] The more usual mathematical notation for expressing ϕ_o would be $\sum_{i=A}^{Z} f_i(f_i-1)$, which is read as "the sum of all the terms for all integral values of f from A to Z inclusive." In turn, $\sum_{i=A}^{Z} f_i(f_i-1)$ would be expanded as $f_A(f_A-1) + f_B(f_B-1) + f_C(f_C-1) + \ldots + f_Z(f_Z-1)$. However, in the interest of simplicity the notation $\Sigma f(f-1)$ is employed; likewise, the notations ϕ_r and ϕ_p are employed in lieu of the more usual $E(\phi_r)$ and $E(\phi_p)$.

[18] Another method of expressing the relative monoalphabeticity of a cryptogram is based upon comparing the *index of coincidence* (abbr. *I. C.*) of the cryptogram under examination with the theoretical I. C. of plain text. The I. C. of a message is defined as the ratio of ϕ_o to ϕ_r; thus, in the example above, the I. C. is $\frac{154}{94}$, which equals 1.64. The theoretical I. C. of English plain text is 1.73, which is the decimal equivalent of $\frac{.0667}{.0385}$, the ratio of the *"plain* constant" to the *"random* constant". The I. C. of random text is 1.00, i. e., $\frac{.0385}{.0385}$.

(2) A B C̃ D E F G̃ H̿ Ĩ J K̃ L M̿ Ñ O P Q̃ R̂ S T̃ U Ṽ W X̃ Ỹ Z̿

    0   0 0 2 0 0 0 6 0 0   0 2   0 0   0 0 2 6   Σf(f−1)=18

Since both distributions have 25 elements, then for both

$$\phi_r = .0385 \times 25 \times 24 = 23, \text{ and}$$
$$\phi_p = .0667 \times 25 \times 24 = 40.$$

Hence distribution (1) is monoalphabetic, while (2) is not.

    e. The student must not assume that statistical tests in cryptanalysis are infallible or absolute in themselves;[19] statistical approaches serve only as a means to the end, in guiding the analyst to the most probably fruitful sources of attack. Since no one test in cryptanalysis gives definite proof of a hypothesis (in fact, not even a battery of tests gives *absolute* proof), all applicable statistical means at the disposal of the cryptanalyst should be used; thus, in examination for monoalphabeticity, the ϕ test, Λ test, and even other tests[20] could profitably be employed. To illustrate this point, if the ϕ test is taken on the distribution of the *plaintext* letters of the phrase

A QUICK BROWN FOX JUMPS OVER THE LAZY DOG

N=33

A̿ B C D̃ E̿ F G̃ H̃ Ĩ J K̃ L̃ M̃ N̿ O P Q̃ R̿ S T̃ U̿ V W̃ X̃ Ỹ Z̃

2   2   12   2   2   Σf(f−1)=20

$$\phi_r = 41; \quad \phi_p = 70$$

it will be noticed that ϕ_o is less than half of ϕ_r, thus conclusively "proving" that the letters of this phrase could not possibly constitute plain text nor a monoalphabetic encipherment of plain text in *any* language! The student should be able to understand the cause of this cryptologic curiosity.

    28. Determining whether a cipher alphabet is standard or mixed.—*a.* Assuming that the uniliteral frequency distribution for a given cryptogram has been made, and that it shows clearly that the cryptogram is a substitution cipher and is monoalphabetic in character, a consideration of the nature of standard cipher alphabets[21] almost makes it obvious how an inspection of the distribution will disclose whether the cipher alphabet involved is a standard cipher alphabet or a mixed cipher alphabet. If the crests and troughs of the distribution occupy positions which correspond to the *relative* positions they occupy in the normal frequency distribution, then the cipher alphabet is a standard cipher alphabet. If this is not the case, then it is highly probable that the cryptogram has been prepared by the use of a mixed cipher alphabet.

    b. The difference between the distribution of a direct standard alphabet cipher and one of a reversed standard alphabet cipher is merely a matter of the *direction* in which the sequence of

---

[19] The following quotation from the Indian mathematician P. C. Mahalanobis, concerning the fallibility of statistics, is particularly appropriate in this connection: "If statistical theory is right, predictions must sometimes come out wrong; on the other hand, if predictions are always right, then the statistical theory must be wrong."--*Sankhyā*, Vol. 10, Part 3, p. 203. Calcutta, 1950.

[20] One of these, the *chi-square test*, will be treated in *Military Cryptanalytics, Part III.*

[21] See par. 12.

crests and troughs progresses—to the right, as is done in normally reading or writing the alphabet (A B C . . . Z), or to the left, that is, in the reversed direction (Z . . . C B A). With a direct standard cipher alphabet the direction in which the crests and troughs of the distribution progress is the normal direction, from left to right; with a reversed standard cipher alphabet this direction is reversed, from right to left.

c. In testing to determine whether a distribution involves encipherment by means of a standard or a mixed alphabet, an attempt is made to locate the more readily-discernible clusters of crests which usually appear in a distribution, such as the distinctive crest-patterns representing the plaintext letters "A . . . E . . . I" and "$\overline{\text{RST}}$." These crest-patterns are searched for, with a quick scanning of the distribution, and then the relative placement with respect to each other is tested to see if it conforms to the expectation for a *direct* standard cipher alphabet, and, if not, then for a *reversed* standard cipher alphabet. During this latter step, which consists of little more than counting in one direction and then (when necessary) in the other, the blank (or nearly-blank) expectation of "$\overline{\text{JK}}_p$" followed by the characteristic curve for "$\overline{\text{LMNOP}}_p$" and the blank "$Q_p$" are also considered.

d. A mechanical test may be applied in doubtful cases arising from lack of material available for study; just what this test involves, and an illustration of its application will be given in the next chapter, using specific examples.

CHAPTER V

UNILITERAL SUBSTITUTION WITH STANDARD CIPHER ALPHABETS

Paragraph

Types of standard cipher alphabets_____ 29
Procedure in encipherment and decipherment by means of uniliteral substitution_____ 30
Principles of solution by construction and analysis of the uniliteral frequency distribution_____ 31
Theoretical example of solution_____ 32
Practical example of solution by the frequency method_____ 33
Solution by completing the plain-component sequence_____ 34
Special remarks on the method of solution by completing the plain-component sequence_____ 35
Value of mechanical solution as a short cut_____ 36
Basic reason for the low degree of cryptosecurity afforded by monoalphabetic cryptograms involving standard cipher alphabets_____ 37

29. Types of standard cipher alphabets.—*a.* Standard cipher alphabets are of two types:

(1) *Direct standard*, in which the cipher component is the normal sequence but shifted to the right or left of its point of coincidence in the normal alphabet.   Example:

Plain: ABCDEFGHIJKLMNOPQRSTUVWXYZ
Cipher: QRSTUVWXYZABCDEFGHIJKLMNOP

It is obvious that the cipher component can be applied to the plain component at any one of 26 points of coincidence, but since the alphabet that results from one of these applications coincides exactly with the normal alphabet, a series of only 25 (direct standard) cipher alphabets results from the shifting of the cipher component.

(2) *Reversed standard*, in which the cipher component is also the normal sequence but runs in the opposite direction from the normal.   Example:

Plain: ABCDEFGHIJKLMNOPQRSTUVWXYZ
Cipher: QPONMLKJIHGFEDCBAZYXWVUTSR

Here the cipher component can be applied to the plain component at any of 26 points of coincidence, each yielding a different cipher alphabet.   There is in this case, therefore, a series of 26 (reversed standard) cipher alphabets.

b. It is often convenient to refer to or designate one of a series of cipher alphabets without ambiguity or circumlocution.   The usual method is to indicate a particular alphabet to which reference is made by citing a pair of equivalents in that alphabet, such as, in the example above, $A_p = Q_c$.   The *key* for the cipher alphabet just referred to, as well as that preceding it, is $A_p = Q_c$, and it is said that the *key letter* for the cipher alphabet is Q_c.

c. The cipher alphabet in subpar. *a* (2), above, is also a *reciprocal alphabet;* that is, the cipher alphabet contains 13 distinct pairs of equivalents which are reversible.   For example, in the alphabet referred to, $A_p = Q_c$ *and* $Q_p = A_c$; $B_p = P_c$ *and* $P_p = B_c$, etc.   The reciprocity exists throughout the alphabet and is a result of the method by which it was formed.   (Reciprocal alphabets may be produced by juxtaposing *any two components which are identical* but progress in opposite directions.)

45

30. Procedure in encipherment and decipherment by means of uniliteral substitution.—
a. When a message is enciphered by means of *monoalphabetic uniliteral substitution*, or *simple substitution* (as it is often called), the individual letters of the message text are replaced by the single-letter equivalents taken from the cipher alphabet selected by prearrangement. Example:

Message: EIGHTEEN PRISONERS CAPTURED
Enciphering alphabet: Direct standard, $A_p = T_c$

Plain: ABCDEFGHIJKLMNOPQRSTUVWXYZ
Cipher: TUVWXYZABCDEFGHIJKLMNOPQRS

Letter-for-letter encipherment:

EIGHTEEN PRISONERS CAPTURED
XBZAMXXG IKBLHGXKL VTIMNKXW

The cipher text is then regrouped, for transmission, into groups of five.

Cryptogram:

XBZAM XXGIK BLHGX KLVTI MNKXW

b. The procedure in decipherment is merely the reverse of that in encipherment. The cipher alphabet selected by prearrangement is set up with the cipher component arranged in the normal sequence and placed above the plain component for ease in deciphering. The letters of the cryptogram are then replaced by their plaintext equivalents, as shown below.

Cipher: ABCDEFGHIJKLMNOPQRSTUVWXYZ
Plain: HIJKLMNOPQRSTUVWXYZABCDEFG

The message deciphers thus:

Cipher: XBZAM XXGIK BLHGX KLVTI MNKXW
Plain: EIGHT EENPR ISONE RSCAP TURED

The deciphering clerk rewrites the text in word lengths:

EIGHTEEN PRISONERS CAPTURED

c. In subpar. *a*, above, the cryptogram was prepared in final form for transmission by dividing the cryptographic text into groups of five. This is generally the case in military communications involving cipher systems. It promotes accuracy in telegraphic communication since an operator knows he must receive a definite number of characters in each group, no more and no less. Also, it usually makes solution of the messages by unauthorized persons more difficult because the length of the words, phrases, and sentences of the plain text is hidden. If the last group of the cipher text in subpar. 30*a* had not been a complete group of five letters, it might have been completed by adding a sufficient number of meaningless letters (called *nulls*).

31. Principles of solution by construction and analysis of the uniliteral frequency distribution.—*a.* The analysis of monoalphabetic cryptograms prepared by the use of standard cipher alphabets follows almost directly from a consideration of the nature of such alphabets. Since the cipher component of a standard cipher alphabet consists either of the normal sequence merely displaced 1, 2, 3, . . . intervals from the normal point of coincidence, or of the normal sequence proceeding in a reversed-normal direction, it is obvious that the uniliteral frequency distribution for a cryptogram prepared by means of such a cipher alphabet employed monoalphabetically will show crests and troughs whose *relative* positions and frequencies will be exactly the same as in the uniliteral frequency distribution for the plain text of that cryptogram.

The only thing that has happened is that the whole set of crests and troughs of the distribution has been displaced to the right or left of the position it occupies in the distribution for the plain text; or else the successive elements of the whole set progress in the opposite direction. Hence, it follows that the correct determination of the plaintext value of the cipher letter marking *any* crest or trough of the uniliteral frequency distribution, coupled with the correct determination of the relative direction in which the plain component sequence progresses, will result at one stroke in the correct determination of the plaintext values of *all* the remaining 25 letters respectively marking the other crests and troughs in that distribution. The problem thus resolves itself into a matter of selecting that point of attack which will most quickly or most easily lead to the determination of the value of *one* cipher letter. The single word *identification* will hereafter be used for the phrase "determination of the value of a cipher letter"; to *identify* a cipher letter is to find its plaintext value.

b. It is obvious that the easiest point of attack is to assume that the letter marking the crest of greatest frequency in the frequency distribution for the cryptogram represents E_p. Proceeding from this initial point, the identifications of the remaining cipher letters marking the other crests and troughs are tentatively made on the basis that the letters of the cipher component proceed in accordance with the normal alphabetic sequence, either direct or reversed. If the actual frequency of each letter marking a crest or a trough approximates to a fairly close degree the normal or theoretical frequency of the assumed plaintext equivalent, then the initial identification $\theta_c = E_p$ may be *assumed to be correct* and therefore the derived identifications of the other cipher letters also may be assumed to be correct.[1] If the original starting point for assignment of plaintext values is not correct, or if the direction of "reading" the successive crests and troughs of the distribution is not correct, then the frequencies of the other 25 cipher letters will not correspond to or even approximate the normal or theoretical frequencies of their hypothetical plaintext equivalents on the basis of the initial identification. A new initial point, that is, a different cipher equivalent, must then be selected to represent E_p; or else the direction of "reading" the crests and troughs must be reversed. This procedure, that is, the attempt to make the actual frequency relations exhibited by the uniliteral frequency distribution for a given cryptogram conform to the theoretical frequency relations of the normal frequency distribution in an effort to solve the cryptogram, is referred to technically as "fitting the actual uniliteral frequency distribution for a cryptogram to the theoretical uniliteral frequency distribution for normal plain text", or, more briefly, as *"fitting the frequency distribution for the cryptogram to the normal frequency distribution"*, or, still more briefly, *"fitting the distribution to the normal."* In statistical work the expression commonly employed in connection with this process of fitting an actual distribution to a theoretical one is "testing the goodness of fit." The goodness of fit may be stated in various ways, mathematical in character.[2]

c. In fitting the actual distribution to the normal, it is necessary to regard the cipher component (that is, the letters A . . . Z marking the successive crests and troughs of the distribution) as partaking of the nature of a circle, that is, a sequence closing in upon itself, so that no matter with what crest or trough one starts, the spatial and frequency relations of the crests and troughs are constant. This manner of regarding the cipher component as being cyclic in nature is valid *because it is obvious that the relative positions and frequencies of the crests and troughs of any uniliteral*

---

[1] The Greek letter θ (theta) is used to represent a character or letter without indicating its identity. Thus, instead of the circumlocution "any letter of the plain text" the symbol θ_p is used; and for the expression "any letter of the cipher text", the symbol θ_c is used.

[2] One of these tests for expressing the goodness of fit, the χ (chi) test, will be treated in *Military Cryptanalytics, Part II.*

47

frequency distribution must remain the same regardless of what letter is employed as the initial point of the distribution. Fig. 5 gives a clear picture of what is meant in this connection, as applied to the normal frequency distribution.

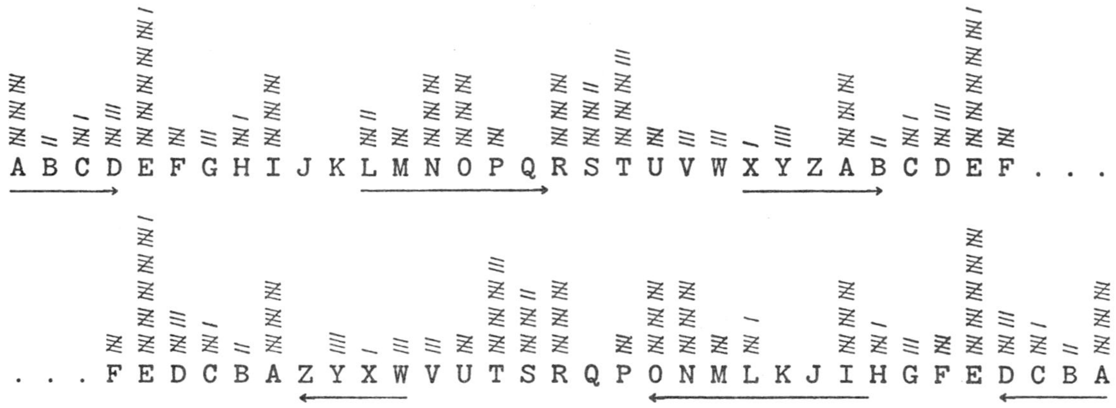

FIGURE 5.

d. In the third sentence of subpar. *b*, the phrase "assumed to be correct" was advisedly employed in describing the results of the attempt to fit the distribution to the normal, because the final test of the goodness of fit in this connection (that is, of the correctness of the assignment of values to the crests and troughs of the distribution) is whether the *consistent* substitution of the plaintext values of the cipher characters in the cryptogram will yield intelligible plain text. If this is not the case, then no matter how close the approximation between actual and theoretical frequencies is, no matter how well the actual frequency distribution fits the normal, the only possible inferences are that (1) either the closeness of the fit is a pure coincidence in this case and that another equally good fit may be obtained from the same data, or else (2) the cryptogram involves something more than simple monoalphabetic substitution by means of a single standard cipher alphabet. For example, suppose a transposition has been applied in addition to the substitution. Then, although an excellent correspondence between the uniliteral frequency distribution and the normal frequency distribution has been obtained, the substitution of the cipher letters by their assumed equivalents will still not yield plain text. However, aside from such cases of double encipherment, instances in which the uniliteral frequency distribution may be easily fitted to the normal frequency distribution and in which at the same time an attempted simple substitution fails to yield intelligible text are rare. It may be said that, in practical operations whenever the uniliteral frequency distribution can be made to fit the normal frequency distribution, substitution of values will result in solution; and, as a corollary, whenever the uniliteral frequency distribution cannot be made to fit the normal frequency distribution, the cryptogram does not represent a case of simple, monoalphabetic substitution by means of a standard alphabet.

48

32. Theoretical example of solution.—*a*. The foregoing principles will become clearer by noting the encryption and solution of a theoretical example. The following message is to be encrypted.

HOSTILE FORCE ESTIMATED AT ONE REGIMENT INFANTRY AND TWO PLATOONS CAVALRY MOVING SOUTH ON QUINNIMONT PIKE STOP HEAD OF COLUMN NEARING ROAD JUNCTION SEVEN THREE SEVEN COMMA EAST OF GREENACRE SCHOOL FIRED UPON BY OUR PATROLS STOP HAVE DESTROYED BRIDGE OVER INDIAN CREEK.

b. First, solely for purposes of demonstrating certain principles, the uniliteral frequency distribution for this plaintext message is presented in Fig. 6.

FIGURE 6.

c. Now let the foregoing message be encrypted monoalphabetically by the following standard cipher alphabet, yielding the cryptogram shown below and the frequency distribution shown in Fig. 7.

Plain	A B C D E F G H I J K L M N O P Q R S T U V W X Y Z
Cipher	G H I J K L M N O P Q R S T U V W X Y Z A B C D E F

Plain	HOSTI	LEFOR	CEEST	IMATE	DATON	EREGI	MENTI	NFANT	RYAND
Cipher	NUYZO	RKLUX	IKKYZ	OSGZK	JGZUT	KXKMO	SKTZO	TLGTZ	XEGTJ

Plain	TWOPL	ATOON	SCAVA	LRYMO	VINGS	OUTHO	NQUIN	NIMON	TPIKE
Cipher	ZCUVR	GZUUT	YIGBG	RXESU	BOTMY	UAZNU	TWAOT	TOSUT	ZVOQK

Plain	STOPH	EADOF	COLUM	NNEAR	INGRO	ADJUN	CTION	SEVEN	THREE
Cipher	YZUVN	KGJUL	IURAS	TTKGX	OTMXU	GJPAT	IZOUT	YKBKT	ZNXKK

Plain	SEVEN	COMMA	EASTO	FGREE	NACRE	SCHOO	LFIRE	DUPON	BYOUR
Cipher	YKBKT	IUSSG	KGYZU	LMXKK	TGIXK	YINUU	RLOXK	JAVUT	HEUAX

Plain	PATRO	LSSTO	PHAVE	DESTR	OYEDB	RIDGE	OVERI	NDIAN	CREEK
Cipher	VGZXU	RYYZU	VNGBK	JKYZX	UEKJH	XOJMK	UBKXO	TJOGT	IXKKQ

Cryptogram

```
N U Y Z O    R K L U X    I K K Y Z    O S G Z K    J G Z U T    K X K M O
S K T Z O    T L G T Z    X E G T J    Z C U V R    G Z U U T    Y I G B G
R X E S U    B O T M Y    U A Z N U    T W A O T    T O S U T    Z V O Q K
Y Z U V N    K G J U L    I U R A S    T T K G X    O T M X U    G J P A T
I Z O U T    Y K B K T    Z N X K K    Y K B K T    I U S S G    K G Y Z U
L M X K K    T G I X K    Y I N U U    R L O X K    J A V U T    H E U A X
V G Z X U    R Y Y Z U    V N G B K    J K Y Z X    U E K J H    X O J M K
U B K X O    T J O G T    I X K K Q
```

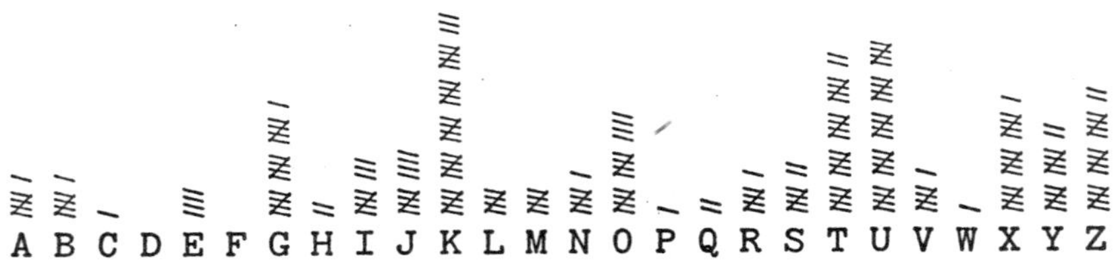

A B C D E F G H I J K L M N O P Q R S T U V W X Y Z

FIGURE 7.

d. Let the student now compare Figs. 6 and 7, which have been superimposed in Fig. 8 for convenience in examination. Crests and troughs are present in both distributions; moreover their relative positions and frequencies have not been changed in the slightest particular. Only the absolute position of the sequence as a whole has been displaced six places to the right in Fig. 7, as compared with the absolute position of the sequence in Fig. 6.

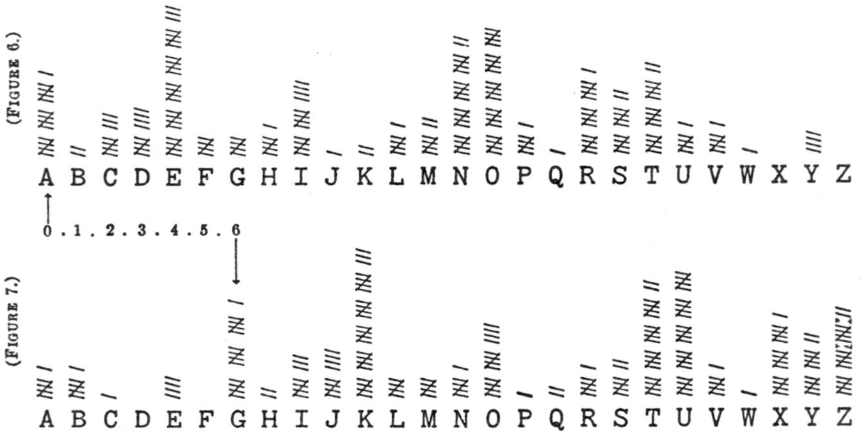

(FIGURE 6.)

A B C D E F G H I J K L M N O P Q R S T U V W X Y Z

0 . 1 . 2 . 3 . 4 . 5 . 6

(FIGURE 7.)

A B C D E F G H I J K L M N O P Q R S T U V W X Y Z

FIGURE 8.

e. If the two distributions are compared in detail the student will clearly understand how easy the solution of the cryptogram would be to one who knew nothing about how it was prepared. For example, the frequency of the highest crest, representing E_p in Fig. 6 is 28; at an interval of four letters before E_p there is another crest representing A_p with frequency 16. Between A and E there is a trough, representing the medium-frequency letters B, C, D. On the other side of E, at an interval of four letters, comes another crest, representing I with frequency 14. Between E and I there is another trough, representing the medium-frequency letters F, G, H. Compare these crests and troughs with their homologous crests and troughs in Fig. 7. In the latter, the letter K marks the highest crest in the distribution with a frequency of 28; four letters before K there is another crest, frequency 16, and four letters on the other side of K there is another crest, frequency 14. Troughs corresponding to B, C, D and F, G, H are seen at H, I, J and L, M, N in Fig. 7. In fact, the two distributions may be made to coincide exactly, by shifting the frequency distribution for the cryptogram six places to the left with respect to the distribution for the equivalent plaintext message, as shown herewith.

50

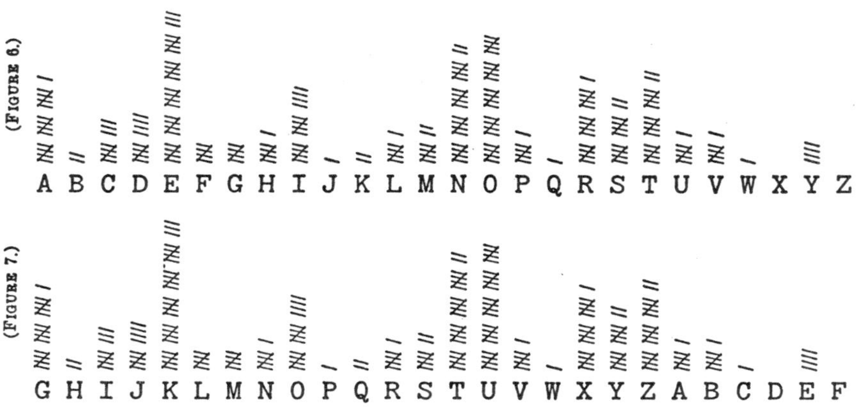

FIGURE 9.

f. Let us suppose now that nothing is known about the process of encryption, and that only the cryptogram and its uniliteral frequency distribution is at hand. It is clear that simply bearing in mind the spatial relations of the crests and troughs in a normal frequency distribution would enable the cryptanalyst to fit the distribution to the normal in this case. He would naturally first assume that $K_c=E_p$, from which it would follow that if a direct standard alphabet is involved, $L_c=F_p$, $M_c=G_p$, and so on, yielding the following (tentative) deciphering alphabet:

Cipher_____A B C D E F G H I J K L M N O P Q R S T U V W X Y Z
Plain_____U V W X Y Z A B C D E F G H I J K L M N O P Q R S T

g. Now comes the final test: If these assumed values are substituted in the cipher text, the plain text immediately appears. Thus:

N U Y Z O   R K L U X   I K K Y Z   O S G Z K   J G Z U T   etc.
H O S T I   L E F O R   C E E S T   I M A T E   D A T O N   etc.

h. It should be clear, therefore, that the initial selection of G_c as the specific key (that is, to represent A_p) in the process of encryption has absolutely no effect upon the relative spatial and frequency relations of the crests and troughs of the frequency distribution for the cryptogram. If Q_c had been selected to represent A_p, these relations would still remain the same, the whole series of crests and troughs being merely displaced further to the right of the positions they occupy when $G_c=A_p$.

33. Practical example of solution by the frequency method.—*a. The case of direct standard alphabet ciphers.* (1) The following cryptogram is to be solved by applying the foregoing principles:

N W N V H   C A X X Y   B J C C J   L T R W P   X D A Y X   B R C R X
W B N J B   C X O W N   F C X W B   C X Y Y N   C N A B L   X U R W O

51

(2) From the presence of so many low-frequency letters such as B, W, and X it is at once suspected that this is a substitution cipher. But to illustrate the steps, that must be taken in difficult cases in order to be certain in this respect, a uniliteral frequency distribution is constructed, and then reference is made to Charts 2 to 5 to note whether the actual numbers of vowels, high-, medium-, and low-frequency consonants fall inside or outside the areas delimited by the respective curves.

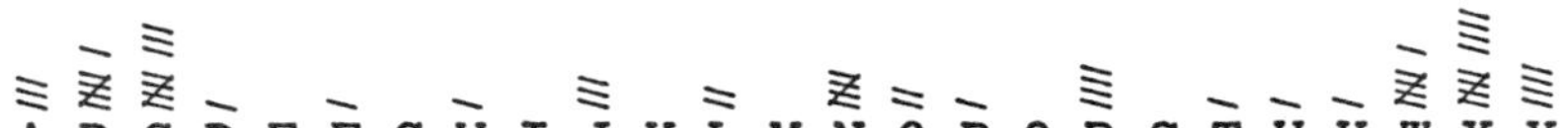

$$\equiv \overset{\equiv}{\underset{\equiv}{\cancel{N}}}\ \overset{\equiv}{\cancel{N}}\ -\ \ -\ \ \overset{\equiv}{\equiv}\ \ \overset{\equiv}{\equiv}\ \ -\ \overset{\equiv}{\cancel{N}}\ \overset{\equiv}{\equiv}\ -\ \overset{\equiv}{\equiv}\ \ -\ -\ -\ \overset{\equiv}{\underset{\cancel{N}}{\cancel{N}}}\ \overset{\equiv}{\underset{\cancel{N}}{||||}}\ \overset{\equiv}{|||}$$

A B C D E F G H I J K L M N O P Q R S T U V W X Y Z

FIGURE 10a.

Letters	Frequency	Position with respect to areas delimited by curves
Vowels (AEIOUY)	10	Outside, Chart 1.
High-frequency Consonants (DNRST)	12	Outside, Chart 2.
Medium-frequency Consonants (BCFGHLMPVW)	26	Outside, Chart 3.
Low-frequency Consonants (JKQXZ)	12	Outside, Chart 4.
Total	60	

(3) All four points falling completely outside the areas delimited by the curves applicable to these four classes of letters, the crypogram is clearly a substitution cipher.

(4) The appearance of the frequency distribution, with marked crests and troughs, indicates that the cryptogram is probably monoalphabetic. At this point the ϕ test is applied to the distribution. The observed value of ϕ is found to be 258, while the expected value of ϕ plain and ϕ random are calculated to be 236 and 136, respectively. The fact that the observed value more closely approximates ϕ_p than it does ϕ_r is taken as statistical evidence that the cryptogram is monoalphabetic. Furthermore, reference being made to Chart 6, the point of intersection of the message length (60 letters) and the number of blanks (8) falls directly on curve P; this is additional evidence that the message is probably monoalphabetic.

(5) The next step is to determine whether a standard or a mixed cipher alphabet is involved. This is done by studying the positions and the sequence of crests and troughs in the frequency distribution, and trying to fit the distribution to the normal.

(6) The first assumption to be made is that a direct standard cipher alphabet is involved. The highest crest in the distribution occurs over X_c. Let it be assumed that $X_c = E_p$. Then Y_c, Z_c, A_c, ... $= F_p$, G_p, H_p, ..., respectively: thus:

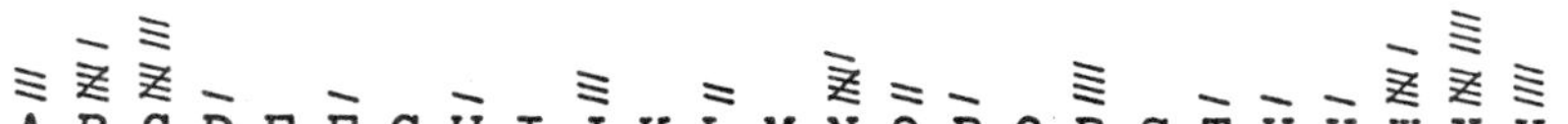

Cipher_____ A B C D E F G H I J K L M N O P Q R S T U V W X Y Z
Plain_____ H I J K L M N O P Q R S T U V W X Y Z A B C D E F G

FIGURE 10b.

52

It may be seen quickly that the approximation to the expected frequencies is very poor. There are too many occurrences of J_p, Q_p, U_p, and F_p and too few occurrences of N_p, O_p, R_p, S_p, T_p and A_p. Moreover, if a substitution is attempted on this basis, the following is obtained for the first two cipher groups:

```
Cipher_____  N W N V H    C A X X Y
"Plain text"_____ U D U C O    J H E E F
```

This is certainly not plain text and it seems clear that X_c is not E_p, if the hypothesis of a direct standard alphabet cipher is correct. A different assumption will have to be made.

(7) Suppose $C_c = E_p$. Going through the same steps as before, again no satisfactory results are obtained. Further trials [3] are made along the same lines, until the assumption $N_c = E_p$ is tested:

```
Cipher_____ A B C D E F G H I J K L M N O P Q R S T U V W X Y Z
Plain_____ R S T U V W X Y Z A B C D E F G H I J K L M N O P Q
```

FIGURE 10c.

(8) The fit in this case is quite good; possibly there are too few occurrences of A_p, D_p, and R_p. But the final test remains: trial of the substitution alphabet on the cryptogram itself. This is done and the results are as follows:

```
C: N W N V H    C A X X Y    B J C C J    L T R W P    X D A Y X    B R C R X
P: E N E M Y    T R O O P    S A T T A    C K I N G    O U R P O    S I T I O

C: W B N J B    C X O W N    F C X W B    C X Y Y N    C N A B L    X U R W O
P: N S E A S    T O F N E    W T O N S    T O P P E    T E R S C    O L I N F
```

ENEMY TROOPS ATTACKING OUR POSITION EAST OF NEWTON. PETERS COL INF.

(9) It is always advisable to note the specific key. In this case the correspondence between any plaintext letter and its cipher equivalent will indicate the key. Although other conventions are possible, and equally valid, it is usual, however, to indicate the key by noting the cipher equivalent of A_p. In this case $A_p = J_c$.

b. The case of reversed standard alphabet ciphers.—(1) Let the following cryptogram and its frequency distribution be studied.

```
F W F X L    Q S V V U    R J Q Q J    H Z B W D    V P S U V    R B Q B V
W R F J R    Q V E W F    N Q V W R    Q V U U F    Q F S R H    V Y B W E
```

(2) The preliminary steps illustrated above, under subpar. *a* (1) to (4) inclusive, in connection with the test for class and monoalphabeticity, will here be omitted, since they are exactly the same in nature. The result is that the cryptogram is obviously a substitution cipher and is monoalphabetic.

(3) Assuming that it is not known whether a direct or a reversed standard alphabet is involved, attempts are at once made to fit the frequency distribution to the normal direct sequence. If the student will try them he will soon find out that these are unsuccessful. All this takes but a few minutes.

---

[3] It is unnecessary, of course, to write out all the alphabets and pseudo-decipherments, as shown above, when testing assumptions. This is usually done mentally, using the scanning procedure treated in subpar. 28c.

(4) The next logical assumption is now made, *viz.*, that the cipher alphabet is a reversed standard alphabet. When on this basis F_c is assumed to be E_p, the distribution can readily be fitted to the normal, practically every crest and trough in the actual distribution corresponding to a crest or trough in the expected distribution.

Cipher_____ A B C D E F G H I J K L M N O P Q R S T U V W X Y Z
Plain_____ J I H G F E D C B A Z Y X W V U T S R Q P O N M L K

FIGURE 10d.

(5) When the substitution is made in the cryptogram, the following is obtained.

Cryptogram_____ F W F X L   Q S V V U   R J Q Q J   etc.
Plain text_____ E N E M Y   T R O O P   S A T T A   etc.

(6) The plaintext message is identical with that in subpar. *a*. The specific key in this case is also $A_p = J_c$. If the student will compare the frequency distributions in the two cases, he will note that the relative positions and extents of the crests and troughs are identical; they merely progress in opposite directions.

34. Solution by completing the plain-component sequence.—*a. The case of direct standard alphabet ciphers.* (1) The foregoing method of analysis, involving as it does the construction of a uniliteral frequency distribution, was termed a *solution by the frequency method* because it involves the construction of a frequency distribution and its study. There is, however, another method which is much more rapid, almost wholly mechanical, and which, moreover, does not necessitate the construction or study of any frequency distribution whatever. An understanding of the method follows from a consideration of the method of encipherment of a message by the use of a single, direct standard cipher alphabet.

(2) Note the following encipherment:

Message_____ TWO CRUISERS SUNK

Enciphering Alphabet

Plain_____ A B C D E F G H I J K L M N O P Q R S T U V W X Y Z
Cipher_____ G H I J K L M N O P Q R S T U V W X Y Z A B C D E F

Encipherment

Plain text_____ T W O   C R U I S E R S   S U N K
Cryptogram_____ Z C U   I X A O Y K X Y   Y A T Q

Cryptogram

Z C U I X   A O Y K X   Y Y A T Q

(3) The enciphering alphabet shown above represents a case wherein the sequence of letters of both components of the cipher alphabet is the normal sequence, with the sequence forming the cipher components merely shifted six places to the left (or 20 positions to the right) of the position it occupies in the normal alphabet. If, therefore, two strips of paper bearing the letters

54

of the normal sequence, equally spaced, are regarded as the two components of the cipher alphabet and are juxtaposed at all of the 25 possible points of coincidence, it is obvious that one of these 25 juxtapositions *must* correspond to the actual juxtaposition shown in the enciphering alphabet directly above.[4] It is equally obvious that if a record were kept of the results obtained by applying the values given at each juxtaposition to the letters of the cryptogram, one of these results would yield the plain text of the cryptogram.

(4) Let the work be systematized and the results set down in an orderly manner for examination. It is obviously unnecessary to juxtapose the two components so that $A_c=A_p$, for on the assumption of a direct standard alphabet, juxtaposing two direct normal components at their normal point of coincidence merely yields plain text. The next possible juxtaposition, therefore, is $A_c=B_p$. Let the juxtaposition of the two sliding strips therefore be $A_c=B_p$, as shown here:

Plain_____   ABCDEFGHIJKLMNOPQRSTUVWXYZ
Cipher_____ ABCDEFGHIJKLMNOPQRSTUVWXYZABCDEFGHIJKLMNOPQRSTUVWXYZ

The values given by this juxtaposition are substituted for the letters of the cryptogram and the following results are obtained.

Cryptogram_____	Z C U I X	A O Y K X	Y Y A T Q
1st Test—"Plain text"___	A D V J Y	B P Z L Y	Z Z B U R

This certainly is not intelligible text; obviously, the two components were not in the position indicated in this first test. The plain component is therefore slid one interval to the left, making $A_c=C_p$, and a second test is made. Thus

Plain_____   ABCDEFGHIJKLMNOPQRSTUVWXYZ
Cipher_____ ABCDEFGHIJKLMNOPQRSTUVWXYZABCDEFGHIJKLMNOPQRSTUVWXYZ

Cryptogram_____	Z C U I X	A O Y K X	Y Y A T Q
2d Test—"Plain text"___	B E W K Z	C Q A M Z	A A C V S

Neither does the second test result in disclosing any plain text. But, if the results of the two tests are studied, a phenomenon that at first seems quite puzzling comes to light. Thus, suppose the results of the two tests are superimposed in this fashion.

Cryptogram_____	Z C U I X	A O Y K X	Y Y A T Q
1st Test—"Plain text"___	A D V J Y	B P Z L Y	Z Z B U R
2d Test—"Plain text"___	B E W K Z	C Q A M Z	A A C V S

(5) Note what has happened. The net result of the two experiments was merely to continue the normal sequence begun by the cipher letters at the heads of the *columns* of letters. It is obvious that if the normal sequence is completed in each column *the results will be exactly the same as though the whole set of 25 possible tests had actually been performed.* Let the columns therefore be completed, as shown in Fig. 11.

---

[4] One of the strips should bear the sequence repeated. This permits juxtaposing the two sequences at all 26 possible points of coincidence so as to have a complete cipher alphabet showing at all times.

```
Z C U I X A O Y K X Y Y A T Q
A D V J Y B P Z L Y Z Z B U R
B E W K Z C Q A M Z A A C V S
C F X L A D R B N A B B D W T
D G Y M B E S C O B C C E X U
E H Z N C F T D P C D D F Y V
F I A O D G U E Q D E E G Z W
G J B P E H V F R E F F H A X
H K C Q F I W G S F G G I B Y
I L D R G J X H T G H H J C Z
J M E S H K Y I U H I I K D A
K N F T I L Z J V I J J L E B
L O G U J M A K W J K K M F C
M P H V K N B L X K L L N G D
N Q I W L O C M Y L M M O H E
O R J X M P D N Z M N N P I F
P S K Y N Q E O A N O O Q J G
Q T L Z O R F P B O P P R K H
R U M A P S G Q C P Q Q S L I
S V N B Q T H R D Q R R T M J
*T W O C R U I S E R S S U N K
U X P D S V J T F S T T V O L
V Y Q E T W K U G T U U W P M
W Z R F U X L V H U V V X Q N
X A S G V Y M W I V W W Y R O
Y B T H W Z N X J W X X Z S P
```

FIGURE 11.

An examination of the successive horizontal lines of the diagram discloses *one and only one* line of plain text, that marked by the asterisk and reading T W O C R U I S E R S S U N K.

(6) Since each column in Fig. 11 is nothing but a normal sequence, it is obvious that instead of laboriously writing down these columns of letters every time a cryptogram is to be examined, it would be more convenient to prepare a set of strips each bearing the normal sequence doubled (to permit complete coincidence for an entire alphabet at any setting), and have them available for examining any future cryptograms. In using such a set of sliding strips in order to solve a cryptogram prepared by means of a single direct standard cipher alphabet, or to make a test to determine whether a cryptogram has been so prepared, it is only necessary to "set up" the letters of the cryptogram on the strips, that is, align them in a single row across the strips (by sliding the individual strips up or down). The successive horizontal lines, called *generatrices* (singular, *generatrix*),[5] are then examined in a search for intelligible text. If the cryptogram really belongs to this simple type of cipher, one of the generatrices will exhibit intelligible text all the way across; this text will almost invariably be the plain text of the message. This method of analysis may be termed *a solution by completing the plain-component sequence.* Sometimes it is

---

[5] Pronounced: *jĕn'ĕr-ȧ-trī'sēz* and *jĕn'ĕr-ā'trĭks*, respectively.

referred to as "running down" the sequence. The principle upon which the method is based constitutes one of the cryptanalyst's most valuable tools.[6]

b. The case of reversed standard alphabets.—(1) The method described under subpar. _a_ may also be applied, in slightly modified form, in the case of a cryptogram enciphered by a single reversed standard alphabet. The basic principles are identical in the two cases, as will now be demonstrated.

(2) Let two sliding components be prepared as before, except that in this case one of the components must be a reversed normal sequence, the other, a direct normal sequence.

(3) Let the two components be juxaposed **A** to **A** as shown below, and then let the resultant values be substituted for the letters of the cryptogram. Thus:

Cryptogram

N K S E P   M Y O C P   O O M T W

Plain _____   ABCDEFGHIJKLMNOPQRSTUVWXYZ
Cipher _____ ZYXWVUTSRQPONMLKJIHGFEDCBAZYXWVUTSRQPONMLKJIHGFEDCBA

| Cryptogram _____ | N K S E P | M Y O C P | O O M T W |
| 1st Test—"Plain text" ___ | N Q I W L | O C M Y L | M M O H E |

(4) This does not yield intelligible text, and therefore the reversed component is slid one space forward and a second test is made. Thus:

Plain _____   ABCDEFGHIJKLMNOPQRSTUVWXYZ
Cipher _____ ZYXWVUTSRQPONMLKJIHGFEDCBAZYXWVUTSRQPONMLKJIHGFEDCBA

| Cryptogram _____ | N K S E P | M Y O C P | O O M T W |
| 2d Test—"Plain text" ___ | O R J X M | P D N Z M | N N P I F |

(5) Neither does the second test yield intelligible text. But let the results of the two tests be superimposed. Thus:

Cryptogram _____	N K S E P	M Y O C P	O O M T W
1st Test—"Plain text" ___	N Q I W L	O C M Y L	M M O H E
2d Test—"Plain text" ___	O R J X M	P D N Z M	N N P I F

(6) It is seen that the letters of the "plain text" given by the _second_ trial are merely the continuants of the normal sequences initiated by the letters of the "plain text" given by the first trial. If these sequences are "run down"—that is, completed within the columns—the results must obviously be the same as though successive tests exactly similar to the first two were applied to the cryptogram, using one reversed normal and one direct normal component. If the cryptogram has really been prepared by means of a single reversed standard alphabet, one of the generatrices of the diagram that results from completing the sequence _must_ yield intelligible text.

(7) Let the diagram be made, or better yet, if the student has already at hand the set of sliding strips referred to in footnote 6, below, let him "set up" the letters given by the _first_ trial. Fig. 12 shows the diagram and indicates the plaintext generatrix.

_____

[6] A set of heavy paper strips, suitable for use in completing the plain-component sequence, has been prepared for use as a training aid in connection with the courses in Military Cryptanalytics.

```
  N K S E P M Y O C P O O M T W
N Q I W L O C M Y L M M O H E
O R J X M P D N Z M N N P I F
P S K Y N Q E O A N O O Q J G
Q T L Z O R F P B O P P R K H
R U M A P S G Q C P Q Q S L I
S V N B Q T H R D Q R R T M J
*T W O C R U I S E R S S U N K
U X P D S V J T F S T T V O L
V Y Q E T W K U G T U U W P M
W Z R F U X L V H U V V X Q N
X A S G V Y M W I V W W Y R O
Y B T H W Z N X J W X X Z S P
Z C U I X A O Y K X Y Y A T Q
A D V J Y B P Z L Y Z Z B U R
B E W K Z C Q A M Z A A C V S
C F X L A D R B N A B B D W T
D G Y M B E S C O B C C E X U
E H Z N C F T D P C D D F Y V
F I A O D G U E Q D E E G Z W
G J B P E H V F R E F F H A X
H K C Q F I W G S F G G I B Y
I L D R G J X H T G H H J C Z
J M E S H K Y I U H I I K D A
K N F T I L Z J V I J J L E B
L O G U J M A K W J K K M F C
M P H V K N B L X K L L N G D
```

FIGURE 12.

(8) The only difference in procedure between this case and the preceding one (where the cipher alphabet was a direct standard alphabet) is that the letters of the cipher text are first "deciphered" by means of *any* reversed standard alphabet and then the columns are "run down", according to the normal A B C . . . Z sequence. For reasons which will become apparent very soon, the first step in this method is technically termed *converting the cipher letters into their plain-component equivalents;* the second step is the same as before, *viz., completing the plain-component sequence.*

35. Special remarks on the method of solution by completing the plain-component sequence.—*a.* The terms employed to denote the steps in the solution set forth in subpar. 34*b* (8), *viz.,* "converting the cipher letters into their plain-component equivalents" and "completing the plain-component sequence", accurately describe the process. Their meaning will become more clear as the student progresses with the work. It may be said that whenever the components of a cipher alphabet are *known* sequences, no matter how they are composed, the difficulty and time required to solve any cryptogram involving the use of those components is considerably reduced. *In some cases this knowledge facilitates, and in other cases is the only thing that makes possible, the solution of a very short cryptogram that might otherwise defy solution.* Later on an example will be given to illustrate what is meant in this regard.

b. The student should take note, however, of two qualifying expressions that were employed in a preceding paragraph to describe the results of the application of the method. It was stated that "one of the generatrices will exhibit intelligible text *all the way across; this text will almost invariably* be the plain text." Will there ever be a case in which more than one generatrix will yield intelligible text through its extent? That obviously depends almost entirely on the number of letters that are aligned to form a generatrix. If a generatrix contains but a very few letters, only five, for example, it may happen as a result of pure chance that there will be two or more generatrices showing what might be "intelligible text." Note in Fig. 12, for example, that there are several cases in which 3-letter and 4-letter English words (LAD, COB, MESH, MAPS, etc.) appear on generatrices that are not correct, these words being formed by pure chance. But there is not a single case, in this diagram, of a 5-letter or longer word appearing fortuitously, because obviously the longer the word the smaller the probability of its appearance purely by chance; and the probability that two generatrices of 15 letters each will both yield intelligible text along their entire length is exceedingly remote, so remote, in fact, that in practical cryptology such a case may be considered nonexistent.[7]

c. The student should observe that in reality there is no difference whatsoever in principle between the two methods presented in subpars. *a* and *b* of par. 34. In the former the preliminary step of converting the cipher letters into their plain-component equivalents is apparently not present but in reality it is there. The reason for its apparent absence is that in that case the plain component of the cipher alphabet is identical in all respects with the cipher component, so that the cipher letters require no conversion, or, rather, they are identical with the equivalents that would result if they were converted on the basis $A_c = A_p$. In fact, if the solution process had been arbitrarily initiated by converting the cipher letters into their plain-component equivalents at the setting $A_c = O_p$, for example, and the cipher component slid one interval to the right thereafter, the results of the first and second tests of par. 34*a* would be as follows:

Cryptogram	Z C U I X A O Y K X Y Y A T Q
1st Test—"Plain text"	N Q I W L O C M Y L M M O H E
2d Test—"Plain text"	O R J X M P D N Z M N N P I F

Thus, the foregoing diagram duplicates in every particular the diagram resulting from the first two tests under par. 34*b:* a first line of cipher letters, a second line of letters derived from them but showing externally no relationship with the first line, and a third line derived immediately from the second line by continuing the direct normal sequence. This point is brought to attention only for the purpose of showing that a single, broad principle is the basis of the general method of solution by completing the plain-component sequence, and once the student has this firmly in mind he will have no difficulty whatsoever in realizing when the principle is applicable, what a powerful cryptanalytic tool it can be, and what results he may expect from its application in specific instances.

d. In the two foregoing examples of the application of the principle, the components were normal sequences; but it should be clear to the student, if he has grasped what has been said in the preceding subparagraph, that these components may be mixed sequences which, if known (that is, if the sequence of letters comprising the sequences is known to the cryptanalyst), can be handled just as readily as can components that are normal sequences.

---

[7] A person with patience and an inclination toward the curiosities of the science might construct a text of 15 or more letters which would yield two "intelligible" texts on the plain-component completion diagram.

e. It is entirely immaterial at what points the plain and the cipher components are juxtaposed in the preliminary step of converting the cipher letters into their plain-component equivalents. For example, in the case of the reversed alphabet cipher solved in subpar. 34*b*, the two components were arbitrarily juxtaposed to give the value $A_p = A_c$, but they might have been juxtaposed at any of the other 25 possible points of coincidence without in any way affecting the final result, *viz.*, the production of one plaintext generatrix in the completion diagram.

36. Value of mechanical solution as a short cut.—*a.* It is evident that *the very first step the student should take in his attempts to solve an unknown cryptogram that is obviously a substitution cipher is to try the mechanical method of solution by completing the plain-component sequence, using the normal alphabet, first direct, then reversed.* This takes only a very few minutes and is conclusive in its results. It saves the labor and trouble of constructing a frequency distribution in case the cipher is of this simple type. Later on it will be seen how certain variations of this simple type may also be solved by the application of this method. Thus, a very easy short cut to solution is afforded, which even the experienced cryptanalyst never overlooks in his first attack on an unknown cipher.

b. It is important now to note that *if neither of the two foregoing attempts is successful in bringing plain text to light and the cryptogram is quite obviously monoalphabetic in character, the cryptanalyst is warranted in assuming that the cryptogram involves a mixed cipher alphabet.*[8]

37. Basic reason for the low degree of cryptosecurity afforded by monoalphabetic cryptograms involving standard cipher alphabets.—The student has seen that the solution of monoalphabetic cryptograms involving standard cipher alphabets is a very easy matter. Two methods of analysis were described, one involving the construction of a frequency distribution, the other not requiring this kind of tabulation, being almost mechanical in nature and correspondingly rapid. In the first of these two methods it was necessary to make a correct assumption as to the value of but one of the 26 letters of the cipher alphabet and the values of the remaining 25 letters at once became known; in the second method it was not necessary to assume a value for even a single cipher letter. The student should understand what constitutes the basis of this situation, *viz.*, the fact that the two components of the cipher alphabet are composed of *known sequences.* What if one or both of these components are for the cryptanalyst *unknown sequences?* In other words, what difficulties will confront the cryptanalyst if the cipher component of the cipher alphabet is a mixed sequence? Will such an alphabet be solvable as a whole at one stroke, or will it be necessary to solve its values individually? Since the determination of the value of one cipher letter in this case gives no direct clues to the value of any other letter, it would seem that the solution of such a cipher should involve considerably more analysis and experiment than has the solution of either of the two types of ciphers so far examined. The steps to be taken in the cryptanalysis of a mixed-alphabet cipher will be discussed in the next chapter.

---

[8] There is but one other possibility, already referred to under subpar. 31*d,* which involves the case where transposition and monoalphabetic substitution processes have been applied in successive steps. This is unusual, however, and will be discussed in a subsequent text.

CHAPTER VI

UNILITERAL SUBSTITUTION WITH MIXED CIPHER ALPHABETS

Paragraph

Literal keys and numerical keys_____ 38
Types of mixed cipher alphabets_____ 39
Additional remarks on cipher alphabets_____ 40
Preliminary steps in the analysis of a monoalphabetic, mixed-alphabet cryptogram_____ 41
Preparation of the work sheet_____ 42
Triliteral frequency distributions_____ 43
Classifying the cipher letters into vowels and consonants_____ 44
Further analysis of the letters representing vowels and consonants_____ 45
Substituting deduced values in the cryptogram_____ 46
Completing the solution_____ 47
General remarks on the foregoing solution_____ 48
The "probable-word" method; its value and applicability_____ 49
Solution of additional cryptograms produced by the same components_____ 50
Recovery of key words_____ 51

38. **Literal keys and numerical keys.**—*a.* As has been previously mentioned, most crypto-systems involve the use of a specific key to control the steps followed in encrypting or decrypting a specific message (see subpar. 9*b*). Such a key may be in literal form or in numerical form.

b. It is convenient to designate a key which is composed of letters as a *literal key*. As already mentioned, a literal key may consist of a single letter, a single word, a phrase, a sentence, a whole paragraph, or even a book; and, of course, it may consist merely of a sequence of letters chosen at random.

c. Certain cryptosystems involve the use of a *numerical key*, which may consist of a relatively long sequence of numbers difficult or impossible for the average cipher clerk to memorize. Several simple methods for deriving such sequences from words, phrases, or sentences have been devised, and a numerical key produced by any of these methods is called a *derived numerical key* (as opposed to a key consisting of randomly-selected numbers). One of the commonly-used methods consists of assigning numerical values to the letters of a selected literal key in accordance with their *relative* positions in the ordinary alphabet, as exemplified in the following subparagraph.

d. Let the prearranged *key word* be the word LOGISTICS. Since C, the penultimate letter of the key word, appears in the normal alphabet before any other letter of the key word, it is assigned the number 1:

```
L O G I S T I C S
              1
```

The next letter of the normal alphabet that occurs in the key word is G, which is assigned the number 2. The letter I, which occurs twice in the key word, is assigned the number 3 for its first occurrence (from left to right) and the number 4 for its second occurrence; and so on. The final result is:

```
L O G I S T I C S
5 6 2 3 7 9 4 1 8
```

This method of assigning the numbers is very flexible and varies with different uses to which numerical keys are put. It may, of course, be applied to phrases or to sentences, so that a very long numerical key, ordinarily impossible to remember, may be thus derived at will from an easily-remembered *key text.*

 e. As far as the cryptanalyst is concerned, the derivation of a numerical key from a specific literal key is of interest to him because this knowledge may assist in subsequent solutions of cryptograms prepared according to the same basic system, or in identifying the source from which the literal key was selected—perhaps an ordinary book, a magazine, etc. However, it should be pointed out that in some instances the cryptanalyst may be unaware that a literal key has in fact been used as the basis for deriving a numerical key.

 39. Types of mixed cipher alphabets.—*a.* It will be recalled that in a mixed cipher alphabet the sequence of letters or characters in one of the components (usually the cipher component) does not correspond to the normal sequence. There are various methods of composing the sequence of letters or elements of this mixed component, and those which are based upon a scheme that is systematic in its nature are very useful because they make possible the derivation of one or more mixed sequences from any easily-remembered word or phrase, and thus do not necessitate the carrying of written memoranda. Alphabets involving a systematic method of mixing are called *systematically-mixed cipher alphabets.*

 b. One of the simplest types of systematically-mixed cipher alphabets is the *keyword-mixed alphabet.* The cipher component consists of a key word or phrase (with repeated letters, if present, omitted after their first occurrence),[1] followed by the letters of the alphabet in their normal sequence (with letters already occurring in the key omitted, of course). Example, with GOVERNMENT as the key word:

Plain: ABCDEFGHIJKLMNOPQRSTUVWXYZ
Cipher: GOVERNMTABCDFHIJKLPQSUWXYZ

 c. It is possible to disarrange the sequence constituting the cipher component even more thoroughly by applying a simple method of transposition to the keyword-mixed sequence. Two common methods are illustrated below, using the key word TELEPHONY.

 (1) *Simple columnar transposition:*

```
T E L P H O N Y
A B C D F G I J
K M Q R S U V W
X Z
```

---

[1] Mixed alphabets formed by including all repeated letters of the key word or key phrase in the cipher component were common in Edgar Allan Poe's day but are impractical because they are ambiguous, making decipherment difficult; an example:

	Plain:	ABCDEFGHIJKLMNOPQRSTUVWXYZ
(a) Alphabet for enciphering _____	Cipher:	NOWISTHETIMEFORALLGOODMENT

	Cipher:	ABCDEFGHIJKLMNOPQRSTUVWXYZ
(b) Inverse form of (a), for deciphering _____	Plain:	P VHMSGD QKAB OEF C
		L J RWYN I
		X T Z
		U

The average cipher clerk would have considerable difficulty in decrypting a cipher group such as TOOET, each letter of which has three or more equivalents, and from which the plaintext fragments (N)INTH., .. FT THI(S), IT THI ... , etc. can be formed on decipherment.

Mixed sequence (formed by transcribing the successive columns from left to right):

TAKXEBMZLCQPDRHFSOGUNIVYJW

(2) *Numerically-keyed columnar transposition:*

```
7-1-3-6-2-5-4-8
T E L P H O N Y
A B C D F G I J
K M Q R S U V W
X Z
```

Mixed sequence (formed by transcribing the columns in a sequence determined by the numerical key derived from the key word itself):

EBMZHFSLCQNIVOGUPDRTAKXYJW

d. The last two systematically-mixed sequences are examples of *transposition-mixed sequences.* Almost any method of transposition may be used to produce such sequences.

e. Another simple method of forming a mixed sequence is the *decimation method.* In this method, letters in the normal alphabet, or in a keyword-mixed sequence, are "counted off" according to any selected interval. As each letter is decimated—that is, eliminated from the basic sequence by counting off—it is entered in a separate list to form the new mixed sequence. For example, to form a mixed sequence by this method from a keyword-mixed sequence based on the key phrase SING A SONG OF SIXPENCE with 7 the interval selected, proceed as follows:
Keyword-mixed (or basic) sequence:

SINGAOFXPECBDHJKLMQRTUVWYZ

When the letters are counted off by 7's from left to right, F will be the first letter arrived at, H the second, T the third:

```
S I N G A O F X P E C B D H J K L M Q R T U V W Y Z
1 2 3 4 5 6 7 1 2 3 4 5 6 7 1 2 3 4 5 6 7
```

These letters are entered in a separate list (F first, H second, T third, and so on) and eliminated from the keyword-mixed sequence. When the end of the keyword-mixed sequence is reached, return to the beginning, skipping the letters already eliminated:

```
S I N G A O F X P E C B D H J K L M Q R T U V W Y Z
                                        1 2 3 4 5
  6 7 1 2 3 4   5 6 7 1 2 3   4 5 6 7
```

The decimation-mixed sequence:

FHTIEMZPQNDWCVBSLXAGOKYJRU

f. Practical considerations, of course, set a limit to the complexities that may be introduced in constructing systematically-mixed alphabets. Beyond a certain point there is no object in

63

further mixing. The greatest amount of mixing by systematic processes will give no more security than that resulting from mixing the alphabet by random selection, such as by putting the 26 letters in a box, thoroughly shaking them up, and then drawing the letters out one at a time. Whenever the laws of chance operate in the construction of a mixed alphabet, the probability of producing a thorough disarrangement of letters is very great. *Random-mixed alphabets* give more cryptographic security than do the less complicated systematically-mixed alphabets, because they afford no clues to positions of letters, given the position of a few of them. Their chief disadvantage is that they must be reduced to writing, since they cannot readily be remembered, nor can they be reproduced at will from an easily-remembered key word.

40. **Additional remarks on cipher alphabets.**—*a.* Cipher alphabets may be classified on the basis of their arrangement as *enciphering* or *deciphering alphabets.* An enciphering alphabet is one in which the sequence of letters in the plain component coincides with the normal sequence and is arranged in that manner for convenience in encipherment. In a deciphering alphabet the sequence of letters in the cipher component coincides with the normal, for convenience in deciphering. For example, (1), below, shows a mixed cipher alphabet arranged as an enciphering alphabet; (2) shows the corresponding deciphering alphabet. An enciphering alphabet and its corresponding deciphering alphabet present an *inverse* relationship to each other.

Enciphering Alphabet

(1)
Plain: ABCDEFGHIJKLMNOPQRSTUVWXYZ
Cipher: JKQVXZWESTRNUIOLGAPHCMYBDF

Deciphering Alphabet

(2)
Cipher: ABCDEFGHIJKLMNOPQRSTUVWXYZ
Plain: RXUYHZQTNABPVLOSCKIJMDGEWF

b. As has been previously mentioned,[2] a series of related reciprocal alphabets may be produced by juxtaposing at all possible points of coincidence two components which are identical but progress in opposite directions. This holds regardless of whether the components are composed of an even or an odd number of elements. The following reciprocal alphabet is one of such a series of 26 alphabets:

Plain: HYDRAULICBEFGJKMNOPQSTVWXZ
Cipher: GFEBCILUARDYHZXWVTSQPONMKJ

A single or isolated reciprocal alphabet may be produced in one of two ways:

(1) By constructing a complete reciprocal alphabet by arbitrary or random assignments of values in pairs. That is, if A_p is made the equivalent of K_c, then K_p is made the equivalent of A_c; if B_p is made R_c, then R_p is made B_c, and so on. If the two components thus constructed are slid against each other no additional reciprocal alphabets will be produced.

(2) By juxtaposing a sequence comprising an *even* number of elements against the same sequence shifted exactly half way to the right (or left), as seen below:

HYDRAULICBEFGJKMNOPQSTVWXZ
HYDRAULICBEFGJKMNOPQSTVWXZHYDRAULICBEFGJKMNOPQSTVWXZ

---

[2] Subpar. 29c.

41. Preliminary steps in the analysis of a monoalphabetic, mixed-alphabet cryptogram.—
a. The student is now ready to resume his cryptanalytic studies. Note the following cryptogram:

```
SFDZF IOGHL PZFGZ DYSPF HBZDS GVHTF UPLVD FGYVJ VFVHT GADZZ AITYD ZYFZJ
ZTGPT VTZBD VFHTZ DFXSB GIDZY VTXOI YVTEF VMGZZ THLLV XZDFM HTZAI TYDZY
BDVFH TZDFK ZDZZJ SXISG ZYGAV FSLGZ DTHHT CDZRS VTYZD OZFFH TZAIT YDZYG
AVDGZ ZTKHI TYZYS DZGHU ZFZTG UPGDI XWGHX ASRUZ DFUID EGHTV EAGXX
```

b. A casual inspection of the text discloses the presence of several long repetitions as well as of many letters of normally low frequency, such as F, G, V, X, and Z; on the other hand, letters of normally high frequency, such as the vowels, and the consonants N and R, are relatively scarce. The cryptogram is obviously a substitution cipher and the usual mechanical tests for determining whether it is possibly of the monoalphabetic, standard-alphabet type are applied. The results being negative, a uniliteral frequency distribution is immediately constructed, as shown in Fig. 13, and the ϕ test is applied to it.

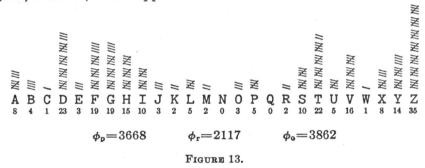

$$\phi_p = 3668 \qquad \phi_r = 2117 \qquad \phi_o = 3862$$

FIGURE 13.

c. The fact that the frequency distribution shows very marked crests and troughs indicates that the cryptogram is very probably monoalphabetic, and the results of the ϕ test further support this hypothesis. The fact that the cryptogram has already been tested by the method of completing the plain-component sequence and found not to be of the monoalphabetic, standard-alphabet type, indicates with a high degree of probability that it involves a mixed cipher alphabet. A few moments might be devoted to making a careful inspection of the distribution to insure that it cannot be made to fit the normal; the object of this would be to rule out the possibility that the text resulting from substitution by a standard cipher alphabet had not subsequently been transposed. But this inspection in this case is hardly necessary, in view of the presence of long repetitions in the message.[3] (See subpar. 25g.)

d. One might, of course, attempt to solve the cryptogram by applying the simple principles of frequency. One might, in other words, assume that Z_c (the letter of greatest frequency) represents E_p, D_c (the letter of next greatest frequency) represents T_p, and so on. If the message

---

[3] This possible step is mentioned here for the purpose of making it clear that the plain-component sequence completion method cannot solve a case in which transposition has followed or preceded monoalphabetic substitution with standard alphabets. Cases of this kind will be discussed in a later text. It is sufficient to indicate at this point that the frequency distribution for such a combined substitution-transposition cipher would present the characteristics of a standard alphabet cipher and yet the method of completing the plain-component sequence would fail to bring out any plain text.

were long enough this simple procedure might more or less quickly give the solution. But the message is relatively short and many difficulties would be encountered. Much time and effort would be expended unnecessarily, because it is hardly to be expected that in a message of only 235 letters the relative order of frequency of the various cipher letters should exactly coincide with, or even closely approximate the relative order of frequency of letters of normal plain text found in a count of 50,000 letters. *It is to be emphasized that the beginner must repress the natural tendency to place too much confidence in the generalized principles of frequency and to rely too much upon them.* It is far better to bring into effective use certain other data concerning normal plain text, such as digraphic and trigraphic frequencies.

42. **Preparation of the work sheet.**—*a.* The details to be considered in this paragraph may at first appear to be superfluous, but long experience has proved that systematization of the work and preparation of the data in the most utilizable, condensed form is most advisable, even if this seems to take considerable time. In the first place, if it merely serves to avoid interruptions and irritations occasioned by failure to have the data in an instantly available form, it will pay by saving mental wear and tear. In the second place, especially in the case of complicated cryptograms, painstaking care in these details, while it may not always bring about success, is often the factor that is of greatest assistance in ultimate solution. The detailed preparation of the data may be irksome to the student, and he may be tempted to avoid as much of it as possible, but, unfortunately, in the early stages of solving a cryptogram he does not know (nor, for that matter, does the expert always know) just which data are essential and which may be neglected. Even though not all of the data may turn out to have been necessary, as a general rule, time is saved in the end if all the usual data are prepared as a regular preliminary to the solution of most cryptograms.

b. First, the cryptogram is recopied in the form of a *work sheet.* This sheet should be of a good quality of paper so as to withstand considerable erasure. If the cryptogram is to be copied by hand, cross-section paper of ¼-inch squares is extremely useful, because each letter may be written in an individual cell. The writing should be in ink, and plain, carefully-made roman capital letters should be used in all cases.[4] If the cryptogram is to be copied on a typewriter, the ribbon employed should be impregnated with an ink that will not smear or smudge under the hand.

c. The arrangement of the characters of the cryptogram on the work sheet is a matter of considerable importance. If the cryptogram as first obtained is in groups of regular length (usually five characters to a group) and if the uniliteral frequency distribution shows the cryp-

---

[4] It is advisable to use, for this purpose, the system of standardized manual printing adopted by Service communications personnel. The use of this system, appended below, assures that work sheets are completely legible, not only to the person preparing them, but to others as well.

togram to be monoalphabetic, the characters should be copied without regard to this grouping. It is advisable to allow one space between letters (this is especially true for work sheets prepared on the typewriter), and to write a constant number of letters per line, approximately 25. At least two spaces, preferably three spaces, should be left between horizontal lines, to allow room for multiple assumptions. Care should be taken to avoid crowding the letters in any case, for this is not only confusing to the eye but also mentally irritating when later it is found that not enough space has been left for making various sorts of marks or indications. If the cryptogram is originally in what appears to be word lengths (and this is the case, as a rule, only with the cryptograms of amateurs), naturally it should be copied on the work sheet in the original groupings.[5] If further study of a cryptogram shows that some special grouping is required, it is often best to recopy it on a fresh work sheet rather than to attempt to indicate the new grouping on the old work sheet.

d. In order to be able to locate or refer to specific letters or groups of letters with speed, certainty, and without possibility of confusion, it is advisable to use coordinates applied to the lines and columns of the text as it appears on the work sheet. To minimize possibility of confusion, it is best to apply letters to the horizontal lines of the text, numbers to the vertical columns. In referring to a letter, the horizontal line in which the letter is located is usually given first. Thus, referring to the work sheet shown below, coordinates A17 designate the letter Y, the 17th letter in the first line. The letter I is usually omitted from the series of line indicators so as to avoid confusion with the figure 1. If lines are limited to 25 letters each, then each set of 100 letters of the text is automatically blocked off by remembering that 4 lines constitute 100 letters.

e. Above each character of the cipher text may be some indication of the frequency of that character in the whole cryptogram. This indication may be the actual number of times the character occurs, or, if colored pencils are used, the cipher letters may be divided up into three categories or groups—high-frequency, medium-frequency, and low-frequency. It is perhaps simpler, if clerical help is available, to indicate the actual frequencies. This saves constant reference to the frequency tables, which interrupts the train of thought, and saves considerable time in the end, since it enables the student better to visualize *frequency-patterns* of words. In any case, it is recommended that the frequencies of the letters comprising the repetitions be inscribed over their respective letters; likewise, the frequencies of the first 10 and last 10 letters should also be inscribed, as these positions often lend themselves readily to attack.[6]

f. After the special frequency distribution, explained in par. 43 below, has been constructed, repetitions of digraphs and trigraphs should be underscored. In so doing, the student should be particularly watchful for trigraphic repetitions which can be further extended into tetragraphs and polygraphs of greater length. If a repetition continues from one line to the next, put an arrow at the end of the underscore to signal this fact. Reversible digraphs and trigraphs should also be indicated by an underscore with an arrow pointing in both directions. Anything which strikes the eye as being peculiar, unusual, or significant as regards the distribution or recurrence of the characters should be noted. All these marks should, if convenient, be made with ink

---

[5] In some cryptosystems, certain low-frequency letters are employed as *word separators* to indicate the end of a word; if the meaning of these letters is discovered, it is tantamount to having the cryptogram in word lengths and thus the work sheet is made accordingly. See also in this connection the treatment on word separators in Chapter VII.

[6] See Appendix 4 in this connection.

so as not to cause smudging. The work sheet will now appear as shown below (not all the repetitions are underscored):

```
         1   2   3   4   5   6   7   8   9  10  11  12  13  14  15  16  17  18  19  20  21  22  23  24  25
        10  19  23  35  19  10   3  19  15   5   5  35  19  19  35  23  14  10   5  19  15   4  35  23  10
     A   S   F   D   Z   F   I   O   G   H   L   P   Z   F   G   Z   D   Y   S   P   F   H   B   Z   D   S
             <--->

        19  16  15  22  19   5   5   5  16  23  19  19  14  16   3  16  19  16  15  22  19   8  23  35  35
     B   G   V   H   T   F   U   P   L   V   D   F   G   Y   V   J   V   F   V   H   T   G   A   D   Z   Z
                                         V   D   F   G

         8  10  22  14  23  35  14  19  35   3  35  22  19   5  22  16  22  35   4  23  16  19  15  22  35
     C   A   I   T   Y   D   Z   Y   F   Z   J   Z   T   G   P   T   V   T   Z   B   D   V   F   H   T   Z
             <--->

        23  19   8  10   4  19  10  23  35  14  16  22   8   3  10  14  16  22   3  19  16   2  19  35  35
     D   D   F   X   S   B   G   I   D   Z   Y   V   T   X   O   I   Y   V   T   E   F   V   M   G   Z   Z

        22  15   5   5  16   8  35  23  19   2  15  22  35   8  10  22  14  23  35  14   4  23  16  19  15
     E   T   H   L   L   V   X   Z   D   F   M   H   T   Z   A   I   T   Y   D   Z   Y   B   D   V   F   H

        22  35  23  19   2  35  23  35  35   3  10   8  10  10  19  35  14  19   8  16  19  10   5  19  35
     F   T   Z   D   F   K   Z   D   Z   Z   J   S   X   I   S   G   Z   Y   G   A   V   F   S   L   G   Z

        23  22  15  15  22   1  23  35   2  10  16  22  14  35  23   3  35  19  19  15  22  35   8  10  22
     G   D   T   H   H   T   C   D   Z   R   S   V   T   Y   Z   D   O   Z   F   F   H   T   Z   A   I   T

        14  23  35  14  19   8  16  23  19  35  35  22   2  15  10  22  14  35  14  10  23  35  19  15   5
     H   Y   D   Z   Y   G   A   V   D   G   Z   Z   T   K   H   I   T   Y   Z   Y   S   D   Z   G   H   U

        35  19  35  22  19   5   5  19  23  10   8   1  19  15   8   8  10   2   5  35  23  19   5  10  23
     J   Z   F   Z   T   G   U   P   G   D   I   X   W   G   H   X   A   S   R   U   Z   D   F   U   I   D

         3  19  15  22  16   3   8  19   8   8
     K   E   G   H   T   V   E   A   G   X   X
```

43. Triliteral frequency distributions.—*a.* In what has gone before, a type of frequency distribution known as a uniliteral frequency distribution was used. This, of course, shows only the number of times each individual letter occurs. In order to apply the normal digraphic and trigraphic frequency data (given in Appendix 2) to the solution of a cryptogram of the type now being studied, it is obvious that the data with respect to digraphs and trigraphs occurring in the cryptogram should be compiled and should be compared with the data for normal plain text. In order to accomplish this in suitable manner, it is advisable to construct a more comprehensive form of distribution termed a *triliteral frequency distribution.*[7]

b. Given a cryptogram of 50 or more letters and the task of determining what trigraphs are present in the cryptogram, there are three ways in which the data may be arranged or assembled. One may require that the data show (1) each letter with its two succeeding letters; (2) each letter with its two preceding letters; (3) each letter with one preceding letter and one succeeding letter.

---

[7] It is felt wise here to distinguish between two closely related terms. A triliteral distribution of A B C D E F would consider the groups A B C, B C D, C D E, D E F; a trigraphic distribution would consider only the trigraphs A B C and D E F. (See also subpar. 23*d.*)

68

c. A distribution of the first of the three foregoing types may be designated as a "triliteral frequency distribution showing two suffixes"; the second type may be designated as a "triliteral frequency distribution showing two prefixes"; the third type may be designated as a "triliteral frequency distribution showing one prefix and one suffix." Quadriliteral and pentaliteral frequency distributions may occasionally be found useful.

d. Which of these three arrangements is to be employed at a specific time depends largely upon what the data are intended to show. For present purposes, in connection with the solution of a monoalphabetic substitution cipher employing a mixed alphabet, possibly the third arrangement, that showing one prefix and one suffix, is most satisfactory.

e. It is convenient to use ¼-inch cross-section paper for the construction of a triliteral frequency distribution in the form of a distribution showing crests and troughs, such as that in Fig. 14. In that figure the prefix to each letter to be recorded is inserted in the left half of the cell directly above the cipher letter being recorded; the suffix to each letter is inserted in the right half of the cell directly above the letter being recorded; and in each case the prefix and the suffix to the letter being recorded occupy the same cell, the prefix being directly to the left of the suffix. The number in parentheses gives the total frequency for each letter.

f. The triliteral frequency distribution is now to be examined with a view to ascertaining what digraphs and trigraphs occur two or more times in the cryptogram. Consider the pair of columns containing the prefixes and suffixes to D_c in the distribution, as shown in Fig. 14. This pair of columns shows that the following digraphs appear in the cryptogram:

Digraphs based on prefixes (arranged as one reads up the column)	Digraphs based on suffixes (arranged as one reads up the column)
FD, ZD, ZD, VD, AD, YD, BD,	DZ, DY, DS, DF, DZ, DZ, DV,
ZD, ID, ZD, YD, BD, ZD, ZD,	DF, DZ, DF, DZ, DV, DF, DZ,
ZD, CD, ZD, YD, VD, SD, GD,	DT, DZ, DO, DZ, DG, DZ, DI,
ZD, ID	DF, DE

The nature of the triliteral frequency distribution is such that in finding what digraphs are present in the cryptogram it is immaterial whether the prefixes or the suffixes to the cipher letters are studied, *so long as one is consistent in the study.* For example, in the foregoing list of digraphs based on the prefixes to D_c, the digraphs FD, ZD, ZD, VD, etc., are found; if now, the student will refer to the suffixes of F_c, Z_c, V_c, etc., he will find the very same digraphs indicated. This being the case, the question may be raised as to what value there is in listing both the prefixes and the suffixes to the cipher letters. The answer is that by so doing the trigraphs are indicated at the same time. For example, in the case of D_c, the following trigraphs are indicated:

FDZ, ZDY, ZDS, VDF, ADZ, YDZ, BDV, ZDF, IDZ, ZDF, YDZ, BDV, ZDF, ZDZ, ZDT, CDZ, ZDO, YDZ, VDG, SDZ, GDI, ZDF, IDE.

g. The *repeated* digraphs and trigraphs can now be found quite readily. Thus, in the case of D_c, examining the list of digraphs based on suffixes, the following repetitions are noted:

DZ appears 9 times; DF appears 5 times; DV appears 2 times

Examining the trigraphs with D_c as central letter, the following repetitions are noted:

ZDF appears 4 times; YDZ appears 3 times; BDV appears 2 times

69

CONDENSED TABLE OF REPETITIONS

Digraphs			*Trigraphs*		*Longer Polygraphs*
DZ–9	TZ–5	VF–4	DZY–4	FHT–3	HTZAITYDZY–2
ZD–9	TY–5	VT–4	HTZ–4	TYD–3	BDVFHTZDF–2
HT–8	FH–4	ZF–4	ITY–4	YDZ–3	ZAITYDZY–3
ZY–6	GH–4	ZT–4	ZDF–4	ZAI–3	FHTZ–3
DF–5	IT–4	ZZ–4	AIT–3		
GZ 5					

Letter	Count	Digraphs (column entries, top to bottom)
A	(8)	EG XS GV ZI GV ZI ZI GD
B	(4)	YD SG ZD HZ
C	(1)	TD
D	(23)	IE ZF GI SZ VG YZ ZO CZ ZT ZZ ZF BV YZ ZF IZ ZF BV YZ AZ VF ZS ZY FZ
E	(3)	VA DG TF
F	(19)	DU ZZ FH ZF VS DK VH DM EV DX VH YZ VV DG TU PH ZG ZI SD
G	(19)	AX EH WH PD TU ZH DZ YA LZ YA SZ MZ BI TP TA FY SV FZ OH
H	(15)	GT GX GU KI FT HT TH FT MT TL FT VT VT FB GL
I	(10)	UD DX HT AT XS AT OY GD AT FO
J	(3)	ZS ZZ VV
K	(2)	TH FZ
L	(5)	SG LV HL PV HP
M	(2)	FH VG
N	(0)	
O	(3)	DZ XI IG
P	(5)	UG GT UL SF LZ
Q	(0)	
R	(2)	SU ZS
S	(10)	AR YD RV FL IG JX XB DG YP –F
T	(22)	HV ZG IY ZK IY HZ VY HC DH HZ IY HZ ZH VE VX HZ VZ PV ZG IY HG HF
U	(5)	FI RZ GP HZ FP
V	(16)	TE AD ST AF DF LX FM YT YT DF TT FH JF YJ LD GH
W	(1)	XG
X	(8)	X– GX HA IW SI VZ TO FS
Y	(14)	ZS TZ ZG TD TZ ZG ZB TD IV ZV ZF TD GV DS
Z	(35)	UD FT UF DG YY ZT GZ DY TA OF YD DR GD GY ZJ DZ KD TD DY TA XD ZT GZ DY TD TB JT FJ DY ZA DZ BD GD PF DF

FIGURE 14.

h. It is unnecessary, of course, to go through the detailed procedure set forth in the preceding subparagraphs in order to find all the repeated digraphs and trigraphs. The repeated trigraphs with D_c as central letter can be found merely from an inspection of the prefixes and suffixes opposite D_c in the distribution. It is necessary only to find those cases in which two or more prefixes are identical at the same time that the suffixes are identical. For example, the distribution shows at once that in four cases the prefix to D_c is Z_c at the same time that the suffix to this letter is F_c. Hence, the trigraph ZDF appears four times. The repeated trigraphs may all be found in this manner.

i. The most frequently repeated digraphs and trigraphs are then assembled in what is termed a *condensed table of repetitions*, so as to bring this information prominently before the eye. As a rule, in messages of average length, digraphs which occur less than four or five times, and trigraphs which occur less than three or four times may be omitted from the condensed table as being relatively of no importance in the study of repetitions. In the condensed table the frequencies of the individual letters forming the most important digraphs, trigraphs, etc., should be indicated.

44. Classifying the cipher letters into vowels and consonants.—*a.* Before proceeding to a detailed analysis of the repeated digraphs and trigraphs, a very important step can be taken which will be of assistance not only in the analysis of the repetitions but also in the final solution of the cryptogram. This step concerns the classification of the high-frequency cipher letters into two groups—(1) those which most probably represent vowels, and (2) those which most probably represent consonants. For if the cryptanalyst can quickly ascertain the equivalents of the four vowels, A, E, I, and O, and of only the four consonants, N, R, S, and T, he will then have the values of approximately two-thirds of all the cipher letters that occur in the cryptogram; the values of the remaining letters can almost be filled in automatically.

b. The basis for the classification will be found to rest upon a comparatively simple phenomenon: the associational or combinatory behavior of vowels is, in general, quite different from that of consonants. If an examination be made of Table 7–B in Appendix 2, showing the relative order of frequency of the 18 digraphs composing 25 per cent of English telegraphic text, it will be seen that the letter E enters into the composition of 9 of the 18 digraphs; that is, in exactly half of all the cases the letter E is one of the two letters forming the digraph. The digraphs containing E are as follows:

ED   EN   ER   ES
  NE   RE   SE   TE   VE

The remaining nine digraphs are as follows:

AN   ND   OR   ST
IN   NT   TH
ON   TO

c. None of the 18 digraphs is a combination of vowels. Note now that of the 9 combinations with E, 7 are with the consonants N, R, S, and T, one is with D, one is with V, and *none is with any vowel.* In other words, E_p combines most readily with consonants but not with other vowels, or even with itself. Using the terms often employed in the chemical analogy, E shows a great "affinity" for the consonants N, R, S, T, but not for the vowels. Therefore, if the letters of highest frequency occurring in a given cryptogram are listed, together with the number of times each of them combines with the assumed cipher equivalent of E_p, those which show con-

71

siderable combining power or affinity for the cipher equivalent of E_p, may be assumed to be the cipher equivalents of N, R, S, T_p; those which do not show any affinity for the cipher equivalent of E_p may be assumed to be the cipher equivalents of A, I, O, U_p. Applying these principles to the problem in hand, and examining the triliteral frequency distribution, it is quite certain that $Z_c = E_p$ not only because Z_c is the letter of highest frequency, but also because it combines with *several* other high-frequency letters, such as D_c, F_c, G_c, etc. The nine letters of next highest frequency are:

$$\begin{array}{ccccccccc} 23 & 22 & 19 & 19 & 16 & 15 & 14 & 10 & 10 \\ D & T & F & G & V & H & Y & S & I \end{array}$$

Let the combinations these letters form with Z_c be indicated in the following manner:

Number of times Z_c occurs as prefix	Cipher letter	Number of times Z_c occurs as suffix
	D(23) T(22) F(19) G(19) V(16) H(15) Y(14) S(10) I(10)	

d. Consider D_c. It occurs 23 times in the message and 18 of those times it is combined with Z_c, 9 times in the form Z_cD_c (=$E\theta_p$), and 9 times in the form D_cZ_c (=θE_p). It is clear that D_c must be a consonant. In the same way, consider T_c, which shows 9 combinations with Z_c, 4 in the form Z_cT_c (=$E\theta_p$) and 5 in the form T_cZ_c (=θE_p). The letter T_c appears to represent a consonant, as do also the letters F_c, G_c, and Y_c. On the other hand, consider V_c, occurring in all 16 times but never in combination with Z_c; it appears to represent a vowel, as do also the letters H_c, S_c, and I_c. So far, then, the following classification would seem logical:

Vowels	Consonants
$Z_c(=E_p)$, V_c, H_c, S_c, I_c	D_c, T_c, F_c, G_c, Y_c

45. Further analysis of the letters representing vowels and consonants.—*a*. O_p is usually the vowel of second highest frequency. Is it possible to determine which of the letters V, H, S, I_c is the cipher equivalent of O_p? Let reference be made again to Table 6 in Appendix 2, where it is seen that the 10 most frequently occurring diphthongs are:

Diphthong	IO	OU	EA	EI	AI	IE	AU	EO	AY	UE
Frequency	41	37	35	27	17	13	13	12	12	11

If V, H, S, I_c are really the cipher equivalents of A, I, O, U_p (not respectively), perhaps it is possible to determine which is which *by examining the combinations they make among themselves and with* Z_c (=E_p). Let the combinations of V, H, S, I, and Z that occur in the message be listed. There are only the following:

$$ZZ_c-4 \qquad VH_c-2 \qquad HH_c-1 \qquad HI_c-1 \qquad IS_c-1 \qquad SV_c-1$$

ZZ_c is of course EE_p. Note the doublet HH_c; if H_c is a vowel, then the chances are excellent that $H_c=O_p$ because the doublets AA_p, II_p, UU_p, are practically non-existent, whereas the double vowel combination OO_p is of next highest frequency to the double vowel combination EE_p. If $H_c=O_p$, then V_c must be I_p because the digraph VH_c occurring two times in the message could hardly be AO_p, or UO_p, whereas the diphthong IO_p is the one of high frequency in English. So far then, the tentative (because so far unverified) results of the analysis are as follows:

$$Z_c=E_p \qquad H_c=O_p \qquad V_c=I_p$$

This leaves only two letters, I_c and S_c (already classified as vowels) to be separated into A_p and U_p. Note the digraphs:

$$HI_c=O\theta_p \qquad IS_c=\theta\theta_p \qquad SV_c=\theta I_p$$

Only two alternatives are open:

(1) either $I_c=A_p$ and $S_c=U_p$,
(2) or $\quad$ $I_c=U_p$ and $S_c=A_p$.

If the first alternative is selected, then

$$HI_c=OA_p \qquad SV_c=UI_p \qquad IS_c=AU_p$$

If the second alternative is selected, then

$$HI_c=OU_p \qquad SV_c=AI_p \qquad IS_c=UA_p$$

The eye finds it difficult to choose between these alternatives; but suppose the frequency values of the plaintext diphthongs as given in Table 6 of Appendix 2 are added for each of these alternatives, giving the following:

$HI_c=OA_p$, frequency value= 7	$HI_c=OU_p$, frequency value=37
$SV_c=UI_p$, frequency value= 5	$SV_c=AI_p$, frequency value=17
$IS_c=AU_p$, frequency value=13	$IS_c=UA_p$, frequency value= 5
Total_____25	Total_____59

Mathematically, the second alternative appears to be more probable than the first.[8] Let it be assumed to be correct and the following (still tentative) values are now at hand:

$$Z_c=E_p \qquad H_c=O_p \qquad V_c=I_p \qquad S_c=A_p \qquad I_c=U_p$$

---

[8] A more accurate guide for choosing between the alternative groups of digraphs could be obtained through a consideration of the *logarithmic weights* of their assigned probabilities, rather than their plaintext *frequency* values. These weights are given in Appendix 2, along with an explanation of the method for their derivation; a detailed treatment of their application is presented in *Military Cryptanalytics, Part II.*

b. Attention is now directed to the letters classified as consonants: How far is it possible to ascertain their values? The letter D_c, from considerations of frequency alone, would seem to be T_p, but its frequency, 23, is not considerably greater than that for T_c. It is not much greater than that for F_c or G_c, with a frequency of 19 each. But perhaps it is possible to ascertain not the value of one letter alone but of two letters at one stroke. To do this one may make use of a tetragraph of considerable importance in English, *viz.*, $TION_p$. For if the analysis pertaining to the vowels is correct, and if $VH_c = IO_p$, then an examination of the letters immediately before and after the digraph VH_c in the cipher text might disclose both T_p and N_p. Reference to the text gives the following:

$$GVHT_c \qquad FVHT_c$$
$$\theta IO\theta_p \qquad \theta IO\theta_p$$

The letter T_c follows VH_c in both cases and very probably indicates that $T_c = N_p$; but as to whether G_c or F_c equals T_p cannot be decided. However, two conclusions are clear: first, the letter D_c is neither T_p nor N_p, from which it follows that it must be either R_p or S_p; second, the letters G_c and F_c must be either T_p and S_p, respectively, or S_p and T_p, respectively, because the only tetragraphs usually found (in English) containing the diphthong IO_p as central letters are $SION_p$ and $TION_p$. This in turn means that as regards D_c, the latter cannot be *either* R_p or S_p; it *must* be R_p, a conclusion which is corroborated by the fact that ZD_c ($=ER_p$) and DZ_c ($=RE_p$) occur 9 times each. Thus far, then, the identifications, when inserted in an *enciphering* alphabet, are as follows:

Plain	A	B	C	D	E	F	G	H	I	J	K	L	M	N	O	P	Q	R	S	T	U	V	W	X	Y	Z
Cipher	S			Z			V							T	H			D	G	F	I					
																			F	G						

46. Substituting deduced values in the cryptogram.—*a.* Thus far the analysis has been almost purely hypothetical, for as yet not a single one of the values deduced from the foregoing analysis has been tried out in the cryptogram. It is high time that this be done, because the final test of the validity of the hypotheses, assumptions, and identifications made in any cryptographic study is, after all, only this: do these hypotheses, assumptions, and identifications ultimately yield verifiable, intelligible plain text when *consistently* applied to the cipher text?

b. At the present stage in the process, since there are at hand the assumed values of but 9 out of the 25 letters that appear, it is obvious that a continuous "reading" of the cryptogram can certainly not be expected from a mere insertion of the values of the 9 letters. However, the substitution of these values should do two things. First, it should immediately disclose the fragments, outlines, or "skeletons" of "good" words in the text; and second, it should disclose no places in the text where "impossible" sequences of letters are established. By the first is meant that the partially deciphered text should show the outlines or skeletons of words such as may be expected to be found in the communication; this will become quite clear in the next subparagraph. By the second is meant that sequences, such as "AOOEN" or "TNRSENO" or the like, obviously not possible or extremely unusual in normal English text, must not result from the substitution of the tentative identifications resulting from the analysis. The appearance of several such extremely unusual or impossible sequences would at once signify that one or more of the assumed values is incorrect.

c. Here are the results of substituting the nine values which have been deduced by the reasoning based on a classification of the high-frequency letters into vowels and consonants and the study of the members of the two groups:

```
     1   2   3   4   5   6   7   8   9   10  11  12  13  14  15  16  17  18  19  20  21  22  23  24  25

A    10  19  23  35  19  10  3   19  15  5   5   35  19  19  35  23  14  10  5   19  15  4   35  23  10
     S   F   D   Z   F   I   O   G   H   L   P   Z   F   G   Z   D   Y   S   P   F   H   B   Z   D   S
     A   T   R   E   T   U       S   O               E   T   S   E   R       A       T   O       E   R   A
         S           S               T                       S   T                           S

B    19  16  15  22  19  5   5   5   16  23  19  19  14  16  3   16  19  16  15  22  19  8   23  35  35
     G   V   H   T   F   U   P   L   V   D   F   G   Y   V   J   V   F   V   H   T   G   A   D   Z   Z
     S   I   O   N   T               I   R   T   S       I       I   T   I   O   N   S   U   R   E   E
     T           S                       S   T                   S           T

C    8   10  22  14  23  35  14  19  35  3   35  22  19  5   22  16  22  35  4   23  16  19  15  22  35
     A   I   T   Y   D   Z   Y   F   Z   J   Z   T   G   P   T   V   T   Z   B   D   V   F   H   T   Z
     U   N   N       R   E       T   E       E   N   S       N   I   N   E       R   I   T   O   N   E
                             S               T                                           S

D    23  19  8   10  4   19  10  23  35  14  16  22  8   3   10  14  16  22  3   19  16  2   19  35  35
     D   F   X   S   B   G   I   D   Z   Y   V   T   X   O   I   Y   V   T   E   F   V   M   G   Z   Z
     R   T       A       S   U   R   E       I   N           U       I   N       T   I       S   E   E
         S               T                                               S               T

E    22  15  5   5   16  8   35  23  19  2   15  22  35  8   10  22  14  23  35  14  4   23  16  19  15
     T   H   L   L   V   X   Z   D   F   M   H   T   Z   A   I   T   Y   D   Z   Y   B   D   V   F   H
     N   O           I       E   R   T       O   N   E   U   N   N       R   E           R   I   T   O
                                     S                                                           S

F    22  35  23  19  2   35  23  35  35  3   10  8   10  10  19  35  14  19  8   16  19  10  5   19  35
     T   Z   D   F   K   Z   D   Z   Z   J   S   X   I   S   G   Z   Y   G   A   V   F   S   L   G   Z
     N   E   R   T       E   R   E   E       A       U   A   S   E       S   U   I   T   A       S   E
                 S                                           T       T           S               T

G    23  22  15  15  22  1   23  35  2   10  16  22  14  35  23  3   35  19  19  15  22  35  8   10  22
     D   T   H   H   T   C   D   Z   R   S   V   T   Y   Z   D   O   Z   F   F   H   T   Z   A   I   T
     R   N   O   O   N       R   E       A   I   N       E   R       E   T   T   O   N   E   U   N   N
                                                                     S   S

H    14  23  35  14  19  8   16  23  19  35  35  22  2   15  10  22  14  35  14  10  23  35  19  15  5
     Y   D   Z   Y   G   A   V   D   G   Z   Z   T   K   H   I   T   Y   Z   Y   S   D   Z   G   H   U
         R   E       S   U   I   R   S   E   E   N       O   U   N       E       A   R   E   S   O
                         T               T                                               T

J    35  19  35  22  19  5   5   19  23  10  8   1   24  15  8   8   10  2   5   35  23  19  5   10  23
     Z   F   Z   T   G   U   P   G   D   I   X   W   G   H   X   A   S   R   U   Z   D   F   U   I   D
     E   T   E   N   S           S   R   U           S   O       U   A           E   R   T       U   R
         S           T               T               T                               S

K    3   19  15  22  16  3   8   19  8   8
     E   G   H   T   V   E   A   G   X   X
         S   O   N   I       U   S
         T               T
```

75

d. No impossible sequences are brought to light, and, moreover, several long words, nearly complete, stand out in the text. Note the following portions:

```
              A21
              H B Z D S G V H T F
          (1) O ? E R A S I O N T
                    T         S
              C15
              T V T Z B D V F H T Z D F
          (2) N I N E ? R I T O N E R T
                        S         S
              F22
              S L G Z D T H H T
          (3) A ? S E R N O O N
                T
```

The words are obviously OPERATIONS, NINE PRISONERS, and AFTERNOON. The value G_c is clearly T_p; that of F_c is S_p; and the following additional values are certain:

$$B_c = P_p \qquad L_c = F_p$$

47. Completing the solution.—*a.* Each time an additional value is obtained, substitution is at once made throughout the cryptogram. This leads to the determination of further values, in an ever-widening circle, until all the identifications are firmly and finally established, and the message is completely solved. In this case the decipherment is as follows:

	1	2	3	4	5	6	7	8	9	10	11	12	13	14	15	16	17	18	19	20	21	22	23	24	25
A	S	F	D	Z	F	I	O	G	H	L	P	Z	F	G	Z	D	Y	S	P	F	H	B	Z	D	S
	A	S	R	E	S	U	L	T	O	F	Y	E	S	T	E	R	D	A	Y	S	O	P	E	R	A
B	G	V	H	T	F	U	P	L	V	D	F	G	Y	V	J	V	F	V	H	T	G	A	D	Z	Z
	T	I	O	N	S	B	Y	F	I	R	S	T	D	I	V	I	S	I	O	N	T	H	R	E	E
C	A	I	T	Y	D	Z	Y	F	Z	J	Z	T	G	P	T	V	T	Z	B	D	V	F	H	T	Z
	H	U	N	D	R	E	D	S	E	V	E	N	T	Y	N	I	N	E	P	R	I	S	O	N	E
D	D	F	X	S	B	G	I	D	Z	Y	V	T	X	O	I	Y	V	T	E	F	V	M	G	Z	Z
	R	S	C	A	P	T	U	R	E	D	I	N	C	L	U	D	I	N	G	S	I	X	T	E	E
E	T	H	L	L	V	X	Z	D	F	M	H	T	Z	A	I	T	Y	D	Z	Y	B	D	V	F	H
	N	O	F	F	I	C	E	R	S	X	O	N	E	H	U	N	D	R	E	D	P	R	I	S	O
F	T	Z	D	F	K	Z	D	Z	Z	J	S	X	I	S	G	Z	Y	G	A	V	F	S	L	G	Z
	N	E	R	S	W	E	R	E	E	V	A	C	U	A	T	E	D	T	H	I	S	A	F	T	E
G	D	T	H	H	T	C	D	Z	R	S	V	T	Y	Z	D	O	Z	F	F	H	T	Z	A	I	T
	R	N	O	O	N	Q	R	E	M	A	I	N	D	E	R	L	E	S	S	O	N	E	H	U	N
H	Y	D	Z	Y	G	A	V	D	G	Z	Z	T	K	H	I	T	Y	Z	Y	S	D	Z	G	H	U
	D	R	E	D	T	H	I	R	T	E	E	N	W	O	U	N	D	E	D	A	R	E	T	O	B
J	Z	F	Z	T	G	U	P	G	D	I	X	W	G	H	X	A	S	R	U	Z	D	F	U	I	D
	E	S	E	N	T	B	Y	T	R	U	C	K	T	O	C	H	A	M	B	E	R	S	B	U	R
K	E	G	H	T	V	E	A	G	X	X
	G	T	O	N	I	G	H	T	(X	X)

76

Message: AS RESULT OF YESTERDAYS OPERATIONS BY FIRST DIVISION THREE HUNDRED SEVENTY NINE PRISONERS CAPTURED INCLUDING SIXTEEN OFFICERS. ONE HUNDRED PRISONERS WERE EVACUATED THIS AFTERNOON, REMAINDER LESS ONE HUNDRED THIRTEEN WOUNDED ARE TO BE SENT BY TRUCK TO CHAMBERSBURG TONIGHT.

b. The solution should, as a rule, not be considered complete until an attempt has been made to discover all the elements underlying the general system and the specific key to a message. In this case, there is no need to delve further into the general system, for it is merely one of uniliteral substitution with a mixed cipher alphabet (with the convention that Q_p may be used to represent a comma and X_p may be used for a period). It is necessary or advisable, however, to reconstruct the cipher alphabet because this may give clues that later may become valuable.

c. Cipher alphabets should, as a rule, be reconstructed by the cryptanalyst in the form of *enciphering* alphabets because they will then usually be in the form in which the encipherer used them. This is important for two reasons. First, if the sequence in the cipher component gives evidence of system in its construction or if it yields clues pointing toward its derivation from a key word or a key phrase, this may often corroborate the identifications already made and may lead directly to additional identifications. A word or two of explanation is advisable here. For example, refer to the skeletonized enciphering alphabet given at the end of subpar. 45*b*:

```
Plain_____ A B C D E F G H I J K L M N O P Q R S T U V W X Y Z
Cipher_____ S     Z     V       T H     D G F I
                                             F G
```

Suppose the crypanalyst, looking at the sequence DGFI or DFGI in the cipher component, suspects the presence of a keyword-mixed alphabet. Then DFGI is certainly a more plausible sequence than DGFI. Examining the skeleton cipher component more carefully, he notes that S . . . Z would allow for insertion of three of the missing letters UWXY since the letters T and V occur later, probably in the key word itself; further, he notes that the key word probably begins under F_p and ends in TH, making it probable that the TH is followed by AB, AC, or BC. This means that if $P_p = A_c$, $Q_p = $ either B_c or C_c; but if $P_p = B_c$, then $Q_p = C_c$. Referring to the frequency distribution, he notes that C_c (with one occurrence) would make an excellent Q_p; however, either A_c (8 occurrences, or 3.4%) or B_c (4 occurrences, or 1.7%) might represent P_p in this single, isolated message. A trial of these values would materially hasten solution because it is often the case in cryptanalysis that if the value of a very low-frequency letter can be surely established it will yield clues to other values very quickly. Thus, if Q_p is definitely identified it almost invariably will identify U_p, and will give clues to the letter following the U_p, since it must be a vowel. For the foregoing reason an attempt should always be made in the early stages of the analysis to determine, if possible, the basis of construction or derivation of the cipher alphabet; as a rule this can be done only by means of the enciphering alphabet, and not the deciphering alphabet. For example, the skeletonized *deciphering* alphabet corresponding to the enciphering alphabet directly above is as follows:

```
Cipher_____ A B C D E F G H I J K L M N O P Q R S T U V W X Y Z
Plain_____     R   T S O U           A N   I       E
                         S T
```

Here no evidences of a keyword-mixed alphabet are seen at all. However, if the enciphering alphabet has been examined and shows no evidences of systematic construction, the deciphering alphabet should then be examined with this in view, because occasionally it is the deciphering alphabet which shows the presence of a key or keying element, or which has been systematically derived from a word or phrase. The second reason why it is important to try to discover the basis of construction or derivation of the cipher alphabet is that it affords clues to the general type of key words or keying elements employed by the enemy. This is a psychological factor, of course, and may be of assistance in subsequent studies of his traffic. It merely gives a clue to the general type of thinking indulged in by certain of his cryptographers.

d. In the case of the foregoing solution, the complete enciphering alphabet is found to be as follows:

```
Plain_____ A B C D E F G H I J K L M N O P Q R S T U V W X Y Z
Cipher_____ S U X Y Z L E A V N W O R T H B C D F G I J K M P
```

Obviously, the letter Q, which is the only letter not appearing in the cryptogram, should follow P in the cipher component. Note now that the latter is based upon the key word LEAVENWORTH, and that this particular cipher alphabet has been composed by shifting the mixed sequence based upon this key word five intervals to the right so that the key for the message is $A_p = S_c$.[9] Note also that the deciphering alphabet fails to give any evidence of keyword construction based upon the word LEAVENWORTH.

```
Cipher_____ A B C D E F G H I J K L M N O P Q R S T U V W X Y Z
Plain_____ H P Q R G S T O U V W F X J L Y Z M A N B I K C D E
```

e. If neither the enciphering nor the deciphering alphabet exhibits characteristics which give indication of derivation from a key word by some form of mixing or disarrangement, the use of such a key word for this purpose is nevertheless not finally excluded as a possibility. For the reconstruction of such mixed alphabets the cryptanalyst must use ingenuity and a knowledge of the more common methods of suppressing the appearance of key words in the mixed alphabets. Several of these methods are given detailed treatment in par. 51 below.

f. It is very important in practical cryptanalytic work to prepare a technical summary of the solution of a system.[10] Step-by-step commentaries should accompany an initial solution, especially those steps leading to the first plaintext entries; the steps taken should be jotted down as they are made, and at the end they should be combined into a complete résumé of the analysis. The résumé should be brief and concise, yet comprehensive enough that at any future time the solution may be reconstructed following the exact manner in which it was originally accomplished. Assumptions of words, etc., should be referred to with worksheet line- and column indicators, and should be couched in the proper cryptologic language or symbols. A short exposition of the mechanics of the general system, enciphering alphabets, enciphering diagrams, etc., as well as all key words (together with their derivation) and specific keys should be included. On the work sheet there should be a letter-for-letter decryptment under the cipher text [11]; the

---

[9] It is usual practice to employ as the specific key the equivalent of either A_p, or the equivalent of the first letter of the plain component when this component is a mixed sequence.

[10] For an illustration of a technical report, see par. 10 of Appendix 7.

[11] It is desirable to standardize work sheets where possible, since it lessens the chance of notations being misread by a cryptanalyst looking over the work of another. The particular reason for printing the plaintext recoveries under the cipher text is that this procedure permits the frequencies and other notations to be placed over the cipher letters.

final plaintext version should be in word lengths, with any errors or garbles corrected. Nulls or indicators showing sentence separation, change of key, etc., may be enclosed in parentheses. *All* work sheets and notes should be kept together with the solution.

48. General remarks on the foregoing solution.—*a.* The example solved above is admittedly a more or less artificial illustration of the steps in analysis, made so in order to demonstrate general principles. It was easy to solve because the frequencies of the various cipher letters corresponded quite well with the normal or expected frequencies. However, all cryptograms of the same monoalphabetic nature can be solved along the same general lines, after a certain amount of experimentation, depending upon the length of the cryptogram, and the skill and experience of the cryptanalyst.[12]

b. It is no cause for discouragement if the student's initial attempts to solve a cryptogram of this type require much more time and effort than were apparently required in solving the foregoing purely illustrative example. It is indeed rarely the case that *every* assumption made by the cryptanalyst proves in the end to have been correct; more often it is the case that a good many of his initial assumptions are incorrect, and that he loses much time in casting out the erroneous ones. The speed and facility with which this elimination process is conducted is in many cases all that distinguishes the expert from the novice.

c. Nor will the student always find that the initial classification into vowels and consonants can be accomplished as easily and quickly as was apparently the case in the illustrative example. The principles indicated are very general in their nature and applicability, and there are, in addition, some other principles that may be brought to bear in case of difficulty. Of these, perhaps the most useful are the following:

(1) In normal English it is unusual to find more than two consonants in succession, each of high frequency. If in a cryptogram a succession of three or four letters of high-frequency appear in succession, it is practically certain that at least one of these represents a vowel.[13]

(2) Successions of three vowels are rather unusual in English.[14] Practically the only time this happens is when a word ends in two vowels and the next word begins with a vowel.[15]

(3) When two letters already classified as vowel-equivalents are separated by a sequence

---

[12] The use of simple substitution in modern military operations is exceedingly rare because of the ease of solution. However, such cases have occurred, and one rather illuminating instance may be cited. In an important communication on 5 August 1918, General Kress von Kressenstein used a single mixed alphabet, and the intercepted radio message was solved at American GHQ very speedily. A day later another message, but in a very much more difficult cipher system, was intercepted and solved. When translated, it read as follows:
"GHQ Kress:
The cipher prepared by General von Kress was at once solved here. Its further use and employment is forbidden.

Chief Signal Officer, Berlin."

[13] Sequences of as many as eight consonants are not impossible, however, as in STRE̲N̲G̲T̲H̲S̲ ̲T̲H̲ROUGH.
[14] Note that the word RAD̲I̲O̲ED, past tense of the verb RADIO, is in use.
[15] A sequence of seven vowels is not impossible, however, as in THE W̲A̲Y̲ ̲Y̲O̲U̲ ̲E̲A̲RN

of six or more letters, it is either the case that one of the supposed vowel-equivalents is incorrect, or else that one or more of the intermediate letters is a vowel-equivalent.[16]

(4) Reference to Table 7–B of Appendix 2 discloses the following:

Distribution of first 18 digraphs forming 25 per cent of English text

Number of consonant-consonant digraphs _ 4
Number of consonant-vowel digraphs _ 6
Number of vowel-consonant digraphs _ 8
Number of vowel-vowel digraphs _ 0

Distribution of first 53 digraphs forming 50 per cent of English text

Number of consonant-consonant digraphs _ 8
Number of consonant-vowel digraphs _ 23
Number of vowel-consonant digraphs _ 18
Number of vowel-vowel digraphs _ 4

The latter tabulation shows that of the first 53 digraphs which form 50 per cent of English text, 41 of them, that is, over 75 per cent, are combinations of a vowel with a consonant. In short, in normal English the vowels and the high-frequency consonants are in the long run distributed fairly evenly and regularly throughout the text.

(5) As a rule, repetitions of trigraphs in the cipher text are composed of high-frequency letters forming high-frequency combinations. The latter practically always contain at least one vowel; in fact, if reference is made to Table 10–A of Appendix 2 it will be noted that 36 of the 56 trigraphs having a frequency of 100 or more contain one vowel, 17 of them contain two vowels, and only three of them contain no vowel. In the case of tetragraphic repetitions, Table 11–A of Appendix 2 shows that no tetragraph listed therein fails to contain at least one vowel; 27 of them contain one vowel, 25 contain two vowels, and 2 contain three vowels.

(6) Quite frequently when two known vowel-equivalents are separated by six or more letters none of which seems to be of sufficiently high frequency to represent one of the vowels A E I O, the chances are good that the cipher-equivalent of the vowel U or Y is present.

d. Another method for the determination of vowels which is of especial importance in a difficult case of monoalphabetic substitution, is that known as the *consonant-line method.* The fact that there is a very strong tendency in English for low-frequency consonants to be flanked on one or both sides by vowels is exploited in this method. If a distribution is made of the contacts of the low-frequency ciphertext letters in a monoalphabetic cryptogram, one or more vowel-equivalents should be identifiable by its high occurrence on both sides of the "consonant-line"

---

[16] Some cryptanalysts place a good deal of emphasis upon this principle as a method of locating the remaining vowels after the first two or three have been located. They recommend that the latter be marked throughout the text and then all sequences of five or more letters showing no marks be studied attentively. Certain letters which occur in several such sequences are sure to be vowels. An arithmetical aid in the study is as follows: Take a letter thought to be a good possibility as the cipher equivalent of a vowel (hereafter termed a *possible vowel-equivalent*) and find the length of each interval from the possible vowel-equivalent to the next *known* (fairly surely determined) vowel-equivalent. Multiply the interval by the number of times this interval is found. Add the products and divide by the total number of intervals considered. This will give the *mean* interval for that possible vowel-equivalent. Do the same for all the other possible vowel-equivalents. The one for which the mean is the greatest is most probably a vowel-equivalent. Mark this letter throughout the text and repeat the process for locating additional vowel-equivalents, if any remain to be located. One convention used for marking vowel-equivalents is to place a *red* dot over these letters; a *blue* dot is reserved for consonant equivalents, when so identified.

diagram. As an example, the consonant-line diagram for the distribution in Fig. 14 is given below. (The letters above the horizontal line are the lowest-frequency cipher letters, i. e., in this case, those letters with a frequency of 4 or less. The letters to the left of the vertical line are those which occurred as prefixes of the low-frequency cipher letters, while the letters to the right of the line are the suffixes of those letters.)

4	1	3	3	2	2	3	2	1
B	C	E	J	K	M	O	R	W
				Y				
	D	D			D	D	D	
	S	S			S	S		
					G	G	G	G
Z	Z	Z	Z		Z	Z	Z	
			H		H	H		
	T	T	T					
	V	V	V		V			
					A			
	F	F			F			
	X	X						
			I		I			
					U			

From this diagram it is easy to see that Z_c in all likelihood is a plaintext vowel-equivalent, and that D_c and S_c are probable vowel-equivalents; furthermore, H_c, V_c, F_c, and I_c are possible vowel-equivalents. (Actually, Z_c, S_c, H_c, V_c, and I_c are vowel-equivalents.)

e. To recapitulate the general principles, vowels may then be distinguished from consonants in that they are usually represented by:

(1) high-frequency letters;

(2) high-frequency letters which do not readily contact each other;

(3) high-frequency letters which have a great variety of contact;

(4) high-frequency letters which have an affinity for low-frequency letters (i. e., low-frequency plaintext consonants).

f. In the foregoing example the amount of experimentation or "cutting and fitting" was practically nil. (This is not true of real cases as a rule.) Where such experimentation is necessary, the underscoring of all repetitions of several letters is very essential, as it calls attention to peculiarities of structure that often yield clues.

g. After a few basic assumptions of values have been made, if short words or skeletons of words do not become manifest, it is necessary to make further assumptions for unidentified letters. This is accomplished most often by assuming a word.[17] Now there are two places in

[17] This process does not involve anything more mysterious than ordinary, logical reasoning; there is nothing of the subnormal or supernormal about it. If cryptanalytic success seems to require processes akin to those of medieval magic, if "hocus-pocus" is much to the fore, the student should begin to look for items that the claimant of such success has carefully hidden from view for the mystification of the uninitiated. If the student were to adopt as his personal motto for all his cryptanalytic ventures the quotation (from Tennyson's poem *Columbus*) appearing on the back of the title page of this text, he will frequently find short cuts to his destination and will not too often be led astray!

every message which lend themselves more readily to successful attack by the assumption of words than do any other places—the very beginning and the very end of the message. The reason is quite obvious, for although words may begin or end with almost any letter of the alphabet, they usually begin and end with but a few very common digraphs and trigraphs. Very often the association of letters in peculiar combinations will enable the student to note where one word ends and the next begins. For example, suppose E, N, S, and T have been definitely identified, and a sequence like the following is found in a cryptogram:

$$. . . E N T S N E . . .$$

Obviously the break between two words should fall either after the S of E N T S or after the T of E N T, so that two possibilities are offered: . . . E N T S / N E . . ., or . . . E N T / S N E . . .. Since in English there are very few words with the initial trigraph S N E, it is most likely that the proper division is . . . E N T S / N E . . .. Of course, when several word divisions have been found, the solution is more readily achieved because of the greater ease with which assumptions of additional new values may be made.

h. Although a considerable amount of detailed treatment has been devoted to vowel-consonant analysis, it is felt advisable again to caution the student against the natural tendency to accept without question the results of any one cryptanalytic technique exclusively, even one such as vowel-consonant analysis which seems quite scientific in character.

49. The "probable-word" method; its value and applicability.—*a.* In practically all cryptanalytic studies, short cuts can often be made by assuming the presence of certain words in the message under study. Some writers attach so much value to this kind of an "attack from the rear" that they practically elevate it to the position of a method and call it the "intuitive method" or the "probable-word method." It is, of course, merely a refinement of what in everyday language is called "assuming" or "guessing" a word in the message. The value of making a "good guess" can hardly be overestimated, and the cryptanalyst should never feel that he is accomplishing a solution by an illegitimate subterfuge when he has made a fortunate guess leading to solution. A correct assumption as to plain text will often save hours or days of labor, and sometimes there is no alternative but to try to "guess a word", for occasionally a system is encountered the solution of which is absolutely dependent upon this artifice.

b. The expression "good guess" is used advisedly. For it is "good" in two respects. First, the cryptanalyst must use care in making his assumptions as to plaintext words. In this he must be guided by extraneous circumstances leading to the assumption of *probable* words—not just any words that come to his mind. Therefore he must use his imagination but he must nevertheless carefully control it by the exercise of *good* judgment. Second, only if the "guess" is correct and leads to solution, or at least puts him on the road to solution, is it a good guess. But, while realizing the usefulness and the time- and labor-saving features of a solution by assuming a probable word, the cryptanalyst should exercise discretion in regard to how long he may continue in his efforts with this method. Sometimes he may actually waste time by adhering to the method too long, if straightforward, methodical analysis will yield results more quickly.

c. Obviously, the "probable-word" method has much more applicability when working upon material the general nature of which is known, than when working upon more or less isolated communications exchanged between correspondents concerning whom or whose activities nothing is known. For in the latter case there is little or nothing that the imagination can seize upon as a background or basis for the assumptions.[18]   However, in the case of military cryptanalysis in time of active operations there is, indeed, so great a probability that certain words and expressions are present in certain cryptograms that those words and expressions ("clichés") are often referred to as "cribs" (as defined in Webster's New Collegiate Dictionary: ". . . a plagiarism; hence, a translation, etc., to aid a student in reciting.").   The cryptanalyst is quite sure they are present in the cryptogram under examination—what he must do is to "fit the crib to the text", that is, locate it in the cipher text.

d. Very frequently, the choice of probable words is aided or limited by the number and positions of repeated letters.   These repetitions may be *patent*—that is, externally visible in the cryptographic text as it originally stands—or they may be *latent*—that is, externally invisible but susceptible of being made patent as a result of the analysis.   For example, in a monoalphabetic substitution cipher, such as that discussed in the preceding paragraph, the repeated letters are directly exhibited in the cryptogram; later the student will encounter many cases in which the repetitions are latent, but are made patent by the analytical process.   When the repetitions are patent, then the *pattern* or *formula* to which the repeated letters conform is of direct use in assuming plaintext words; and when the text is in word lengths, the pattern is obviously of even greater assistance.   Suppose the cryptanalyst is dealing with military text, in which case he may expect such words as DIVISION, BATTALION, etc., to be present in the text. The positions of the repeated letter I in DIVISION, of the reversible digraph AT, TA in BATTALION, and so on, constitute for the experienced cryptanalyst telltale indications of the presence of these words, even when the text is not divided up into its original word lengths.

e. The important aid that a study of word patterns can afford in cryptanalysis warrants the use of definite terminology and the establishment of certain data having a bearing thereon. The phenomenon herein under discussion, namely, that many words are of such construction as regards the number and positions of repeated letters as to make them readily identifiable, will be termed *idiomorphism* (from the Greek "idios"=one's own, individual, peculiar+"morphe"= form).   Words which show this phenomenon will be termed *idiomorphic*.   It will be useful to deal with the idiomorphisms symbolically and systematically as described below.

f. The most usual practice in designating idiomorphic patterns and classifying them into systematic lists is to assign a literal nomenclature to that portion of a word (or sequence of plaintext letters) which contains the distinctive pattern, beginning with the first letter which is repeated in the pattern and ending with the last letter which is repeated in the pattern.   Thus, the word DIVISION would be termed an idiomorph of the *abaca* class (based on the sequence $\overline{IVISI}$ contained therein), and the word BATTALION as an idiomorph of the *abba* class (based on the sequence $\overline{ATTA}$).   In Appendix 3 will be found a compendium of the more frequent military words in English, arranged according to word lengths in alphabetical order and in rhyming order;

---

[18] General Givierge in his *Cours de Cryptographie* (p. 121) says: "However, expert cryptanalysts often employ such details as are cited above [in connection with assuming the presence of 'probable words'], and the experience of the years 1914 to 1918, to cite only those, proves that in practice one often has at his disposal elements of this nature, permitting assumptions much more audacious than those which served for the analysis of the last example.   The reader would therefore be wrong in imagining that such fortuitous elements are encountered only in cryptographic works where the author deciphers a document that he himself enciphered.   Cryptographic correspondence, if it is extensive, and if sufficiently numerous working data are at hand, often furnishes elements so complete that an author would not dare use all of them in solving a problem for fear of being accused of obvious exaggeration."

in addition, there will be found in this appendix a listing of idiomorphs arranged first according to pattern and then according to the first letter of the idiomorphic sequence.[19]

50. Solution of additional cryptograms produced by the same components.—a. To return, after a rather long digression, to the cryptogram solved in pars. 44–47, once the components of a cipher alphabet have been reconstructed, subsequent messages which have been enciphered by means of the same components may be solved very readily, and without recourse to the principles of frequency, or application of the probable-word method. It has been seen that the illustrative cryptogram treated in pars. 41–47 was enciphered by juxtaposing the cipher component against the normal sequence so that $A_p = S_c$. It is obvious that the cipher component may be set against the plain component at any one of 26 different points of coincidence, each yielding a different cipher alphabet. After the components have been reconstructed, however, they become *known* sequences and the method of converting the cipher letters into their plain-component equivalents and then completing the plain-component sequence [20] begun by each equivalent can be applied to solve any cryptogram which has been enciphered by these components.

b. An example will serve to make the process clear. Suppose the following message, passing between the same two stations as before, was intercepted shortly after the first message had been solved:

    I Y E W K   C E R N W   O F O S E   L F O O H   E A Z X X

It is assumed that the same components were used, but with a different key letter. First the initial two groups are converted into their plain-component equivalents by setting the cipher component against the plain component at any arbitrary point of coincidence. The initial letter of the former may as well be set against A of the latter, with the following result:

Plain_____ A B C D E F G H I J K L M N O P Q R S T U V W X Y Z
Cipher_____ L E A V N W O R T H B C D F G I J K M P Q S U X Y Z

    Cryptogram_____ I Y E W K   C E R N W   . . .
    Equivalents_____ P Y B F R   L B H E F   . . .

The plain component sequence initiated by each of these conversion equivalents is now completed, with the results shown in Fig 15. Note the plaintext generatrix, CLOSEYOURS, which manifests itself without further analysis. The rest of the message may be read either by continuing the same process, or, what is even more simple, the key letter of the message may now be determined quite readily and the message deciphered by its means.

---

[19] When dealing with cryptograms in which the word lengths are determined or specifically shown, it might be convenient to indicate their lengths and their patterns in a slightly modified form, such as is illustrated below:

                3/aba: DID, EVE, EYE, etc.
                  abb: ADD, ALL, ILL, OFF, etc.
               4/abac: ARAB, AWAY, etc.
                 abbc: ALLY, BEEN, etc.
                 abca: AREA, BOMB, DEAD, etc.
                 abcb: ANON, CEDE, etc.
                 etc. etc.

[20] It must be noted that if the plain component is a *mixed* sequence, then it is this mixed sequence which must be used to complete the columns.

```
I Y E W K C E R N W
P Y B F R L B H E F
Q Z C G S M C I F G
R A D H T N D J G H
S B E I U O E K H I
T C F J V P F L I J
U D G K W Q G M J K
V E H L X R H N K L
W F I M Y S I O L M
X G J N Z T J P M N
Y H K O A U K Q N O
Z I L P B V L R O P
A J M Q C W M S P Q
B K N R D X N T Q R
*C L O S E Y O U R S
D M P T F Z P V S T
E N Q U G A Q W T U
F O R V H B R X U V
G P S W I C S Y V W
H Q T X J D T Z W X
I R U Y K E U A X Y
J S V Z L F V B Y Z
K T W A M G W C Z A
L U X B N H X D A B
M V Y C O I Y E B C
N W Z D P J Z F C D
O X A E Q K A G D E
```

FIGURE 15.

c. In order that the student may understand without question just what is involved in the latter step, that is, discovering the key letter after the first two or three groups have been deciphered by the conversion-completion process, the foregoing example will be used. It was noted that the first cipher group was finally deciphered as follows:

Cipher _____ I Y E W K
Plain _____ C L O S E

Now set the cipher component against the normal sequence so that $C_p = I_c$. Thus:

Plain _____ A B C D E F G H I J K L M N O P Q R S T U V W X Y Z
Cipher _____ F G I J K M P Q S U X Y Z L E A V N W O R T H B C D

It is seen here that when $C_p = I_c$ then $A_p = F_c$. This is the key for the entire message. The decipherment may be completed by direct reference to the cipher alphabet. Thus:

Cipher _____ I Y E W K   C E R N W   O F O S E   L F O O H   E A Z X X
Plain _____ C L O S E   Y O U R S   T A T I O   N A T T W   O P M(X X)

Message: CLOSE YOUR STATION AT TWO PM

d. The student should make sure that he understands the fundamental principles involved in this quick solution, for they are among the most important principles in cryptanalytics. How useful they are will become clear as he progresses into more and more complex cryptanalytic studies.

e. It must be kept in mind that there are *four* ways that two basic sequences may be used to form a cipher alphabet, subject to the instructions guiding the cryptographer in the use of his cryptosystem; this fact must be considered when additional cryptograms appear in a particular cryptosystem for which the primary components have been recovered. Assuming that the sequences just recovered are labelled "A" and "B", then the following contingencies might arise in the encryption of subsequent messages:

(1) "A" direct for the plain component, and "B" direct for the cipher component (as in the original recovery);

(2) "A" direct for the plain, and "B" reversed for the cipher;

(3) "B" direct for the plain, and "A" direct for the cipher; and

(4) "B" direct for the plain, and "A" reversed for the cipher.

51. Recovery of key words.—*a.* Concurrent with the solution of a cryptogram, there should be a simultaneous effort in the reconstruction of cipher alphabets and recovery of key words. Much labor can thus be saved as recovery of the keys early in the stages of solution may transform the process of cryptanalysis into one of decipherment.

b. A mixed cipher alphabet falls into one of five categories, according to the composition of its components, *viz.,*

(1) the plain component is the normal sequence and the cipher component is mixed;

(2) the cipher component is the normal sequence and the plain component is mixed;

(3) both components are the same mixed sequence;

(4) both components are the same mixed sequence, but running in reverse; or

(5) the components are different mixed sequences.

c. Let us examine several types of mixed sequences, using the key word HYDRAULIC as an example. The ordinary keyword-mixed sequence produced from this key word is:

(1) H Y D R A U L I C B E F G J K M N O P Q S T V W X Z

The two principal transposition-mixed types based on this key word are derived from the diagram:

```
H Y D R A U L I C
B E F G J K M N O
P Q S T V W X Z   and read:
```

(2) *Simple columnar*

H B P Y E Q D F S R G T A J V U K W L M X I N Z C O and

(3) *Numerically-keyed columnar*

A J V C O D F S H B P I N Z L M X R G T U K W Y E Q

Other types may arise from various types of route transpositions such as the following, using the foregoing diagram:

86

(4) *Alternate vertical*

H B P Q E Y D F S T G R A J V W K U L M X Z N I C O

(5) *Alternate diagonal*

H Y B P E D R F Q S G A U J T V K L I M W X N C O Z

(6) *Simple diagonal*

P B Q H E S Y F T D G V R J W A K X U M Z L N I O C

(7) *Alternate horizontal*

H Y D R A U L I C O N M K J G F E B P Q S T V W X Z

(8) *Spiral counterclockwise*

O C I L U A R D Y H B P Q S T V W X Z N M K J G F E

Still other types are possible from the foregoing diagram which do not follow a simple, clear-cut route, such as the following:

(9) H Y E B P Q S T G F D R A U K J V W X Z N M L I C O
(10) C P I O Q B L N S E H U M Z T F Y A K X V G D R J W

Any transposition system may be employed to produce a systematically-mixed sequence; practicability of method is the only determining factor. It must be remembered that the greatest amount of systematic mixing will produce a sequence inherently no more secure than a random-mixed alphabet.

d. The student would do well to construct both enciphering and deciphering versions of cipher alphabets recovered, as has been previously mentioned. For example, in the following case

Plain: J Q N M F H L E B R S K G Y Z O T I C D U V A W P X
Cipher: A B C D E F G H I J K L M N O P Q R S T U V W X Y Z

no semblance of a key is apparent; but in the inverse form

Plain: A B C D E F G H I J K L M N O P Q R S T U V W X Y Z
Cipher: W I S T H E M F R A L G D C P Y B J K Q U V X Z N O

the key phrase "NOW IS THE TIME FOR ALL GOOD MEN TO COME TO THE AID OF THEIR PARTY" is quite clear. In other types of mixed sequences, first the one form is attacked, and then if negative results are obtained the inverse form is treated.

e. Let us consider the following cipher alphabet:

P: A B C D E F G H I J K L M N O P Q R S T U V W X Y Z
C: D W Z M S O C R Y A T X B E F U G Q H I V J K L N P

The section $\begin{smallmatrix} V & W & X \\ J & K & L \end{smallmatrix}$ seems to comprise superimposed parts of the non-keyword portions of mixed sequences. Adding Y Z to the plain component, we get $\begin{smallmatrix} V & W & X & Y & Z \\ J & K & L & N & P \end{smallmatrix}$ which is certainly consistent as far as alphabetical progression goes, and indicates that the letters M and O are present in the key word of the cipher component. Continuing in this vein, the section

$$\begin{matrix} M & N & O & Q & S & T & V & W & X & Y & Z \\ B & E & F & G & H & I & J & K & L & N & P \end{matrix}$$

is rapidly established by correlating both sequences. It is obvious that the plain component key word begins right after the Z, and that the cipher component key word probably just precedes the B. Going to the right, $\begin{smallmatrix} Z & R & H \\ P & Q & R \end{smallmatrix}$ suggests key words like RHOMBOID, RHEUMATISM etc. These trials are quickly repudiated; therefore we go on to $\begin{smallmatrix} Z & R & E \\ P & Q & S \end{smallmatrix}$ which is acceptable. $\begin{smallmatrix} Z & R & E & K \\ P & Q & S & T \end{smallmatrix}$ is found wanting, but $\begin{smallmatrix} Z & R & E & P \\ P & Q & S & U \end{smallmatrix}$ is very satisfactory, and this is soon expanded to $\begin{smallmatrix} Z & R & E & P & U & B & L & I & C \\ P & Q & S & U & V & W & X & Y & Z \end{smallmatrix}$, and in a moment or two we recover the complete cipher alphabet:

P: R E P U B L I C A N D F G H J K M O Q S T V W X Y Z
C: Q S U V W X Y Z D E M O C R A T B F G H I J K L N P

f. In the example below the student will observe that the alphabets are reciprocal: this is an indication that identical sequences at a shift of 13 have been employed, or that a mixed sequence is running against itself in reverse. In this case the $\begin{smallmatrix} W & X & Y & Z \\ Z & Y & X & W \end{smallmatrix}$ points to the latter hypothesis.

P: A B C D E F G H I J K L M N O P Q R S T U V W X Y Z
C: H O J F T D N A K C I M L G B S U V P E Q R Z Y X W

Starting with the $\begin{smallmatrix} V & W & X & Y & Z & R \\ R & Z & Y & X & W & V \end{smallmatrix}$ cluster, we see that the key word begins with the letter R; therefore the next letter should be a vowel. $\begin{smallmatrix} Z & R & A \\ W & V & H \end{smallmatrix}$ is not acceptable, but $\begin{smallmatrix} Z & R & E \\ W & V & T \end{smallmatrix}$ is fine, showing that the letter U appears in the key word. Continuing the same line of reasoning as in the preceding example, and with a little further experimentation, the final alphabet is discovered to be

P: R E P U B L I C A N D F G H J K M O Q S T V W X Y Z
C: V T S Q O M K J H G F D N A C I L B U P E R Z Y X W

g. In the next example, all efforts to derive key words on the basis of keyword-mixed sequences are fruitless. The conclusion is therefore drawn that this is a case of a transposition.

P: A B C D E F G H I J K L M N O P Q R S T U V W X Y Z
C: A C S E J Y I G W L F V M H X N K Z P B Q R D U T O

Considering the mechanics of the cryptography involved, and assuming for the time being that Z is at the bottom of the matrix and not in the key word, we start with the letters to the left of Z in the cipher component (or if this fails, with the letters to the right of Z), obtaining the column

N
K which is not incompatible if N is in the key word on the top row.   If we place Y to the left of Z
Z

```
                    E N                                        I M E N
and build up its column, we get J K which is excellent.  This is expanded into G H J K which
                    Y Z                                        W X Y Z
```

```
                7 1 8 4 3 5 2 6 9
                P A R L I M E N T
quickly becomes B C D F G H J K O
                Q S U V W X Y Z
```

This last example was very easy because none of the letters V W X Y Z appeared in the key word; but other cases should hardly prove more difficult.

h. Two additional methods that have been encountered for deriving mixed sequences may be mentioned.   One is a slight modification of the system in the preceding subparagraph, when the key word contains repeated letters:

```
        1 8 7 3 4 9 5 2 6
        C O M . I T . E .
        A B D F G H J K L
        N P Q R S U V W X
        Y Z                    which produces the mixed sequence:
```

C A N Y E K W F R I G S J V L X M D Q O B P Z T H U

The other method is an interrupted-key columnar transposition system:[21]

```
        5 1 3 4 2 6
        V A L . E Y
        B C)
        D F G H I)
        J K M)
        N O P Q)
        R)
        S T U W X Z)    which produces the mixed sequence:
```

A C F K O T E I X L G M P U H Q W V B D J N R S Y Z

The first example will succumb to the treatment outlined in subpar. *g*, whereas the second method is vulnerable owing to the presence of the fragments D J N, F K O, and G M P in the sequence

---

[21] It is to be noted that in this particular case the numerical key serves two purposes: (1) determining the cut-off point (and therefore the number of letters) in each *row* of the diagram, after the appearance of the key word; and (2) determining the order of transcription of the *columns*.

which may be anagrammed. Note the fair-sized fragment B D J N R S, composed of an ascending sequence of letters; this is an outward manifestation of the interrupted-key columnar method.

i. There are still other methods used for the production of mixed sequences, but space does not permit giving further examples. However, the student should by this time be able to devise methods of attack for any special cases that may present themselves, based upon the cryptanalytically exploitable weaknesses or peculiarities inherent in the system of cryptography involved.

CHAPTER VII

MULTILITERAL SUBSTITUTION WITH SINGLE-EQUIVALENT CIPHER ALPHABETS

	Paragraph
General types of multiliteral cipher alphabets	52
The Baconian and Trithemian ciphers	53
Analysis of multiliteral, monoalphabetic substitution ciphers	54
Historically interesting examples	55
The international (Baudot) teleprinter code	56

52. General types of multiliteral cipher alphabets.—*a.* Monoalphabetic substitution methods in general may be classified into uniliteral and multiliteral systems. In the former there is a strict "one-to-one" correspondence between the length of the units of the plain and those of the cipher text; that is, each letter of the plain text is replaced by a single character in the cipher text. In the latter this correspondence is no longer $1_p:1_c$ but may be $1_p:2_c$, where each letter of the plain text is replaced by a combination of two characters in the cipher text; or $1_p:3_c$, where a three-character combination in the cipher text represents a single letter of the plain text, and so on. A cipher in which the correspondence is of the $1_p:1_c$ type is termed *uniliteral* in character; one in which it is of the $1_p:2_c$ type, *biliteral;* $1_p:3_c$, *triliteral,* and so on. Ciphers in which one plaintext letter is represented by cipher characters of two or more elements are classed as multiliteral.[1]

b. Biliteral alphabets are usually composed of a set of 25 or 26 combinations of a limited number of characters taken in pairs. An example of such an alphabet is the following:

Plain	A	B	C	D	E	F	G	H	I	J	K	L	M
Cipher	WW	WH	WI	WT	WE	HW	HH	HI	HT	HT	HE	IW	IH

Plain	N	O	P	Q	R	S	T	U	V	W	X	Y	Z
Cipher	II	IT	IE	TW	TH	TI	TT	TE	EW	EH	EI	ET	EE

This alphabet is derived from the *cipher square* or *matrix* shown in Fig. 16. The cipher equivalent of each plaintext element is made up of two letters from outside the cipher matrix, one letter being the letter beside the row, the other being the letter above the column in which the plaintext letter is located. In other words, the letters at the side and top of the matrix have been used to designate, according to a coordinate system, the cell occupied by each letter within the matrix. The letters (or figures) at the side and top of the matrix are termed *row and column coordinates,* respectively, or row and column *indicators.*

---

[1] The terms uniliteral and multiliteral, although originally applied only to cipher text composed of letters, are used here in their broader sense to embrace cipher text in letters, digits, and even other symbols. In more precise terminology, these terms would probably be *monosymbolic* and *polysymbolic,* respectively, but the terms uniliteral and multiliteral are too well established in literature to be changed at this late time.

$$\theta_{\mathrm{p}}^{2}$$

	W	H	I	T	E
W	A	B	C	D	E
H	F	G	H	IJ	K
θ_{p}^{1} I	L	M	N	O	P
T	Q	R	S	T	U
E	V	W	X	Y	Z

FIGURE 16.

c. If a message is enciphered by means of the foregoing biliteral alphabet, the cryptogram is still monoalphabetic in character. A frequency distribution based upon pairs of letters will obviously have all the characteristics of a simple, uniliteral distribution for a monoalphabetic substitution cipher.

d. The cipher alphabets shown thus far in this text have involved only letters, but alphabets in which the cipher component consists of figures, or groups of figures, are not uncommon in military cryptography.[2] Since there are but 10 digits it is obvious that, in order to represent an alphabet of more than 10 characters by means of figure ciphers, combinations of at least two digits are necessary. The simplest kind of such an alphabet is that in which $A_p=01$, $B_p=02$, . . . $Z_p=26$; that is, one in which the plaintext letters have as their equivalents two-digit numbers indicating their positions in the normal alphabet.

e. Instead of a simple alphabet of the preceding type, it is possible to use a diagram of the type shown in Fig. 17. In this cipher the letter A_p is represented by the *dinome*[3] 11, B_p by the dinome 12, etc. Furthermore, this matrix includes provision for the encipherment of some of the frequently-used punctuation marks in addition to the 26 letters.

	1	2	3	4	5	6	7	8	9	Ø
1	A	B	C	D	E	F	G	H	I	J
2	K	L	M	N	O	P	Q	R	S	T
3	U	V	W	X	Y	Z	.	,	:	;

FIGURE 17.

f. Other types of biliteral cipher alphabets are illustrated in the examples below:

	5	6	7	8	9	Ø
1	A	B	C	D	E	F
2	G	H	IJ	K	L	M
3	N	O	P	Q	R	S
4	T	U	V	W	X	Y	Z

FIGURE 18.

	1	2	3	4	5	6	7	8	9
1	A	B	C	D	E	F	G	H	I
2	J	K	L	M	N	O	P	Q	R
3	S	T	U	V	W	X	Y	Z	*

FIGURE 19.

---

[2] Although, as an extension of this idea, cipher components employing signs and symbols are possible, such alphabets are not suitable for modern cryptography because they can be neither telegraphed nor telephoned with any degree of accuracy, speed, or facility.

[3] A pair of digits is called a *dinome*; similarly, a *trinome* is a set of three digits; a *tetranome*, a set of four digits; etc. Although a single digit would properly be termed a mononome, for the sake of euphony it is shortened into the term *monome*.

	M	U	N	I	C	H
B	A	7	E	5	R	M
E	G	1	N	Y	B	2
R	C	3	D	4	F	6
L	H	8	I	9	J	∅
I	K	L	O	P	Q	S
N	T	U	V	W	X	Z

FIGURE 20.

	A	B	C	D	E	F	G	H	I
A	A	D	G	J	M	P	S	V	Y
B	B	E	H	K	N	Q	T	W	Z
C	C	F	I	L	O	R	U	X	1
D	2	3	4	5	6	7	8	9	∅

FIGURE 21.

g. It is to be noted that in alphabets of the foregoing types, the row indicators may be distinct from the column indicators (e. g., Fig. 18), or they may not (e. g., Fig. 19); of course, when there is any duplication beween the row and column indicators, it is necessary to agree beforehand upon which indicator will be given as the first half of the equivalent for a letter, in order to avoid ambiguity. (In all of the systems described in this and subsequent sections of this text, the row indicator will always form the first part of an equivalent.) When letters are used as row and column indicators they may form a key word (e. g., Fig. 20), or they may not (e. g., Fig. 21); the key words, if formed, may be identical (e. g., Fig. 16) or different (e. g., Fig. 20). Furthermore, the plaintext letters may be arranged within the matrix as a mixed sequence (e. g., Fig. 20), either systematically- or random-mixed; and the matrix may contain, in addition to the letters of the alphabet, punctuation symbols (Fig. 17), numbers (Figs. 20, 21), etc., permitting their encipherment as such, instead of having to be spelled out. When the digits are included within a matrix they are usually inscribed in sequence (such as in Fig. 21), or in some systematic fashion (such as in Fig. 20, where A is followed by "1," B by "2," . . . ., J by "∅".

h. When letters are used as row and column indicators, they may be selected so as to result in producing cipher text that resembles artificial words; that is, words composed of alternate vowels and consonants. For example, if in Fig. 16 the row indicators consisted of the vowels A E I O U in this sequence from the top down, and the column indicators consisted of the consonants B C D F G in this sequence from left to right, the word RAIDS would be enciphered as OCABE FAFOD, which very closely resembles code of the type formerly called artificial code language. Such a system may be called a *false,* or *pseudo-code* system.[4]

i. As a weak type of subterfuge, ciphers which are essentially biliteral may involve a third character appended to the basic two-character cipher unit; this is done to "camouflage" the biliteral nature of the cipher text. This third character may be produced through the use of a cipher matrix of the type illustrated in Fig. 22 (wherein A_p=611, B_p=612 etc.); or the third character may be a "sum-checking" digit which is the *noncarrying sum* (i. e., the sum modulo 10)[5] of the preceding two digits, such as in the trinomes 25<u>7</u>, 83<u>1</u>, and 66<u>2</u>; or it may involve "self-summing" groups, such as the trinomes 254, 83∅, and 669, all of which sum to a constant "1"; or it may merely be a randomly-selected character (inserted solely for the purpose of leading the cryptanalyst astray).

---

[4] Prior to 1934, international telegraph regulations required code words of five letters to contain at least one vowel and code words of ten letters to contain at least three vowels. The International Telegraph Conference held in Madrid in 1932 amended these regulations to permit the use of 5-letter code groups containing any combination of letters. These unrestricted code groups were authorized for use after 1 January 1934.

[5] The term *modulo* (abbreviated *mod*) pertains to a cyclic scale or basis of arithmetic; thus, in the *modulus* of 7, the numbers 8 and 15 are equivalent to 1, and 9 and 16 are equivalent to 2, etc.; or expressed differently, 8 mod 7 is 1, 9 mod 7 is 2. In cryptology, many operations are expressed mod 10 and mod 26.

```
     1 2 3 4 5
61 │ A B C D E │
72 │ F G HIJ K │
83 │ L M N O P │
94 │ Q R S T U │
05 │ V W X Y Z │
```

FIGURE 22.

j. Another possibility that lends itself to certain multiliteral ciphers is the use of a *word spacer* or *word separator*. This word separator might be represented by a value in the matrix; i. e., the separator is *enciphered* (for instance, the dinome "39" in Fig. 19 might stand for a word separator). The word separator might instead be a *single* element not otherwise used in the cryptosystem; i. e., *unenciphered*, thus not giving rise to any possible ambiguity. Thus, in Fig. 19 the digit Ø and in Fig. 21 the letter J might be used as word separators, since no confusion would arise in decrypting.

k. The alphabets yielded by the matrices of Figs. 16–22 may also be termed *bipartite*, because the cipher units of these alphabets may be divided into two separate *parts* whose functions are clearly defined, *viz.*, row indicators and column indicators. As will be discussed later, this bipartite nature of most biliteral alphabets produced from cipher matrices constitutes one of the weaknesses of these alphabets which make them recognizable as such to a cryptanalyst. However, it is possible to employ a cipher matrix in a manner which will produce a biliteral alphabet *not* bipartite in character. For example, using the matrix of Fig. 23 one could produce the following biliteral cipher alphabet in which the equivalent for any letter in the matrix is the sum

```
     1 2 3 4 5
09 │ H Y D R A │
15 │ U LIJ C B │
21 │ E F G K M │
27 │ N O P Q S │
33 │ T V W X Z │
```

FIGURE 23.

of the two coördinates which indicate its cell in the matrix:

Plain	A	B	C	D	E	F	G	H	I	J	K	L	M
Cipher	14	20	19	12	22	23	24	10	18	18	25	17	26

Plain	N	O	P	Q	R	S	T	U	V	W	X	Y	Z
Cipher	28	29	30	31	13	32	34	16	35	36	37	11	38

The cipher units of this alphabet are, of course, biliteral; but they are not bipartite. Note the equivalent of A_p, that is 14—if divided, it yields the digits 1 and 4 which have no meaning *per se*: plaintext letters whose cipher equivalents begin with 1 may be found in *two* different rows of the matrix, and those whose equivalents end in 4 appear in *three* different columns.

94

53. The Baconian and Trithemian ciphers.—*a.* An interesting example in which the cipher equivalents are five-letter groups and yet the resulting cipher is strictly monoalphabetic in character is found in the cipher system invented by Sir Francis Bacon (1561–1626) over 300 years ago. Despite its antiquity the system possesses certain features of merit which are well worth noting.[6] Bacon proposes the following 24-element cipher alphabet, composed of arrangements of five elements, each of which may be chosen from one of two categories:[7]

A=aaaaa	I–J=abaaa	R=baaaa
B=aaaab	K=abaab	S=baaab
C=aaaba	L=ababa	T=baaba
D=aaabb	M=ababb	U–V=baabb
E=aabaa	N=abbaa	W=babaa
F=aabab	O=abbab	X=babab
G=aabba	P=abbba	Y=babba
H=aabbb	Q=abbbb	Z=babbb

If this were all there were to Bacon's invention it would be hardly worth bringing to attention. But what he pointed out, with great clarity and simple examples, was how such an alphabet might be used to convey a secret message by enfolding it in an innocent, external message which might easily evade the strictest kind of censorship. As a very crude example, suppose that a message is written in capital and lower-case letters, any capital letter standing for an "a" element of the cipher alphabet, and any small letter, for a "b" element. Then the external sentence "All is well with me today" can be made to contain the secret message "Help."

Thus:

```
A  L  l     i  s     W  E  l  L  W     I  t  H     m  E     T  o  d  a  Y
a  a  b     b  b     a  a  b  a  a     a  b  a     b  a     a  b  b  a  a
    H                    E                 L                    P
```

Instead of employing a device so obvious as capital and small letters, suppose that an "A" element be indicated by a very slight shading, or a very slightly heavier stroke. Then a secret message might easily be thus enfolded within an external message of exactly opposite meaning. The number of possible variations of this basic scheme is very high. The fact that the characters of the cryptographic text are hidden in some manner or other has, however, no effect upon the strict monoalphabeticity of the scheme.

---

[6] For a true picture of this cipher, the explanation of which is often distorted beyond recognition even by cryptographers, see Bacon's own description of it as contained in his *De Augmentis Scientiarum* (*The Advancement of Learning*), as translated by any first class editor, such as Gilbert Watts (1640) or Ellis, Spedding, and Heath (1857, 1870). The student is cautioned, however, not to accept as true any alleged "decipherments" obtained by the application of Bacon's cipher to literary works of the 16th century. These readings are purely subjective.

[7] Bacon's alphabet was called by him a "biliteral alphabet" because it employs permutations of two letters. But from the cryptanalytic standpoint the significant point is that each plaintext letter is represented by a 5-character equivalent. Hence, present terminology requires that this alphabet be referred to as a *quinqueliteral alphabet*. Although the quinqueliteral alphabet affords 32 permutations, Bacon used only 24 of them, because in the 16th century the letters I and J, U and V were used interchangeably. Note the regularity of construction of Bacon's biliteral alphabet, a feature which easily permits its reconstruction from memory.

b. Another historical multiliteral cipher, sometimes attributed to the abbot Trithemius, born Johann von Heydenberg (1462–1516), is that incorporating a *triliteral alphabet.* Trithemius was said to have invented this alphabet for use in a fashion similar to Bacon's alphabet; i. e., as a means of disguise or cover for a secret text. This alphabet, modified to include the 26 letters of the present-day English alphabet, is shown in Fig. 23, below; it consists of all the permutations (with repetitions allowed) of three things taken three at a time, i. e., 3^3 or 27 in all.

A=111	D=121	G=131	J=211	M=221	P=231	S=311	V=321	Y=331
B=112	E=122	H=132	K=212	N=222	Q=232	T=312	W=322	Z=332
C=113	F=123	I=133	L=213	O=223	R=233	U=313	X=323	*=333

FIGURE 23.

The cipher text of course does not have to be restricted to digits; any groupings of three things taken three at a time will do.

54. Analysis of multiliteral, monoalphabetic substitution ciphers.—*a.* Biliteral ciphers and those of the other multiliteral (triliteral, quadriliteral, . . .) types are often readily detected externally by the fact that the cryptographic text is usually composed of but a very limited number of different characters. They are handled in exactly the same manner as are uniliteral, monoalphabetic substitution ciphers. So long as the same character, or combination of characters, is always used to represent the same plaintext letter, and so long as a given letter of the plain text is always represented by the same character or combination of characters, the substitution is strictly monoalphabetic and can be handled in the simple manner described in the preceding chapter of this text.

b. In the case of biliteral ciphers in which the row and column indicators are not identical, and the direction of reading the cipher pairs is chosen at will for each succeeding cipher pair, an analysis of the *contacts* of the letters comprising the cipher pairs will disclose that there are *two* distinct families of letters, and a cipher pair will never consist of two letters of the same family. With this fact discovered, the cipher may be quickly reduced to uniliteral terms and solved in the manner previously mentioned.

c. If a multiliteral cipher includes provision for the encipherment of a word separator, the cipher equivalent of this word separator may be readily identified because it will have the *highest* frequency of any cipher unit.[8] On the other hand, if the word separator is a *single* character (see subpar. 52*j*, on the use of the digit Ø and the letter J), this character may be identified throughout the encrypted text by its positional appearance spaced "wordlength-wise" in the cipher text, and by the fact that it never contacts itself. If this single character is used as a null indiscriminately throughout the cipher text, instead of as a word separator, the analysis is a bit more complicated but not as great as might be thought.

d. As a general rule, it is advisable to reduce multiliteral cipher text to uniliteral equivalents, especially if a triliteral frequency distribution is to be made. If not more than 36 different

---

[8] For English, since the average word length is 5.2 letters, the word separator will have a percentage frequency of 16%. The letters of the alphabet will now take on new percentage frequencies as follows:

A	6.2	F	2.3	K	0.25	O	6.3	S	5.1	W	1.3
B	0.84	G	1.3	L	3.0	P	2.3	T	7.7	X	0.41
C	2.6	H	2.9	M	2.1	Q	0.25	U	2.2	Y	1.6
D	3.5	I	6.2	N	6.6	R	6.4	V	1.3	Z	0.08
E	11.0	J	0.16								

combinations are present in a cryptogram, the extra values over 26 may be represented by digits for the purpose of this reduction. If, however, more than 36 different combinations are found in the encrypted text, it is usually not worth the trouble to attempt any uniliteral reduction, and the cipher text can be attacked in its multiliteral groupings.

e. As one of the first steps in the solution of any multiliteral cipher in letters which appears to involve the use of a cipher matrix, it is generally advisable to anagram the letters comprising the row and column indicators in an attempt to disclose any key words for these indicators. When the anagramming process *does* disclose such a key word or words, the next step is to make a skeleton reconstruction matrix which is a duplicate of the original enciphering matrix in that the indicators are arranged in the same order as on the original. Then, as plain text is recovered in the cryptogram by any of the methods outlined in the previous chapter of this text, the recovered plaintext letters should be inserted in the proper cells of the reconstruction matrix, so that any systematic arrangement of the plaintext letters, if present in the original, may be disclosed prior to recovery of the complete plain text. Furthermore, it may in some instances be found worthwhile, immediately after successfully uncovering the key words used as indicators, to make a frequency distribution of the particular cryptogram in the form of tally marks within the properly arranged frame of the reconstruction matrix, because a few moments' study of the *locations* of the crests and troughs in the distribution made in that form may, if the letters of the underlying plain component have been arranged in the normal sequence or in a keyword-mixed sequence (especially if it is related to the key words for the indicators), provide a basis for the recovery of this sequence at one stroke, without recourse to analysis of the cipher text.

55. Historically interesting examples.—*a.* Two examples of multiliteral ciphers of historical interest will be cited as illustrations. During the campaign for the presidential election of 1876 (Hayes vs. Tilden) many cipher messages were exchanged between the Tilden managers and their agents in several states where the voting was hotly contested. Two years later the New York Tribune [9] exposed many irregularities in the campaign by publishing the decipherments of many of these messages. These decipherments were achieved by two investigators employed by the Tribune, and the plain text of the messages seems to show that illegal attempts and measures to carry the election for Tilden were made by his managers. Here is one of the messages:

JACKSONVILLE, Nov. 16 (1876).

GEO. F. RANEY, Tallahassee.

```
    P p y y e m n s n y y y p i m a s h n s y y s s i t e p a a e n s h n
s p e n s s h n s m m p i y y s n p p y e a a p i e i s s y e s h a i n s
s s p e e i y y s h n y n s s s y e p i a a n y i t n s s h y y s p y y p
i n s y y s s i t e m e i p i m m e i s s e i y y e i s s i t e i e p y y
p e e i a a s s i m a a y e s p n s y y i a n s s s e i s s m m p p n s p
i n s s n p i n s i m i m y y i t e m y y s s p e y y m m n s y y s s i t
s p y y p e e p p p m a a a y y p i i t
```
L'Engle goes up tomorrow.

DANIEL.

Examination of the message discloses that only ten different letters are used. It is probable, therefore, that what one has here is a cipher which employs a multiliteral alphabet. First

[9] New York Tribune, Extra No. 44, *The Cipher Dispatches*, New York, 1879.

assuming that the alphabet is one in which combinations of two letters represent single letters of the plain text, the message is rewritten in pairs and substitution of arbitrary letters for the pairs is made, as seen below:

```
PP  YY  EM  NS  NY  YY  PI  MA  SH  NS  YY  SS  etc.
A   B   C   D   E   B   F   G   H   D   B   I   etc.
```

A triliteral frequency distribution is then made and analysis of the message along the lines illustrated in the preceding chapter of this text yields solution, as follows:

Jacksonville, Nov. 16.

GEO. F. RANEY, Tallahassee:
Have Marble and Coyle telegraph for influential men from Delaware and Virginia. Indications of weakening here. Press advantage and watch Board. L'Engle goes up tomorrow.

DANIEL.

b. The other example, using numbers, is as follows:

Jacksonville, Nov. 17.

S. PASCO and E. M. L'ENGLE:
```
84  55  84  25  93  34  82  31  31  75  93  82  77  33  55  42
93  20  93  66  77  66  33  84  66  31  31  93  20  82  33  66
52  48  44  55  42  82  48  89  42  93  31  82  66  75  31  93
```
DANIEL.

There were, of course, several messages of like nature, and examination disclosed that only 26 different dinomes in all were used. Solution of these ciphers followed very easily, the decipherment of the one given above being as follows:

Jacksonville, Nov. 17.

S. PASCO and E. M. L'ENGLE:
Cocke will be ignored, Eagan called in. Authority reliable.

DANIEL.

c. The Tribune experts gave the following alphabets as the result of their decipherments:

AA=O	EN=Y	IT=D	NS=E	PP=H	SS=N
AI=U	EP=C	MA=B	NY=M	SH=L	YE=F
EI=I	IA=K	MM=G	PE=T	SN=P	YI=X
EM=V	IM=S	NN=J	PI=R	SP=W	YY=A
20=D	33=N	44=H	62=X	77=G	89=Y
25=K	34=W	48=T	66=A	82=I	93=E
27=S	39=P	52=U	68=F	84=C	96=M
31=L	42=R	55=O	75=B	87=V	99=J

They did not attempt to correlate these alphabets, or at least they say nothing about a possible relationship. The author [W. F. F.] has, however, reconstructed the square upon which these alphabets are based, and it is given below (Fig. 24).

1st Letter or Number \ 2d Letter or Number	H 1	I 2	S 3	P 4	A 5	Y 6	M 7	E 8	N 9	T 0
H 1										
I 2				K			S			D
S 3	L		N	W					P	
P 4		R		H				T		
A 5		U			O					
Y 6		X					A	F		
M 7				B			G			
E 8		I		C			V		Y	
N 9			E				M		J	
T 0										

FIGURE 24.

It is amusing to note that the conspirators selected as their key a phrase quite in keeping with their attempted illegalities—HIS PAYMENT—for bribery seems to have played a considerable part in that campaign. The blank cells in the matrix probably contained proper names, numbers, etc.

56. The international (Baudot) teleprinter code.—*a.* Modern printing telegraph systems,[10] or *teleprinter systems* as they are more often called, make use of a five-unit code[11] or alphabet which is similar to the Baconian alphabet treated in par. 53. The teleprinter alphabet is composed of all the possible permutations (with repetitions allowed) of five elements, each of which may be chosen from one of two categories, making it possible to obtain 32 different permutations, 26 of which are assigned to the letters of the alphabet, leaving 1 for an "idle condition" and 5 for certain printer operations called *functions*, such as "space," "figure shift," "letter shift," etc.

---

[10] Such systems are characterized by the transmission and *reception printing* of messages by electrical means, incorporating two electrically-connected instruments resembling typewriters. When a key of the keyboard on the transmitting instrument is depressed, an electrical signal is transmitted to the receiving instrument, causing the corresponding character to be printed therein. Usually the message is printed at the local as well as the distant station. The system has been adapted to radio as well as wire and overseas cable transmission.

[11] The five-unit code was first applied to teleprinter systems by Jean Maurice Emile Baudot (1845–1903), and is commonly known as the Baudot Code. It is worthwhile to point out that Baudot apparently constructed his alphabet to correspond with normal frequencies of characters (with certain exceptions), since the most frequent ones are represented by permutations requiring the least electrical energy on the basis of "marking" and "spacing." In this respect Baudot "took a leaf out of Morse's note-book." Seven-unit codes are also in existence; the characters in these alphabets are always composed of 3 mark impulses, so that the adding or dropping of an impulse will at once be recognized as an error.

b. During electrical transmission, the two distinct elements of which each character is composed take the form of (1) a timed interval of electrical current and (2) a timed interval of no current, which are commonly referred to as "mark" impulses and "space" impulses, respectively, and these impulses are transmitted serially. In certain operations, a paper tape is prepared of the traffic to be transmitted, or a paper tape may be prepared of the incoming traffic at the receiving end; in such tapes, the elements of the Baudot characters take the form of punched holes ("mark" impulses) and imperforate positions ("space" impulses).

c. The teleprinter code in international use is given in Chart 7, below, wherein the mark and space impulses (known collectively as *bauds*) are illustrated as the holes (shown as black dots) and "no-holes" of a teleprinter tape. The letter equivalents ("lower case") are self-explanatory.

UPPER CASE — WEATHER SYMBOLS / COMMUNICATIONS	A	B	C	D	E	F	G	H	I	J	K	L	M	N	O	P	Q	R	S	T	U	V	W	X	Y	Z	BLANK	C.R.	L.F.	SPACE	LTR. SHIFT	FIG. SHIFT
COMMUNICATIONS	-	?	:	$	3	!	&	£	8	'	(	)	.	,	9	Ø	1	4	△	5	7	;	2	/	6	"						
1	●	●		●	●	●				●	●						●		●		●		●	●	●	●					●	●
2	●		●				●		●	●	●	●				●	●	●			●	●	●								●	●
3			●			●		●	●		●		●	●		●	●		●		●	●		●	●					●	●	
4		●	●	●		●	●			●	●		●	●	●			●				●		●				●			●	●
5		●					●	●				●	●		●	●	●			●		●	●	●	●	●					●	●

CHART 7. International teleprinter code.

The *figure shift* is used to change the meaning of a particular character to an "upper case" equivalent, and when it is desired to return to lower case, the *letter shift* is used; in regular teleprinter usage, the "communications" set of upper-case equivalents are the ones recorded on the typed copy by the teleprinter, whereas the "weather symbols" are the upper-case equivalents which are printed in teleprinter systems designed for the sending and receiving of weather information. The *space* is used to separate words; the *carriage return* (C. R.) effects the return of the teleprinter carriage to the right and the *line feed* (L. F.) rolls the platen to the next line for printing (cf. the corresponding functions of an ordinary typewriter). In addition, when the upper-case equivalent of "S" is used, a bell rings in the receiving teleprinter as a signal to call the operator to his machine, or to indicate that traffic is about to be sent.

d. In Fig. 25 is shown a portion of a teleprinter tape containing the beginning of the phrase "Now is the time for all good men . . ."

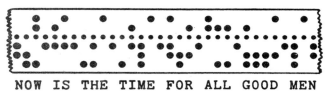

NOW   IS   THE   TIME   FOR   ALL   GOOD   MEN

FIGURE 25.

The small holes, one of which appears in every position of the tape between the second and third levels, are sprocket holes used for advancing the tape through the teleprinter unit. Tapes may be of two kinds: (a) tapes in which the holes are fully perforated, called "chad tape" or "fully-

100

chadded tape"; or (b) tapes in which the holes are cut as little round flaps or lids (i. e., the punchings are left attached to the body of the tape), called "chadless tape." This latter tape was developed so as to permit an easily readable typed record on a perforated tape without increasing the width of the standard tape or changing punching dimensions.

e. It is to be emphasized that messages are *not* made secure from unauthorized reading merely by sending them by means of an ordinary teleprinter system—the teleprinter alphabet is internationally known, just as the English, Russian, etc. alphabets are. In order to provide security for a teleprinter message, it is just as necessary to apply thereto some sort of cryptographic treatment as it is to any other kind of message. The cryptosystems used for teleprinter encryption may involve either, or both, of the two classes of cryptographic treatment, *viz.*, substitution and transposition. A substitution treatment might involve changing certain of the mark impulses of the characters comprising a message to space impulses, and vice versa, according to a prearranged system; a transposition treatment might involve changing the *order* of the 5 impulses in the Baudot equivalents for the characters comprising a message; and so on. The cryptographic treatment can be accomplished by a special cipher attachment (called an "appliqué unit") to a teleprinter; thus no modification of the teleprinter itself would be necessary. There are, of course, self-contained cipher teleprinters designed as such for engineering or cryptographic reasons, or both.

f. In the analysis of encrypted teleprinter systems, recourse is had to special tables [12] of the frequencies of single Baudot characters, digraphs, trigraphs, etc., as they appear in teleprinter traffic. It is important to note that in teleprinter traffic, as in any other type of traffic involving the use of a word separator, this character has the highest frequency of any plaintext element. Furthermore, one of the highest-frequency plaintext digraphs, in addition to those wherein the word separator constitutes one of the elements, will be the combination "carriage-return/line-feed", since this combination of characters is used in the normal procedure of typing each line of text on the teleprinter.

---

[12] In such tables, as is common in cryptanalytic practice, the mark impulses are designated by a plus symbol (+), and the space impulses are designated by a minus symbol (−). In addition, it is usual in such tables to denote the character representing the carriage return by the digit "3," the line feed by "4," the figure shift by "5." the blank by "7," the letter shift by "8," and the space by "9."

Chapter VIII

MULTILITERAL SUBSTITUTION WITH VARIANTS

	Paragraph
Purpose of providing variants in monoalphabetic substitution	57
Simple types of cipher alphabets with variants	58
More complicated types of cipher alphabets with variants	59
Analysis of simple examples	60
Analysis of more complicated examples	61
Analysis involving the use of isologs	62
Further remarks on variant systems	63

57. Purpose of providing variants in monoalphabetic substitution.—*a.* It has been seen that the individual letters composing ordinary intelligible plain text are used with varying frequencies; some, such as (in English) E, T, R, I, and N, are used much more often than others, such as J, K, Q, X, and Z. In fact, each letter has a *characteristic frequency* which affords definite clues in the solution of simple monoalphabetic ciphers, such as those discussed in the preceding chapters of this text. In addition, the associations which individual letters form in combining to make up words, and the peculiarities which certain of them manifest in plain text, afford further direct clues by means of which ordinary monoalphabetic substitution encipherments of such plain text may be more or less speedily solved. This has led cryptographers to devise methods for disguising, suppressing, or eliminating the foregoing characteristics manifested in cryptograms produced by the simpler methods of monoalphabetic substitution. One category of such methods, the one to be discussed in this chapter, is that in which the letters of the plain component of a cipher alphabet are assigned two or more cipher equivalents, which are called *variant values* (or, more simply, *variants*).

b. Basically, systems involving variants are multiliteral [1] and, in such systems, because of the large number of equivalents made available by the combinations and permutations of a limited number of elements, each letter of the plain text may be represented by several multiliteral cipher equivalents which may be selected at random. For example, if 3-letter combinations are employed as the multiliteral equivalents, there are available 26^3 or 17,576 such equivalents for the 26 letters of the plain text; they may be assigned in equal numbers of different equivalents for the 26 letters, in which case each letter would be representable by 676 different 3-letter equivalents; or they may be assigned on some other basis, for example, proportionately to the

---

[1] *Uniliteral* substitution with variants is also possible, but not very practical. Note the following cipher alphabet, illustrated by Captain Roger Baudouin in his excellent treatise, *Eléments de Cryptographie*, p. 101 (Paris, 1939):

```
Plain:   A B C D E F G H I L M N O P Q R S T U V X Z
Cipher:  L G O R F Q A H C M B T I D N P U S Y E W J
             K             X             Z
             V
```

Baudouin proposed that J_p and Y_p be replaced by I_p; K_p by C_p or Q_p; and W_p by VV_p—thus four cipher letters would be available as variants for the high-frequency plaintext letters in French. (Cf. the variant scheme in Edgar Allan Poe's day, in footnote 1 on p. 62, in which the decipherment may be ambiguous.)

relative frequencies of plaintext letters. For this reason this type of system may be more completely described as a *monoalphabetic, multiliteral substitution with a multiple-equivalent cipher alphabet.*[2] Some authors term such a system "simple substitution with multiple equivalents"; others term it "monoalphabetic substitution with variants", or *multiliteral substitution with variants*. For the sake of brevity and precise terminology, the latter designation will be employed in this text, it being understood without further restatement that only such systems as are monoalphabetic will be discussed.

c. The primary object of substitution with variants is, as has been mentioned above, to provide several values which may be employed at random in a simple substitution of cipher equivalents for the plaintext letters.

d. A word or two concerning the underlying theory of (monoalphabetic) multiliteral substitution with variants may not be amiss. Whereas in simple or single-equivalent substitution it has been seen that

(1) the same letter of the plain text is invariably represented by but one and always the same character or cipher unit of the cryptogram, and

(2) the same character or cipher unit of the cryptogram invariably represents one and always the same letter of the plain text,

in multiliteral substitution with variants it will be seen that

(1) the same letter of the plain text may be represented by one or more different cipher units of the cryptogram, but

(2) the same cipher unit of the cryptogram nevertheless invariably represents one and always the same letter of the plain text.

58. **Simple types of cipher alphabets with variants.**—*a.* The matrices shown below represent some of the simpler means for accomplishing monoalphabetic substitution with variants. The systems incorporating these matrices are extensions of the basic ideas of multiliteral substitution treated in par. 52. The variant equivalents for any plaintext letter may be chosen at will; thus, in Fig. 26, E_p=10, 15, 60, or 65; in Fig. 27, E_p=AU_c, AZ_c, FU_c, FZ_c, LU_c, or LZ_c; etc.

		6	7	8	9	0
		1	2	3	4	5
6	1	A	B	C	D	E
7	2	F	G	H	IJ	K
8	3	L	M	N	O	P
9	4	Q	R	S	T	U
0	5	V	W	X	Y	Z

FIGURE 26.

			V	W	X	Y	Z
			Q	R	S	T	U
L	F	A	A	B	C	D	E
M	G	B	F	G	H	IJ	K
N	H	C	L	M	N	O	P
O	I	D	Q	R	S	T	U
P	K	E	V	W	X	Y	Z

FIGURE 27.

				A	E	I	O	U
T	N	H	B	A	B	C	D	E
V	P	J	C	F	G	H	IJ	K
W	Q	K	D	L	M	N	O	P
X	R	L	F	Q	R	S	T	U
Z	S	M	G	V	W	X	Y	Z

FIGURE 28.

[2] Cf. the title of the preceding chapter, "Multiliteral substitution with *single*-equivalent cipher alphabets."

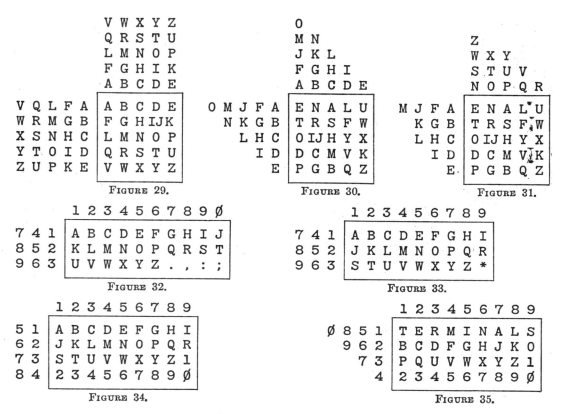

```
        V W X Y Z                    O                        Z
        Q R S T U                    M N                      W X Y
        L M N O P                    J K L                    S T U V
        F G H I K                    F G H I                  N O P Q R
        A B C D E                    A B C D E

V Q L F A  | A B C D E |   O M J F A  | E N A L U |   M J F A  | E N A L'U |
W R M G B  | F G H IJK |   N K G B    | T R S F W |   K G B    | T R S F,W |
X S N H C  | L M N O P |   L H C      | O IJ H Y X |  L H C    | O IJ H Y X |
Y T O I D  | Q R S T U |   I D        | D C M V K |   I D      | D C M V,K |
Z U P K E  | V W X Y Z |   E          | P G B Q Z |   E.       | P G B Q Z |

    FIGURE 29.                 FIGURE 30.                FIGURE 31.

    1 2 3 4 5 6 7 8 9 Ø            1 2 3 4 5 6 7 8 9

7 4 1  | A B C D E F G H I J |   7 4 1  | A B C D E F G H I |
8 5 2  | K L M N O P Q R S T |   8 5 2  | J K L M N O P Q R |
9 6 3  | U V W X Y Z . , : ; |   9 6 3  | S T U V W X Y Z * |

    FIGURE 32.                         FIGURE 33.

    1 2 3 4 5 6 7 8 9            1 2 3 4 5 6 7 8 9

5 1  | A B C D E F G H I |    Ø 8 5 1  | T E R M I N A L S |
6 2  | J K L M N O P Q R |    9 6 2    | B C D F G H J K O |
7 3  | S T U V W X Y Z 1 |    7 3      | P Q U V W X Y Z 1 |
8 4  | 2 3 4 5 6 7 8 9 Ø |    4        | 2 3 4 5 6 7 8 9 Ø |

    FIGURE 34.                         FIGURE 35.
```

b. It is to be noted that encipherment by means of the matrices in Figs. 27, 28, and 31 is *commutative;* i. e., the coordinates may be read in either row-column or column-row order without cryptographic ambiguity, since there is no duplication between the row and column coordinates. The remaining matrices above are *noncommutative;* therefore a convention must be agreed upon as to the order of reading the coordinates. It should also be noted that in Figs. 30 and 31 the letters in the square have been inscribed in such a manner that, coupled with the particular arrangement of the row and column coordinates, the number of variants available for each plaintext letter is roughly proportional to the frequencies of the letters in plain text. A similar idea is found in Fig. 35, wherein the top row of the rectangle contains a word composed of high-frequency letters, and the coordinates are arranged in a manner roughly corresponding to the frequencies of plaintext letters. The matrix in Fig. 28 is a modification of the pseudo-code system described in par. 52*h,* with the added feature of variants.

c. Other simple ideas for producing variant systems are matrices such as the following:

```
A  B  C  D  E  F  G  H IJ K  L  M  N  O  P  Q  R  S  T  U  V  W  X  Y  Z

08 09 10 11 12 13 14 15 16 17 18 19 20 21 22 23 24 25 01 02 03 04 05 06 07
35 36 37 38 39 40 41 42 43 44 45 46 47 48 49 50 26 27 28 29 30 31 32 33 34
68 69 70 71 72 73 74 75 51 52 53 54 55 56 57 58 59 60 61 62 63 64 65 66 67
87 88 89 90 91 92 93 94 95 96 97 98 99 00 76 77 78 79 80 81 82 83 84 85 86
```

FIGURE 36.

105

A	B	C	D	E	F	G	H	I	J	K	L	M	N	O	P	Q	R	S	T	U	V	W	X	Y	Z
14	15	16	17	18	19	20	21	22	23	24	25	26	01	02	03	04	05	06	07	08	09	10	11	12	13
27	28	29	30	31	32	33	34	35	36	37	38	39	40	41	42	43	44	45	46	47	48	49	50	51	52
58	59	60	61	62	63	64	65	66	67	68	69	70	71	72	73	74	75	76	77	78	53	54	55	56	57
81	82	83	84	85	86	87	88	89	90	91	92	93	94	95	96	97	98	99	00	/////////////				79.80	

FIGURE 37.

In these two matrices there has been a regular inscription of the dinomes in the rows. Furthermore, in Fig. 36 the dinomes 01, 26, 51, and 76 (i. e., the lowest number in each of the four sequences) give the key word (TRIP) for that matrix; and in Fig. 37, the dinomes 01, 27, 53, and 79 denote the key word (NAVY) for that matrix. The security of systems involving such matrices would of course be greatly improved if the dinomes were assigned in a random manner; but then the easy mnemonic feature of the four sequences and the key word would be lost.

d. An interesting adaptation in a disc form of the type of matrix illustrated in Fig. 37 is the following device reputedly once used by the Mexican Army:

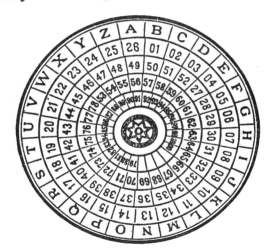

The device consisted of five concentric discs, the outer disc bearing the 26 letters of the alphabet, and the other four bearing the sequences 01–26, 27–52, 53–78, and 79–00. The rotatable discs made it possible to change the keys at frequent intervals, without the necessity of writing out a new matrix each time.

59. **More complicated types of cipher alphabets with variants.**—*a.* Matrices such as those in Figs. 38, 39, and 40 below are termed *frequential matrices*, since the number of cipher values available for any given plaintext letter closely approximates its relative plaintext frequency.

b. In the fragmentary matrix illustrated in Fig. 38, the number of occurrences of a particular letter within the matrix is proportional to its frequency in plain text; the letters are inscribed in a random manner, in order to enhance further the security of the system. In Fig. 39, we have a modification of the idea set forth in Fig. 38, except that the size of the matrix has been reduced from 26 x 26 to 10 x 10; in this case, the letters (with appropriate number of repetitions) have been inscribed in a simple diagonal route (lower left to upper right) within the square, and the coordinates have been scrambled, for greater security. In Fig. 40, there is illustrated a type of

106

```
          A B C D E        V W X Y Z

    A |  T G A U R   . . . I E C A P
    B |  S L I E Y         F R N S T
    C |  C N D O M   . . . E L T I H
    D |  R A P T F         O Y S O V
    E |  N T X N E         C E R E D
            .                 .
            .                 .          (676—cell matrix)
            .                 .
    V |  N O A T E         A L E Z H
    W |  I H R O Q         E T R B T
    X |  O I E T A   . . . C N P E S
    Y |  F T L O S         A M T I U
    Z |  I S N D R   . . . I E D O N
```

FIGURE 38.

```
        6 8 9 1 5 4 3 7 2 0

    7 | A A A C D E E I L N
    1 | A A C D E E H K N O
    3 | A B D E E H J N O R
    8 | A D E E H I N O R S
    9 | C E E G I N O R S T
    2 | E E F I M O Q S T T
    0 | E F I M O P R T T U
    5 | F I L N P R S T U X
    6 | I L N P R S T U W Y
    4 | L N O R S T T V Y Z
```

FIGURE 39.

```
        0 1 2 3 4 5 6 7 8 9

    0 | E N T R U C K I N G
    1 | Q U A R A N T I N E
    2 | U N E X P E N D E D
    3 | I M P O S S I B L E
    4 | V I C T O R I O U S
    5 | A D J U D I C A T E
    6 | L A B O R A T O R Y
    7 | E I G H T E E N T H
    8 | N A T U R A L I Z E
    9 | T W E N T Y F I V E
```

FIGURE 40.

cipher square which is known in cryptologic literature as the *Grandpré cipher;* in this square there are inscribed ten 10-letter words containing all the letters of the alphabet in their approximate plaintext frequencies. These ten words are further linked together by a 10-letter word which appears vertically in the first column, as a mnemonic feature for the inscription of the words in the rows.

c. The frequential-type system represented in Fig. 41a (enciphering matrix) and 41b (deciphering matrix) was described by Sacco,[3] who proposed that the dinomes inscribed in the enciphering matrix be thoroughly disarranged by applying a double transposition to the dinomes 00–99 as a means of suppressing any patent relationships among the variant values for the various plaintext letters; furthermore, the nulls incorporated in the matrix were to be used occasionally during the encryption of a message, in order to throw a cryptanalyst off the track. In this example the number of variant values for each plaintext letter has been established, of course, from the standpoint of Italian letter frequencies.

[3] Sacco, Generale Luigi, *Manuale di Crittografia*, 3d Ed., Rome, 1947, p. 22.

107

Enciphering Table

Nulls	A	E	I	M	Q	V	one	seven
48–56	03–25	18–35	10–23	39	20	02–86	44	46
21–09	52–62	37–65	53–75	68	77		66	
76–54	79–69	71–78	82–87					**eight**
42–12	**B**	**F**	**J**	**N**	**R**	**W**	**two**	29
64–74	40	24	81	13–73	26–94	95	84	
55–14	93	57						**nine**
83–90	**C**	**G**	**K**	**O**	**S**	**X**	**three**	31
63–06	28	38	96	07–30	11–58	85	50	
47–45	70	97		51–67	**T**	**Y**	**four**	**zero**
				72–89	33–88	22	27	19
								92
	D	**H**	**L**	**P**	**U**	**Z**	**five**	**period**
	08	17	05	41	00–15	34	60–91	16–91
	80	43	49	98	36–99	59		
					01		**six**	**comma**
							04	32

FIGURE 41a.

Deciphering Table

	1	2	3	4	5	6	7	8	9	Ø
1	S	—	N	—	U	period	H	E	zero	I
2	—	Y	I	F	A	R	four	C	eight	Q
3	nine	comma	T	Z	E	U	E	G	M	O
4	P	—	H	one	—	seven	—	—	L	B
5	O	A	I	—	—	—	F	S	Z	three
6	period	A	—	—	E	one	O	M	A	five
7	E	O	N	—	I	—	Q	E	A	C
8	J	I	—	two	X	V	I	T	O	D
9	five	zero	B	R	W	K	G	P	U	—
Ø	U	V	A	six	L	—	O	D	—	U

FIGURE 41b.

108

d. The Baconian cipher described in subpar. 53a may be used as a basis for superimposing additional complexities. For instance, the "a" elements may be represented by any one of the 20 consonants as variants, while the "b" elements may be represented by any one of the six vowels; or the letters A–M may be used to represent the "a" elements and the letters N–Z for the "b" elements; digits may be used for the "a" and "b" elements, either on the basis of the first five and last five digits, or on the basis of the odd and even digits; or the first 10 consonants (B–M) and the last 10 consonants (N–Z) may be used for the "a" and "b" elements, with the vowels used occasionally as nulls—thus the resultant cryptograms will resemble those of a fairly complex cryptosystem. However, once the cryptanalyst assumes the possibility of such a system, its complexity is more apparent than real. Similarly, variations of this genre may be superimposed on triliteral systems such as the Trithemian cipher illustrated in subpar. 53b; variants for the "1", "2", and "3" elements may be chosen in such a way as to provide a large number of equivalents for each basic triliteral combination.

e. Another scheme for a complex variant system is a *summing-trinome system*. In this cryptosystem, each plaintext letter is assigned a unique value of 1 to 26; this value is then expressed as a trinome, *the digits of which sum to the designated value of the letter*. For example, if a letter has been assigned the value "4", it may be represented by any one of the following permutations and combinations:[4]

```
004   031   112   202   301
013   040   121   211   310
022   103   130   220   400
```

Since the values toward the middle of the range 1–26 may be represented by a very considerable number of summing-trinomes (e. g., for the values 13 and 14 there are 75 variants each), such a system would offer a cryptographer wide latitude in the choice of cipher equivalents in enciphering, especially if the basic values of the plaintext letters were chosen to correspond with the scale of their relative frequencies, such as the following:

J	Q	B	W	Y	U	F	H	D	I	O	N	E	T	R	A	S	L	C	P	M	G	V	X	K	Z		
0	1	2	3	4	5		7	8	9	10	11	12	13	14	15	16	17	18	19	20	21	22	23	24	25	26	27

[4] The representations of an integer (i. e., a whole number) as the sum of integers in all possible ways are termed the *partitions* of that number. The members of the partitions in this subparagraph are one-digit numbers, including the digit Ø in order to form trinome equivalents out of all the possible permutations.

The tallies beneath each value represent the number of variants possible for the particular value. The unused values for Ø and 27 (uniquely represented by 000 and 999, respectively) may be used for punctuation marks, nulls, or other special-purpose symbols. Since such a system, once suspected, would offer little difficulty [5] to a cryptanalyst, certain modifications would be necessary in order to pose any real obstacles in the way of solution. For instance, if the numerical value of a letter is expressed by permutations of 3 letters (instead of digits) out of a set of the 10 letters A–J wherein the sequence of the letters A–J represents a *disarranged* sequence of the digits Ø–9, such a system may be among the most complex types of ciphers in the realm of monoalphabetic substitution, requiring the solution of many simultaneous equations. A further refinement would involve the use of all 26 letters as variants, in predetermined groups, to represent the digits Ø–9. Fortunately for the cryptanalyst, such systems are impracticable for field military use; but if they were encountered, a sufficiently large volume of text, coupled with Hitt's four essentials quoted in Chapter I, would eventually make a solution possible. The actual cryptanalytic complexity of certain apparently exceedingly complex cryptosystems is dependent on their being correctly used at all times, which is not always the case with military ciphers.

60. Analysis of simple examples.—*a*. The following cryptogram is available for study:

```
Q M D C V   P L F N F   D H N W J   W L K D K   N H B P V   R L T V M
B K L W D   W V H V K   S H B C L   P Q K J R   V W S M L   K G C N R
L R N K V   M G F X W   J R G M V   W G T J H   Q K X F N   Z V F D M
L T B P L   P V F L M   D C N W N   H B C V Z   N M L W Q   F D H D W
V Z B R V   K L C V C   V R D H L   R V T L F   N C D K G   M X W X M
D T S C B   C L Z L R   L M V T S   Z N K B W   V P B R N   C L R X R
D C N K V   P B T N T   G H J Z L   F Q F V K   B W D Z X   P N H S P
G H L K L   F V Z L T   V M L K D   P Q R N Z   L Z D T B   M N T G M
N Z V F X   K S F D C   L Z V T V   F D F V R   G C L P Q   P N C D W
V R J T N   H L Z L M   V W N P V   P D Z D W   J P N W L   R J K V M
X M D T S   M G F D R   D K L W J   F L P J M   S F Q W B   F N C B Z
D K V W G   Z S H B H   D H J C X
```

The first thing that strikes the eye is the total absence of A, E, I, O, U, and Y, remarkable not only because six letters are missing (cf. the Λ test) in a text of this size, but also because all six of these letters fall into an identical limited category, namely, they are all vowels—a significant nonrandom phenomenon. Since a uniliteral substitution *alphabet* with six letters missing is highly improbable, the conclusion of multiliteral substitution is obvious. Upon closer inspection it is found that, if the cipher text is divided into pairs of letters, only ten consonants (B D G J L N Q S V X) are used as initial letters, and the remaining ten consonants

---

[5] The solution would involve simply dividing the cipher text into groups of 3 digits, summing the trinomes thus produced to yield 28 possible basic values, and solving these basic values as in any simple monoalphabetic substitution cipher.

(C F H K M P R T W Z) are used as final letters—thus the biliteral (and *bipartite*) characteristics of the cipher text are disclosed. A digraphic distribution is therefore constructed:[6]

	C	F	H	K	M	P	R	T	W	Z
B	≡	~	~	~	~	≈	≈	~	≈	~
D	≡	~	≡	≡	~	~	~	≡	≡	≈
G	≈	≈	≈		≡			~		~
J	~	~	~	~	~	~	≈	~	~	~
L	~	≣		≣	≡	≣	≣	≡	≡	≣
N	≡	~	≡	≡	~	~	~	≈	≡	≡
Q		≈		≈	~	~	~		~	
S	~	≈	≈		≈	~				~
V	~	≣	~	≣	≣	≣	≣	≡	≣	≣
X		~		~	≈	~	~		≈	

b. It is possible that the cryptogram under study may involve the use of a small enciphering matrix with variants for the rows and columns. Since there is available an easily-applied special solution which permits the determination of the row indicators which are equivalent (i. e., interchangeable variants) and the column indicators which are equivalent, merely from a study of the digraphic distribution, this possibility is examined. The special solution is based on the following considerations: in a message of moderate length for such a cryptosystem, it may be assumed that the various possible cipher digraphs for a given plaintext letter will be used with approximately equal frequency; for this reason, the column indicators which pair with one of the letters used to indicate any particular row of the enciphering matrix may be expected to pair equally often with any other cipher letter which has been used to indicate the same row. Thus, in the digraphic distribution of such a cryptogram, sets of rows appear which have similar "profiles" and, likewise, sets of similar columns.[7] First a study will be made of the rows of the distribution just compiled, in an attempt to locate and isolate those which *match* with each other; then, the same will be done with the columns of the distribution.

c. It is noted that the "L" and "V" distributions have pronounced similarities (Fig. 42a)—these rows came under consideration first because of the unique "heaviness" of their frequency characteristics. Likewise, the "D" and "N" rows have homologous attributes in their appearance (Fig. 42b). However, the further grouping of the rows by ocular inspection may present difficulties to the student, since he may not yet trust his eye in matching distributions; and he may feel the need for some kind of statistical assurance. In the following subparagraphs there is given the technique of a more precise method for matching, mathematical in nature.

---

[6] If it had not been noticed that the cryptogram should be divided into pairs for analysis, a *biliteral* distribution (see subpar. 23d) might have been made, in order to reveal contact affinities of the cipher letters.

[7] These similarities are especially pronounced when the encipherer uses a "check-off" procedure for choosing his variants for each letter, that is, when he systematically checks off the variants used during encryption to insure that all possible variants are used in approximately equal proportions.

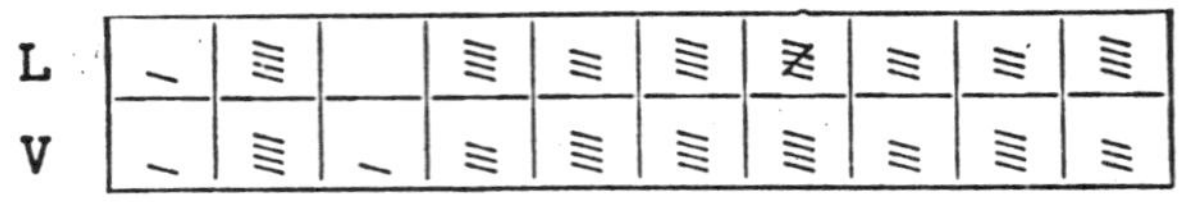

FIGURE 42a.

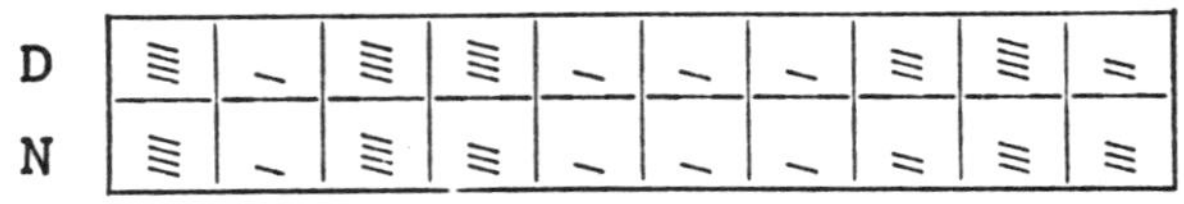

FIGURE 42b.

d. This method of matching in an attempt to "equate" interchangeable variants involves computing a separate value for each trial matching of a particular row (or column) against each of a series of other rows (or columns, as appropriate)—such a value is taken as an indication of the "goodness of match" exhibited by the particular trial, the theory being that the correct match will produce the highest value.[8] The value for a particular trial match is computed by multiplying the number of tallies in each cell of one row (or column) by the number of tallies in each corresponding cell in the other row (or column) and then totaling the products thus obtained. Because of the way in which it is produced, such a value is termed a "cross-products sum".

e. In subpar. *c* above, it was determined that the "L" and "V" rows were equivalent, and that the "D" and "N" rows also formed an equivalent pair. The next "heavy" row is the "G" row; this is to be tested for match with the five remaining unmatched rows. Let the "G" row be tested first against the "B" row. These two rows are given below, with their cross-products sum. For convenience, the cross-products sum is symbolized by $\chi(\theta^1, \theta^2)$, where θ^1 and θ^2 represent the designators of the distributions to be matched.[9]

$$
\begin{array}{l}
\text{"G": } 2\ 2\ 2 - 3 - - 1 - 1 \\
\text{"B": } 3\ 1\ 1\ 1\ 1\ 2\ 2\ 1\ 2\ 1 \\
\chi(G,B): 6\ 2\ 2 - 3 - - 1 - 1 = 15
\end{array}
$$

The complete table of the comparisons of the "G" row with the five available rows is as follows:

$$
\begin{array}{l}
\chi(G,B): 6\ 2\ 2 - 3 - - 1 - 1 = 15 \\
\chi(G,J): 2\ 2\ 2 - 3 - - 1 - 1 = 11 \\
\chi(G,Q): - 4 - - 3 - - - - - = 7 \\
\chi(G,S): 2\ 4\ 4 - 6 - - - - 1 = 17 \\
\chi(G,X): - 2 - - 6 - - - - - = 8
\end{array}
$$

The results indicate that the most probable match with the "G" row is the "S" row.

f. Since the next "heaviest" row to be tested is the "B" row, its matchings with the three remaining rows are made, and are given below:

$$
\begin{array}{l}
\chi(G,J): 3\ 1\ 1\ 1\ 1\ 2\ 4\ 1\ 2\ 1 = 17 \\
\chi(B,Q): - 2 - 2\ 1\ 2\ 2 - 2\ 1 = 12 \\
\chi(B,X): - 1 - 1\ 2\ 2 - 4 - = 12
\end{array}
$$

---

[8] In this connection, note the considerations treated in subpar. 60*j*.

[9] The Greek letter χ (chi) is often used in cryptology to symbolize matching operations.

The correct matching of the "B" and "J" rows is indicated by the results. This leaves only the "Q" and "X" rows, which are presumed to go together, since not only is their cross-products sum satisfactory (when compared to the χ values for some of the other rows which have been matched), but, equally important, their patterns of *crests* and *troughs* are similar. Since we have not found more than *two* rows for any one set of interchangeable values, it appears that the original matrix had only five rows, with two variants for each row. The rows of the distribution diagram are therefore combined in the following diagram:

		C	F	H	K	M	P	R	T	W	Z
B	J	4	2	2	2	2	3	4	2	3	2
D	N	8	2	8	7	2	2	2	5	7	5
G	S	3	4	4	–	5	1	–	1	–	2
L	V	2	8	1	7	7	8	9	6	7	7
Q	X	–	3	–	3	3	2	2	–	3	–

FIGURE 43.

g. Ocular inspection of the distributions of the columns of Fig. 43 quickly reveals that columns "C" and "H" may be matched as a pair, and likewise columns "F" and "M", and columns "P" and "R". In order to decide the groupings of the remaining columns, the six possible χ values are derived:

$\chi(K,T)$: 4 35 – 42 – = 81

$\chi(K,W)$: 4 49 – 49 9 = 113   Combinations:

$\chi(K,Z)$: 4 35 – 49 – = 88   KT, WZ: 81 + 90 = 171

$\chi(T,W)$: 6 35 – 42 – = 83   KW, TZ: 113 + 73 = 186

$\chi(T,Z)$: 4 25 2 42 – = 73   KZ, TW: 88 + 83 = 171

$\chi(W,Z)$: 6 35 – 49 – = 90

It appears that the proper pairings of the columns are "K" and "W", "T" and "Z".

h. The groupings of the columns having been determined, the frequency diagram is reduced to its basic 5 x 5 square, and the ϕ test is taken as further statistical assurance of the matchings

		C	F	K	P	T
		H	M	W	R	Z
B	J	6	4	5	7	4
D	N	16	4	14	4	10
G	S	7	9	–	1	3
L	V	3	15	14	17	13
Q	X	–	6	6	4	–

$\phi_p = 1962$

$\phi_r = 1132$

$\phi_o = 1670$

Although ϕ_o in this case does not come up to the best expectations, we feel nevertheless that the matching has been carefully and correctly accomplished, and so the next step is continued with a conversion of the multiliteral text into uniliteral equivalents, using the following reduction square containing an arbitrary sequence:

```
            C F K P T
            H M W R Z
    B J  | A B C D E |
    D N  | F G H I K |
    G S  | L M N O P |
    L V  | Q R S T U |
    Q X  | V W X Y Z |
```

The converted cryptogram is now easily solved, using the principles set forth in Chapter VI. The first fifteen letters of the plaintext message are found to read "WEATHER FORECAST.....", and the original enciphering matrix is recovered, based on the key word ATMOSPHERIC, as follows:

```
            P F C K T
            R M H W Z
    L V  | A T M O S |
    D N  | P H E R I |
    B J  | C B D F G |
    G S  | K L N Q U |
    Q X  | V W X Y Z |
```

i. The method of matching rows and columns just described in the preceding subparagraphs applies equally well to all the matrices in Figs. 26–35, and similar variations. If in the process of equating indicators the cryptanalyst sees that the row indicators are falling into the same groupings as the column indicators, he might be able to accelerate the equating process by taking advantage of this feature alone, as would be the case if he had encountered a cryptogram involving a matrix with indicators arranged in a manner similar to that shown in Figs. 29 and 30. Furthermore, a cryptogram enciphered in a commutative system, wherein the equivalents have been taken in row-column and column-row order indiscriminately, may be recognized as such through a study of the digraphic distribution of the cryptogram since the "α" row of the distribution will have an appearance similar to the "α" column, the "β" row will be similar to the "β" column, etc;[10] this matter is discussed further in subpar. 61*d*.

___

[10] It is often convenient to use arbitrary symbols in cryptanalytic work, to prevent confusion with designations of actual elements of plain text, cipher text, or key (see footnote 1 on page 47). For this purpose Greek letters are often used; for reference, the 24 letters of the Greek alphabet and their names are appended in the chart below:

A α alpha	E ϵ epsilon	I ι iota	N ν nu	P ρ rho	Φ ϕ phi
B β beta	Z ζ zeta	K κ kappa	Ξ ξ xi	Σ σ sigma	X χ chi
Γ γ gamma	H η eta	Λ λ lambda	O o omicron	T τ tau	Ψ ψ psi
Δ δ delta	Θ θ theta	M μ mu	Π π pi	Υ υ upsilon	Ω ω omega

j. It is important to point out that in matching, the cryptanalyst should begin with the "best" rows or columns—best not only from the standpoint of "heaviness" of the distribution, but also best from the point of view of a distinctive pattern of crests and troughs. If insufficient text is available to allow equating all the interchangeable coordinates of a particular enciphering matrix, it may still be possible that a conversion of the cipher test by means of a partially-reduced reconstruction matrix may yield enough idiomorphic patterns and other data to make possible an entry into the text. If the cryptographer has not used a "check-off" process in enciphering, but instead has favored certain equivalents for the various plaintext letters, matching may not be possible; nevertheless, an entry into the text may be facilitated in this case, because some of the resultant peaks in the cipher text may be correctly identified. Furthermore, since *no* variant system can possibly disguise the *letters of low frequency* in plain text, their low-frequency equivalents in the cipher text may provide possible approaches to solution. (See also subpar. 61*e*).

k. In addition to the method of solution by matching and combining rows and columns of a digraphic distribution of a multiliteral cipher, there is also the *general* approach applicable without exception to *any* variant system. This method, involving the correlation of cipher elements suspected to be the equivalents of specific but unknown plaintext letters, is treated in detail in pars. 61 and 62.

l. Systems such as the 4-level dinome cipher illustrated in Fig. 36 are susceptible to a very easy solution, if the dinomes have been inscribed in numerical order as indicated. Assuming such a case in a specific cryptogram, the first six groups of which are

68321　09022　48057　65111　88648　42036　...

a four-part frequency distribution of the entire message is taken, as illustrated in Fig. 44 below:

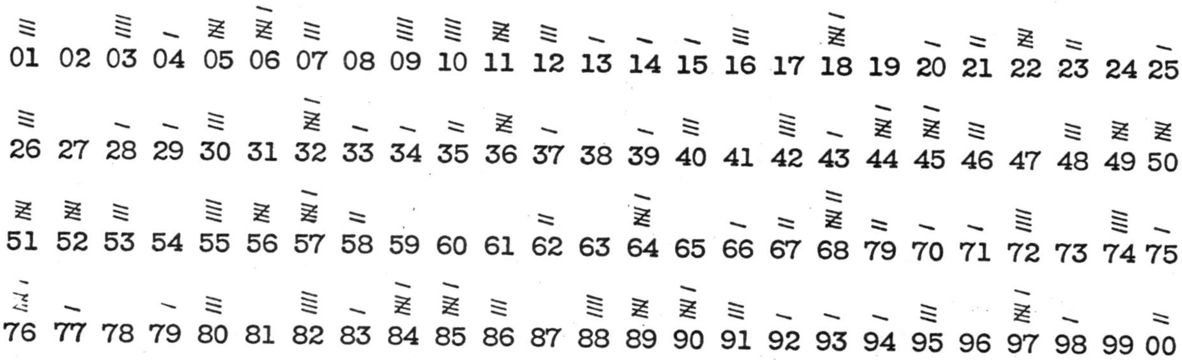

01 02 03 04 05 06 07 08 09 10 11 12 13 14 15 16 17 18 19 20 21 22 23 24 25

26 27 28 29 30 31 32 33 34 35 36 37 38 39 40 41 42 43 44 45 46 47 48 49 50

51 52 53 54 55 56 57 58 59 60 61 62 63 64 65 66 67 68 79 70 71 72 73 74 75

76 77 78 79 80 81 82 83 84 85 86 87 88 89 90 91 92 93 94 95 96 97 98 99 00

FIGURE 44.

If the student will bring to bear upon this problem the principles he learned in Chapter V of this text, he will soon realize that what he now has before him are four simple, monoalphabetic frequency distributions similar to those involved in a monoalphabetic substitution cipher using standard alphabets. The realization of this fact immediately provides the clue to the next step: "fitting each of the distributions to the normal". (See par. 31.) This can be done without difficulty in this case (remembering that a 25-letter alphabet is involved and assuming that I and J are combined) and the following alphabets result:

01—I–J	26—U	51—N	76—E
02—K	27—V	52—O	77—F
03—L	28—W	53—P	78—G
04—M	29—X	54—Q	79—H
05—N	30—Y	55—R	80—I–J
06—O	31—Z	56—S	81—K
07—P	32—A	57—T	82—L
08—Q	33—B	58—U	83—M
09—R	34—C	59—V	84—N
10—S	35—D	60—W	85—O
11—T	36—E	61—X	86—P
12—U	37—F	62—Y	87—Q
13—V	38—G	63—Z	88—R
14—W	39—H	64—A	89—S
15—X	40—I–J	65—B	90—T
16—Y	41—K	66—C	91—U
17—Z	42—L	67—D	92—V
18—A	43—M	68—E	93—W
19—B	44—N	69—F	94—X
20—C	45—O	70—G	95—Y
21—D	46—P	71—H	96—Z
22—E	47—Q	72—I–J	97—A
23—F	48—R	73—K	98—B
24—G	49—S	74—L	99—C
25—H	50—T	75—M	00—D

The key word is seen to be JUNE and the beginning of the cryptogram is deciphered as "EASTERN ENTRANCE....."

m. If instead of 25-element alphabets, a system such as that in Fig. 37 has been used, only a slight modification of the procedure in subpar. *l* would have been necessary, i. e., the distributions would have had to be considered on a basis of 26, and the process of fitting the distributions to the normal would have gone on as in the previous example.

n. One further application of principles learned in Chapter V deserves to be mentioned here, in connection with the solution of systems such as those of Fig. 36. Let the following short message be considered:

```
4 8 2 2 6    8 8 4 2 3    5 2 0 9 9    9 3 6 0 4    7 6 0 5 9    0 5 6 5 1
3 6 6 8 3    5 2 2 6 7    9 7 1 1 4    5 4 4 6 6    7 6
```

If it is known that the correspondents have been using a variant system such as that in Fig. 36, a special solution may be employed in those cases wherein there is insufficient cipher text to permit analysis by the method of fitting the frequency distributions to the normal. Thus, a short cryptogram may be solved by a variation of the plain-component completion method described in par. 34.[11] First, let the cryptogram be copied in dinomes, with an indication of the *level* (i. e., the "alphabet") the dinome would occupy in the 4-level matrix; thus:

```
48 22 68 84 23 52 09 99 36 04 76 05 90 56 51 36 68 35 22 67 97 11 45 44 66 76
 2  1  3  4  1  3  1  4  2  1  4  1  4  3  3  2  3  2  1  3  4  1  2  2  3  4
```

The dinomes belonging to the four levels are as follows:

    (1)   22 23 09 04 05 22 11
    (2)   48 36 36 35 45 44
    (3)   68 52 56 51 68 67 66
    (4)   84 99 76 90 97 76

These dinomes are converted into terms of the plain component by setting each of the cipher sequences against the plain component at an arbitrary point of coincidence, such as in the following example:

A	B	C	D	E	F	G	H	IJ	K	L	M	N	O	P	Q	R	S	T	U	V	W	X	Y	Z
01	02	03	04	05	06	07	08	09	10	11	12	13	14	15	16	17	18	19	20	21	22	23	24	25
26	27	28	29	30	31	32	33	34	35	36	37	38	39	40	41	42	43	44	45	46	47	48	49	50
51	52	53	54	55	56	57	58	59	60	61	62	63	64	65	66	67	68	69	70	71	72	73	74	75
76	77	78	79	80	81	82	83	84	85	86	87	88	89	90	91	92	93	94	95	96	97	98	99	00

    (1) 22=W;   23=X;   09=I;   04=D;   05=E;   22=W;   11=L
    (2) 48=X;   36=L;   36=L;   35=K;   45=U;   44=T
    (3) 68=S;   52=B;   56=F;   51=A;   68=S;   67=R;   66=Q
    (4) 84=I;   99=Y;   76=A;   90=P;   97=W;   76=A

---

[11] It should be clear to the student that the reason this method can be applied in this instance is that both the plain component (ABC.....Z) and the cipher component (01, 02, 03 ..... 25; 26–50, 51–75, 76–00) are *known* sequences (or thus assumed).

o. The plain-component sequence is now completed on the letters of the four levels, **as** follows:

1st level	2d level	3d level	4th level
W X I D E W L	X L L K U T	S B F A S R Q	I Y A P W A
X Y K E F X M	Y M M L V U	T C G B T S R	K Z B Q X B
Y Z L F G Y N	Z N N M W V	U D H C U T S	L A C R Y C
Z A M G H Z O	A O O N X W	V E I D V U T	M B D S Z D
A B N H I A P	B P P O Y X	W F K E W V U	N C E T A E
B C O I K B Q	C Q Q P Z Y	X G L F X W V	O D F U B F
C D P K L C R	D R R Q A Z	Y H M G Y X W	P E G V C G
D E Q L M D S	E S S R B A	Z I N H Z Y X	Q F H W D H
E F R M N E T	F T T S C B	A K O I A Z Y	R G I X E I
F G S N O F U	G U U T D C	B L P K B A Z	S H K Y F K
G H T O P G V	H V V U E D	C M Q L C B A	T I L Z G L
H I U P Q H W	I W W V F E	D N R M D C B	U K M A H M
I K V Q R I X	K X X W G F	E O S N E D C	V L N B I N
K L W R S K Y	L Y Y X H G	F P T O F E D	W M O C K O
L M X S T L Z	M Z Z Y I H	G Q U P G F E	X N P D L P
M N Y T U M A	N A A Z K I	H R V Q H G F	Y O Q E M Q
N O Z U V N B	O B B A L K	I S W R I H G	Z P R F N R
O P A V W O C	P C C B M L	K T X S K I H	A Q S G O S
P Q B W X P D	Q D D C N M	L U Y T L K I	B R T H P T
Q R C X Y Q E	R E E D O N	M V Z U M L K	C S U I Q U
R S D Y Z R F	S F F E P O	N W A V N M L	D T V K R V
S T E Z A S G	T G G F Q P	O X B W O N M	E U W L S W
T U F A B T H	U H H G R Q	P Y C X P O N	F V X M T X
U V G B C U I	V I I H S R	Q Z D Y Q P O	G W Y N U Y
V W H C D V K	W K K I T S	R A E Z R Q P	H X Z O V Z

It is seen that the generatrices with the best assortment [12] of high-frequency letters for the four levels are:

1st level	2d level	3d level	4th level
E F R M N E T	R E E D O N	E O S N E D C	N C E T A E

If the letters of these generatrices are arranged in the order of appearance of their dinome equivalents, according to the way they fall into the various levels,

```
48 22 68 84 23 52 09 99 36 04 76 05 90 56 51 36 68 35 22 67 97 11 45 44 66 76
    E       F   R       M   N               E   D       E       T
 R               E               E   D                       O N
    E       O                           S   N       E           D               C
       N           C       E   T                           A               E
```

the plain text "REENFORCEMENTS NEEDED AT ONCE" is clearly seen. Or, more simply, if we examine the equivalents of 01, 26, 51, and 76 after the generatrix determination has been made,

---

[12] In evaluating generatrices, the sum of the arithmetical frequencies of the letters in each row may be used **as** an indication of their relative "goodness". A statistically much more accurate method of evaluating generatrices involves the use of logarithms of the probabilities of the plaintext letters forming the generatrices. This method is treated in detail in *Military Cryptanalytics, Part II*. (See also footnote 8 on p. 73.)

the key word JUNE is revealed. If an error had been made in the selection of a generatrix, the error could be resolved by hypothesizing the probable key word, or by deciphering the text on the basis of the assumed diagram and then noting and degarbling the systematic errors (which, it would be noticed, all come from one level).

p. The student should note that no one generatrix will yield plain text all the way across as in the example in par. 34. Instead, the generatrices must be considered separately for the four levels, since it is within each of the four levels that there is a homogeneous relationship of dinomes. Obviously if dinomes from more than one level were used to complete the plain component sequence, the generatrices would not consist of a homogeneous group of letters but instead would represent an assortment of letters from two or more "alphabets".

61. Analysis of more complicated examples.—*a.* As soon as a beginner in cryptography realizes the consequences of the fact that letters are used with greatly varying frequencies in normal plain text, a brilliant idea very speedily comes to him. Why not disguise the natural frequencies of letters by a system of substitution using many equivalents, and let the numbers of equivalents assigned to the various letters be more or less in direct proportion to the normal frequencies of the letters? Let E, for example, have 13 equivalents; T, 9; N, 8; etc., and thus (he thinks) the enemy cryptanalyst can have nothing in the way of telltale or characteristic frequencies to use as an entering wedge.

b. If the text available for study is small in amount and if the variant values are wholly independent of one another, the problem can become exceedingly difficult. But in practical military communications such methods are rarely encountered, *because the volume of text is usually great enough to permit of the establishment of equivalent values.* To illustrate what is meant, suppose a number of cryptograms produced by a monoalphabetic-variant method of the type mentioned above show the following two sets of groupings [13] of cipher elements in the text, Set "A" being assumed to be different representations of one particular underlying plaintext word or phrase and Set "B" assumed to be representations of another underlying plaintext word or phrase:

Set "A"	Set "B"
(12–37–02–79–68–13–03–37–77)	(71–12–02–51–23–05–77)
(82–69–02–79–13–68–23–37–35)	(11–82–51–02–03–05–35)
(82–69–51–16–13–13–78–05–35)	(11–91–02–02–23–37–35)
(91–05–02–01–68–42–78–37–77)	(97–12–51–02–78–69–77)

An examination of these groupings would lead to the following tentative conclusions with regard to probable equivalents:

(12,82,91) (02,51) (13,42,68) (35,77)
(05,37,69) (01,16,79) (03,23,78) (11,71,97)

The establishment of these equivalencies would sooner or later lead to the finding of additional sets of equal values. The completeness with which this can be accomplished will determine the ease or difficulty of solution. Of course, if many equivalencies can be established the problem can then be reduced practically to monoalphabetic terms and a speedy solution can be attained.

c. Theoretically, the determination of equivalencies may seem to be quite an easy matter, but practically it may be very difficult, because the cryptanalyst can never be *certain* that a

[13] The alert student might be able to determine the underlying plain text of the two sets of ciphertext groupings.

combination showing what may appear to be a variant value is really such and does not represent a part of a *different* plaintext sequence. For example, take the groups—

$$17-82-31-82-14-63, \text{ and}$$
$$27-82-40-82-14-63$$

Here one might suspect that 17 and 27 represent the same letter, 31 and 40 another letter. But it happens that one group represents the word MANAGE, the other DAMAGE. There are hundreds of such cases in English and in other languages.

d. When reversible combinations are used as variants, the problem is perhaps a bit more

	K,Z	Q,V	B,H	M,R	D,L
W,S	N	H	A	O	E
F,X	D	T	M	F	P
G,J	Q	B	U	I	V
C,N	G	X	R	C	S
P,T	Z	L	Y	W	K

FIGURE 45.

simple. For example, using the accompanying Fig. 45 for encipherment, two messages with the same initial words, REFERENCE YOUR, may be enciphered as follows:

	R	E	F	E	R	E	N	C	E	Y	O	U	R
(1)	N H W D R	X L S H C	D W W Z N	R S L H P	S R B J C			H
(2)	C H D W R	X S L H N	D W Z W N	R L S H P	R W J B N			H

The experienced cryptanalyst, noting the appearance of the very first few cipher groups, assumes that not only have the messages identical beginnings in their plain texts, but also that he is here confronted with a variant system involving biliteral reversible equivalents. One of the manifestations of such a cryptosystem is that in the digraphic distribution of the cipher text the "B" row will have an appearance similar to the "B" column, the "C" row will resemble the "C" column, etc.; thus the cryptanalyst will almost immediately realize that he has encountered a commutative system involving a matrix smaller than that indicated by the size of matrix necessary for making the digraphic distribution.

e. The probable-word method of solution may be used, but with a slight variation introduced because of the fact that, regardless of the system, *letters of low frequency in plain text remain infrequent in the cryptogram.* Hence, suppose a word containing low-frequency letters, but in itself a rather common word striking idiomorphic in character is sought as a "probable word"; for example, a word such as C<u>A</u>VAL<u>R</u>Y, ATTA<u>C</u>K, or <u>P</u>RE<u>P</u>ARE. Such a word may be written on a slip of paper and slid one interval at a time under the text, which has been marked so that the high- and low-frequency characters are indicated. Each coincidence of a low-frequency letter of the text with a low-frequency letter of the assumed word is examined carefully to see whether the adjacent text letters correspond in frequency with the other letters of the assumed word, and whether there are correspondences between repetitions in the cipher text and those in the word. Many trials are necessary but this method will produce results when the difficulties are otherwise too much for the cryptanalyst to overcome.

62. **Analysis involving the use of isologs.**—*a.* In military communications it is not unusual that cryptograms are produced containing identical plain text but which have been subjected to different cryptographic treatment, thus yielding different cipher texts. This difference in cryptographic treatment may be caused by the use of an entirely different general system, or by the use of a different specific key, or merely by the choice of equivalents in a variant system. Messages which present different encrypted texts but which contain identical plain text are called *isologs* (from the Greek *isos*="equal" and *logos*="word"). One of the easily-noted indications of the possible presence of isologs is equality or near-equality in the lengths of two (or more) cryptograms. Isologs, no matter how the cryptographic treatment varies, are among the most powerful media available to the cryptanalyst for the successful solution of a difficult cryptosystem—and, in some cases, may provide the only possible entries into a complex cryptosystem. An inkling of the help afforded by isologs was revealed by the example contained in subpar. 61*d* above; however, a much more striking illustration is given in the next few subparagraphs.

b. The following two cryptograms, suspected to be isologs, are available for study:

Message "A"

```
82265   63103   74839   69842   32529   70115
80277   89106   94000   13828   54082   40065
63629   33918   43158   81048   26458   45039
81713   52538   73309   20749   61752   16476
38728   91147   99926   41468   13365   33881
89697   93816   51750   57074   11804   43255
28120   27730   31199   79962   27865   60653
90870   40867   46594   19855   10822   22987
46729   36245
```

Message "B"

```
30150   87497   14511   97360   49676   50106
45647   99181   69672   53889   41563   25203
90628   77536   20351   10570   89277   75011
35199   90138   99974   50232   04115   89216
38463   17547   14648   00646   85864   53898
26121   83878   94889   33728   11272   20504
06484   32103   98715   42662   80760   89880
44105   52900   59728   22855   87300   70893
59682   46253
```

On the possibility that some dinome system (or systems) is involved, the messages are written under each other in dinomes to facilitate the examination of the *similarities and differences* of such a grouping of the cipher texts, as shown below:

					5					10					15
A	82	26	56	31	03	74	83	96	98	42	32	52	97	01	15
A'	30	15	08	74	97	14	51	19	73	60	49	67	65	01	06
B	80	27	78	91	06	94	00	01	38	28	54	08	24	00	65
B'	45	64	79	91	81	69	67	25	38	89	41	56	32	52	03
C	63	62	93	39	18	43	15	88	10	48	26	45	84	50	39
C'	90	62	87	75	36	20	35	11	05	70	89	27	77	50	11
D	81	71	35	25	38	73	30	92	07	49	61	75	21	64	76
D'	35	19	99	01	38	99	97	45	02	32	04	11	58	92	16
E	38	72	89	11	47	99	92	64	14	68	13	36	53	38	81
E'	38	46	31	75	47	14	64	80	06	46	85	86	45	38	98
F	89	69	79	38	16	51	75	05	70	74	11	80	44	32	55
F'	26	12	18	38	78	94	88	93	37	28	11	27	22	05	04
G	28	12	02	77	30	31	19	97	99	62	27	86	56	06	53
G'	06	48	43	21	03	98	71	54	26	62	80	76	08	98	80
H	90	87	04	08	67	46	59	41	98	55	10	82	22	29	87
H'	44	10	55	29	00	59	72	82	28	55	87	30	07	08	93
J	46	72	93	62	45										
J'	59	68	24	62	53										

The dinome distributions for the two messages are as follows:

	1	2	3	4	5	6	7	8	9	0
1	2	1	1	1	2	1	–	1	1	2
2	1	1	–	1	1	2	2	2	1	–
3	2	2	–	–	1	1	–	5	2	2
4	1	1	1	1	2	2	1	1	1	–
5	1	1	2	1	2	2	–	–	1	1
6	1	3	1	2	1	–	1	1	1	–
7	1	2	1	2	2	1	1	1	1	1
8	2	2	1	1	–	1	2	1	2	2
9	1	2	2	1	–	1	2	2	2	1
0	2	1	1	1	1	2	1	2	–	2

Distribution for Message "A"

	1	2	3	4	5	6	7	8	9	0
1	4	1	–	2	1	1	–	1	2	1
2	1	1	–	1	1	2	2	2	1	1
3	1	2	–	–	2	1	1	5	–	2
4	1	–	1	1	3	2	1	1	1	–
5	1	1	1	1	2	1	–	1	2	1
6	–	3	–	2	1	–	2	1	1	1
7	1	1	1	1	2	1	1	1	1	1
8	1	1	–	–	1	1	2	1	2	3
9	1	1	2	1	–	–	2	3	2	1
0	2	1	2	2	2	3	1	3	–	1

Distribution for Message "B"

122

c. Since a general absence of marked crests and troughs is noted in both distributions, if the division of these cryptograms into dinomes is correct, *and* if they are both monoalphabetic, it is quite probable that some type of variant system (or systems) has been used. With this in mind, the encrypted texts and their distributions are scrutinized further for some indication of the kind of relationship which exists between the methods of encipherment of the two messages. The distributions are seen to be strikingly similar, not only with respect to the location of the one predominant peak in each, but also in the close correlation of the locations of the blanks in each.[14] Furthermore, upon examination of the superimposed messages themselves, it is

[14] For the benefit of the student with a statistical background, it might be interesting to point out certain applications of cryptomathematics in connection with these two distributions. First of all, each of the two distributions is *much flatter* than that which would be expected for a sample of 125 dinomes of *random* text; i. e., a drawing (with replacement) and recording from an urn containing equal numbers of counters in each of 100 categories labeled 00–99 consecutively. That is, the samples at hand exhibit phenomena even *flatter* (or "worse") than that expected for random, approaching the theoretical (and fantastically nonrandom) "equilibrium" of exactly the same number of tallies in each cell of a distribution. The following table gives the observed number of x-fold repetitions in the two distributions, together with the expected numbers of x-fold repetitions in a sample of like size of random text, which expected numbers have been computed from tables of the Poisson exponential distribution (see *Military Cryptanalytics, Part III*):

x	Observed Msg. "A"	Observed Msg. "B"	Expected
Ø	14	17	29
1	51	52	36
2	33	23	22
3	1	6	9
4	–	1	3
5	1	1	1

It is to be noted that in the distribution for Message "A", the observed number of blanks (14) when compared with the expected number of blanks in random text (29) may be evaluated and found to represent a very small probability indeed. Likewise, the other entries besides Ø (in particular, the x-values of 1 and 2, and the *cumulative* values of 3-and-better) may be evaluated, and the conclusion would be reached that the two distributions have a most remote chance of being as flat as they are through mere chance. Moreover, the observed frequency distribution for Message "A" may be fitted against the expected distribution by means of the chi-square test, again getting an extremely small probability. In addition, by means of the chi-square test, the I. C. of Message "A" (found to be 0.59 as against the I. C. of random of 1.0) has an extremely small probability of occurring at random in a sample of this size. Similarly, the distribution for Message "B" could be studied, and it would be found that this too has characteristics that have a very small probability of occurrence by pure chance. Since the distributions of the two messages are much worse than would even be expected for random chance, the conclusion is drawn that the *dinome grouping* is highly significant and therefore *must* be correct, and further that the cryptosystem involves variants in sufficient numbers for the plaintext letters to permit the encipherer to select the cipher equivalents with a view to suppressing as much of the phenomena of repetition as possible. Furthermore, the χ test of the two distributions gives a χ value of 206, as against the expected χ value of 156 for a random matching of these two samples; the sigmage of this event could be computed and its significance estimated and the conclusion drawn that the ratio $\frac{206}{156}$ is extremely unlikely of happening by pure chance, i. e., if the cryptograms were not in the same general system and specific keys. Therefore, it is a foregone conclusion *statistically* that not only do the cryptosystems involve dinomes as the ciphertext grouping, but that the identical cryptosystem is involved in the two messages; and that because of the close correlation of the patterns of the two distributions, there is a good probability that the cryptograms contain identical plain text and therefore are isologs. This specific illustration of the potentialities of cryptomathematics indicates the important role that this branch of science may play in the art cryptanalysis.

observed that there are several instances wherein a value in Message "A" coincides with the same value in Message "B" (e. g., see positions A/A' 14, B/B' 9). This observation, taken in conjunction with the marked similarity of the distributions, strongly indicates that not only has the same *general* cryptosystem been used for the encryption of both messages, but that the *same enciphering matrix* has been used for both. Also, in the case of the value 38 and 62, it is noted that wherever either occurs in one message the same value occurs in the other message, a phenomenon explainable on the assumption that the plaintext equivalents of these values are of such low frequency that no variant values have been provided for these plaintext letters in the cryptosystem.

d. With the foregoing details determined, it is now realized that it should be possible to form, between the two messages, "chains" of those cipher values which represent identical plaintext letters, as exemplified below. Beginning with the first value in each message, 82 and 30, a partial chain of equivalent variants is started; now locating some other occurrence of either value elsewhere (e. g., 82 at position H'8), and noting the cipher value coinciding with it (in this case, 41), the partial chain may be extended (including now 82, 30, and 41). After this particular chain is extended to include as many values as possible, another chain is formed by starting with any value which has not already been included in the preceding chain, this procedure being repeated until all possible chains are completed. It is found that the following chains, arbitrarily arranged here according to length, may be derived from the two messages:

```
(06 14 15 26 28 31 35 73 74 81 89 98 99)
(02 07 20 22 43 44 63 90)
(12 37 48 51 69 70 83 94)
(03 30 41 54 65 82 97)
(05 10 24 32 49 87 93)
(16 18 36 76 78 79 86)
(27 45 53 64 80 92)
(11 39 75 88)
(21 58 77 84)
(46 59 68 72)
(00 52 67)
(04 55 61)
(08 29 56)
(19 71 96)
(01 25)                     Single dinomes:
(13 85)
(42 60)                     (38)  (47)  (50)  (62)  (91)
```

If we now make an arbitrary assignment of a different letter to represent each chain (and one for each single dinome) and convert either of the messages to uniliteral terms by means of these arbitrarily-assigned values, we note the pattern of the opening stereotype "REFERENCE YOUR MESSAGE.....", and quickly recover the plain text.

e. The plaintext values when inserted into a 10 x 10 matrix having arbitrarily-arranged coordinates yield the following:

	1	2	3	4	5	6	7	8	9	Ø
1	D	N	H	E	E	A	–	A	C	O
2	I	T	–	O	M	E	S	E	F	T
3	E	O	–	–	E	A	N	B	D	R
4	R	Y	T	T	S	L	V	N	O	–
5	N	U	S	R	P	F	–	I	L	X
6	P	W	T	S	R	–	U	L	N	Y
7	C	L	E	E	D	A	I	A	A	N
8	E	R	N	I	H	A	O	D	E	S
9	G	S	O	N	–	C	R	E	E	T
Ø	M	T	R	P	O	E	T	F	–	U

Manipulating the rows and columns with a view to uncovering some symmetry or systematic phenomena, the latent diagonal pattern of the equivalents for certain of the letters (such as E_p, N_p, O_p, R_p, and S_p) is revealed, and the rows and columns of the reconstruction diagram are permuted to yield the following original enciphering matrix:

	6	8	9	1	5	4	3	7	2	Ø
7	A	A	A	C	D	E	E	I	L	N
1	A	A	C	D	E	E	H	(K)	N	O
3	A	B	D	E	E	(H)	(J)	N	O	R
8	A	D	E	E	H	I	N	O	R	S
9	C	E	E	G	(I)	N	O	R	S	T
2	E	E	F	I	M	O	(Q)	S	T	T
Ø	E	F	I	M	O	P	R	T	T	U
5	F	I	L	N	P	R	S	(T)	U	X
6	(I)	L	N	P	R	S	T	U	W	Y
4	L	N	O	R	S	T	T	V	Y	Z

There are no observable relationships in or between the sequences of digits in the row and column coordinates; therefore for want of any visible phenomena or further information on the derivation (if any) of these digits, it is assumed that they must have been assigned at random. The student will note that the final matrix is identical to that of Fig. 39 in par. 59.

f. It should be emphasized that in the example of the preceding subparagraphs it was only possible to form chains of values from both messages *reciprocally* because the same enciphering matrix had been used for both. A nonreciprocal chaining procedure would have been required if only the general system had been the same for both but the enciphering matrices had differed in some respect, or if two completely different variant systems had been used (e. g., one using a frequential matrix and the other involving a less complex type of variant matrix, such as Fig. 29). Specifically, it would have been necessary to maintain two separate groups of chains, one group for each message; otherwise heterogeneous values would have become intermingled. For instance, if the two messages on p. 121 had been enciphered with two different matrices, then we would build up chains of equivalencies in Message "B" against *one* value of Message "A", and, likewise, chains of equivalencies in Message "A" against *one* value of Message "B". Thus, we note at position A2 we have $\frac{26}{15}$, and at position C11 we have $\frac{26}{89}$; this means that 15 and 89 are in one chain *in Message "B"*. Likewise, the $\frac{28}{89}$ at position B1Ø and the $\frac{26}{89}$ at position C11 demonstrates that 26 and 28 are in one chain *in Message "A"*. This process would of course be continued so as to expand chains wherever possible.

g. Although an analysis of but one isolated example by means of isologs was presented, the student should be able to appreciate the significance and potentially enormous value of isologs to a cryptanalyst. This value goes far beyond the simple variant encryption in a mono-alphabetic substitution system; isologs produced by the use of two different code books, or two different enciphered code versions of the same underlying plain text, or two encryptions of identical plain text by two different "settings" of a cipher machine, may all prove of inestimable value in the attack on a difficult cryptosystem.

63. **Further remarks on variant systems.**—*a.* A few words should be added with regard to certain subterfuges which are sometimes encountered in monoalphabetic substitution with variants, and which, if not recognized in time, cause considerable delays. The considerations treated before in subpars. 52*i* and *j* on the disguise of the length of the basic multiliteral group apply equally here to multiliteral substitution with variants; thus, in dinome systems, a sum-checking digit or a null might be added in specified positions of the group to form a trinome. In complex variant systems, the presence of a *null* as one of the digits of a trinome would add greatly to the complexities of cryptanalysis of that system. The most important of the subterfuges have to deal with the use of nulls which are of a *different size than the real cryptographic units,* inserted occasionally to prevent the cryptanalyst from breaking up the text into its proper units. The student should take careful note of the last phrase; the mere insertion of symbols having the same characteristics as the symbols of the cryptographic text, except that they have no meaning, is not what is meant. *This* class of nulls rarely achieves the purpose intended. What is really meant can best be explained by an example. Suppose that a 5 x 5 variant matrix with the row and column indicators shown in Fig. 46 is adopted for encipherment. Normally, the cipher units would consist of 2-letter combinations of the indicators, invariably giving the row indicator first (by agreement).

				V	G	I	W	D
				A	H	P	S	M
				T	O	E	B	N
				F	U	R	L	C
V A T F	A	B	C	D	E
G H O U	F	G	H	IJ	K
I P E R	L	M	N	O	P
W S B L	Q	R	S	T	U
D M N C	V	W	X	Y	Z

FIGURE 46.

126

The phrase "COMMANDER OF SPECIAL TROOPS" might be enciphered thus:

```
C   O    M    M    A    N    D    E    R    O    F  . . .
VI  EB   PH   IU   FT   IE   AB   TM   WO   PW   GT . . .
```

These would normally then be arranged in 5-letter groups, thus:

```
V I E B P   H I U F T   I E A B T   M W O P W   G T . . .
```

b. It will be noted, however, that only 20 of the 26 letters of the alphabet have been employed as row and column indicators, leaving J, K, Q, X, Y, and Z unused. Now, suppose these six letters are used as nulls, *not in pairs, but as individual letters inserted at random* just before the real text is arranged in 5-letter groups. Occasionally, a *pair* of letters might be inserted, in order to mask the characteristics of "avoidance" of these letters for each other. Thus, for example:

```
V I E X B   P H K I U   F J X T I   E A J B T   M W O Q P   W G K T Y
```

The cryptanalyst, after some study suspecting a biliteral cipher, proceeds to break up the text into pairs:

```
VI  EX  BP  HK  IU  FJ  XT  IE  AJ  BT  MW  OQ  PW  GK  TY
```

Compare this set of 2-letter combinations with the correct set. Only 4 of the 15 pairs are "proper" units. It is easy to see that without a knowledge of the *existence* of the nulls—and even with a knowledge, if he does not know *which* letters are nulls—the cryptanalyst would be confronted with a problem for the solution of which a fairly large amount of text might be necessary. The careful employment of the variants also very materially adds to the security of the method because repetitions can be rather effectively suppressed.

c. Similarly in the examples under par. 58, the letter J in Figs. 27 and 29 may be used as a null; the letter Y in Fig. 28; and the digit Ø in Figs. 33 and 34. In Fig. 30, any letters in the range of P–Z might be used as nulls, but this usage would be weak because of the extremely low frequency of these letters as compared with the letters A–O; this is an important point to consider in the examination of encrypted text for possible poor usages of nulls.

d. From the cryptographic standpoint, usage of nulls in the manner outlined above results in cryptographic text even more than twice as long as the plain text, thus constituting a serious disadvantage. From the cryptanalytic standpoint, the masking of the cipher units in the system described in subpar. *b* above constitutes the most important obstacle to solution; this, coupled with the use of variants, makes this system considerably more difficult to solve, despite its monoalphabeticity.

CHAPTER IX

POLYGRAPHIC SUBSTITUTION SYSTEMS

Paragraph

General remarks on polygraphic substitution _____ 64
Polygraphic substitution methods employing large tables _____ 65
Polygraphic substitution methods employing small matrices _____ 66
Methods for recognizing polygraphic substitution _____ 67
General procedure in the identification and analysis of polygraphic substitution ciphers _____ 68
Analysis of four-square matrix systems _____ 69
Analysis of two-square matrix systems _____ 70
Analysis of Playfair cipher systems _____ 71
Analysis of polygraphic systems involving large tables _____ 72
Further remarks on polygraphic substitution systems _____ 73

64. **General remarks on polygraphic substitution.**—*a.* The substitution systems dealt with thus far have involved plaintext units consisting of single elements (usually single letters). The major distinction between them has been made simply on the basis of the number of elements constituting the *ciphertext units* of each; i. e., those involving single-element ciphertext units were termed *uniliteral,* and those involving ciphertext units composed of two or more elements were termed *multiliteral.*[1] That is to say, when the terms "uniliteral", "biliteral", "triliteral", etc., were used, it was to have been inferred automatically that the plaintext units were composed of single elements.

b. This chapter of the text will deal with substitution systems involving *plaintext units* composed of more than one element; such systems are termed *polygraphic.*[2] (By comparing this new term with the terms "uniliteral" and "multiliteral" it may then be deduced—and correctly so—that a term involving the suffix "-literal" is descriptive of the composition of the ciphertext units of a cryptosystem, and that a term containing the suffix "-graphic" describes the composition of the plaintext units.[3]) Polygraphic systems in which the plaintext units are composed of two elements are called *digraphic,* those in which the plaintext units are composed of three elements are *trigraphic,* etc. The *ciphertext* units of polygraphic systems usually consist of the same number of elements as the plaintext units.[4] Thus, if a system is called "digraphic", it may be assumed that the ciphertext units of the system consist of two elements, as do the plaintext units; if this were not the case, the term "digraphic" by itself would not be adequate to describe the

[1] See also subpar. 52a.

[2] Systems involving plaintext units composed of single elements may, on this basis, be termed monographic; however, as has been stated in connection with the terms "uniliteral" and "multiliteral", the plaintext units of a system are understood (without restatement) to be monographic unless otherwise specified.

[3] In this connection, it is further pointed out that since the root "literal" derives from the Latin "litera", it is conventionally prefixed by modifiers of Latin origin, such as "uni-", "bi-", and "multi-"; similarly, "graphic", deriving from the Greek "graphikos", is prefixed by modifiers of Greek origin, such as "mono-", "di-", and "poly-".

[4] The qualifying adverb "usually" is employed because this correspondence is not essential. For example, if one should draw up a set of 676 arbitrary single signs, it would be possible to represent the 2-letter pairs from AA to ZZ by single symbols. This would still be a digraphic system.

system completely, and an additional modifying word or phrase would have to be used to indicate this fact.[5]

c. In polygraphic substitution, the *combinations* of elements which constitute the plaintext units are considered as indivisible compounds. The units are composite in character and the individual elements composing the units affect the equivalent cipher units *jointly*, rather than separately. The basic important factor in true polygraphic substitution is that *all* the letters of each plaintext unit participate in the determination of its cipher equivalent; the identity of *each* element of the plaintext unit affects the composition of the *whole* cipher unit.[6] Thus, in a certain digraphic system, $\overline{AB}_p$ may be enciphered as $\overline{XP}_c$; and $\overline{AC}_p$, on the other hand, may be enciphered as $\overline{NK}_c$; a difference in the identity of but one of the letters of the plaintext pair here produces a difference in the identity of *both* letters of the cipher pair.[7]

d. The fundamental purpose of polygraphic substitution is again the suppression or the elimination of the frequency characteristics of single letters of plain text, just as is the case in monoalphabetic substitution with variants; but here this is accomplished by a different method, the latter arising from a somewhat different approach to the problem involved in producing cryptographic security. When the substitution involves replacement of *single* letters in a monoalphabetic system, even a single cryptogram can be solved rather readily; basically the reason for this is that the principles of frequency and the laws of probability, applied to individual units (single letters) of the plain text, have a very good opportunity to manifest themselves. However, when the substitution involves replacement of plaintext units composed of two or more letters—that is, when the substitution is polygraphic in nature—the principles of frequency and laws of probability have a much lesser opportunity to manifest themselves. If the substitution is digraphic, then the units are pairs of letters and the normal frequencies of plaintext *digraphs* become of first consideration; if the substitution is trigraphic, the units are sets of three letters and the normal frequencies of plaintext trigraphs are involved. In these cases the data that can be employed in the solution are meager; that is why, generally speaking, the solution of polygraphic substitution ciphers is often extremely difficult.

e. By way of example, a given plaintext message of say N letters, enciphered by means of a uniliteral substitution system, affords N cipher characters, and the same number of cipher units. The same message, enciphered digraphically, still affords N cipher characters but only $\frac{N}{2}$ cipher units. Statistically speaking, the sample to which the laws of probability now are to be applied has been cut in half. Furthermore, from the point of view of frequency, the very noticeable diversity in the frequencies of individual letters, leading to the marked crests and troughs of the uniliteral frequency distribution, is no longer so strikingly in evidence in the frequencies of digraphs. Therefore, although digraphic encipherment, for example, simply cuts the cryptographic textual units in half, the number of cipher units which must be identified has been *squared*; and the difficulty of solution is not merely doubled but, if a matter of judgment arising

---

[5] See subpars. 65e and 66f for examples of two such systems and their names.

[6] An analogy is found in chemistry, when two elements combine to form a molecule, the latter usually having properties quite different from those of either of the constituent elements. For example: sodium, a metal, and chlorine, a gas, combine to form sodium chloride, common table salt. However, sodium and fluorine, also a gas similar in many respects to chlorine, combine to form sodium fluoride, which is much different from table salt.

[7] For this reason the two letters are marked by a ligature; that is, by a bar across their tops. In cryptologic notation, the symbol $\overline{\theta\theta}_p$ means "any plaintext digraph", the symbol $\overline{\theta\theta}_c$, "any ciphertext digraph". To refer specifically to the 1st, 2d, 3d, . . . member of a ligature, the exponent 1, 2, 3, . . . will be used. Thus θ_p^2 of $\overline{REM}_p$ is the letter E; θ_c^3 of $\overline{XRZ}_c$ is Z. See also footnote 1 on p. 47.

from practical experience can be expressed or approximated mathematically, squared or cubed.

f. The following two paragraphs will treat various polygraphic substitution methods. The most practical of these methods are digraphic in character and for this reason their treatment herein will be more detailed than that of trigraphic methods.

65. Polygraphic substitution methods employing large tables.—*a.* The simplest method of effecting polygraphic substitution involves the use of tables similar to that shown in Fig. 47a. This table merely provides equivalents for digraphs, by means of the coordinate system. Specifically, in obtaining the cipher equivalent of any plaintext digraph, the initial letter of the plaintext digraph is used to indicate the row in which the equivalent is found, and the final letter of the plaintext digraph indicates the column; the cipher digraph is then found at the intersection of the row and column thus indicated. For example, $\overline{KG}_p = \overline{FC}_c$; $\overline{WM}_p = \overline{OY}_c$; etc.

$$\theta_p^2$$

	A	B	C	D	E	F	G	H	I	J	K	L	M	N	O	P	Q	R	S	T	U	V	W	X	Y	Z
A	WG	EE	SN	TR	IA	NL	GC	HT	OI	UO	AM	RP	BY	KB	CD	DF	FH	JJ	LK	MQ	PS	QU	VV	XW	YX	ZZ
B	EG	SE	TN	IR	NA	GL	HC	OT	UI	AO	RM	BP	KY	CB	DD	FF	JH	LJ	MK	PQ	QS	VU	XV	YW	ZX	WZ
C	SG	TE	IN	NR	GA	HL	OC	UT	AI	RO	BM	KP	CY	DB	FD	JF	LH	MJ	PK	QQ	VS	XU	YV	ZW	WX	EZ
D	TG	IE	NN	GR	HA	OL	UC	AT	RI	BO	KM	CP	DY	FB	JD	LF	MH	PJ	QK	VQ	XS	YU	ZV	WW	EX	SZ
E	IG	NE	GN	HR	OA	UL	AC	RT	BI	KO	CM	DP	FY	JB	LD	MF	PH	QJ	VK	XQ	YS	ZU	WV	EW	SX	TZ
F	NG	GE	HN	OR	UA	AL	RC	BT	KI	CO	DM	FP	JY	LB	MD	PF	QH	VJ	XK	YQ	ZS	WU	EV	SW	TX	IZ
G	GG	HE	ON	UR	AA	RL	BC	KT	CI	DO	FM	JP	LY	MB	PD	QF	VH	XJ	YK	ZQ	WS	EU	SV	TW	IX	NZ
H	HG	OE	UN	AR	RA	BL	KC	CT	DI	FO	JM	LP	MY	PB	QD	VF	XH	YJ	ZK	WQ	ES	SU	TV	IW	NX	GZ
I	OG	UE	AN	RR	BA	KL	CC	DT	FI	JO	LM	MP	PY	QB	VD	XF	YH	ZJ	WK	EQ	SS	TU	IV	NW	GX	HZ
J	UG	AE	RN	BR	KA	CL	DC	FT	JI	LO	MM	PP	QY	VB	XD	YF	ZH	WJ	EK	SQ	TS	IU	NV	GW	HX	OZ
K	AC	RE	BN	KR	CA	DL	FC	JT	LI	MO	PM	QP	VY	XB	YD	ZF	WH	EJ	SK	TQ	IS	NU	GV	HW	OX	UZ
L	RG	BE	KN	CR	DA	FL	JC	LT	MI	PO	QM	VP	XY	YB	ZD	WF	EH	SJ	TK	IQ	NS	GU	HV	OW	UX	AZ
M	BG	KE	CN	DR	FA	JL	LC	MT	PI	QO	VM	XP	YY	ZB	WD	EF	SH	TJ	IK	NQ	GS	HU	OV	UW	AX	RZ
N	KG	CE	DN	FR	JA	LL	MC	PT	QI	VO	XM	YP	ZY	WB	ED	SF	TH	IJ	NK	GQ	HS	OU	UV	AW	RX	BZ
O	CG	DE	FN	JR	LA	ML	PC	QT	VI	XO	YM	ZP	WY	EB	SD	TF	IH	NJ	GK	HQ	OS	UU	AV	RW	BX	KZ
P	DG	FE	JN	LR	MA	PL	QC	VT	XI	YO	ZM	WP	EY	SB	TD	IF	NH	GJ	HK	OQ	US	AU	RV	BW	KX	CZ
Q	FG	JE	LN	MR	PA	QL	VC	XT	YI	ZO	WM	EP	SY	TB	ID	NF	GH	HJ	OK	UQ	AS	RU	BV	KW	CX	DZ
R	JG	LE	MN	PR	QA	VL	XC	YT	ZI	WO	EM	SP	TY	IB	ND	GF	HH	OJ	UK	AQ	RS	BU	KV	CW	DX	FZ
S	LG	ME	PN	QR	VA	XL	YC	ZT	WI	EO	SM	TP	IY	NB	GD	HF	OH	UJ	AK	RQ	BS	KU	CV	DW	FX	JZ
T	MG	PE	QN	VR	XA	YL	ZC	WT	EI	SO	TM	IP	NY	GB	HD	OF	UH	AJ	RK	BQ	KS	CU	DV	FW	JX	LZ
U	PG	QE	VN	XR	YA	ZL	WC	ET	SI	TO	IM	NP	GY	HB	OD	UF	AH	RJ	BK	KQ	CS	DU	FV	JW	LX	MZ
V	QG	VE	XN	YR	ZA	WL	EC	ST	TI	IO	NM	GP	HY	OB	UD	AF	RH	BJ	KK	CQ	DS	FU	JV	LW	MX	PZ
W	VG	XE	YN	ZR	WA	EL	SC	TT	II	NO	GM	HP	OY	UB	AD	RF	BH	KJ	CK	DQ	FS	JU	LV	MW	PX	QZ
X	XG	YE	ZN	WR	EA	SL	TC	IT	NI	GO	HM	OP	UY	AB	RD	BF	KH	CJ	DK	FQ	JS	LU	MV	PW	QX	VZ
Y	YG	ZE	WN	ER	SA	TL	IC	NT	GI	HO	OM	UP	AY	RB	BD	KF	CH	DJ	FK	JQ	LS	MU	PV	QW	VX	XZ
Z	ZG	WE	EN	SR	TA	IL	NC	GT	HI	OO	UM	AP	RY	BB	KD	CF	DH	FJ	JK	LQ	MS	PU	QV	VW	XX	YZ

θ_p^1 (left margin label) $\overline{\theta\theta}_c$ (right margin label)

FIGURE 47a.

b. In the preceding table two mixed sequences were employed to form the cipher equivalents, one sequence being based on the key phrase WESTINGHOUSE AIR BRAKE and the other on GENERAL ELECTRIC COMPANY. The table in Fig. 47a could have been drawn up in a slightly different manner, as shown in Fig. 47b, and still yield the same cipher equivalents as before. Using this latter table, θ_c^1 for any plaintext digraph is found at the intersection of the row and column identified by θ_p^1 and θ_p^2, respectively; θ_{c}^2 is found in the sequence below the table and is taken from the position directly under the column identified by θ_p^2. A few trial encipherments will illustrate that this table is cryptographically equivalent to that of Fig. 47a.

131

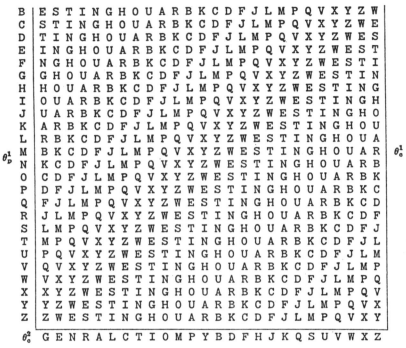

FIGURE 47b.

c. Figs. 48 and 49, below, contain other possible types of tables for digraphic substitution. In Fig. 48, it will be seen that there are *two* vertical sequences to the left of this table and no horizontal sequence below it. θ_p^1 is located in the leftmost sequence, θ_c^1 being found directly to its side in the right-hand sequence; θ_c^2 is then found at the intersection of the row and column identified by θ_p^1 and θ_p^2, respectively. The table in Fig. 49 provides digraphic equivalents by means of the coordinate system (e. g., $\overline{RE}_p = \overline{JZ}_c$), in the same manner as in Fig. 47a, and a cursory examination of the inside of the table might disclose nothing new about this table at all. But, if one were to scan closely the diagonals formed by each θ_c^1 from upper right to lower left, he would see that each such diagonal changes below the "M_p row"; similarly, if the diagonals formed by θ_c^2 are scanned from upper left to lower right, it will be seen that each of them also changes after the "M_p row". In effect, the inside of the table is divided into two separate portions by an imaginary line extending horizontally between the M and N rows; but within each portion a straightforward type of symmetry is exhibited and the same two mixed sequences have been employed in each. Actually, in a 26 x 26 table, it is *not* possible to maintain the diagonals formed thus by θ_c^1 and θ_c^2 in a completely "unbroken" sequence without producing repeated digraphs within the table and without consequent cryptographic ambiguity; thus, Fig. 49 illustrates one type of limited diagonal symmetry which must be resorted to in the systematic construction of such a table.

132

θ^1_p	θ^1_o	A	B	C	D	E	F	G	H	I	J	K	L	M	N	O	P	Q	R	S	T	U	V	W	X	Y	Z
A	W	G	E	N	R	A	L	C	T	I	O	M	P	Y	B	D	F	H	J	K	Q	S	U	V	W	X	Z
B	E	E	N	R	A	L	C	T	I	O	M	P	Y	B	D	F	H	J	K	Q	S	U	V	W	X	Z	G
C	S	N	R	A	L	C	T	I	O	M	P	Y	B	D	F	H	J	K	Q	S	U	V	W	X	Z	G	E
D	T	R	A	L	C	T	I	O	M	P	Y	B	D	F	H	J	K	Q	S	U	V	W	X	Z	G	E	N
E	I	A	L	C	T	I	O	M	P	Y	B	D	F	H	J	K	Q	S	U	V	W	X	Z	G	E	N	R
F	N	L	C	T	I	O	M	P	Y	B	D	F	H	J	K	Q	S	U	V	W	X	Z	G	E	N	R	A
G	G	C	T	I	O	M	P	Y	B	D	F	H	J	K	Q	S	U	V	W	X	Z	G	E	N	R	A	L
H	H	T	I	O	M	P	Y	B	D	F	H	J	K	Q	S	U	V	W	X	Z	G	E	N	R	A	L	C
I	O	I	O	M	P	Y	B	D	F	H	J	K	Q	S	U	V	W	X	Z	G	E	N	R	A	L	C	T
J	U	O	M	P	Y	B	D	F	H	J	K	Q	S	U	V	W	X	Z	G	E	N	R	A	L	C	T	I
K	A	M	P	Y	B	D	F	H	J	K	Q	S	U	V	W	X	Z	G	E	N	R	A	L	C	T	I	O
L	R	P	Y	B	D	F	H	J	K	Q	S	U	V	W	X	Z	G	E	N	R	A	L	C	T	I	O	M
M	B	Y	B	D	F	H	J	K	Q	S	U	V	W	X	Z	G	E	N	R	A	L	C	T	I	O	M	P
N	K	B	D	F	H	J	K	Q	S	U	V	W	X	Z	G	E	N	R	A	L	C	T	I	O	M	P	Y
O	C	D	F	H	J	K	Q	S	U	V	W	X	Z	G	E	N	R	A	L	C	T	I	O	M	P	Y	B
P	D	F	H	J	K	Q	S	U	V	W	X	Z	G	E	N	R	A	L	C	T	I	O	M	P	Y	B	D
Q	F	H	J	K	Q	S	U	V	W	X	Z	G	E	N	R	A	L	C	T	I	O	M	P	Y	B	D	F
R	J	J	K	Q	S	U	V	W	X	Z	G	E	N	R	A	L	C	T	I	O	M	P	Y	B	D	F	H
S	L	K	Q	S	U	V	W	X	Z	G	E	N	R	A	L	C	T	I	O	M	P	Y	B	D	F	H	J
T	M	Q	S	U	V	W	X	Z	G	E	N	R	A	L	C	T	I	O	M	P	Y	B	D	F	H	J	K
U	P	S	U	V	W	X	Z	G	E	N	R	A	L	C	T	I	O	M	P	Y	B	D	F	H	J	K	Q
V	Q	U	V	W	X	Z	G	E	N	R	A	L	C	T	I	O	M	P	Y	B	D	F	H	J	K	Q	S
W	V	V	W	X	Z	G	E	N	R	A	L	C	T	I	O	M	P	Y	B	D	F	H	J	K	Q	S	U
X	X	W	X	Z	G	E	N	R	A	L	C	T	I	O	M	P	Y	B	D	F	H	J	K	Q	S	U	V
Y	Y	X	Z	G	E	N	R	A	L	C	T	I	O	M	P	Y	B	D	F	H	J	K	Q	S	U	V	W
Z	Z	Z	G	E	N	R	A	L	C	T	I	O	M	P	Y	B	D	F	H	J	K	Q	S	U	V	W	X

θ^2_o

FIGURE 48.

d. All of the foregoing tables have exhibited a symmetry in the arrangement of their contents, which is undesirable from the standpoint of cryptographic security. This systematic internal arrangement could be detected by a cryptanalyst early in his attack on cryptograms produced through their use, permitting rapid reconstruction of the particular table involved; this subject will be given a more detailed treatment in par. 72. The table in Fig. 50 is an example of one type of table which would provide more security than the foregoing. This table is constructed by random assignment of values and shows no symmetry whatsoever in its arrangement of contents. It will be noted that this table is reciprocal in nature; that is $\overline{AF}_p = \overline{YG}_c$ and $\overline{YG}_p = \overline{AF}_c$. Thus, this single table serves for deciphering as well as for enciphering. Reciprocity is, however, not an essential factor; in fact, greater security is provided by nonreciprocal tables. But, in the case of such nonreciprocal, randomly constructed tables, each enciphering table must have its complementary deciphering table.

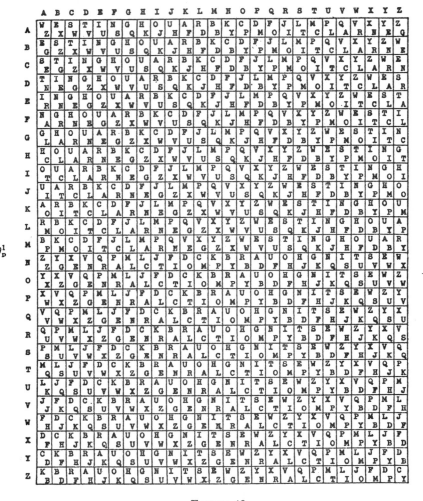

FIGURE 49.

e. Digraphic tables employing numerical equivalents instead of letter equivalents may be encountered. However, since 676 equivalents are required (there being 676, or 26 x 26 different pairs of letters), this means that combinations of three figures must be used; such systems are termed *trinome-digraphic* systems, indicating clearly the number of elements which comprise

134

$$\theta_p^2$$

θ_p^1	A	B	C	D	E	F	G	H	I	J	K	...	X	Y	Z	
A	FX	CH	XE	YY	ZA	YG	FB	CD	EF	XJ	ZX	...	EA	DJ	FH	A
B	NY	DC	NB	ZI	XX	DX						...				B
C	—			AH				AB				...		ND		C
D			BB		YA					AY		...	BF			D
E	AX					AI						...				E
F		AG			NZ			AZ				...	AA			F
⋮												...				⋮
N		BC		CY								...		BA	FE	N
⋮												...				⋮
X					AC					AJ		...	BE			X
Y	DE						AF					...		AD		Y
Z	AE								BD			...	AK			Z
	A	B	C	D	E	F	G	H	I	J	K		X	Y	Z	

FIGURE 50.

the cipher units. By way of an example, the following figure contains a fragment of a table [8] which provides trinome equivalents for the plaintext digraphs:

```
        J   U   P   I   T   E   R   A   B              X   Y   Z
  V  | 001 002 003 004 005 006 007 008 009 ... ... ... 024 025 026
  E  | 027 028 029 030 031 032 033 034 035           050 051 052
  N  | 053 054 055 056 057
  U  | 079 080 081 082
  S  | 105 106 107
  A  | 131 132
  B  | 157
     |  . . .
     |  . . .
     |  . . .
  X  | 599 600                                        622 623 624
  Y  | 625 626                                        648 649 650
  Z  | 651 652                            ... ... ... 674 675 676
```

FIGURE 51.

[8] It is interesting to note that this comparatively bulky and unwieldy table can be reduced to the following two alphabets with numerical equivalents for the letters:

(1)   V   E   N   U   S   B   X   Y   Z
      000 026 052 078 104 130 156 ... ... 598 624 650

(2)   J   U   P   I   T   E   R   X   Y   Z
      1   2   3   4   5   6   7 ... ... 24 25 26

In enciphering, the first letter of the plaintext digraph is converted into its numerical value from alphabet (1), and the second plaintext letter is converted by means of alphabet (2); the two numerical values thus derived are added together, and their *sum* is taken as the cipher equivalent of the particular plaintext digraph. Of course, this simple reduction would not be possible if the trinomes, in ascending order, had been arranged in the table in, say, a diagonal manner.

f. All of the foregoing tables have been digraphic in nature, but a kind of false trigraphic substitution may also be accomplished by means of similar tables, as illustrated in Fig. 52, wherein the table is the same as that in Fig. 48 with the addition of one more sequence at the top of the table. In using this table, θ_p^1 is located in sequence I, and its equivalent, θ_c^1, taken from sequence II; θ_p^2 is located in sequence III, and its equivalent, θ_c^2, taken from sequence IV; θ_c^3 is the letter lying at the intersection of the row indicated by θ_p^3 in sequence I and the column determined by θ_p^2. Thus, FIRE LINES would be enciphered $\overline{NNZ}$ $\overline{IEQ}$ $\overline{KOV}$. Various other agreements may be made with respect to the alphabets in which each plaintext letter will be sought in such a table, but the basic cryptographic principles are the same as in the case described.

```
 III.   A B C D E F G H I J K L M N O P Q R S T U V W X Y Z
  IV.   R A D I O C P T N F M E B G H J K L Q S U V W X Y Z
I. II.
A  W   G E N R A L C T I O M P Y B D F H J K Q S U V W X Z
B  E   E N R A L C T I O M P Y B D F H J K Q S U V W X Z G
C  S   N R A L C T I O M P Y B D F H J K Q S U V W X Z G E
D  T   R A L C T I O M P Y B D F H J K Q S U V W X Z G E N
E  I   A L C T I O M P Y B D F H J K Q S U V W X Z G E N R
F  N   L C T I O M P Y B D F H J K Q S U V W X Z G E N R A
G  G   C T I O M P Y B D F H J K Q S U V W X Z G E N R A L
H  H   T I O M P Y B D F H J K Q S U V W X Z G E N R A L C
I  O   I O M P Y B D F H J K Q S U V W X Z G E N R A L C T
J  U   O M P Y B D F H J K Q S U V W X Z G E N R A L C T I
K  A   M P Y B D F H J K Q S U V W X Z G E N R A L C T I O
L  R   P Y B D F H J K Q S U V W X Z G E N R A L C T I O M
M  B   Y B D F H J K Q S U V W X Z G E N R A L C T I O M P
N  K   B D F H J K Q S U V W X Z G E N R A L C T I O M P Y
O  C   D F H J K Q S U V W X Z G E N R A L C T I O M P Y B
P  D   F H J K Q S U V W X Z G E N R A L C T I O M P Y B D
Q  F   H J K Q S U V W X Z G E N R A L C T I O M P Y B D F
R  J   J K Q S U V W X Z G E N R A L C T I O M P Y B D F H
S  L   K Q S U V W X Z G E N R A L C T I O M P Y B D F H J
T  M   Q S U V W X Z G E N R A L C T I O M P Y B D F H J K
U  P   S U V W X Z G E N R A L C T I O M P Y B D F H J K Q
V  Q   U V W X Z G E N R A L C T I O M P Y B D F H J K Q S
W  V   V W X Z G E N R A L C T I O M P Y B D F H J K Q S U
X  X   W X Z G E N R A L C T I O M P Y B D F H J K Q S U V
Y  Y   X Z G E N R A L C T I O M P Y B D F H J K Q S U V W
Z  Z   Z G E N R A L C T I O M P Y B D F H J K Q S U V W X
```

FIGURE 52.

g. Tables such as those illustrated in Figs. 47–52, above, have been encountered in operational systems, but their use has not been very widespread because of their relatively large size and the inconvenience in their production and handling. In lieu of these large tables it is possible to employ much smaller matrices or geometrical designs to accomplish digraphic substitution; methods involving their use will be discussed in the following paragraph.

66. Polygraphic substitution methods employing small matrices.[9]—*a.* A simple method for accomplishing digraphic substitution involves the use of the *four-square matrix,* a matrix consisting of four 5 x 5 squares in which the letters of a 25-element alphabet (combining I and J) are inserted in any prearranged order. In a four-square matrix, θ_p^1 of $\overline{\theta\theta}_p$ is sought in Section 1; θ_p^2, in Section 2. Thus, θ_p^1 and θ_p^2 will always form the northwest-southeast corners of an imaginary rectangle delimited by these two letters as located in these two sections of the square. Then θ_c^1 and θ_c^2 are, respectively, the letters at the northeast-southwest corners of this same rectangle. Thus, $\overline{TG}_p = \overline{XS}_c$; $\overline{WD}_p = \overline{CH}_c$; $\overline{OR}_p = \overline{YV}_c$; $\overline{UR}_p = \overline{XB}_c$; etc. In decrypting, θ_c^1 and θ_c^2 are sought in Sections 3 and 4, respectively, and their equivalents, θ_p^1 and θ_p^2, noted in Sections 1 and 2, respectively.

Sec. 1 (θ_p^1)
Sec. 3 (θ_c^1)

```
A B C D E | F O U R T
F G H I K | L M P Q E
L M N O P | K Y Z S N
Q R S T U | I X W V A
V W X Y Z | H G D C B
----------+----------
T H I R E | A B C D E
O P Q S N | F G H I K
M Y Z U A | L M N O P
L X W V B | Q R S T U
K G F D C | V W X Y Z
```

Sec. 4 (θ_c^2)
Sec. 2 (θ_p^2)

FIGURE 53.

b. It is possible to effect digraphic substitution with a matrix consisting of but two sections by a modification in the method of finding equivalents. In a *horizontal two-square matrix,* such as that shown in Fig. 54, θ_p^1 of $\overline{\theta\theta}_p$ is located in the square at the left; θ_p^2, in the square at the right.

$\theta_p^1\theta_c^2$

```
M A N U F | A U T O M
C T R I G | B I L E S
B D E H K | C D F G H
L O P Q S | K N P Q R
V W X Y Z | V W X Y Z
```

$\theta_p^2\theta_c^1$

FIGURE 54.

When θ_p^1 and θ_p^2 are at the opposite ends of the diagonal of an imaginary rectangle defined by these letters, the ciphertext equivalent comprises the two letters appearing at the opposite ends of the other diagonal of the same rectangle; θ_c^1 is the particular one which is in the same row as θ_p^1, and θ_c^2 is the one in the same row as θ_p^2. For example, $\overline{AL}_p = \overline{TT}_c$; $\overline{DO}_p = \overline{GA}_c$. When θ_p^1 and θ_p^2 happen to be in the same row, the ciphertext equivalent is merely the reverse of the plaintext digraph; for example, $\overline{AT}_p = \overline{TA}_c$ and $\overline{EH}_p = \overline{HE}_c$.

---

[9] The word *matrix* as employed in this paragraph refers to checkerboard-type diagrams smaller than the tables illustrated in the preceding paragraph. These matrices are usually composed of sections containing 25 cells each.

c. Digraphic substitution may also be effected by means of *vertical two-square matrices*, in which one section is directly above the other, as in Fig. 55; it will be noted that matrices of this type have a feature of reciprocity when employed according to the usual rules, which follow.

$\theta_p^1\theta_c^1$
$\theta_p^2\theta_c^2$

```
M A N U F
C T R I G
B D E H K
L O P Q S
V W X Y Z
─────────
A U T O M
B I L E S
C D F G H
K N P Q R
V W X Y Z
```

FIGURE 55.

When θ_p^1 and θ_p^2 are at the opposite ends of a diagonal, the rule for encipherment is the same as that for horizontal two-square encipherment (e. g., $\overline{MO}_p = \overline{UA}_c$ and $\overline{UA}_p = \overline{MO}_c$); when both θ_p^1 and θ_p^2 happen to be in the same column, the plaintext digraphs are self-enciphered (e. g., $\overline{MA}_p = \overline{MA}_c$ and $\overline{EL}_p = \overline{EL}_c$), a fact which constitutes an important weakness of this method.[10] This disadvantage is only slightly less obvious in the preceding case of horizontal two-square methods wherein the cipher equivalent of $\overline{\theta\theta}_p$ consists merely of the plaintext letters in reversed order.

d. One-square digraphic methods, with a necessary modification of the method for finding equivalents, are also possible. The first of this type to appear as a practical military system was that known as the *Playfair cipher*.[11] It was used for a number of years as a field cipher by the British Army, before and during World War I, and for a short time, also during that war, by certain units of the American Expeditionary Forces. Fig. 56 shows a typical Playfair square.

```
M A N U F
C T R I G
B D E H K
L O P Q S
V W X Y Z
```

FIGURE 56.

The modification in the method of finding cipher equivalents has been found useful in imparting a greater degree of security than that afforded in the preceding small matrix methods. The usual method of encipherment can be best explained by examples given under four categories:

(1) Members of the plaintext pair, θ_p^1 and θ_p^2, are at opposite ends of the diagonal of an imaginary rectangle defined by the two letters; the members of the ciphertext pair, θ_c^1 and θ_c^2,

[10] See subpar. 73*b* on other enciphering conventions which remove this weakness.

[11] This cipher was really invented by Sir Charles Wheatstone but receives its name from Lord Playfair, who apparently was its sponsor before the British Foreign Office. See Wemyss Reid, *Memoirs of Lyon Playfair*, London, 1899. It is of interest to note that, to students of electrical engineering, Wheatstone is generally not known for his contributions to cryptography but is famed for something he did not invent—the so-called "Wheatstone bridge", really invented by Samuel H. Christie.

are at the opposite ends of the other diagonal of this imaginary rectangle. Examples: $\overline{MO}_p = \overline{AL}_c$; $\overline{MI}_p = \overline{UC}_c$; $\overline{LU}_p = \overline{QM}_c$; $\overline{VI}_p = \overline{YC}_c$.

(2) θ_p^1 and θ_p^2 are in the same row; the letter immediately to the *right* of θ_p^1 forms θ_c^1; the letter immediately to the right of θ_p^2 forms θ_c^2. When either θ_p^1 or θ_p^2 is at the extreme right of the row, the first letter in the row becomes its cipher equivalent. Examples: $\overline{MA}_p = \overline{AN}_c$; $\overline{MU}_p = \overline{AF}_c$; $\overline{AF}_p = \overline{NM}_c$; $\overline{FA}_p = \overline{MN}_c$.

(3) θ_p^1 and θ_p^2 are in the same column; the letter immediately *below* θ_p^1 forms θ_c^1, the letter immediately below θ_p^2 forms θ_c^2. When either θ_p^1 or θ_p^2 is at the bottom of the column, the top letter in that column becomes its cipher equivalent. Examples: $\overline{MC}_p = \overline{CB}_c$; $\overline{AW}_p = \overline{TA}_c$; $\overline{WA}_p = \overline{AT}_c$; $\overline{QU}_p = \overline{YI}_c$.

(4) θ_p^1 and θ_p^2 are identical; they are to be separated by inserting a null, usually the letter X or Q, and subsequently enciphered by the pertinent rule from above. For example, the word BATTLES would be enciphered thus:

```
BA TX TL ES
DM RW CO KP
```

The Playfair square is automatically reciprocal so far as encipherments of type (1) above are concerned; but this is not true of encipherments of type (2) and (3).

e. It is not essential that the small matrices used for digraphic substitution be in the shape of perfect squares; rectangular designs will serve equally well, with little or no modification in procedure.[12]   For example, each section of, say, a four-square matrix could be constructed with four rows containing six letters each by having U_p serve for V_p, as well as I_p for J_p.   Furthermore, it is possible to expand the sections of a digraphic matrix to 28, 30, or more characters by the following subterfuge, without introducing digits or symbols into the cipher text.[13]   One of the letters of the alphabet may be omitted from the set of 26 letters, and this letter may then be replaced by 2, 3, or more *pairs* of letters, each pair having as one of its members the omitted single letter.   The 5 x 6 Playfair square of Fig. 57a has been derived thus; the letter K has

W	A	S	H	I	N
G	T	O	B	C	D
E	F	J	KA	KE	KI
KO	KU	L	M	P	Q
R	U	V	X	Y	Z

FIGURE 57a.

been omitted as a single letter, and the number of characters in the rectangle has been made a total of 30 by the addition of five combinations of K with other letters.   An interesting consequence of this modification is that certain irregularities are introduced in any cryptogram produced through its use; for example, (1) occasionally a plaintext digraph is replaced by a ciphertext trigraph or tetragraph, such as $\overline{AM}_p = \overline{HKU}_c$ and $\overline{EP}_p = \overline{KEKO}_c$; and (2) variant values may

---

[12] However, because the terms "four-*square* matrix", "two-*square* matrix", and "Playfair *square*" have become firmly fixed in cryptologic literature and practice, they continue to be applied to all such matrices, even when the "squares" of such matrices do not contain an equal number of rows and columns (that is, even when they are not square).

[13] The addition of any symbols such as the digits 1, 2, 3, . . . into a matrix solely to augment the number of elements to 27, 28, 30, 32, or 36 characters would not be considered practicable, since such a procedure would result in producing cryptograms containing intermixtures of letters and figures.

139

appear—$\overline{\text{BKE}}_c$, $\overline{\text{DKE}}_c$, $\overline{\text{KEP}}_c$, $\overline{\text{GP}}_c$, and $\overline{\text{TP}}_c$ all may be used to represent $\overline{\text{CK}}_p$. As far as the deciphering is concerned, there is no difficulty because any K occurring in the cipher text is considered as invariably forming a ligature with the succeeding letter, taking the pair of letters as a unit; and, when a plaintext unit is obtained containing one of the K-pairs, the letter after

$$
\theta_p^1 \quad
\begin{array}{cccccc|cccccc}
B & 2 & E & 5 & R & L & A & B & C & D & E & F \\
I & 9 & N & A & 1 & C & G & H & I & J & KA & KE \\
3 & D & 4 & F & 6 & G & KI & KO & KU & KY & L & M \\
7 & H & 8 & J & \emptyset & K & N & O & P & QA & QE & QI \\
M & O & P & Q & S & T & QO & QU & QY & R & S & T \\
U & V & W & X & Y & Z & U & V & W & X & Y & Z \\
\hline
A & B & C & D & E & F & M & U & N & I & 9 & C \\
G & H & I & J & KA & KE & 3 & H & 8 & A & 1 & B \\
KI & KO & KU & KY & L & M & 2 & D & 4 & E & 5 & F \\
N & O & P & QA & QE & QI & 6 & G & 7 & J & \emptyset & K \\
QO & QU & QY & R & S & T & L & O & P & Q & R & S \\
U & V & W & X & Y & Z & T & V & W & X & Y & Z \\
\end{array}
\quad \theta_c^1
$$

θ_c^2 (left of lower left square), θ_p^2 (right of lower right square)

FIGURE 57b.

the K is disregarded; for example, $\overline{\text{CKO}}_p$ is read as CK. The four-square matrix in Fig. 57b has also been constructed using the foregoing subterfuge. With this latter matrix, numbers in the plain text may be enciphered, still without producing *cipher* text containing numbers; for example, the plain text "HILL 3406" would be represented by the cipher QAB AT KUKI NQE which would be regrouped into groups of five letters and sent as QABAT KUKIN QE...

f. Fig. 58 shows a numerical four-square matrix which presents a rather interesting feature in that it makes possible the substitution of 3-figure combinations for digraphs in a unique manner. To encipher a message one proceeds as usual to find the numerical equivalents of a pair, and then these numbers are added together. Thus:

Plain text:	PR	OC	EE	DI	NG
	275	350	100	075	325
	9	13	24	18	7
Cipher text:	284	363	124	093	332

Sec. 1 (θ_p^1) / Sec. 3 (θ_c^1) / Sec. 4 (θ_c^2) / Sec. 2 (θ_c^2)

A	B	C	D	E	000	025	050	075	100
F	G	H	I	K	125	150	175	200	225
L	M	N	O	P	250	275	300	325	350
Q	R	S	T	U	375	400	425	450	475
V	W	X	Y	Z	500	525	550	575	600
$\emptyset$	1	2	3	4	V	Q	L	F	A
5	6	7	8	9	W	R	M	G	B
10	11	12	13	14	X	S	N	H	C
15	16	17	18	19	Y	T	O	I	D
20	21	22	23	24	Z	U	P	K	E

FIGURE 58.

140

In deciphering, the greatest multiple of 25 contained in the group of three digits is determined; then this multiple and its remainder are used to form the elements for determining the plaintext pair in the usual manner. Thus, 284=275+9=PR.

g. Thus far all the small-matrix methods have involved only digraphic substitution. The two matrices together illustrated in Figs. 59*a* and *b* may be used to provide a system for encipherment which is partly trigraphic; the adverb "partly" has been used because this particular system will yield trigraphic encipherment approximately 88.5% of the time in ordinary text and digraphic encipherment approximately 11.5% of the time.[14] In this case the cipher equivalents of the trigraphs (or digraphs, as the case may be) are tetranomes. Encipherment is best illustrated by an example; this is given in the next subparagraph.

Sec. 1

H_1	H_2	H_3	H_4	Y_1	Y_2	Y_3	Y_4	D_1	D_2
D_3	D_4	R_1	R_2	R_3	R_4	A_1	A_2	A_3	A_4
U_1	U_2	U_3	U_4	L_1	L_2	L_3	L_4	I_1	I_2
I_3	I_4	C_1	C_2	C_3	C_4	B_1	B_2	B_3	B_4
E_1	E_2	E_3	E_4	F_1	F_2	F_3	F_4	G_1	G_2
G_3	G_4	K_1	K_2	K_3	K_4	M_1	M_2	M_3	M_4
N_1	N_2	N_3	N_4	O_1	O_2	O_3	O_4	P_1	P_2
P_3	P_4	Q_1	Q_2	Q_3	Q_4	S_1	S_2	S_3	S_4
T_1	T_2	T_3	T_4	V_1	V_2	V_3	V_4	W_1	W_2
W_3	W_4	X_1	X_2	X_3	X_4	Z_1	Z_2	Z_3	Z_4

00	01	02	03	04	05	06	07	08	09
10	11	12	13	14	15	16	17	18	19
20	21	22	23	24	25	26	27	28	29
30	31	32	33	34	35	36	37	38	39
40	41	42	43	44	45	46	47	48	49
50	51	52	53	54	55	56	57	58	59
60	61	62	63	64	65	66	67	68	69
70	71	72	73	74	75	76	77	78	79
80	81	82	83	84	85	86	87	88	89
90	91	92	93	94	95	96	97	98	99

Sec. 3

Sec. 4

00	01	02	03	04	05	06	07	08	09
10	11	12	13	14	15	16	17	18	19
20	21	22	23	24	25	26	27	28	29
30	31	32	33	34	35	36	37	38	39
40	41	42	43	44	45	46	47	48	49
50	51	52	53	54	55	56	57	58	59
60	61	62	63	64	65	66	67	68	69
70	71	72	73	74	75	76	77	78	79
80	81	82	83	84	85	86	87	88	89
90	91	92	93	94	95	96	97	98	99

Q_1	Q_2	Q_3	Q_4	U_1	U_2	U_3	U_4	E_1	E_2
E_3	E_4	S_1	S_2	S_3	S_4	T_1	T_2	T_3	T_4
I_1	I_2	I_3	I_4	O_1	O_2	O_3	O_4	N_1	N_2
N_3	N_4	A_1	A_2	A_3	A_4	B_1	B_2	B_3	B_4
L_1	L_2	L_3	L_4	Y_1	Y_2	Y_3	Y_4	C_1	C_2
C_3	C_4	D_1	D_2	D_3	D_4	F_1	F_2	F_3	F_4
G_1	G_2	G_3	G_4	H_1	H_2	H_3	H_4	K_1	K_2
K_3	K_4	M_1	M_2	M_3	M_4	P_1	P_2	P_3	P_4
R_1	R_2	R_3	R_4	V_1	V_2	V_3	V_4	W_1	W_2
W_3	W_4	X_1	X_2	X_3	X_4	Z_1	Z_2	Z_3	Z_4

Sec. 2

	1	2	3	4
1	–	E	T	N
2	R	O	A	I
3	S	D	L	H
4	C	F	P	U

FIGURE 59*b*.

FIGURE 59*a*.

h. Let the text to be enciphered be a message beginning with the words "REFERRING TO YOUR MESSAGE NUMBER FIVE STOP . . ." This is rewritten into trigraphs, with the proviso that the third letter of the trigraph be one of the letters contained in the small square in Fig. 59*b*; if the third letter is not one of these 15 letters, the plaintext grouping is left as a digraph; then the grouping into trigraphs (or digraphs) continues. Thus, the foregoing plain text would be written as follows:

REF   ERR   IN–   GTO   YOU   RME   SSA   GEN   UM–   BER   FI–   VES   TOP   . . .

In encipherment, it is to be noticed that R_p occurs four times in Section 1 (as do all the letters) and E_p occurs four times in Section 2; the proper combination of the 16 possibilities is determined by the *coordinates of the third letter of the trigraph* as indicated in the small square, Fig. 59*b*.

[14] These figures are based on the number of trigraphs ending in one of the 15 highest-frequency letters (ETNROAISDLHCFPU), and on the number of trigraphs ending with other letters.

141

Since the coordinates of F_p in this square are 42, then it is the *4th* occurrence of R_p in Section 1 and the *2d* occurrence of E_p in Section 2 which are used to obtain the equivalent for the trigraph $\overline{REF}_p$; this equivalent is 1905. When the plaintext unit as obtained above is only a digraph, it is the *1st* occurrence of θ_p^1 which is used in Section 1 and the *1st* occurrence of θ_p^2 which is used in Section 2; thus, "IN–" from the sample message beginning, above, would be enciphered 2828. The encipherment of the plaintext example above is then

```
REF   ERR   IN–   GTO   YOU   RME   SSA   GEN   UM–   BER   FI–   VES   TOP
1905  4081  2828  4719  0727  1372  7417  4118  2270  3807  4024  8806  8623
```

The cipher text could then be transmitted in groups of four digits, or, as a subterfuge to conceal the basic group length, the transmission could be in five-digit groups. In decipherment, the ciphertext tetranome is deciphered in the manner of the usual four-square matrix, and the location of the particular values for θ_p^1 and θ_p^2 will indicate the identity of the third plaintext letter, if any.

i. Now that the student has become familiar with the details of typical polygraphic substitution systems, he is ready to continue his cryptanalytic study with the treatment of methods for recognizing polygraphic substitution; these methods are described in the next paragraph.

67. Methods for recognizing polygraphic substitution.—*a.* The methods used to determine whether or not a given cryptogram is digraphic in character are usually rather simple. If there are many repetitions in a cryptogram or a set of cryptograms and yet the uniliteral frequency distribution gives no clear-cut indications of monoalphabeticity; if most of the repetitions contain an even number of letters and these repetitions for the most part begin on the odd letters and end on the even letters of the message, yet the cipher text does not yield to solution as a biliteral cipher when the procedures outlined in Chapters VII and VIII are applied to it; if the cryptograms usually contain an even number of letters (exclusive of nulls); and if the cipher text is in letters and all 26 letters are not present and J or U are among the absent letters (or if the cipher is in digits and there is a limitation in the range of the text when divided into trinomes, this range usually being not greater than 001–676); then the encipherment may be assumed to be digraphic in nature.

b. Although the foregoing general remarks are true as far as they go, occasionally they may be difficult to apply with any clear-cut results unless a large volume of cipher text is available for study. To supplement them there are statistical tests which may be applied for the recognition of digraphic substitution. Just as the ϕ test and the Λ test may be applied to the uniliteral distribution of a cryptogram to help determine whether it is monoalphabetic with respect to single-letter plaintext units, so may these same tests be applied to the *digraphic* distribution of a cryptogram for the purpose of determining whether the cryptogram in question is monoalphabetic when considered as a digraphic cipher.

c. The basic *form* of the ϕ test is the same when applied to digraphic distributions as when applied to monographic—that is, uniliteral—distributions (see par. 27). It is only the plain and random constants that change, and "N" in the formulas now pertains to the number of *digraphs* under consideration, instead of the number of single letters. To illustrate this, the formulas for computing the "digraphic phi plain" ($_2\phi_p$) and "the digraphic phi random" ($_2\phi_r$) are shown below:[15]

$$_2\phi_p = .0069 \, N(N-1)$$

$$_2\phi_r = .0015 \, N(N-1)$$

The "digraphic phi observed" ($_2\phi_o$) is calculated in the usual manner, that is, by multiplying each f (which in this case is found in each one of the cells of a digraphic distribution) by $f-1$, and then totalling all the values thus derived.

d. The digraphic Λ test (or the "digraphic blank-expectation test") may be applied to a digraphic distribution just as easily as its monographic counterpart is applied to a uniliteral frequency distribution. For this purpose, Chart 8 is given below, showing the average number of blanks theoretically expected in digraphic distributions for plain text and for random text containing various numbers of digraphs (up to 200 digraphs). As can be seen, the chart contains two curves. The one labeled P applies to the average number of blanks theoretically expected in digraphic distributions based upon normal *plaintext* messages containing the indicated number of digraphs. The other curve, labeled R, applies to the average number of blanks theoretically expected in digraphic distributions based upon perfectly random assortments of digraphs. In using this chart one finds the point of intersection of the vertical line corresponding to the number of digraphs in the message, with the horizontal line corresponding to the observed number of blanks in the digraphic distribution for the message. If this point of intersection falls closer to curve P than it does to curve R, this is evidence that the cryptogram is digraphic in nature [16]; if it falls closer to curve R than to curve P, this is evidence that the cryptogram is not digraphic in character.

e. Although it may not be necessary to resort to the use of the digraphic ϕ and Λ tests to determine whether or not a particular cryptogram has been digraphically enciphered, it is well to know the application of these tests, since use has been made of them in difficult cases in operational practice. They may be helpfully employed in cases where the cryptanalyst is uncertain as to whether or not a single null has been added at the *beginning* of a cryptogram suspected to

---

[15] The digraphic plain constant, .0069, was obtained by summing the squares of the probabilities of digraphs in English plain text; the digraphic random constant, .0015 (or .00148 to three significant figures), is merely the decimal equivalent of 1/676. The digraphic I. C. for English plain text is 4.66, i. e., $\dfrac{.0069}{.00148}$, as compared with the digraphic I. C. for random text of 1.0, i. e., $\dfrac{.00148}{.00148}$. Further elaboration on the use of these constants, among others, will be given in *Military Cryptanalytics, Part III.*

[16] Unfortunately, such would also be the case if the cryptogram under consideration were a polyalphabetic cipher involving two alphabets. However, to distinguish between a digraphic cipher and a polyalphabetic cipher with two alphabets, a digraphic distribution could be made "off the cut", that is, made of those ciphertext digraphs which are formed by omitting the first letter of text and then dividing the remaining text into groups of two letters. If the system were digraphic, such a distribution would exhibit a poor $_2\phi_o$; if the system were a two-alphabet substitution system, the $_2\phi_o$ would be as satisfactory as that of the regular distribution, taken "on the cut".

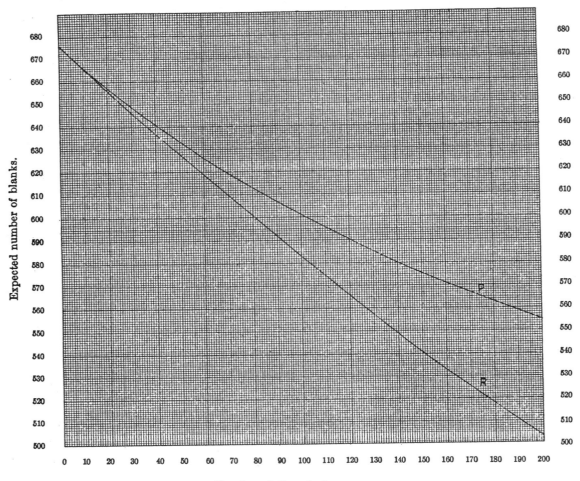

Number of digraphs in message.

CHART 8. Curves showing the average number of blanks theoretically expected in digraphic distributions for plain text (P) and for random text (R) for messages comprising various numbers of digraphs. (See subpar. 67d.)

be a digraphic cipher; and these tests may also be found useful in the analysis of complex cases where the digraphic encipherment has been applied, not to adjacent letters of the plaintext message, but to digraphs composed of more-or-less *separated* letters in the message. Elaborations of these ideas will be treated in *Military Cryptanalytics, Part II*.

f. As for the recognition of *trigraphic* substitution ciphers—if most of the repetitions are a multiple of three letters in length, if these repetitions for the most part begin (when the cipher text is divided into trigraphs) with the first letters and end with the third letters of the trigraphs, and if the length of the cryptograms is for the most part a multiple of three letters, yet the cipher text does not yield to solution as a triliteral cipher, then the encipherment may be assumed to be trigraphic in nature.

144

g. Just as the φ test may be used as an aid in the recognition of digraphicity, it may theoretically be used for recognizing the trigraphic, tetragraphic, etc., nature of cryptograms, but its use for these latter purposes is much more limited because of the large amount of text which would be required to permit a valid application of the pertinent polygraphic φ test.

68. General procedure in the identification and analysis of polygraphic substitution ciphers.—*a.* Certain systems which at first glance seem to be polygraphic, in that groupings of plaintext letters are treated as units, are on closer inspection seen to be only partly polygraphic in character. Such is true of systems involving large tables of the type illustrated in Figs. 47a and *b*, and 48 (in par. 65, above), wherein encipherment is by pairs but one of the letters in each pair is enciphered monoalphabetically, making these systems only *pseudo*-polygraphic. For example, using the table in Fig. 48, any plaintext digraph beginning with "A" must be enciphered by a ciphertext digraph beginning with "W"; any plaintext digraph beginning with "B" must be enciphered by a ciphertext digraph beginning with "E"; etc. A cryptogram involving the use of this table may then be identified as such merely from a study of the uniliteral frequency distribution made on the initial letters of the cipher digraphs, since such a distribution would perforce be monoalphabetic.[17]

b. In certain other systems—namely, the four-square, two-square, and Playfair square systems of par. 66, above—the method of encipherment is by pairs, but the encipherments of the left-hand and right-hand members of the pairs show group relationships; this is not pseudo-polygraphic but, rather, *partially*-polygraphic. Cryptograms enciphered by means of systems of this latter type may not be readily identified as such merely through an examination of their cipher text, but their solution may be effected rather rapidly as soon as a few correct plaintext assumptions have been made therein. A more detailed treatment of this matter will be given in succeeding paragraphs of this chapter.

c. The analysis of cryptograms which have been produced by digraphic substitution is accomplished largely by the application of the simple principles of frequency of digraphs,[18] with the additional aid of digraphic idiomorphs and such special circumstances as may be known to or suspected by the cryptanalyst. The latter refer to peculiarities which may be the result of the particular method employed in obtaining the equivalents of the plaintext digraphs in the encrypting process, such as those mentioned in subpars. *a* and *b*, above. In general, if there is sufficient text to disclose the normal phenomena of repetition and idiomorphism, or if cribs are available to be used as an entering wedge, solution will be feasible. The foregoing general statements will be expanded upon in the following two subparagraphs, *d* and *e*.

d. When a digraphic system is employed in regular service, there is little doubt that traffic will rapidly accumulate to an amount more than sufficient to permit of solution by simple principles of frequency. Sometimes only two or three long messages, or a half-dozen of average length, are sufficient. For with the identification of only a few cipher digraphs, larger portions of messages may be read because the skeletons of words formed from the few high-frequency

---

[17] For this purpose, the simplest and most economical way to obtain the uniliteral distributions for the initial and final letters of digraphs is to make a digraphic distribution and then add the tallies in each row to yield the distribution for the initial letters, and add the tallies in each column to obtain the distribution for the final letters.

[18] In this connection, it would be well for the student to familiarize himself with that portion of Appendix 2 which contains digraphic frequency data, if he has not already done so.

digraphs very definitely limit the values that can be inserted for the intervening unidentified digraphs. For example, suppose that the plaintext digraphs RE, IN, ON, ND, NO, SI, NT, and TO are among those that have been identified by frequency considerations, corroborated by a tentatively identified long repetition; and suppose also that the enemy is known to be using a large table of 676 cells containing digraphs showing reciprocal equivalence between plaintext and ciphertext digraphs. Suppose the message begins as follows (in which the assumed values have been inserted):

XQ	VO	ZI	LK	AP	OL	ZX	PV	CK	IK	OL	UK	AT	HN	LK
	ND	IN		NT		RE				NT	NO			IN

VL	BN	OZ	BZ	DY	TY	LE	GI
	SI		ON	TO			

The initial words SECOND INFANTRY REGIMENT are readily recognized. Furthermore, if $\overline{CK}_c = \overline{GI}_p$ then $\overline{GI}_c = \overline{CK}_p$, which suggests ATTACK as the last word in the message beginning. This fragment of the message may now be completely recovered: SECOND INFANTRY REGIMENT NOT YET IN POSITION TO ATTACK......

e. Just as the choice of probable words in the solution of uniliteral systems is aided or limited by the positions of repeated letters (see subpar. 49*d*), so, in digraphic ciphers, is the placing of cribs aided or limited by the positions of repeated *digraphs*. In this connection, several frequent words and phrases containing repeated digraphs have been tabulated for the student's aid, and this list of *digraphic idiomorphs* is presented as Section D in Appendix 3 (q. v.). Thus, if one is confronted by a ciphertext message containing the following repeated sequence (therefore likely to represent an entire word)

VI FW HM AZ FF FW RO

he may refer to the appropriate section of Appendix 3 which will disclose, on the basis of the idiomorphic pattern "AB -- -- -- AB" starting with the second cipher digraph, that the underlying plaintext word may be RE EN FO RC EM EN T, among others. Once a good start has been made and a few words have been solved, subsequent work is quite simple and straightforward. A knowledge of enemy correspondence, including data regarding its most common words and phrases, is of as much assistance in breaking down digraphic systems as it is in the solution of any other cryptosystems.

f. In the case of trigraphic substitution, analysis is made considerably more complex by the large amount of traffic required, not only for the initial entries, but also for further exploitation of the entering wedges. In effect, the solution of a trigraphic system closely parallels the solution of the syllabary portion of a large two-part code; these techniques will be discussed in *Military Cryptanalytics, Part V*.

69. **Analysis of four-square matrix systems.**—*a.* In all the small-matrix methods illustrated in par. 66, the encipherment is only partially digraphic because there are certain relationships between those plaintext digraphs which have common elements and their corresponding ciphertext digraphs, which will also have common elements. For example, in the four-square matrix given in Fig. 53, it will be noted that $\overline{AA}_p = \overline{FT}_c$, $\overline{AF}_p = \overline{FO}_c$, $\overline{AL}_p = \overline{FM}_c$, $\overline{AQ}_p = \overline{FL}_c$, and $\overline{AV}_p = \overline{FK}_c$. In each of these cases when A_p is the initial letter of the plaintext pair, the initial letter of the ciphertext equivalent is F_c. This, of course, is the direct result of the method; it means that the encipherment is monoalphabetic for the first half of each of *these five* plaintext pairs. This relationship holds true for *four* other groups of five pairs beginning with A_p; in effect, there

are five cipher alphabets employed, not 25. Thus, this case differs from the case discussed under subpar. 68a only in that the monoalphabeticity is complete, not for half of all the pairs but only among the members of certain groups of pairs. In a *true* digraphic system, such as a system making use of a 676-cell randomized table, relationships of the foregoing type are entirely absent, and for this reason such a system is cryptographically more secure than small-matrix systems.

b. From the foregoing it is clear that when solution has progressed sufficiently to disclose a few values, the insertion of letters within the cells of the matrix to give the plaintext-ciphertext relationships indicated by the solved values immediately leads to the disclosure of additional values. Thus, the solution of only a few values soon leads to the breakdown of the entire matrix.

c. The following example will serve to illustrate the procedure.

(1) Let the message be as follows:

A. H F C A P   G O Q I L   B S P K M   N D U K E   O H Q N F   B O R U N

B. Q C L C H   Q B Q B F   H M A F X   S I O K O   Q Y F N S   X M C G Y

C. X I F B E   X A F D X   L P M X H   H R G K G   Q K Q M L   F E Q Q I

D. G O I H M   U E O R D   C L T U F   E Q Q C G   Q N H F X   I F B E X

E. F L B U Q   F C H Q O   Q M A F T   X S Y C B   E P F N B   S P K N U

F. Q I T X E   U Q M L F   E Q Q I G   O I E U E   H P I A N   Y T F L B

G. F E E P I   D H P C G   N Q I H B   F H M H F   X C K U P   D G Q P N

H. C B C Q L   Q P N F N   P N I T O   R T E N C   C B C N T   F H H A Y

J. Z L Q C I   A A I Q U   C H T P C   B I F G W   K F C Q S   L Q M C B

K. O Y C R Q   Q D P R X   F N Q M L   F I D G C   C G I O G   O I H H F

L. I R C G G   G N D L N   O Z T F G   E E R R P   I F H O T   F H H A Y

M. Z L Q C I   A A I Q U   C H T P

(2) The cipher having been tested for standard alphabets (by the method of completing the plain-component sequence) and found to give negative results, a uniliteral frequency distribution is made. It is as follows:

```
A   B   C   D   E   F   G   H   I   J   K   L   M   N   O   P   Q   R   S   T   U   V   W   X   Y   Z
11  15  26  8   16  30  17  23  23  0   8   14  11  18  15  16  33  9   6   11  11  0   1   12  7   3
```

(3) At first glance this may appear to the untrained eye to be a monoalphabetic frequency distribution, but upon closer inspection it is noted that, aside from the frequencies of four or five letters, the frequencies for the remaining letters are not very dissimilar. There are, in

147

reality, no very marked crests and troughs—certainly not as many as would be expected in a a monoalphabetic substitution cipher of equal length. The ϕ test, if taken (this test, as a rule, is not necessary with samples of text of sizes such as this), would show unsatisfactory results (ϕ_o=6082, as against ϕ_p=7870 and ϕ_r=4543).

(4) The message is carefully examined for repetitions of 4 or more letters, and all of them are listed:

	Frequency	Located in lines
TFHHAYZLQCIAAIQUCHTP (20 letters)	2	H and L.
QMLFEQQIGOI (11 letters).	2	C and F.
XIFBEX (6 letters).	2	C and D.
FEQQ.	3	C, D, F.
QMLF.	3	C, F, K.
BFHM.	2	B and G.
BSPK.	2	A and E.
GOIH.	2	D and K.

Since there are quite a few repetitions, two of considerable length, since all but one of them contain an even number of letters, since these repetitions with but two exceptions begin on odd letters and end on even letters, and since the message also contains an even number of letters (344), the cryptogram is retranscribed into 2-letter groups for further study. It is as follows:

				5					10					15
A	HF	CA	PG	OQ	IL	BS	PK	MN	DU	KE	OH	QN	FB	OR	UN
B	QC	LC	HQ	BQ	BF	HM	AF	XS	IO	KO	QY	FN	SX	MC	GY
C	XI	FB	EX	AF	DX	LP	MX	HH	RG	KG	QK	QM	LF	EQ	QI
D	GO	IH	MU	EO	RD	CL	TU	FE	QQ	CG	QN	HF	XI	FB	EX
E	FL	BU	QF	CH	QO	QM	AF	TX	SY	CB	EP	FN	BS	PK	NU
F	QI	TX	EU	QM	LF	EQ	QI	GO	IE	UE	HP	IA	NY	TF	LB
G	FE	EP	ID	HP	CG	NQ	IH	BF	HM	HF	XC	KU	PD	GQ	PN
H	CB	CQ	LQ	PN	FN	PN	IT	OR	TE	NC	CB	CN	TF	HH	AY
J	ZL	QC	IA	AI	QU	CH	TP	CB	IF	GW	KF	CQ	SL	QM	CB
K	OY	CR	QQ	DP	RX	FN	QM	LF	ID	GC	CG	IO	GO	IH	HF
L	IR	CG	GG	ND	LN	OZ	TF	GE	ER	RP	IF	HO	TF	HH	AY
M	ZL	QC	IA	AI	QU	CH	TP								

It is noted that all the repetitions listed above break up properly into digraphs except in one case, viz., FEQQ in lines C, D, and F. This latter seems rather strange, and at first thought one might suppose that a letter was dropped out or was added in the vicinity of the FEQQ in line D. But it may be assumed that the FE QQ in line D has no relation at all to the .F EQ Q. in lines C and F and is merely an accidental repetition.

(5) A digraphic distribution is made as follows:

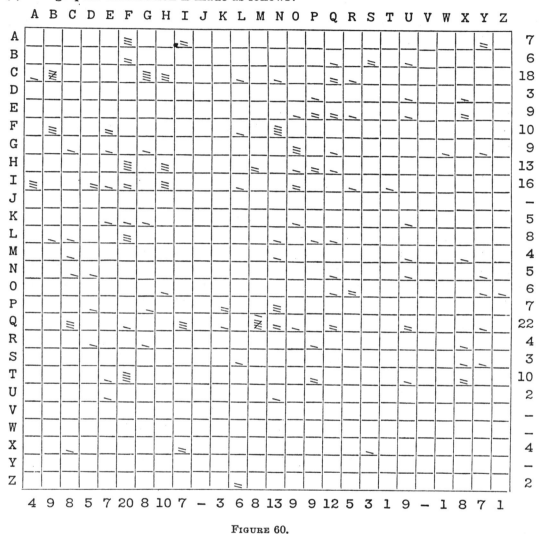

FIGURE 60.

(6) The appearance of the foregoing distribution for this message is quite characteristic of that for a digraphic substitution cipher   Although there are 676 possible digraphs, only 107 are present in the distribution; this parallels what is expected of normal plain text, since out of the 676 possible two-letter combinations (including "impossible plaintext digraphs" such as QQ, JK, etc., which *might* have been used for special indicators, punctuation marks, etc.) only about 300 are usually used in the construction of plain text.[19] The number of blank cells, 569, closely approximates the 566 which would be expected in a distribution made on a sample of plain text of this size, as shown by Chart 8. Furthermore, although there are many cases in

---

[19] The 300 most frequent digraphs comprise 95% of normal English plain text (Appendix 2, Table 7–A).

149

which a digraph appears only once, there are quite a few in which a digraph appears two or three times, four cases in which a digraph appears four times, one case in which a digraph appears five times, and one in which a digraph appears six times. All of the foregoing observations concerning the distribution are reflected by the ϕ test: the observed digraphic phi value, 210, compares very favorably with the expected plain value ($=.0069\times172\times171 = 203$) as against the expected random value ($=.0015\times172\times171=44$). Thus all indications point to a *digraphic* substitution system.

(7) Since neither the ϕ_o (1780) and Λ_o (4) for the initial letters of the cipher digraphs nor the ϕ_o (1496) and Λ_o (2) for the final letters are too satisfactory in their approximation to the values expected for monoalphabetic distributions ($\phi_p=1962$ and $\phi_r=1133$; $\Lambda_p=5$ and $\Lambda_r=0$), the possibility of a *pseudo*-digraphic system is ruled out for the time being. There remain the possibilities of a *partially*-digraphic system employing a small matrix, or a *true* digraphic system employing a large, randomized table. In one common type of small-matrix system, the Playfair cipher, one of the telltale indications besides the absence of (usually) the letter J is the absence of cipher doublets, that is, two successive identical cipher letters. The occurrence of the double letters GG, HH, and QQ in the message under investigation eliminates the possibility of its being a normal Playfair cipher. For want of more accurate diagnostic criteria [20] *at this stage*,[21] the simplest thing to assume, from among the various hypotheses that remain to be considered, is that a four-square matrix is involved. One with normal alphabets (as being the simplest case) in Sections 1 and 2 is therefore set down (Fig. 61*a*).

	A B C D E	
	F G H I K	
1	L M N O P	3
	Q R S T U	
	V W X Y Z	
		A B C D E
		F G H I K
4		L M N O P	2
		Q R S T U
		V W X Y Z

FIGURE 61*a*.

[20] Even a medical practitioner often cannot successfully diagnose a condition on the first visit. Cryptanalytically speaking, we are still on our "first visit". Subsequent probing will, we hope, reject or substantiate this or that hypothesis or assumption, until the patient (the cipher text) is recovered (i. e., brought back to plain text).

[21] However, see the treatment on the diagnosis of various types of digraphic systems in subpar. 73*j*.

(8) The recurrence of the group QMLF, three times, and at intervals suggesting that it might be a sentence separator, leads to the assumption that it represents the word STOP. The letters Q, M, L, and F are therefore inserted in the appropriate cells in Sections 3 and 4 of the diagram. Thus (Fig. 61*b*):

FIGURE 61*b*.

These placements seem rather good from the standpoint that keyword-mixed sequences may have been used in these two sections. Moreover, in Section 3 the number of cells between L and Q is just one less than enough to contain all the letters M to P, inclusive; this suggests that one of these letters, probably N or O, is in the keyword portion of the sequence; that is, near the top of Section 3. Without making a commitment in the matter, let us suppose that M follows L and that P precedes Q; then let both N and O, for the present, be inserted in the cell between M and P. Thus (Fig. 61*c*):

FIGURE 61*c*.

(9) Now, *if* the placement of P in Section 3 is correct, the cipher equivalent of $\overline{\text{TH}}_\text{p}$ will be $\overline{\text{P}\theta}_\text{o}$, and there should be a group of adequate frequency to correspond. Noting that $\overline{\text{PN}}_\text{o}$ occurs three times, it is assumed to represent $\overline{\text{TH}}_\text{p}$ and the letter N is inserted in the appropriate cell in Section 4. Thus (Fig. 61*d*):

	A	B	C	D	E		
	F	G	H	I	K		
1	L	M	N	O	P		L	3
	Q	R	S	T	U	M $\overset{N}{O}$ P Q	
	V	W	X	Y	Z		

FIGURE 61*d*.

(10) It is about time to try out these assumed values in the message. The proper insertions are made, with the following results:

					5					10					15
A	HF	CA	PG	OQ	IL	BS	PK	MN	DU	KE	OH	QN	FB	OR	UN
B	QC	LC	HQ	BQ	BF	HM	AF	XS	IO	KO	QY	FN	SX	MC	GY
C	XI	FB	EX	AF	DX	LP	MX	HH	RG	KG	QK	QM ST	LF OP	EQ	QI
D	GO	IH	MU	EO	RD	CL	TU	FE	QQ	CG	QN	HF	XI	FB	EX
E	FL	BU	QF	CH	QO	QM ST	AF	TX	SY	CB	EP	FN	BS	PK	NU
F	QI	TX	EU	QM ST	LF OP	EQ	QI	GO	IE	UE	HP	IA	NY	TF	LB
G	FE	EP	ID	HP	CG	NQ	IH	BF	HM	HF	XC	KU	PD	GQ	PN TH
H	CB	CQ	LQ	PN TH	FN	PN TH	IT	OR	TE	NC	CB	CN	TF	HH	AY
J	ZL	QC	IA	AI	QU	CH	TP	CB	IF	GW	KF	CQ	SL	QM ST	CB
K	OY	CR	QQ	DP	RX	FN	QM ST	LF OP	ID	GC	CG	IO	GO	IH	HF
L	IR	CG	GG	ND	LN	OZ	TF	GE	ER	RP	IF	HO	TF	HH	AY
M	ZL	QC	IA	AI	QU	CH	TP								

152

(11) So far no impossible combinations are in evidence. Beginning with group H4 in the message is seen the following sequence:

```
PN  FN  PN
TH  ..  TH
```

Assume it to be THAT THE. Then $\overline{AT}_p=\overline{FN}_e$, and the letter N is to be inserted in row 4 column 1 of Section 4. But this is inconsistent with previous assumptions, since N in Section 4 has already been tentatively placed in row 2 column 4. Other assumptions for $\overline{FN}_e$ are made: that it is $\overline{IS}_p$ (THIS TH. . .); that it is $\overline{EN}_p$ (THEN TH. . .); but the same inconsistency is apparent. In fact the student will see that $\overline{FN}_e$ must represent a digraph ending in F, G, H, I–J, or K, since N_e is tentatively located on the same line as these letters in Section 2. Now $\overline{FN}_e$ occurs 4 times in the message. The digraph it represents *must* be one of the following:

```
DF, DG, DH, DI, DJ, DK        OF, OG, OH, OI, OJ,
IF, IG, IH, II, IJ, IK        TK,
JF, JG, JH, JI, JJ, JK        YF, YG, YH, YI, YJ, YK
```

Of these the only one likely to be repeated 4 times is OF, yielding

```
PN FN PN
TH OF TH
```
which may be a part of

```
CQ LQ PN FN PN IT        CQ LQ PN FN PN IT
.N OR TH OF TH E.   or   .S OU TH OF TH E.
```

In either case, the position of the F in Section 3 is excellent: F . . . L in row 3. There are 3 cells intervening between F and L, into which G, H, I–J, and K may be inserted. It is not nearly so likely that G, H, and K are in the key word as that I should be in it. Let it be assumed that this is the case, and let the letters G, H, and K be placed in the appropriate cells in Section 3. Thus (Fig. 61*e*):

	A	B	C	D	E						
	F	G	H	I	K						
1	L	M	N	O	P	F	G	H	K	L	3
	Q	R	S	T	U	M	N/O	P	Q		
	V	W	X	Y	Z						
						A	B	C	D	E	
				N		F	G	H	I	K	
4				F		L	M	N	O	P	2
			M	Q		Q	R	S	T	U	
						V	W	X	Y	Z	

FIGURE 61*e*.

Let the resultant derived values be checked against the frequency distribution. If the position of H in Section 3 is correct, then the digraph $\overline{ON}_p$, normally of high frequency, should be represented several times by $\overline{HF}_c$. Reference to Fig. 60 shows $\overline{HF}_c$ to have a frequency of 4. And $\overline{HM}_c$, with 2 occurrences, represents $\overline{NS}_p$. There is no need to go through all the possible corroborations.

(12) Going back to the assumption that TH $\ldots$ TH is part of the expression

PN FN PN

$$
\begin{array}{llllll}
\text{CQ} & \text{LQ} & \text{PN} & \text{FN} & \text{PN} & \text{IT} \\
\text{.N} & \text{OR} & \text{TH} & \text{OF} & \text{TH} & \text{E.}
\end{array}
\quad \text{or} \quad
\begin{array}{llllll}
\text{CQ} & \text{LQ} & \text{PN} & \text{FN} & \text{PN} & \text{IT} \\
\text{.S} & \text{OU} & \text{TH} & \text{OF} & \text{TH} & \text{E.,}
\end{array}
$$

it is seen at once from Fig. 61e that the latter is apparently correct and not the former, because $\overline{LQ}_c$ equals $\overline{OU}_p$ and not $\overline{OR}_p$. If $\overline{OS}_p = \overline{CQ}_c$, this means that the letter C of the digraph $\overline{CQ}_c$, must be placed in row 1 column 3 or row 2 column 3 of Section 3. Now the digraph $\overline{CB}_c$ occurs 5 times; $\overline{CG}_c$, 4 times; $\overline{CH}_c$, 3 times; $\overline{CQ}_c$, 2 times. Let an attempt be made to deduce the exact position of C in Section 3 and the positions of B, G, and H in Section 4. Since F is already placed in Section 4, assume G and H directly follow it, and that B comes before it. How much before? Suppose a trial be made. Thus (Fig. 61f):

Figure 61f.

By referring now to the frequency distribution, Fig. 60, after a very few minutes of experimentation it becomes apparent that the following is correct:

Figure 61g.

(13) The identifications given by these placements are inserted in the text, and solution is very rapidly completed. The final matrix and deciphered text are given below.

$$
\begin{array}{c|ccccc|ccccc|c}
 & A & B & C & D & E & S & O & C & I & E & \\
 & F & G & H & I & K & T & Y & A & B & D & \\
1 & L & M & N & O & P & F & G & H & K & L & 3 \\
 & Q & R & S & T & U & M & N & P & Q & R & \\
 & V & W & X & Y & Z & U & V & W & X & Z & \\
\hline
 & E & X & P & U & L & A & B & C & D & E & \\
 & S & I & O & N & A & F & G & H & I & K & \\
4 & B & C & D & F & G & L & M & N & O & P & 2 \\
 & H & K & M & Q & R & Q & R & S & T & U & \\
 & T & V & W & Y & Z & V & W & X & Y & Z & \\
\end{array}
$$

FIGURE 61h.

		5						10						15	
A	HF ON	CA EH	PG UN	OQ DR	IL ED	BS FI	PK RS	MN TF	DU IE	KE LD	OH AR	QN TI	FB LL	OR ER	UN YF
B	QC RO	LC MP	HQ OS	BQ IT	BF IO	HM NS	AF IN	XS VI	IO CI	KO NI	QY TY	FN OF	SX BA	MC RL	GY OW
C	XI WI	FB LL	EX BE	AF IN	DX GE	LP NE	MX RA	HH LS	RG UP	KG PO	QK RT	QM ST	LF OP	EQ DU	QI RI
D	GO NG	IH AT	MU TA	EO CK	RD SP	CL EC	TU IA	FE LA	QQ TT	CG EN	QN TI	HF ON	XI WI	FB LL	EX BE
E	FL PA	BU ID	QF TO	CH AS	QO SI	QM ST	AF IN	TX GA	SY DV	CB AN	EP CE	FN OF	BS FI	PK RS	NU TB
F	QI RI	TX GA	EU DE	QM ST	LF OP	EQ DU	QI RI	GO NG	IE AD	UE VA	HP NC	IA EI	NY TW	TF IL	LB LP
G	FE LA	EP CE	ID CO	HP NC	CG EN	NQ TR	IH AT	BF IO	HM NS	HF ON	XC WO	KU OD	PD SN	GQ OR	PN TH
H	CB AN	CQ DS	LQ OU	PN TH	FN OF	PN TH	IT AY	OR ER	TE FA	NC RM	CB AN	CN DH	TF IL	HH LS	AY IX
J	ZL ZE	QC RO	IA EI	AI GH	QU TD	CH AS	TP HA	CB AN	IF DO	GW NW	KF OO	CQ DS	SL EA	QM ST	CB AN
K	OY DW	CR ES	QQ TT	DP HE	RX RE	FN OF	QM ST	LF OP	ID CO	GC MM	CG EN	IO CI	GO NG	IH AT	HF ON
L	IR ET	CG EN	GG PM	ND SM	LN OK	OZ EW	TF IL	GE LB	ER EU	RP SE	IF DO	HO NH	TF IL	HH LS	AY IX
M	ZL ZE	QC RO	IA EI	AI GH	QU TD	CH AS	TP HA								

155

d. In the solution of four-square cryptograms, advantage may be taken not only of the general type of digraphic idiomorphs mentioned in subpar. 68*e*, above, but also of a special type of *partial* idiomorphism present in any four-square cryptograms involving the use of a matrix in which the *plain components consist of normal alphabets* normally inscribed.[22] As an illustration, let the digraphs $\overline{SO}$ $\overline{UT}$ (H.) be enciphered by means of any four-square having normal alphabets in Sections 1 and 2, and it will be found that *in the encipherment* the initial letter of the cipher digraph representing $\overline{SO}_p$ will be identical to the initial letter of the cipher digraph representing $\overline{UT}_p$, regardless of how the cipher components are constructed. On this basis, a brief list of *specialized single-letter patterns* have been compiled for use in the solution of such a digraphic system; this list of "four-square digraphic idiomorphs" constitutes Section F of Appendix 3.

e. It is interesting to note how much simpler the technique of analysis is in the case of so-called *inverse four-square* ciphers, which involve the use of a matrix wherein the *ciphertext* sections contain normal alphabets, the plain components being mixed. For example, referring to Fig. 53, suppose that Sections 3 and 4 are used as the source of the plaintext pairs, and Sections 1 and 2 as the source of the ciphertext pairs; then $ON_p = ET_c$, $EH_p = GE_c$, etc. The simplicity of the analytic procedure will be made clear by the following exposition.

(1) To solve a message enciphered with an inverse four-square matrix, it is necessary to perform two steps. First, convert the ciphertext pairs into their plain-component equivalents by "deciphering" the message with a matrix in which all four sections contain normal alphabets; this operation yields two uniliteral substitution "ciphers", one composed of the odd letters, the other of the even letters. The second step is to solve these two monoalphabetic portions.

(2) As an example, let us consider the following cipher text, known (or assumed) to have been encrypted with a trinome-digraphic [23] system incorporating a four-square matrix similar to that illustrated in Fig. 58, except that the plain-component sections have been changed:

```
2 0 3 2 3    8 5 0 8 1    8 3 4 5 0    2 7 9 3 4    1 1 5 0 3    0 9 1 6 8
2 7 8 3 5    4 1 8 0 4    5 0 4 1 3    2 7 4 1 6    3 3 0 9 1    0 1 0 9 2
2 0 8 0 5    7 4 1 3 5    3 5 4 7 3    3 2 6 2 6    9 1 1 6 0    0 3 2 1 8
4 6 8 1 8    3 3 9 3 0    9 1 3 9 3    4 1 1 0 4    4 1 3 3 1    1 7 2 9 6
2 4 3 0 2    8 3 8 3 2    2 8 3 5 9    3 8 0 2 2    6 1 0 4 3    6 9 1 3 0
1 5 3 1 3    6 1 0 4 1    0 0 1 4 4    1 0 1 0 1    8 2 4 0 3    3 6 1 6 8
4 6 5 3 6    6 2 6 6 3    4 4 0 0 7    1 8 3 4 5    0 1 4 0 2    8 8 1 5 2
4 7 8 2 1    7 3 9 3 3    8 1 1 9 3    4 7 9 2 4    0 4 0 3 2    4 1 3 0 6
0 8 7 0 3    7 0 9 1 4    1 9 3 9 1    1 1 6 0 7    7 1 3 7 1    5 3 5 9 5
0 0 7 4 1    3 3 3 8 1    3 3 5 9 3    3 9 3 4 0    6 3 5 3 1    8 8 1 3 3
```

---

[22] If any other *known* plain components were involved, the procedure of deriving a list of idiomorphic patterns would be modified to fit the particular case.

[23] If the cipher text were being examined "from cryptanalytic scratch", the limitations (003–595) of the cipher text when the latter is divided into trinomes for examination would have at once indicated that this grouping is the one which merits detailed analysis. The digraphic ϕ test would then give an indication of the digraphic nature of the cryptographic treatment.

(3) The first thing to be done is to construct a four-square matrix with the known cipher-text sections, and inscribe arbitrary alphabets in the plaintext sections, as follows:

A	B	C	D	E	000	025	050	075	100
F	G	H	I	K	125	150	175	200	225
L	M	N	O	P	250	275	300	325	350
Q	R	S	T	U	375	400	425	450	475
V	W	X	Y	Z	500	525	550	575	600
Ø	1	2	3	4	A	B	C	D	E
5	6	7	8	9	F	G	H	I	K
10	11	12	13	14	L	M	N	O	P
15	16	17	18	19	Q	R	S	T	U
20	21	22	23	24	V	W	X	Y	Z

(4) The cipher text is then written in trinomes, and these trinomes are "deciphered" by means of the foregoing matrix, yielding the converted cipher text as follows:

				5					10					15	
A	203	238	508	183	450	279	341	150	309	168	278	354	180	450	413
	ID	IP	YF	IH	QD	PB	MT	FB	PH	IR	OB	PE	FH	QD	TM
B	274	163	309	101	092	208	057	413	535	473	326	269	116	003	218
	PV	IM	PH	BE	CT	II	CH	TM	VM	TY	MD	PQ	BU	DA	IT
C	468	183	393	091	393	411	044	133	117	296	243	028	383	228	359
	TT	IH	TQ	BT	TQ	RM	ER	IF	CU	MW	IU	DB	TF	IE	PK
D	380	226	104	369	130	153	136	104	100	144	101	018	240	336	168
	QF	GE	EE	PU	FF	IB	GL	EE	AE	KQ	BE	DQ	FU	MO	IR
E	465	366	266	344	007	183	450	140	288	152	478	217	393	381	193
	QT	MU	MQ	PT	CF	IH	QD	FQ	OM	HB	TE	HT	TQ	RF	IS
F	479	240	403	241	306	087	037	091	419	391	116	077	137	153	595
	UE	FU	TB	GU	MH	CO	CM	BT	UR	RQ	BU	CD	HL	IB	VY
G	007	413	338	133	593	393	406	353	188	133					
	CF	TM	OO	IF	YT	TQ	RG	OE	IN	IF					

157

The distributions of the letters constituting the initial letters and final letters of the converted digraphs are as follows:

(Initial Letters) A B C D E F G H I K L M N O P Q R S T U V W X Y Z

(Final Letters) A B C D E F G H I K L M N O P Q R S T U V W X Y Z

(5) Using straightforward principles of frequency and partial idiomorphs,[24] the plain text (beginning with the opening words ENEMY RECONNAISSANCE...) is recovered, and the following equivalents are obtained for the converted cipher letters of the two alphabets:

(Initial Letters)   C: A B C D E F G H I K L M N O P Q R S T U V W X Y Z
                    P: B R A H M S C D E F   I   L N O P   T U V   Y

(Final Letters)   C: A B C D E F G H I K L M N O P Q R S T U V W X Y Z
                    P: W A   N E R B C D F H I K L M O P Q S T U V   Y

Keyword-mixed sequences directly manifest themselves because the original enciphering matrix contained such sequences in Sections 1 and 2, inscribed in the same manner as were the arbitrary A–Z sequences which were used for the conversion. In fact, the key words of the two distributions might have been recovered from an analysis of the "profiles" of the distributions above, as described in subpar. 54e.

(6) The original enciphering matrix is then reconstructed, thus:

B	R	A	H	M	000	025	050	075	100
S	C	D	E	F	125	150	175	200	225
G	I	K	L	N	250	275	300	325	350
O	P	Q	T	U	375	400	425	450	475
V	W	X	Y	Z	500	525	550	575	600
Ø	1	2	3	4	W	A	G	N	E
5	6	7	8	9	R	B	C	D	F
10	11	12	13	14	H	I	K	L	M
15	16	17	18	19	O	P	Q	S	T
20	21	22	23	24	U	V	X	Y	Z

[24] Note the ABA pattern of the first word in the message (ENEMY), made patent by the two-alphabet conversion process. Also note the 3-fold repetition (representing the plaintext word STOP) which, although hidden in the original cipher text, now comes to light.

(7) Although the example illustrated was that of a numerical digraphic system, it is obvious that this technique of solution also applies to *literal* four-square systems in which the cipher components are known sequences. It should be clear to the student the tremendous difference it makes when it is possible to convert a *digraphic* system into a *two-alphabet* system; in a digraphic system, we are plagued by a potential 676 different elements in the cipher, whereas in a two-alphabet system we still have only 26 elements (in each of two sets, it is true) in the cipher text to be solved. This principle of conversion of cipher text into a secondary cipher text has application in some of the most complex types of cryptosystems; the student would do well to keep this in mind.

(8) As a further observation on inverse four-square systems, it is pointed out that where the *same* mixed alphabet is present in the two plaintext sections, the problem is still easier, since the letters resulting from the conversion into plain-component equivalents all belong to the same, *single* mixed alphabet; thus such a digraphic system is reduced to an ordinary simple substitution cipher.

f. The solution of cryptograms enciphered by other types of small matrices is accomplished along lines very similar to those set forth in subpar. *c* on the solution of a four-square cipher; this will be illustrated in subsequent paragraphs. There are, unfortunately, few means or tests which can be applied to determine in the early stages of the analysis *exactly* what type of digraphic system is involved in the first case under study. The author freely admits that the solution outlined in subpar. *c* is quite artificial in that nothing is demonstrated in step (7) that obviously leads to or warrants the assumption that a four-square matrix is involved. The point was passed over with the quite bald statement that this was "from among the various hypotheses that remain to be considered"—and then the solution proceeded exactly as though this mere hypothesis had been definitely established. For example, the very first results obtained were based upon our assuming that a certain 4-letter repetition represented the word STOP and *immediately inserting certain letters in appropriate cells in a four-square matrix with normal sequences in Sections 1 and 2.* Several more assumptions were built on top of that, and very rapid strides were made. What if it had not been a four-square matrix at all? What if it had been some other type of not readily identifiable digraphic system? The only defense that can be made of what may seem to the student to be purely arbitrary procedure based upon the author's advance information or knowledge is the following: In the first place, in order to avoid making the explanation a too-long-drawn-out affair, it is necessary (and pedagogical experience warrants) that certain alternative hypotheses be passed over in silence. In the second place it may now be added, *after* the principles and procedure have been elucidated (which at this stage is the primary object of this text), that if good results do not follow from a first hypothesis, the only thing the cryptanalyst can do is to reject that hypothesis and formulate a second hypothesis. In actual practice he may have to reject a second, third, fourth, . . . *n*th hypothesis. In the end he may strike the right one—or he may not. There is no assurance of success in the matter. In the third place, one of the objects of this text is to show how certain cryptosystems, if employed for military purposes, can readily be broken down. Assuming that some type of digraphic system is in use, and that daily changes in key words are made, it is possible that the traffic of the first day might give considerable difficulty in solution if the *specific* type of digraphic system were not known to the cryptanalyst. But by the time two or three days' traffic had accumulated it would be easy to solve, because probably by that time the cryptanalytic personnel would have successfully analyzed the cryptosystem and thus learned what type of matrix or table the enemy is using.

70. Analysis of two-square matrix systems.—*a.* Cryptosystems involving either vertical two-square or horizontal two-square matrices may be identified as such and solved by capitalizing on the cryptographic peculiarities and idiosyncracies of these systems. It will be noted that, considering the mechanics of the cryptosystems, in vertical two-square matrices employing the normal enciphering conventions,[25] exactly 20% of the 625 "possible" plaintext digraphs will be "transparent" (i. e., self-enciphered) in cipher text; in horizontal two-square systems, exactly 20% of the 625 digraphs will be characterized by an "inverse transparency" (i. e., enciphered by the same digraphs reversed).[26] Therefore, if an examination of a cryptogram or a set of cryptograms discloses a goodly portion of what appear to be *direct* transparencies (cipher digraphs which could well be plaintext digraphs), it may then be assumed that a *vertical* two-square matrix has been used for the encryption. On the other hand, if a large number of cipher digraphs could be "good" plaintext digraphs when the positions of the letters were *reversed*, then it may be assumed that the cryptosystem involved a *horizontal* two-square matrix. Sometimes skeletons of words or even of whole phrases are self-evident in such cipher text, thus affording an easy entering wedge into the cryptosystem.

b. An example will best serve to illustrate the techniques of identification and subsequent solution of a two-square matrix cipher. The following naval message is to be studied:

```
U O D L C    E N O A N    S I G L B    B E I R I    R C R G L    N M M L C
P T E R G    R B B O E    G P A B Q    W N N K S    I P C R M    M O R A P
D E A M H    A N X R A    I E D A I    R M A G B    E K H S L    C D D L C
T Q O R E    N D T M D    T I A Q F    I E Q T A    N N B F N    O U O O S
S N N N R    K T A S E    S N H L P    O N N K S    I P C R C    E N O I S
H L I R K    P L O N O    N Z U C T    A L T O I    I H O C N    O C E R A
O S D I N    O E E K R    L C U B R    A O S D I    I P D A R    C O G G R
O L N O C    W D I L P    O I L N Q    X D I G L    R B B Q Y    F S S R A
V Y O I G    R S L X X
```

Preliminary steps in analysis are made according to the procedures already described in this text, and the hypothesis of monographic, uniliteral encipherment (with either standard or

---

[25] That is, for vertical two-square systems, digraphs are self-enciphered if θ_p^1 and θ_p^2 fall in the same column in the matrix; and, for horizontal two-square systems, if θ_p^1 and θ_p^2 are in the same row, the ciphertext digraphs are the *reversed* plaintext digraphs.

[26] Although 625 "possible" plaintext digraphs are involved, the identity of digraphs actually used in plain text limit this figure considerably. Furthermore, the *frequencies* of the plaintext digraphs actually used come into consideration, in conjunction with the location of the letters of these digraphs in any particular two-square matrix. Thus, from the cryptanalyst's standpoint, there are "excellent" two-square matrices giving a high self-encipherment rate for high-frequency plaintext digraphs, and there are "poor" two-square matrices which have a potentially high self-encipherment rate only for those low-frequency plaintext digraphs which may not occur at all in a given cryptogram.

mixed cipher alphabets) is rejected. Multiliteral substitution, or digraphic substitution, comes next into consideration. The cipher text is written in digraphs, as follows:

			5							10					15
A	UO	DL	CE	NO	AN	SI	GL	BB	EI	RI	RC	RG	LN	MM	LC
B	PT	ER	GR	BB	OE	GP	AB	QW	NN	KS	IP	CR	MM	OR	AP
C	DE	AM	HA	NX	RA	IE	DA	IR	MA	GB	EK	HS	LC	DD	LC
D	TQ	OR	EN	DT	MD	TI	AQ	FI	EQ	TA	NN	BF	NO	UO	OS
E	SN	NN	RK	TA	SE	SN	HL	PO	NN	KS	IP	CR	CE	NO	IS
F	HL	IR	KP	LO	NO	NZ	UC	TA	LT	OI	IH	OC	NO	CE	RA
G	OS	DI	NO	EE	KR	LC	UB	RA	OS	DI	IP	DA	RC	OG	GR
H	OL	NO	CW	DI	LP	OI	LN	QX	DI	GL	RB	BQ	YF	SS	RA
J	VY	OI	GR	SL	XX										

FIGURE 62.

Noting the 8-letter repetition 90 letters apart, the 6-letter repetition 16 letters apart, and the 4-letter repetition at an interval of 220 letters, and that those repetitions begin on odd letters and end on even letters, credence is given to the grouping of the cipher text into pairs of letters. A digraphic distribution is then made, illustrated in Fig. 63.

c. The $_2\phi_o$, 152, is most satisfactory when compared with $_2\phi_p$ (107) and $_2\phi_r$ (23). Since the cryptogram has all the earmarks of a digraphic cipher, and no manifestations are found to support the hypothesis of a multiliteral system, the next problem is the specific determination of the particular kind of digraphic system involved. It may be noted that there are quite a few digraphs in the cipher text which resemble good plaintext digraphs, proportionally more so than, for instance, in the cryptogram in subpar. 69c; the cryptologic finger points to the possibility of a two-square system. However, since the words "good digraphs" are semantically elusive, let us attempt to determine statistically whether or not a two-square system might be involved and, if a two-square, whether it is more probably a vertical or a horizontal two-square.[27]

[27] The test to be described in the following subparagraphs is based on an evaluation of those instances wherein the observed frequency of any particular ciphertext digraph approximates the frequency with which the particular digraph, or its reversal, would be expected to occur if considered as a plaintext digraph. Any such correlation which occurs in a four-square or Playfair cipher, or in a cryptogram produced by a large randomized digraphic table, is purely accidental because it is not a result of the mechanics of the system. However, in two-square cryptograms such correlation *is* caused by the mechanics of the system in the encipherment of 20% of the possible plaintext digraphs, and these causal instances of correlation occur *in addition* to any accidental instances which may arise in the encipherment of the remaining 80%. Thus, if a digraphic cipher exhibits *merely the random* expectation of correlation both when the particular ciphertext digraphs are considered as they are *and* when their reversals are considered, the cryptogram may be assumed to involve a system other than two-square. If a digraphic cipher exhibits more than the random expectation of correlation, either when the particular digraphs are considered direct or when considered reversed, it may be assumed to involve two-square encipherment; and the particular consideration—that of the digraphs direct or that of the digraphs reversed—which gives rise to the greater degree of correlation indicates whether the cryptogram involves a vertical two-square or a horizontal two-square, respectively.

161

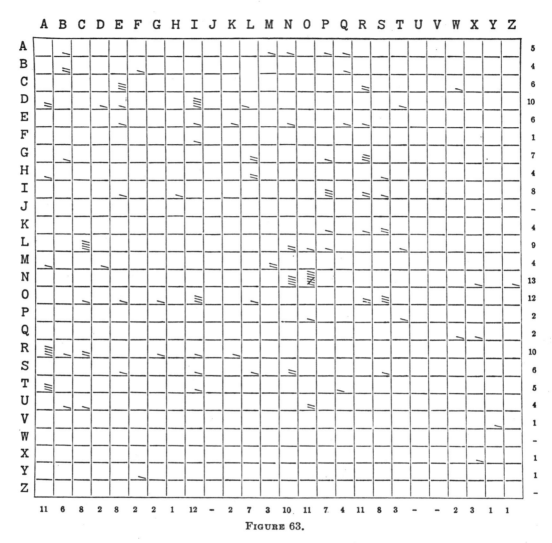

FIGURE 63.

d. First, for the purpose of determining whether "direct transparencies" or "inverse transparencies" predominate in this cryptogram, the digraphs of the distribution in Fig. 63 will be set down in tabular form, with an indication of their frequency in the cryptogram, and with data relative to the probability of these digraphs as *plaintext digraphs*, and as plaintext digraphs when *reversed*. In the table on p. 163, col. (1) is a listing of the ciphertext digraphs; col. (2) is the frequency of the ciphertext digraph as it occurs in the cryptogram; col. (3) is the logarithm of the theoretical *plaintext* frequency of the particular digraph (from Table 15, Appendix 2); col. (4) represents the products of the entries in cols. (2) and (3); col. (5) is the logarithm of the theoretical plaintext frequency of the *reversed* digraph (from Table 15, Appendix 2); and col. (6) represents the products of the entries in cols. (2) and (5). From this, the sum of the values in col. (4), 58.42, is taken to be the "direct transparency" value, and the sum of the values in col. (6), 62.76, is taken to be the "inverse transparency" value. Thus, since this particular cryptogram

162

has an "inverse transparency" value which is higher than the "direct transparency" value, it may be assumed [28] to involve a *horizontal* two-square—if, indeed, two-square encipherment has been employed. It is now for us to establish whether or not this latter *is* the case, and this will be done by determining whether or not the foregoing observed value, 62.76, is representative of the degree of transparency which may be expected in a horizontal two-square cipher. (If the "*direct* transparency" value had been the higher of the two, then it would have been more probable that a *vertical* two-square were involved, and it would be necessary to determine whether or not *this* observed value was representative of the degree of transparency expected in a *vertical* two-square cipher.)

(1)	(2)	(3)	(4)	(5)	(6)	(1)	(2)	(3)	(4)	(5)	(6)	(1)	(2)	(3)	(4)	(5)	(6)
AB	1	.45	0.45	.38	0.38	HA	1	.67	0.67	.25	0.25	OR	2	.89	1.78	.74	1.48
AM	1	.61	0.61	.78	0.78	HL	2	.13	0.26	.13	0.26	OS	3	.61	1.83	.62	1.86
AN	1	.89	0.89	.72	0.72	HS	1	.38	0.38	.72	0.72	PO	1	.64	0.64	.72	0.72
AP	1	.58	0.58	.61	0.61	IE	1	.59	0.59	.73	0.73	PT	1	.51	0.51	.25	0.25
AQ	1	.00	0.00	.00	0.00	IH	1	.00	0.00	.77	0.77	QW	1	.00	0.00	.00	0.00
BB	2	.00	0.00	.00	0.00	IP	3	.48	1.44	.45	1.35	QX	1	.00	0.00	.00	0.00
BF	1	.00	0.00	.00	0.00	IR	2	.73	1.46	.75	1.50	RA	4	.80	3.20	.82	3.28
BQ	1	.00	0.00	.00	0.00	IS	1	.78	0.78	.77	0.77	RB	1	.25	0.25	.25	0.25
CE	3	.76	2.28	.76	2.28	KP	1	.00	0.00	.00	0.00	RC	2	.53	1.06	.38	0.76
CR	2	.38	0.76	.53	1.06	KR	1	.00	0.00	.13	0.13	RG	1	.48	0.48	.42	0.42
CW	1	.13	0.13	.00	0.00	KS	2	.13	0.26	.13	0.26	RI	1	.75	0.75	.73	0.73
DA	2	.76	1.52	.73	1.46	LC	4	.33	1.32	.42	1.68	RK	1	.13	0.13	.00	0.00
DD	1	.51	0.51	.51	0.51	LN	2	.13	0.26	.42	0.84	SE	1	.84	0.84	.86	0.86
DE	1	.77	0.77	.88	0.88	LO	1	.59	0.59	.67	0.67	SI	1	.77	0.77	.78	0.78
DI	4	.73	2.92	.45	1.80	LP	1	.33	0.33	.59	0.59	SL	1	.25	0.25	.45	0.45
DL	1	.33	0.33	.53	0.53	LT	1	.51	0.51	.42	0.42	SN	2	.38	0.76	.71	1.42
DT	1	.62	0.62	.45	0.45	MA	1	.78	0.78	.61	0.61	SS	1	.67	0.67	.67	0.67
EE	1	.81	0.81	.81	0.81	MD	1	.13	0.13	.42	0.42	TA	3	.74	2.22	.83	2.49
EI	1	.73	0.73	.59	0.59	MM	2	.59	1.18	.59	1.18	TI	1	.82	0.82	.73	0.73
EK	1	.00	0.00	.45	0.45	NN	4	.51	2.04	.51	2.04	TQ	1	.13	0.13	.00	0.00
EN	1	.99	0.99	.87	0.87	NO	7	.66	4.62	.92	5.74	UB	1	.33	0.33	.25	0.25
EQ	1	.58	0.58	.00	0.00	NX	1	.00	0.00	.13	0.13	UC	1	.33	0.33	.38	0.38
ER	1	.94	0.94	.96	0.96	NZ	1	.00	0.00	.00	0.00	UO	2	.13	0.26	.79	1.58
FI	1	.80	0.80	.55	0.55	OC	1	.51	0.51	.80	0.80	VY	1	.00	0.00	.00	0.00
GB	1	.00	0.00	.00	0.00	OE	1	.33	0.33	.58	0.58	XX	1	.00	0.00	.00	0.00
GL	2	.25	0.50	.13	0.26	OG	1	.25	0.25	.45	0.45	YF	1	.56	0.56	.13	0.13
GP	1	.25	0.25	.00	0.00	OI	3	.42	1.26	.80	2.40		125		58.42		62.76
GR	3	.42	1.26	.48	1.44	OL	1	.67	0.67	.59	0.59						

(1) Identity of cipher digraph appearing in the cryptogram.
(2) Frequency of the particular digraph as it occurs in the cryptogram.
(3) Logarithm of theoretical *plaintext* frequency of the particular digraph (from Table 15, Appendix 2).
(4) Product of entries in columns (2) and (3).
(5) Logarithm of theoretical *plaintext* frequency of the digraph's *reversal* (from Table 15, Appendix 2).
(6) Product of entries in columns (2) and (5).

---

[28] The difference between the higher inverse transparency value and the direct value is indicative of the degree of probability of the horizontal hypothesis over the vertical hypothesis. In this case, the difference of 4.34 (i. e., 62.76 − 58.42) represents a difference of *log scores*; but since the cipher text is expected to contain 20% plaintext digraphs (or their reversals) "diluted" with 80% random digraphs, it can be proved mathematically that the correct allowance to compensate for this is to divide the log score by 5—that is, $\frac{4.34}{5}$ or 0.87. This adjusted value is then employed as an exponent of the log base (224); the number produced, 110 (i. e., $224^{0.87}$), is the factor in favor of the hypothesis of a horizontal two-square. Statistical interpretation of scoring techniques will be treated in detail in *Military Cryptanalytics, Part III.*

163

e. The observed "inverse transparency" value (selected in this case because it is the higher observed value) will be compared with the value *expected* from a horizontal two-square cryptogram of the same size, and if this observed value is *as great as or greater than* the transparency value expected for horizontal two-squares, the cryptogram may be considered to be a horizontal two-square cipher; if the observed value is lower than the expected two-square value, decision will have to be suspended.[29] The transparency value expected in a horizontal two-square cipher containing N digraphs is computed by multiplying N by .3388, which in this case yields 42.35 (=.3388×125).[30] The observed value for the cryptogram, 62.76, is much higher than the expected value, 42.35. Thus, it has been proven statistically that the cryptogram at hand involves two-square encipherment, particularly, *horizontal* two-square encipherment.

f. Having now proved that the cryptogram at hand is a horizontal two-square cipher, the next step is to assume some plain text in the message, guided by probable inverse transparencies (*inverse* because the system has been identified as a horizontal two-square) in the cipher text. Referring to the work sheet in Fig. 62, the repeated sequence at B9 and E9 is assumed to represent the plain text TA SK FO RC (E–), on the basis of $\overline{KS}_c = \overline{SK}_p$, and $\overline{CR}_c = \overline{RC}_p$. The plaintext-ciphertext

---

[29] For the benefit of the student with a background in statistics, it is pointed out that by abiding by the stipulation "as great or greater", some cryptograms which actually *are* the result of two-square encipherment may be rejected by this stipulation, but it will insure that only a relatively few non-two-square cryptograms will be accepted. A better approach of a statistical nature would involve, first, computing the expected value for non-two-squares as well as that for two-squares. Then, any observed value falling below the expected two-square value could be expressed in terms of the number of standard deviations (i. e., the sigmage) from this expected two-square value and from the expected *non*-two-square value. Finally, the particular expected value which would be considered as significant would be the one from which the observed value differed by the smaller number of standard deviations. The concept of standard deviation will be treated in *Military Cryptanalytics, Part III.*

[30] In the case of *vertical* two-squares, N would be multiplied by the constant .3610. The mathematical considerations underlying this test and their proofs (involving Bayes' theorem and Bayes' factors) are beyond the scope of this text; however, for the benefit of the mathematician, the derivation of the foregoing constants is explained below, along with the derivation of the constant used for computing the expected transparency value for *non*-two-squares. In the formulas, below,

$$\sum_{AB} = \text{the summation over all digraphs AA—ZZ}$$

F_{AB} = the frequency of a given digraph AB as found in Table 6A, Appendix 2

α_{AB} = the logarithm (to the base 224) of the frequency of a given digraph AB as found in Table 15, Appendix 2

For vertical two-squares,

$$k = \sum_{AB} \alpha_{AB} \left[.80(.0015) + \frac{.20\,F_{AB}}{5000} \right] = .3610$$

For horizontal two-squares,

$$k = \sum_{AB} \alpha_{BA} \left[.80(.0015) + \frac{.20\,F_{AB}}{5000} \right] = .3388$$

For *non*-two square digraphic systems,

$$k = \frac{\alpha_{AB}}{676} = .2737$$

values are now recorded [31] in a skeleton reconstruction diagram as illustrated in Fig. 64a. At A3, the assumption of (–R) EC ON NA IS SA NC (E–) is tossed off without much ado, since four of the six diagraphs concerned are transparent. The plain-cipher relationships from this assumption are added to the reconstruction diagram, as shown in Fig. 64b. Continuing in this vein, the plain text (–A) IR CR AF (T–) is inserted at A1Ø, and the plain text (–B) AT TL

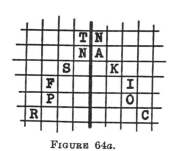

FIGURE 64a.

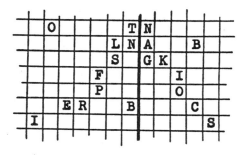

FIGURE 64b.

ES HI (P–) is inserted at F8; the successive cumulative reconstruction diagrams for these two assumptions are shown in Figs. 64c and d below. It is to be noted that at F12, $\overline{OC}_c = \overline{P\theta}_p$; but

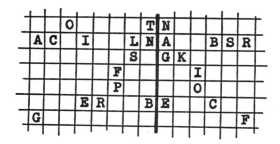

FIGURE 64c.

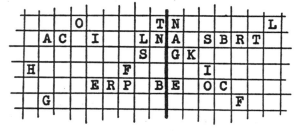

FIGURE 64d.

since in Fig. 64d it has already been determined that $\overline{OC}_c = \overline{\theta S}_p$, then $\overline{OC}_c$ must equal $\overline{PS}_p$, making the word BATTLESHIP$\underline{S}$ rather than BATTLESHIP.

---

[31] During the reconstruction of the squares of the matrix, the student should keep clear in his skeleton diagram which letters are in the same row, and which are in the same column. It will be found expeditious to draw a dividing line (either horizontal or vertical, depending on the type of two-square matrix involved) on the page to keep the elements of the two squares independent, recording the values which are in the same row or column and writing down the letters as they are assumed. In the early stages of this process the student must exercise care in recording the letters so that no false relationships are formed; in other words, the values should be written down so that they are not in the same row or column with any letters other than those with which they are known to be related. This will entail spreading the work rather widely over the page initially, then gradually telescoping and reducing the size of the reconstruction diagram as the work progresses, until in the end it will be reduced to a concise matrix of two 5 x 5 squares.

g. At this point the partially filled-in work sheet will look as follows:

	1	2	3	4	5	6	7	8	9	10	11	12	13	14	15
A	UO	DL	CE	NO	AN	SI	GL	BB	EI	RI	RC	RG	LN	MM	LC
		-R	EC	ON	NA	IS	SA	NC	EA	IR	CR	AF	T-	E-	
B	PT	ER	GR	BB	OE	GP	AB	QW	NN	KS	IP	CR	MM	OR	AP
		RE	-E	NC	EO	-E	NE		TA	SK	FO	RC	E-	RO	-E
C	DE	AM	HA	NX	RA	IE	DA	IR	MA	GB	EK	HS	LC	DD	LC
					AR	-O		-O		-E					
D	TQ	OR	EN	DT	MD	TI	AQ	FI	EQ	TA	NN	BF	NO	UO	OS
		RO	BA			IT		-R		AT	TA		ON		
E	SN	NN	RK	TA	SE	SN	HL	PO	NN	KS	IP	CR	CE	NO	IS
	NS	TA		AT	IO	NS			TA	SK	FO	RC	EC	ON	
F	HL	IR	KP	LO	NO	NZ	UC	TA	LT	OI	IH	OC	NO	CE	RA
		-O		OL	ON		-B	AT	TL	ES	HI	PS	ON	EC	AR →
G	← OS	DI	NO	EE	KR	LC	UB	RA	OS	DI	IP	DA	RC	OG	GR
			ON	EE				AR			FO		CR		-E
H	OL	NO	CW	DI	LP	OI	LN	QX	DI	GL	RB	BQ	YF	SS	RA
	-S	ON				ES	T-			SA	N-			L-	AR
J	VY	OI	GR	SL	XX										
		ES	-E	LS											

Skeletons of additional plain text, such as the word OUR at A1, PRESENCE OF ENEMY at B1, PROBABLE at D1, ATTACK ON OUR INSTALLATIONS at D10, CARRIER at F14, and VESSELS at J1, may now clearly be seen. The complete recovery of the plain text follows, and the reconstruction diagram is completed and telescoped into the form shown in Fig. 64e. Since phenomena of keyword-mixed sequences are observed, the rows and columns of Fig. 64e are permuted to yield the original two-square matrix as shown in Fig. 64f.

```
Q M O K T | N - Q L P
A I C L N | A B S R T
G D F S H | G K I F H
U E P R B | E C O D M
Y - X V - | W Z Y - X
```
FIGURE 64e.

```
R E P U B | D E M O C
L I C A N | R A T S B
S D F G H | F G H I K
K M O Q T | L N P Q U
V W X Y Z | V W X Y Z
```
FIGURE 64f.

h. The solution of vertical two-square systems follows analogous lines, with the necessary modifications of the reconstruction diagram in consonance with the difference in mechanics between horizontal and vertical two-square systems.

i. A few additional remarks concerning the test applied in subpars. *d* and *e*, above, are in order. First, the exceptionally high transparency value observed in this cryptogram is a direct result of the very favorable manner in which the keyword-mixed sequences in the two squares interact; in the foregoing cryptogram, 47 of the 125 digraphs present (approx. 38%) were inverse transparencies. It is also pointed out that, although some actual two-square cryptograms may be rejected by that portion of the test which was described in subpar. *e*, the other phase of the test (described in subpar. *d*)—by which one may determine whether a cryptogram is more probably a vertical two-square encipherment or more probably a horizontal two-square encipherment—is sensitive and accurate to a high degree. The foregoing statistical method is not merely valuable *per se* as an application of cryptomathematics in the analysis of two-square matrix systems, but is included as being illustrative of the general principles of special techniques that may be developed in the attack on any particular cryptosystem, the mechanics of which are known to the cryptanalyst. The field of actual operational cryptanalysis is replete with special methods of attack of this nature.

71. Analysis of Playfair cipher systems.—*a.* Of all digraphic cryptosystems employing small matrices, the one which has been most frequently encountered is the Playfair cipher. Certain variations of this cipher have been incorporated in several complex manual ciphers used in actual operational practice; because of this it is important that the student gain familiarity with the methods of solution of the classic Playfair system.

b. The first published solutions [32] for this cipher are quite similar basically and vary only in minor details. The earliest, that by Lieut. Mauborgne (later to become Chief Signal Officer of the U. S. Army), used straightforward principles of frequency to establish the values of three or four of the most frequent digraphs. Then, on the assumption that in most cases in which a key word appears on the first and second rows the last five letters of the normal alphabet, VWXYZ, will rarely be disturbed in sequence and will occupy the last row of the square, he "juggles" the letters given by the values tentatively established from frequency considerations, placing them in various positions in the square, together with VWXYZ, to correspond to the plaintext-ciphertext relationships tentatively established. A later solution by Lieut. Frank Moorman, as described in Hitt's manual, assumes that in a Playfair cipher prepared by means of a square in which the key word occupies the first and second rows, if a digraphic frequency distribution is made, it will be found that the letters having the greatest combining power are very probably letters of the key. A still later solution, by Lieut. Commander Smith, is perhaps the most lucid and systematized of the three. He sets forth in definite language certain considerations which the other two writers certainly entertained but failed to indicate.

c. The following details have been summarized from Smith's solution:

(1) The Playfair cipher may be recognized by virtue of the fact that it always contains an even number of letters, and that when divided into groups of two letters each, no group contains a repetition of the same letter, as NN or EE. Repetitions of digraphs, trigraphs, and polygraphs will be evident in fairly long messages.

(2) Using the square [33] shown in Fig. 65, there are two general cases to be considered, as regards the results of encipherment:

[32] Mauborgne, Lieut. J. O., U. S. A. *An advanced problem in cryptography and its solution,* Leavenworth, 1914. Hitt, Captain Parker, U. S. A. *Manual for the solution of military ciphers,* Leavenworth, 1918.

Smith, Lieut. Commander W. W., U. S. N. In *Cryptography* by André Langie, translated by J. C. H. Macbeth, New York, 1922.

[33] The Playfair square accompanying Smith's solution is based upon the key word BANKRUPTCY "to be distributed between the first and fourth lines of the square." This is a simple departure from the original Playfair scheme in which the letters of the key word are written from left to right and in consecutive lines from the top downward.

```
B A N K R
D E F G H
I L M O Q
U P T C Y
S V W X Z
```

FIGURE 65.

Case 1. Letters at opposite corners of a rectangle. The following illustrative relationships are found:

$$\overline{TH}_p = \overline{YF}_c$$
$$\overline{HT}_p = \overline{FY}_c$$
$$\overline{YF}_p = \overline{TH}_c$$
$$\overline{FY}_p = \overline{HT}_c$$

Reciprocity and reversibility.[34]

Case 2. Two letters in the same row or column. The following illustrative relationships are found:

$$\overline{AN}_p = \overline{NK}_c$$
$$\overline{NA}_p = \overline{KN}_c$$

But $\overline{NK}_p$ does not equal $\overline{AN}_c$ nor does $\overline{KN}_p = \overline{NA}_c$.

Reversibility only.

(3) The foregoing gives rise to the following:

Rule I. (a) Regardless of the position of the letters in the square, if

$$1.2 = 3.4, \quad \text{then}$$
$$2.1 = 4.3$$

This rule is of particular aid in selecting probable words in the solution of Playfair ciphers, as will be shown shortly.[35]

(b) If 1 and 2 form opposite corners of a rectangle, the following equations obtain:

$$1.2 = 3.4$$
$$2.1 = 4.3$$
$$3.4 = 1.2$$
$$4.3 = 2.1$$

(4) A letter considered as occupying a position in a row can be combined with but four other letters in the same row; the same letter considered as occupying a position in a column can be combined with but four other letters in the same column. Thus, this letter can be combined with only 8 other letters all told, under Case 2, above. But the same letter considered as occupying a corner of a rectangle can be combined with 16 other letters, under Case 1, above. Smith derives from these facts the conclusion that "it would appear that Case 1 is twice as probable as Case 2". He continues thus (notation my own):

---

[34] By way of explaining what is meant by *reciprocity* and by *reversibility*, in the case of digraphic systems, the following examples are given: $\overline{TH}_p = \overline{YF}_c$ and $\overline{YF}_p = \overline{TH}_c$ constitute a *reciprocal* relationship; $\overline{TH}_p = \overline{YF}_c$ and $\overline{HT}_p = \overline{FY}_c$ constitute a *reversible* relationship.

[35] In this connection, a list of frequently-encountered words and phrases which contain reversed digraphs (so-called "ABBA patterns") has been compiled and is included as Section E, "Digraphic idiomorphs: Playfair", in Appendix 3.

168

"Now in the square, note that:

$$\overline{AN}_p = \overline{NK}_e \qquad\qquad \overline{EN}_p = \overline{FA}_e$$
$$\overline{GN}_p = \overline{FK}_e \qquad\qquad \overline{EM}_p = \overline{FL}_e$$
$$\overline{ON}_p = \overline{MK}_e \quad also \quad \overline{ET}_p = \overline{FP}_e$$
$$\overline{CN}_p = \overline{TK}_e \qquad\qquad \overline{EW}_p = \overline{FV}_e$$
$$\overline{XN}_p = \overline{WK}_e \qquad\qquad \overline{EF}_p = \overline{FG}_e$$

"From this it is seen that of the 24 equations that can be formed when each letter of the square is employed either as the initial or final letter of the group, five will indicate a repetition of a corresponding letter of plain text.

"Hence, *Rule II*. After it has been determined, in the equation 1.2=3.4, that, say, $\overline{EN}_p = \overline{FA}_e$, there is a probability of one in five that any other group beginning with F_e indicates $\overline{E\theta}_p$, and that any group ending in A_e indicates θN_p.[36]

"After such combinations as $\overline{ER}_p$, $\overline{OR}_p$, and $\overline{EN}_p$ have been assumed or determined, the above rule may be of use in discovering additional digraphs and partial words."

---

[36] The probability of "one in five" is only an approximation. Take for example, the 24 equations having F as an initial letter:

Case		Case		Case		Case	
1.	$FB_e = DN_p$	2.	$FE = ED$	2.	$FT = NM$	1.	$FX = GW$
2.	$FD = EH$	1.	$FL = EM$	2.	$FW = NT$	1.	$FR = HN$
1.	$FI = DM$	1.	$FP = ET$	1.	$FK = GN$	2.	$FH = EG$
1.	$FU = DT$	1.	$FV = EW$	2.	$FG = EF$	1.	$FQ = HM$
1.	$FS = DW$	2.	$FN = NW$	1.	$FO = GM$	1.	$FY = HT$
1.	$FA = EN$	2.	$FM = NF$	1.	$FC = GT$	1.	$FZ = HW$

Here, the initial letter F_e represents the following initial letters of plaintext digraphs:

$$D\theta_p, E\theta_p, N\theta_p, G\theta_p, \text{ and } H\theta_p.$$

It is seen that F_e represents D_p, N_p, G_p, H_p 4 times each, and E_p, 8 times. Consequently, supposing that it has been determined that $FA_e = EN_p$, the probability that F_e will represent E_p is not 1 in 5 but 8 in 24, or 1 in 3; but supposing that it has been determined that $FW_e = NT_p$, the probability that F_e will represent N_p is 4 in 24 or 1 in 6. The difference in these probabilities is occasioned by the fact that the first instance, $FA_e = EN_p$ corresponds to a Case 1 encipherment, the second instance, $FW_e = NT_p$, to a Case 2 encipherment. But there is no way of knowing initially, and without other data, whether one is dealing with a Case 1 or Case 2 encipherment. Only as an approximation, therefore, may one say that the probability of F_e representing a given θ_p is 1 in 5. A probability of 1 in 5 is of almost trivial importance in this situation, since it represents such a "long shot" for success. The following rule might be preferable: If the equation 1.2=3.4 has been established, where all the letters represented by 1, 2, 3, and 4 are different, then there is a probability of 4/5 that a Case 1 encipherment is involved. Consequently, if at the same time another equation, 3.6=5.2, has been established, where 2 and 3 represent the same letters as in the first equation, and 5 and 6 are different letters, also different from 2 and 3, there is a probability of 16/25 that the equation 1.6=5.4 is valid; or if at the same time that the equation 1.2=3.4 has been determined, the equation 1.6=5.4 has also been established, then there is a probability of 16/25 that the equation 3.6=5.2 is valid. (Check this by noting the following equations based upon Fig. 65: $\overset{1\,2}{CE} = \overset{3\,4}{PG}$, $\overset{3\,6}{PH} = \overset{5\,2}{YE}$, $\overset{1\,6}{CH} = \overset{5\,4}{YG}$. Note the positions occupied in Fig. 65 by the letters involved.) Likewise, if the equations 1.2=3.4 and 1.6=3.5 have been simultaneously established, then there is a probability that the equation 2.5=4.6 is valid; or if the equations 1.2=3.4 and 2.5=4.6 have been simultaneously established, then there is a probability that the equation 2.5=4.6 is valid. (Check this by noting the following equations: $\overset{1\,2}{CE} = \overset{3\,4}{PG}$; $\overset{1\,6}{CA} = \overset{3\,5}{PK}$; $\overset{2\,5}{EK} = \overset{4\,6}{GA}$; note the positions occupied in Fig. 65 by the letters involved.) However, it must be added that these probabilities are based upon assumptions which fail to take into account any considerations whatever as to frequency of letters or specificity of composition of the matrix. For instance, suppose the 5 high-frequency letters E, T, N, R, O all happen to fall in the same row or column in the matrix; the number of Case 2 encipherments would be much greater than expectancy and the probability that the equation 1.2=3.4 represents a Case 1 encipherment falls much below 4/5.

169

Rule III. In the equation 1.2=3.4, 1 and 3 can never be identical, nor can 2 and 4 ever be identical. Thus, $\overline{AN}_p$ could not possibly be represented by $\overline{AY}_c$, nor could $\overline{ER}_p$ be represented by $\overline{KR}_c$. This rule is useful in elimination of certain possibilities when a specific message is being studied.

Rule IV. In the equation $1.2_p=3.4_c$, if 2 and 3 are identical, the letters are all in the same row or column, and in the relative order 1–2–4 from left to right or top to bottom, respectively. In the square shown, $\overline{AN}_p=\overline{NK}_c$ and the absolute order is ANK. The relative order 1–2–4 includes five absolute orders which are cyclic permutations of one another. Thus: ANK.., NK..A, K..AN, ..ANK, and .ANK..

Rule V. In the equation $1.2_p=3.4_c$, if 1 and 4 are identical, the letters are all in the same row or column, and in the relative order 2–4–3 from left to right or top to bottom. In the square shown, $\overline{KN}_p=\overline{RK}_c$ and the absolute order is NKR. The relative order 2–4–3 includes five absolute orders which are cyclic permutations of one another. Thus NKR.., KR..N, R..NK, ..NKR, and .NKR..

Rule VI. "Analyze the message for group recurrences. Select the groups of greatest recurrence and assume them to be high-frequency digraphs.[37] Substitute the assumed digraphs throughout the message, testing the assumptions in their relation to other groups of the cipher. The reconstruction of the square proceeds simultaneously with the solution of the message and aids in hastening the translation of the cipher."

d. (1) When solutions for the Playfair cipher system were first developed, based upon the fact that the letters were inserted in the cells in keyword-mixed order, cryptographers thought it desirable to place stumbling blocks in the path of such solution by departing from strict, keyword-mixed order. One of the simplest methods is illustrated in Fig. 65, wherein it will be noted that the last five letters of the key word proper are inserted in the fourth row of the square instead of the second, where they would naturally fall. Another method involves inserting the letters within the cells from left to right and top downward but using a sequence that is derived from a columnar transposition instead of a keyword-mixed sequence. Thus, using the keyword BANKRUPTCY:

```
2 1 5 4 7 9 6 8 3 10
B A N K R U P T C Y
D E F G H I L M O Q
S V W X Z
```

Sequence: A E V B D S C O K G X N F W P L R H Z T M U I Y Q

The Playfair square is as follows:

```
A E V B D
S C O K G
X N F W P
L R H Z T
M U I Y Q
```

FIGURE 66a.

---

[37] A more accurate guide to the determination of the plaintext equivalents of high-frequency cipher digraphs would involve the consideration of the difference in frequency of a particular digraph and its reversal. Thus, an example of a high-frequency $\overline{\theta\theta}_p$ which is also high-frequency in its reversal, is $\overline{RE}_p$; an example of a high-frequency $\overline{\theta\theta}_p$ which is rarely found in its reversed form, is $\overline{TH}_p$.

(2) Note the following three squares:

Z	T	L	R	H
Y	Q	M	U	I
B	D	A	E	V
K	G	S	C	O
W	P	X	N	F

FIGURE 66b.

O	K	G	S	C
F	W	P	X	N
H	Z	T	L	R
I	Y	Q	M	U
V	B	D	A	E

FIGURE 66c.

N	F	W	P	X
R	H	Z	T	L
U	I	Y	Q	M
E	V	B	D	A
C	O	K	G	S

FIGURE 66d.

At first glance they all appear to be different, but closer examination shows them to be *cyclic permutations* of one another and of the square in Fig. 66a. They yield identical cryptographic equivalents in all cases. However, if an attempt be made to reconstruct the original key word, it would be much easier to do so from Fig. 66a than from any of the others, because in Fig. 66a the original mixed sequence has not been disturbed as much as in Figs. 66b, c, and d. In working with Playfair ciphers, the student should be on the lookout for such instances of cyclic permutation of the original Playfair square, for during the course of solution he will not know whether he is building up the original or an equivalent cyclic permutation of the original matrix; usually only after he has completely reconstructed the matrix will he be able to determine this point.

e. (1) The steps in the solution of a typical example of this cipher will now be illustrated. Let the message be as follows:

```
V T Q E U   H I O F T   C H X S C   A K T V T   R A Z E V   T A G A E

O X T Y M   H C R L Z   Z T Q T D   U M C Y C   X C T G M   T Y C Z U

S N O P D   G X V X S   C A K T V   T P K P U   T Z P T W   Z F N B G

P T R K X   I X B P R   Z O E P U   T O L Z E   K T T C S   N H C Q M

V T R K M   W C F Z U   B H T V Y   A B G I P   R Z K P C   Q F N L V

O X O T U   Z F A C X   X C P Z X   H C Y N O   T Y O L G   X X I I H

T M S M X   C P T O T   C X O T T   C Y A T E   X H F A C   X X C P Z

X H Y C T   X W L Z T   S G P Z T   V Y W C E   T W G C C   M B H M Q

Y X Z P W   G R T I V   U X P U M   Q R K M W   C X T M R   S W G H B

X C P T O   T C X O T   M I P Y D   N F G K I   T C O L X   U E T P X

X F S R S   U Z T D B   H O Z I G   X R K I X   Z P P V Z   I D U H Q

O T K T K   C C H X X
```

171

(2) Without going through the preliminary tests in detail, with which it will be assumed that the student is now familiar,[38] the conclusion is reached that the cryptogram is digraphic in nature. The digraphic frequency distribution for the cryptogram is shown in Fig. 67.

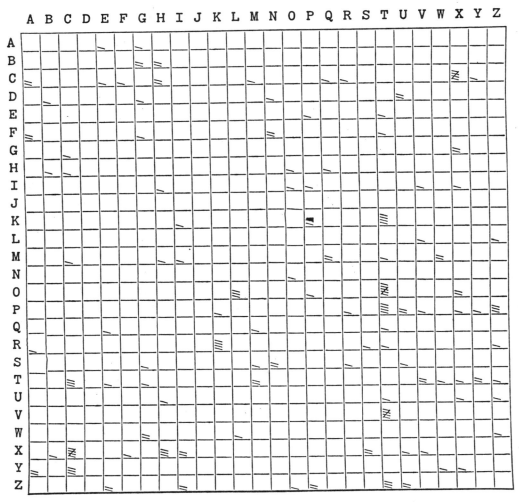

FIGURE 67.

Since there are no double-letter groups (termed "doublets"), the conclusion is reached that a Playfair cipher is involved. The message, having been rewritten in digraphs, is given below.

[38] See par. 69c.

					5					10					15
A	VT	QE	UH	IO	FT	CH	XS	CA	KT	VT	RA	ZE	VT	AG	AE
B	OX	TY	MH	CR	LZ	ZT	QT	DU	MC	YC	XC	TG	MT	YC	ZU
C	SN	OP	DG	XV	XS	CA	KT	VT	PK	PU	TZ	PT	WZ	FN	BG
D	PT	RK	XI	XB	PR	ZO	EP	UT	OL	ZE	KT	TC	SN	HC	QM
E	VT	RK	MW	CF	ZU	BH	TV	YA	BG	IP	RZ	KP	CQ	FN	LV
F	OX	OT	UZ	FA	CX	XC	PZ	XH	CY	NO	TY	OL	GX	XI	IH
G	TM	SM	XC	PT	OT	CX	OT	TC	YA	TE	XH	FA	CX	XC	PZ
H	XH	YC	TX	WL	ZT	SG	PZ	TV	YW	CE	TW	GC	CM	BH	MQ
J	YX	ZP	WG	RT	IV	UX	PU	MQ	RK	MW	CX	TM	RS	WG	HB
K	XC	PT	OT	CX	OT	MI	PY	DN	FG	KI	TC	OL	XU	ET	PX
L	XF	SR	SU	ZT	DB	HO	ZI	GX	RK	IX	ZP	PV	ZI	DU	HQ
M	OT	KT	KC	CH	XX										

(3) The following three fairly lengthy repetitions are noted:

Lines

F: OT UZ FA CX XC PZ XH CY NO

G: TE XH FA CX XC PZ XH YC TX

A: FT CH XS CA KT VT RA ZE VT

C: DG XV XS CA KT VT PK PU TZ

G: TM SM XC PT OT CX OT TC YA

K: WG HB XC PT OT CX OT MI PY

The first long repetition, with the sequent reversed digraphs **CX** and **XC** immediately suggests the word **BATTALION** (see Section E, Appendix 3), split up into **—B AT TA LI ON** and the sequence containing this repetition in lines F and G becomes as follows:

Line F _____ OX OT UZ FA CX XC PZ XH CY NO TY
                                  B   AT TA LI ON

Line G _____ YA TE XH FA CX XC PZ XH YC TX WL
                                  B   AT TA LI ON

(4) Because of the frequent use of numerals before the word **BATTALION** (as mentioned in Section B of Appendix 4) and because of the appearance of $\overline{ON}_p$ before this word in line G, the possibility suggests itself that the word before BATTALION in line G is either **ONE** or **SECOND**. The identical cipher digraph $\overline{FA}$ in both cases gives a hint that the word BATTALION in line F may also be preceded by a numeral; if ONE is correct in line G, then **THREE** is possible in line F. On the other hand, if SECOND is correct in line G, then **THIRD** is possible in line F. Thus:

Line F	OX	OT	UZ	FA	CX	XC	PZ	XH	CY	NO	TY
1st hypothesis	—	TH	RE	EB	AT	TA	LI	ON			
2d hypothesis	—	TH	IR	DB	AT	TA	LI	ON			

Line G	YA	TE	XH	FA	CX	XC	PZ	XH	YC	TX	WL
1st hypothesis	—	—	ON	EB	AT	TA	LI	ON			
2d hypothesis	–S	EC	ON	DB	AT	TA	LI	ON			

First, note that if either hypothesis is true, then $\overline{OT}_c=\overline{TH}_p$. The frequency distribution shows that $\overline{OT}$ occurs 6 times and is in fact the most frequent digraph in the message. Moreover, by Rule I of subpar. *b*, if $\overline{OT}_c=\overline{TH}_p$ then $\overline{TO}_c=\overline{HT}_p$. Since $\overline{HT}_p$ is a very rare digraph in normal plain text, $\overline{TO}_c$ should either not occur at all in so short a message or else it should be very infrequent. The frequency distribution shows that it does not occur. Hence, there is nothing inconsistent with the supposition that the word in front of BATTALION in line F is THREE or THIRD and there is some evidence that it is actually one of these.

(5) But can evidence be found for the support of one hypothesis against the other? Let the frequency distribution be examined with a view to throwing light upon this point. If the first hypothesis is true, then $\overline{UZ}_c=\overline{RE}_p$, and, by Rule I, $\overline{ZU}_c=\overline{ER}_p$. The frequency distribution shows but one occurrence of $\overline{UZ}_c$ and but two occurrences of $\overline{ZU}_c$. These do not look very good for $\overline{RE}_p$ and $\overline{ER}_p$. On the other hand, if the second hypothesis is true, then $\overline{UZ}_c=\overline{IR}_p$, and, by Rule I, $\overline{ZU}_c=\overline{RI}_p$. The frequencies are much more favorable in this case. Is there anything inconsistent with the assumption, on the basis of the second hypothesis, that $\overline{TE}_c=\overline{EC}_p$? The frequency distribution shows no inconsistency, for $\overline{TE}_c$ occurs once and $\overline{ET}_c(=\overline{CE}_p$, by Rule I) occurs once. As regards whether $\overline{FA}_c=\overline{EB}_p$ or $\overline{DB}_p$, both hypotheses are tenable; possibly the second hypothesis is a shade better than the first, on the following reasoning: By Rule I, if $\overline{FA}_c=\overline{EB}_p$ then $\overline{AF}_c=\overline{BE}_p$, or if $\overline{FA}_c=\overline{DB}_p$ then $\overline{AF}_c=\overline{BD}_p$. The fact that no $\overline{AF}_c$ occurs, whereas at least one $\overline{BE}_p$ may be expected in this message, inclines one to the second hypothesis, since $\overline{BD}_p$ is very rare.

(6) Let the second hypothesis be assumed to be correct. The additional values are tentatively inserted in the text, and in lines G and K two interesting repetitions are noted:

Line G	TM	SM	XC	PT	OT	CX	OT	TC	YA	TE	XH	FA	CX	XC	PZ	XH
			TA		TH	AT	TH		–S	EC	ON	DB	AT	TA	LI	ON

Line K	WG	HB	XC	PT	OT	CX	OT	MI	PY	DN	FG	KI	TC	OL	XU	ET
			TA		TH	AT	TH									

This certainly looks like STATE THAT THE . . . , which would make $\overline{TE}_p=\overline{PT}_c$. Furthermore, in line G the sequence STATETHATTHE. .SECONDBATTALION can hardly be anything else than

STATE THAT THEIR SECOND BATTALION, which would make $\overline{TC}_c=\overline{EI}_p$ and $\overline{YA}_c=\overline{RS}_p$. Also $\overline{SM}_c=\overline{-S}_p$.

(7) It is perhaps high time that the whole list of tentative equivalent values be studied in relation to their consistency with the positions of letters in the Playfair square; moreover, by so doing, additional values may be obtained in the process. The complete list of values is as follows:

Assumed values	*Derived by Rule I*
$\overline{AT}_p=\overline{CX}_c$	$\overline{TA}_p=\overline{XC}_c$
$\overline{LI}_p=\overline{PZ}_c$	$\overline{IL}_p=\overline{ZP}_c$
$\overline{ON}_p=\overline{XH}_c$	$\overline{NO}_p=\overline{HX}_c$
$\overline{TH}_p=\overline{OT}_c$	$\overline{HT}_p=\overline{TO}_c$
$\overline{IR}_p=\overline{UZ}_c$	$\overline{RI}_p=\overline{ZU}_c$
$\overline{DB}_p=\overline{FA}_c$	$\overline{BD}_p=\overline{AF}_c$
$\overline{EC}_p=\overline{TE}_c$	$\overline{CE}_p=\overline{ET}_c$
$\overline{TE}_p=\overline{PT}_c$	$\overline{ET}_p=\overline{TP}_c$
$\overline{EI}_p=\overline{TC}_c$	$\overline{IE}_p=\overline{CT}_c$
$\overline{RS}_p=\overline{YA}_c$	$\overline{SR}_p=\overline{AY}_c$
$\overline{-S}_p=\overline{SM}_c$	$\overline{S-}_p=\overline{MS}_c$

(8) By Rule V, the equation $\overline{TH}_p=\overline{OT}_c$ means that H, O, and T are all in the same row or column and in the absolute order HTO; similarly, C, E, and T are in the same row or column and in the absolute order CET. Further, E, P, and T are in the same row and column, and their absolute order is ETP. That is, these sequences must occur some place in the square, in either rows or columns, taking into consideration of course the probability of cyclic displacements of these sequences within the square:

(a) HTO   (b) CET   (c) ETP

(9) Noting the common letters E and T in the second and third sequences, these two sequences may be combined into one sequence of four letters, *viz.*, CETP. Since only one position remains to be filled in this row (or column) of the square, and noting in the list of equivalents that $\overline{EI}_p=\overline{TC}_c$, it is obvious that the letter I belongs to the CETP sequence; the complete sequence is therefore ICETP.

(10) Since the sequence HTO has a common letter (T) with the sequence ICETP, it follows that if the HTO sequence occupies a row, then the ICETP sequence must occupy a column; or, if the HTO sequence occupies a column, then the ICETP sequence must occupy a row; and they may be combined by means of their common letter, T, *viz.*:

The proof of whether the ICETP sequence, for example, properly belongs in a row or a column of the Playfair square lies in the establishment of a *rectangular* relationship, instead of the *linear* relationships constructed thus far.

(11) We note that, from the assumptions in subpar. $d(6)$, $\overline{AT}_p=\overline{CX}_c$ and $\overline{ON}_p=\overline{XH}_c$. The relationship $\overline{ON}_p=\overline{XH}_c$ might be either a rectangular one, such as O   X, or it might be linear, *viz.*, HTOXN or H. Since, however,

```
                    O       X
                      \   /
                       \ /
                       / \
H                     /   \
T                   H       N
O
X
N
```

$\overline{AT}_p=\overline{CX}_c$ must be a rectangular relationship, then only the configuration

```
 ┌ ─ ─ ─ ─ ─ ┐
 │ I         │
 │ C    A    │
 │ E         │
 │ H  T  O  X  N │
 │ P         │
 └ ─ ─ ─ ─ ─ ┘
```
will be valid, since the alternative form
```
 ┌ ─ ─ ─ ─ ─ ┐
 │        H  │
 │ I C E T P │
 │        O  │
 │    A   X  │
 │        N  │
 └ ─ ─ ─ ─ ─ ┘
```
will not

satisfy the equation $\overline{AT}_p=\overline{CX}_c$.

(12) The fragmentary Playfair square [39] has been established, in one of its 25 possible cyclic permutations, as follows:

```
┌───────────┐
│ I         │
│ C     A   │
│ E         │
│ H T O X N │
│ P         │
└───────────┘
```

FIGURE 68a.

Scanning the list of plain-cipher equivalents given in subpar. $d(7)$ in order to insert possible additional values, note is made of $\overline{IR}_p=\overline{UZ}_c$, which means that U must be in the same row as I; and since Z cannot be in the same column as I the square must be one of the two following possibilities:

```
┌───────────┐
│ I U R Z   │
│ C     A   │
│ E         │
│ H T O X N │
│ P         │
└───────────┘
```

FIGURE 68b.

```
┌───────────┐
│ Z I U   R │
│ C     A   │
│ E         │
│ H T O X N │
│ P         │
└───────────┘
```

FIGURE 68c.

---

[39] In actual practice, it is more usual to start with a much larger diagram than a simple 5 x 5 square; as relationships develop, the diagram is gradually condensed, until finally a 5 x 5 square emerges. This procedure is quite similar to that employed in the reconstruction diagrams for two-square matrices.

(13) Now note that $\overline{RS}_p = \overline{YA}_c$; this eliminates one of the two squares above, thus the correct square is now

```
┌─────────┐
│ Y I U R Z │
│ S C   A │
│   E     │
│ H T O X N │
│   P     │
└─────────┘
```
FIGURE 68d.

Since $\overline{LI}_p = \overline{PZ}_c$, this places L in the square:

```
┌─────────┐
│ Y I U R Z │
│ S C   A │
│   E     │
│ H T O X N │
│   P   L │
└─────────┘
```
FIGURE 68e.

Finally, since $\overline{DB}_p = \overline{FA}_c$, the new letters can be placed in the square in the three following ways:

```
┌─────────┐
│ Y I U R Z │
│ S C B A │
│   E F D │
│ H T O X N │
│   P   L │
└─────────┘
```
FIGURE 68f.

```
┌─────────┐
│ Y I U R Z │
│ S C   A B │
│   E   D F │
│ H T O X N │
│   P   L │
└─────────┘
```
FIGURE 68g.

```
┌─────────┐
│ Y I U R Z │
│ S C B A │
│   E     │
│ H T O X N │
│   P F D L │
└─────────┘
```
FIGURE 68h.

Checking back to the cipher text at A5, of the three possibilities for $\overline{FT}_c$ ($=\overline{EO}_p$, $\overline{EN}_p$, or $\overline{PO}_p$), the obvious choice is $\overline{PO}_p$ in the word —O UT PO ST, so this confirms Fig. 68h as the correct square of the three possibilities.

(14) It is now a simple matter to decipher the cryptogram and make the few assumptions in the text necessary to permit filling in the remaining six letters in the square, which will result in its completion as follows:

```
┌─────────┐
│ Y I U R Z │
│ S C B A G │
│ M E Q K V │
│ H T O X N │
│ W P F D L │
└─────────┘
```
FIGURE 68i.

177

f. Reconstruction of the square in Playfair ciphers is normally carried on concurrently with the synthesis of the plain text, once a few correct assumptions have been made. Now, having just reconstructed the square as shown in Fig. 68*i*, the question to be answered is whether this square is identical with the original enciphering matrix or whether it is a cyclic permutation of the original square (which may have contained, say, a transposition-mixed sequence). Even though the cryptogram in subpar. 71*e* has been solved, this point is still of interest.

(1) The square that is derived may not necessarily be the original enciphering square; more than likely it will be one of the 24 possible cyclic permutations of the original square. If the Playfair square consisted of a keyword-mixed sequence, a permutation of the square will cause no difficulty in recovering the original matrix and hence the key word. For example, if the square derived in some other instance is

Q T L N O   then the square   P Y R A M   is easily
X Z U V W   I D S B C
A M P Y R   E F G H K
B C I D S   L N O Q T
H K E F G   U V W X Z

recovered because of the telltale letters UVWXZ occurring in a row of the derivative square. But when the Playfair square consists of a transposition-mixed sequence, then a different procedure must be adopted.

(2) As an example, let us take the transposition matrix 5 8 6 1 4 3 2 7 from which

P Y R A M I D S
B C E F G H K L
N O Q T U V W X
Z

A F T D K is the original square. Using the methods illustrated in par. 51*g*, scanning suc-
W I H V M
G U P B N
Z R E Q S
L X Y C O

cessive rows of the square will disclose sequences of letters which could have appeared as columns in the transposition matrix. For example, discovery of the columns

I|D|S   will afford rapid
H|K|L
V|W|X

recovery of the key word. But if instead of the original square we had one of its permutations such as Q S Z R E, then treatment of the "columns", e. g.,
C O L X Y
D K A F T
V M W I H
B N G U P

F|V|O|L|Q, of the tentative trans-
T|M|L|X|S
V|W|X|Y|Z

position matrix (assuming that some or all of the letters V, W, X, Y, Z are in the last row of the transposition matrix) will be without significance; therefore the procedure above is inapplicable without a slight modification.

(3) Since it will be noted that a permutation of the rows will not affect the procedure of keyword recovery, then we construct a 9 x 5 rectangle Q S Z R E Q S Z R which contains
C O L X Y C O L X
D K A F T D K A F
V M W I H V M W I
B N G U P B N G U

178

the five squares which result simply from successive permutations of the columns. A 5 x 5 cut-out square will be found convenient in testing each permutation in turn. Recovery of the key word will be possible when the correct permutation is reached, which in this case is the third square in the rectangle, namely, Z R E Q S. After recovery of the key word from

```
L X Y C O
A F T D K
W I H V M
G U P B N
```

this permuted square it is probable then that the original enciphering square must have been

```
A F T D K
W I H V M
G U P B N
Z R E Q S
L X Y C O
```

(4) In the case of the square recovered in Fig. 68*i*, it is found that, following the procedure outlined in subpars. (1), (2), and (3), above, the key word is based on COMPANY, recoverable from the following diagram:

```
2 5 3 6 1 4 7
C O M P A N Y
B D E F G H I
K L Q R S T U
V W X Z
```

The original square must have been this:

```
A G S C B
K V M E Q
X N H T O
D L W P F
R Z Y I U
```

FIGURE 68*j*.

g. Continued practice in the solution of Playfair ciphers will make the student quite expert in the matter and will enable him to solve shorter and shorter messages.[40] Also, with practice it will become a matter of indifference to him as to whether the letters are inserted in the square with any sort of regularity, such as simple keyword-mixed order, transposition-mixed order, or in a purely random order.

h. It may perhaps seem to the student that the foregoing steps are somewhat too artificial, a bit too "cut and dried" in their accuracy to portray the process of analysis as it is applied in practice. For example, the critical student may well object to some of the assumptions and the reasoning in subpar. *e* (5), above, in which the words THREE and ONE (1st hypothesis) were rejected in favor of the words THIRD and SECOND (2d hypothesis). This rested largely upon the rejection of $\overline{RE}_p$ and $\overline{ER}_p$ as the equivalents of $\overline{UZ}_c$ and $\overline{ZU}_c$, and the adoption of $\overline{IR}_p$ and $\overline{RI}_p$ as their equivalents. Indeed, if the student will examine the final plain text with a

---

[40] The author once had a student who "specialized" in Playfair ciphers and became so adept that he could solve messages containing as few as 50–60 letters within 30 minutes.

critical eye, he will find that while the bit of reasoning in step (5) is perfectly logical, the assumption upon which it is based is in fact wrong; for it happens that in this case $\overline{ER}_p$ occurs only once and $\overline{RE}_p$ does not occur at all. Consequently, although most of the reasoning which led to the rejection of the first hypothesis and the adoption of the second was logical, it was in fact based upon erroneous assumption. In other words, despite the fact that the assumption was incorrect, a correct deduction was made. *The student should take note that in cryptanalysis situations of this sort are not at all unusual.* Indeed they are to be expected, and a few words of explanation at this point may be useful.

i. Cryptanalytics is a science in which deduction, based upon observational data, plays a very large role. But it is also true that in this science most of the deductions usually rest upon assumptions. It is most often the case that the cryptanalyst is forced to make his assumptions based upon a quite limited amount of text. It cannot be expected that assumptions based upon statistical generalizations will always hold true when applied to data comparatively very much smaller in quantity than the total data used to derive the generalized rules. Consequently, as regards assumptions made in specific messages, *most of the time* they will be correct, but *occasionally* they will be incorrect.[41] In cryptanalysis it is often found that among the correct deductions there will be cases in which subsequently discovered facts do not bear out the assumptions on which the deduction was based. Indeed, it is sometimes true that if the *facts* had been known *before* the deduction was made, this knowledge would have prevented making the correct deduction. For example, suppose the cryptanalyst had somehow or other divined that the message under consideration contained no RE, only one ER, one IR, and two RI's (as is actually the case). He would certainly not have been able to choose between the words THREE and ONE (1st hypothesis) as against THIRD and SECOND (2d hypothesis). But because he assumes that there should be more $\overline{ER}_p$'s and $\overline{RE}_p$'s than $\overline{IR}_p$'s and $\overline{RI}_p$'s in the message, he deduces that $\overline{UZ}_0$ cannot be $\overline{RE}_p$, rejects the first hypothesis and takes the second. It later turns out, after the problem has been solved, that the deduction was correct, although the assumption on which it was based (expectation of more frequent appearance of $\overline{RE}_p$ and $\overline{ER}_p$) was, in fact, *not* true in this particular case. The cryptanalyst can only hope that the number of times when his deductions are correct, even though based upon assumptions which later turn out to be erroneous, will abundantly exceed the number of times when his deductions are wrong, even though based upon assumptions which later prove to be correct. If he is lucky, the making of an assumption which is really not true will make no difference in the end and will not delay solution; but if he is specially favored with luck, it may actually help him solve the message—as was the case in this particular example.

j. Another comment of a general nature may be made in connection with this specific example. The student may ask what would have been the procedure in this case if the message had not contained such a telltale repetition as the word BATTALION, which formed the point of departure for the solution, or, as it is often said, permitted an "entering wedge" to be driven into the message. The answer to his query is that if the word BATTALION had not been repeated, there would probably have been some other repetition which would have permitted the same sort of attack. If the student is looking for cut and dried, straightforward, unvarying methods of attack, he should remember that cryptanalytics, while considered a branch of mathematics by some, is not a science which has many "general solutions" such as are found and expected in

---

[41] See footnote 19 on p. 43.

mathematics proper. It is inherent in the very nature of cryptanalytics that, *as a rule*, only general principles can be established; their practical application must take advantage of peculiarities and particular situations which are noted in specific messages. This is especially true in a text on the subject. The illustration of a general principle requires a specific example, and the latter must of necessity manifest characteristics which make it different from any other example. The word BATTALION was not purposely repeated in this example in order to make the demonstration of solution easy; "it just happened that way". In another example, some other entering wedge would have been found. The student can be expected to learn only the *general principles* which will enable him to take advantage of the *specific characteristics* manifested in *specific cases*. Here it is desired to illustrate the general principles of solving Playfair ciphers and to point out the fact that entering wedges must and can be found. The specific nature of the entering wedge varies with specific examples.

72. **Analysis of polygraphic systems involving large tables.**—*a.* The analysis of systems incorporating large digraphic tables is accomplished by entering, within the appropriate cells of a 26 x 26 chart, data corresponding to the plain-cipher relationships of assumed cribs, and examining the charts for evidences of symmetry or systematic construction in their compilation. The initial plaintext entries may, in the absence of cribs, be made on the basis of digraphic frequency considerations, aided by idiomorphisms and repetitions.

b. In pseudo-digraphic systems, such as those incorporating tables similar to Figs. 47*a* and *b*, and 48, the identification of the monoalphabetically-enciphered component of cipher digraphs will greatly accelerate plaintext entries, since advantage may be taken of this monoalphabeticity. Tables with a feature of reciprocity, such as the example in Fig. 50, may be exploited on the basis of *this* weakness, even if the reciprocal pairs are assigned at random. Tables such as that in Fig. 49 and the one for trinome digraphic encipherment shown in Fig. 51 may also be exploited with facility, once enough plain text has been correctly assumed and inserted to disclose their systematic construction. A word of warning is inserted here against making incautious assumptions concerning the exact internal composition of tables such as that in Fig. 49, since their unusual construction could easily mislead the analyst who jumps to premature conclusions. In the case of a table such as Fig. 51 wherein the trinomes have been inscribed in straight horizontals, if the dimensions of the table have been correctly assumed the simplest solution involves a reduction to two alphabets, reflecting the sequences of letters for the side and top of the matrix; this solution closely parallels that of the numerical four-square system described in subpar. 69*e*.

c. Because the foregoing principles are rather straightforward, it is not considered necessary to illustrate their application with examples. Of course, when digraphic tables of random construction have been used, no refinements in solution are possible. However, the recording of as few as 225 different plaintext digraphs and their ciphertext equivalents will theoretically enable the automatic decryption of approximately 92% of the cipher digraphs of messages, and the recording of 335 plaintext-ciphertext values will enable the automatic decryption of 98% of the cipher digraphs; thus almost every message may be read in its entirety without recourse to further assumptions. Actually, it should be pointed out that having only 122 matched plaintext-ciphertext equivalencies will theoretically enable the decryption of 75% of the cipher digraphs, and enough skeletons of plain text may then be manifest to permit the decryption of the complete message texts.

d. It might be well to point out in connection with large digraphic tables that there exist literal types which give rise to monoalphabetic distributions for *both* the initial letters and final letters of pairs. Such a table is illustrated in Fig. 69 below:

$$\theta_p^2$$

	A	B	C	D	E	F	G	H	I	J	K	L	M	N	O	P	Q	R	S	T	U	V	W	X	Y	Z
A	HQ	YQ	DQ	RQ	AQ	UQ	LQ	IQ	CQ	BQ	EQ	FQ	GQ	JQ	KQ	MQ	NQ	OQ	PQ	QQ	SQ	TQ	VQ	WQ	XQ	ZQ
B	HU	YU	DU	RU	AU	UU	LU	IU	CU	BU	EU	FU	GU	JU	KU	MU	NU	OU	PU	QU	SU	TU	VU	WU	XU	ZU
C	HE	YE	DE	RE	AE	UE	LE	IE	CE	BE	EE	FE	GE	JE	KE	ME	NE	OE	PE	QE	SE	TE	VE	WE	XE	ZE
D	HS	YS	DS	RS	AS	US	LS	IS	CS	BS	ES	FS	GS	JS	KS	MS	NS	OS	PS	QS	SS	TS	VS	WS	XS	ZS
E	HT	YT	DT	RT	AT	UT	LT	IT	CT	BT	ET	FT	GT	JT	KT	MT	NT	OT	PT	QT	ST	TT	VT	WT	XT	ZT
F	HI	YI	DI	RI	AI	UI	LI	II	CI	BI	EI	FI	GI	JI	KI	MI	NI	OI	PI	QI	SI	TI	VI	WI	XI	ZI
G	HO	YO	DO	RO	AO	UO	LO	IO	CO	BO	EO	FO	GO	JO	KO	MO	NO	OO	PO	QO	SO	TO	VO	WO	XO	ZO
H	HN	YN	DN	RN	AN	UN	LN	IN	CN	BN	EN	FN	GN	JN	KN	MN	NN	ON	PN	QN	SN	TN	VN	WN	XN	ZN
I	HA	YA	DA	RA	AA	UA	LA	IA	CA	BA	EA	FA	GA	JA	KA	MA	NA	OA	PA	QA	SA	TA	VA	WA	XA	ZA
J	HB	YB	DB	RB	AB	UB	LB	IB	CB	BB	EB	FB	GB	JB	KB	MB	NB	OB	PB	QB	SB	TB	VB	WB	XB	ZB
K	HL	YL	DL	RL	AL	UL	LL	IL	CL	BL	EL	FL	GL	JL	KL	ML	NL	OL	PL	QL	SL	TL	VL	WL	XL	ZL
L	HY	YY	DY	RY	AY	UY	LY	IY	CY	BY	EY	FY	GY	JY	KY	MY	NY	OY	PY	QY	SY	TY	VY	WY	XY	ZY
M	HC	YC	DC	RC	AC	UC	LC	IC	CC	BC	EC	FC	GC	JC	KC	MC	NC	OC	PC	QC	SC	TC	VC	WC	XC	ZC
N	HD	YD	DD	RD	AD	UD	LD	ID	CD	BD	ED	FD	GD	JD	KD	MD	ND	OD	PD	QD	SD	TD	VD	WD	XD	ZD
O	HF	YF	DF	RF	AF	UF	LF	IF	CF	BF	EF	FF	GF	JF	KF	MF	NF	OF	PF	QF	SF	TF	VF	WF	XF	ZF
P	HG	YG	DG	RG	AG	UG	LG	IG	CG	BG	EG	FG	GG	JG	KG	MG	NG	OG	PG	QG	SG	TG	VG	WG	XG	ZG
Q	HH	YH	DH	RH	AH	UH	LH	IH	CH	BH	EH	FH	GH	JH	KH	MH	NH	OH	PH	QH	SH	TH	VH	WH	XH	ZH
R	HJ	YJ	DJ	RJ	AJ	UJ	LJ	IJ	CJ	BJ	EJ	FJ	GJ	JJ	KJ	MJ	NJ	OJ	PJ	QJ	SJ	TJ	VJ	WJ	XJ	ZJ
S	HK	YK	DK	RK	AK	UK	LK	IK	CK	BK	EK	FK	GK	JK	KK	MK	NK	OK	PK	QK	SK	TK	VK	WK	XK	ZK
T	HM	YM	DM	RM	AM	UM	LM	IM	CM	BM	EM	FM	GM	JM	KM	MM	NM	OM	PM	QM	SM	TM	VM	WM	XM	ZM
U	HP	YP	DP	RP	AP	UP	LP	IP	CP	BP	EP	FP	GP	JP	KP	MP	NP	OP	PP	QP	SP	TP	VP	WP	XP	ZP
V	HR	YR	DR	RR	AR	UR	LR	IR	CR	BR	ER	FR	GR	JR	KR	MR	NR	OR	PR	QR	SR	TR	VR	WR	XR	ZR
W	HV	YV	DV	RV	AV	UV	LV	IV	CV	BV	EV	FV	GV	JV	KV	MV	NV	OV	PV	QV	SV	TV	VV	WV	XV	ZV
X	HW	YW	DW	RW	AW	UW	LW	IW	CW	BW	EW	FW	GW	JW	KW	MW	NW	OW	PW	QW	SW	TW	VW	WW	XW	ZW
Y	HX	YX	DX	RX	AX	UX	LX	IX	CX	BX	EX	FX	GX	JX	KX	MX	NX	OX	PX	QX	SX	TX	VX	WX	XX	ZX
Z	HZ	YZ	DZ	RZ	AZ	UZ	LZ	IZ	CZ	BZ	EZ	FZ	GZ	JZ	KZ	MZ	NZ	OZ	PZ	QZ	SZ	TZ	VZ	WZ	XZ	ZZ

θ_p^1 (left-hand label for rows)

FIGURE 69.

In effect, encipherment by means of such a system yields the equivalent of a two-alphabet cipher, with a transposition within each of the pairs of letters. The cipher text produced by such a system may be characterized by a large number of repetitions which begin with the initial letter of digraphs and end on the final letter of digraphs and which are preceded by digraphs having repeated *initial* letters or which are followed by digraphs having repeated *final* letters; for example, ciphertext passages of the following type might often arise: S̲F̲ B̲D̲ G̲B̲ H̲K̲ and S̲Q̲ B̲D̲ G̲B̲ W̲K̲ (wherein the repeated plain text is actually represented by SDBBGK, affected by the transposition). This system is included here as being illustrative of many simple systems which are capable of leading the student very much astray; in this instance, if one were unaware of the transposition feature involved and were to attempt what appears to be the simple task of fitting plain text into the two monoalphabetic portions on the basis of single-letter frequency considerations, he could spend a great deal of time without success—probably without any idea of what was causing his difficulties.

e. A pseudo-trigraphic cipher involving a table such as that in Fig. 52 may be readily recognized as such, since two letters of each trigraph enciphered by means of such a table are treated monoalphabetically. If three separate uniliteral frequency distributions are made—one for each of the three letters of the cipher trigraphs—two of the distributions should be monoalphabetic. Then, exploiting the monoalphabeticity (i. e., the *positional* monoalphabeticity) thus disclosed in the cipher text, plain text can be fitted to the cipher on the basis of single-letter frequency considerations; in addition, advantage may be taken of *partial* idiomorphisms, if these idiomorphisms involve the particular positions of the trigraphs which have been treated monoalphabetically.

f. Fortunately, it is unlikely that trigraphic systems other than the foregoing pseudo-trigraphic type will be encountered, because they are difficult to manipulate without extensive tables or complicated rules for encryption.[42] The subject can be passed over with the simple statement that their analysis requires much text to permit of solution by the frequency method—and blood, sweat, toil, and tears.[43]

73. **Further remarks on polygraphic substitution systems.**—*a.* In the treatment of the cryptography of the various digraphic systems in this chapter, the rules for encryption and decryption which have been illustrated are the "standard" rules (i. e., the rules extant in cryptologic literature, or the rules most commonly encountered in operational practice). Needless to say, however, there is no cryptologic counterpart of the Geneva Convention making these rules sacrosanct, nor forbidding the use of other rules for enciphering and deciphering.

b. In two-square systems and Playfair systems there are possible (and, in fact, there have been encountered in operational practice) modifications of the usual enciphering and deciphering rules which, if not suspected, may pose difficulties in the identification of such systems and in their cryptanalysis. For example, in a vertical two-square system, when two plaintext letters fall in the same column, their cipher equivalents might be taken as the letters immediately to the right of or immediately below these plaintext letters. Similarly, in a horizontal two-square system, if two plaintext letters are in the same row, their cipher equivalents might be taken as those immediately below or to the right of these letters. In Playfair cipher systems, two plaintext letters in the same row might be represented by the letters immediately below; two plaintext letters in the same column might be represented by the letters immediately to the right; a plaintext doublet might be represented by a ciphertext *doublet* formed by doubling the letter immediately to the right, or below, or diagonally to the right and below, thus removing one of the identifying ciphertext characteristics of the *normal* Playfair system. In one case encountered, instead of the normal Playfair linear relationship $\overline{AB}_p = \overline{BC}_c$, the rule was changed to $\overline{AB}_p = \overline{CB}_c$ (thus allowing a letter to "represent itself"—an "impossibility" in Playfair encipherment); even this simple modification caused difficulties in cryptanalysis because variant rules for encryption had not been considered.

c. The placing of cribs in small-matrix digraphic systems may be guided by the cryptographic peculiarities of these systems, when the general system is known to, or suspected by the cryptanalyst; conversely, the placing of a known crib may assist in the determination of the type of cryptosystem, or in the rejection of other types of systems. For example, cribs may be placed in Playfair ciphers on the basis of the "non-crashing" feature of the normal Playfair; that is, on the basis that in the equation 1.2=3.4 neither 1 and 3 nor 2 and 4 can be identical. Further-

---

[42] However, see in this connection subpar. 73*h*, which treats of a relatively simple mathematical method for enciphering polygraphs of *any* size.

[43] If a trigraphic system is encountered in operational cryptanalysis, special solutions would be made possible by the application of cribs, the aid furnished by isologs (not only in the same system, but also *between* systems), etc.

more, in the normal Playfair, $\alpha\beta_c$ cannot equal $\beta\alpha_p$. In horizontal two-square systems, if $\alpha\beta_c =$ $-\alpha_p$, then $\alpha\beta_c$ must equal $\beta\alpha_p$; and if $\alpha\beta_c = \beta-_p$, then $\alpha\beta_c$ must equal $\beta\alpha_p$. If, by placing a known crib in a cryptogram, evidence of *non*-reciprocity is disclosed (e. g., if $\overline{AB}_p = \overline{CD}_c$, but $\overline{CD}_p = \overline{XY}_c$), the cryptogram may be assumed to be other than a vertical two-square cipher, since vertical two-square encipherment yields complete reciprocity. In either type of two-square system, if one of the two squares is known (for example, a vertical two-square might be employed in which the upper square is always a normal alphabet), the placement of cribs is materially facilitated.

d. The ϕ test performed separately on the initial letters and final letters of ciphertext pairs from cryptograms produced by small-matrix digraphic systems will give results neither close to that expected for plain text, nor close to that for random text. The reason for the comparative "roughness" or pronounced differences among the relative frequencies in these distributions, as contrasted with the "smoothness" expected of random, is that small-matrix digraphic systems are only *partially* digraphic in nature and that the encryption involves characteristics similar to those of monoalphabetic substitution with variants. This roughness of the uniliteral frequency distributions for the initial and final letters, and, for that matter, for the over-all cipher text, reflects the partially digraphic nature of the encipherment.

e. If the cipher letters V, W, X, Y, and Z are of very low frequency in the over-all uniliteral frequency distribution of a digraphic cryptogram or set of cryptograms, this may be taken as evidence that the cryptosystem is a small-matrix digraphic system employing keyword-mixed sequences in the matrix or matrices. Furthermore, in small-matrix systems involving keyword-mixed squares, if θ_c^1 of $\overline{\theta\theta}_c$ is one of the letters VWXYZ, the θ_p^1 of the corresponding $\overline{\theta\theta}_p$ is likely to be one of these same letters. Similarly, if θ_c^2 is one of the letters VWXYZ, then θ_p^2 of the corresponding $\overline{\theta\theta}_p$ is likely to be one of these letters.

f. In trinome-digraphic systems employing large tables, the trinomes may run from 001 to 676, as in Fig. 51, or any consecutive set of 676 trinomes in the scale of 1000 possible trinomes may be used. For that matter, the entire span of trinomes 000–999 might be used in such a table, with occasional gaps, to hide the limitations of this system. As another means of disguising the limitation of 676 trinomes in such a system, three of the initial digits of the trinomes might have one variant each—thus no limitation would exist in the first position of trinomes. The 001, or other starting point in the cyclic scale, need not be at the upper left-hand corner of the table. The 676 trinomes in such tables may be inscribed in straight horizontals (i. e., in the normal manner of writing) as in Fig. 51, or they might be inscribed according to some other route; they probably would *not* be inscribed in a random manner because clumsy "deciphering tables" would then be necessary. It is also possible that the trinomes in a trinome-digraphic system might be converted into tetranomes by the addition of a sum-check (to assist in error-correction).

g. The cryptanalysis of tetranome-trigraphic systems with matrices similar to that illustrated in Fig. 59 involves a modification of the technique used in solving inverse four-square systems. If the plain-component and cipher-component sections of the large square have been inscribed according to the normal manner of writing (or any other manner, *if known*), the first two elements of the trigraphs may be reduced to a pair of cipher alphabets, and these two monoalphabetic substitutions may be solved as indicated in subpar. 69*e*. The applicability of inverse four-square solution principles to this tetranome-trigraphic system of course rests on the fact that the ciphertext sections are known or assumed to contain the dinomes 00–99 in numerical order, inscribed in the normal manner of writing; the conversion of the first two elements of the trigraphs depends upon the knowledge of the manner of inscription of the letters of the plain component sections, in order that the *four occurrences of the initial letters* and the *four occurrences* *of the final letters* may be correctly combined into two monoalphabetic distributions. Of course, if the composition of the small square (for the third element of trigraphs) is known, the third letter of trigraphs may be automatically deciphered. If the composition of the small square is not known, a consideration of the frequencies of the converted dinomes for the small square (i. e., the coordinates of the square to indicate the third member of trigraphs) may be used to obtain an entering wedge into this *third* monoalphabetic substitution.

h. There are but a very limited number of known cipher mechanisms which employ the polygraphic encipherment principle in any form. U. S. Patent No. 1515680 issued to A. Henkels in 1924 and U. S. Patent No. 1845947 issued to Weisner and Hill in 1932 describe two such mechanisms which produce polygraphic substitution. The latter, that of Weisner and Hill, is of particular interest because it is based on a rather simple mathematical process which can yield true polygraphic encipherment for polygraphs of any size. The underlying mathematical process, invented by Prof. Lester S. Hill of Hunter College and described in the "American Mathematical Monthly" in 1929 (Vol. XXXVI, p. 306) and 1931 (Vol. XXXVIII, p. 135), is treated briefly, below.

(1) Since Professor Hill's system is mathematical in nature, the first step in its use involves the conversion of the plaintext letters into numbers by means of a conversion alphabet which shows a correspondence between the 26 letters of the alphabet and the 26 numbers from 0 to 25, such as the following:

$$\begin{array}{cccccccccccccccccccccccccc} \text{A} & \text{B} & \text{C} & \text{D} & \text{E} & \text{F} & \text{G} & \text{H} & \text{I} & \text{J} & \text{K} & \text{L} & \text{M} & \text{N} & \text{O} & \text{P} & \text{Q} & \text{R} & \text{S} & \text{T} & \text{U} & \text{V} & \text{W} & \text{X} & \text{Y} & \text{Z} \\ 0 & 9 & 3 & 5 & 24 & 6 & 18 & 8 & 11 & 1 & 21 & 14 & 15 & 12 & 4 & 10 & 25 & 17 & 7 & 19 & 20 & 2 & 22 & 16 & 23 & 13 \end{array}$$

(2) The numbers obtained through the conversion of the plaintext letters are next treated arithmetically through the application of algebraic linear functions, this treatment being performed by means of mod 26 arithmetic.[43] The numerical results yielded by the algebraic treatment are then converted back into letters by means of the conversion alphabet, to yield the cipher equivalent of the original plain text.

(3) For example, suppose that the message, "NOTHING TO REPORT" is to be enciphered by trigraphs, and that, for this purpose, the enciphering keys [44] are (1, 2, 1); (5, 11, 3); (2, 4, 13). The message would be divided into trigraphs NOT–HIN–GTO–REP–ORT and the letters which result from the following operation would be taken as the cipher equivalent of the first trigraph:

Using the conversion alphabet in (1), above, "N–O–T" is converted into "12–4–19"; then the foregoing keys are applied—

$$(1\times\underline{12})+(2\times\underline{4})+(1\times\underline{19})=12+8+19=13+(1\times26)=\text{Z}$$
$$(5\times\underline{12})+(11\times\underline{4})+(3\times\underline{19})=60+44+57=5+(6\times26)=\text{D}$$
$$(2\times\underline{12})+(4\times\underline{4})+(13\times\underline{19})=24+16+247=1+(11\times26)=\text{J}$$

Thus, $\overline{\text{NOT}}_p$ is enciphered as $\overline{\text{ZDJ}}_c$. The complete encipherment would read ZDJ XMH HQH YMA DOI.

---

[43] Using "mod 26 arithmetic", one considers as the sum or product of two numbers, the number from 0–25 which is obtained by subtracting 26 (or a multiple of 26) from the ordinary arithmetical sum or product of the numbers.

[44] Encipherment of polygraphs containing *n* letters requires the use of n^2 keys. Thus, 9 keys are necessary for trigraphic encipherment; digraphic encipherment requires only 4 keys, whereas tetragraphic and pentagraphic encipherment necessitate the use of 16 and 25 keys, respectively. The numbers selected for use as keys must be chosen according to rather definite rules which evolve from the solution of simultaneous linear equations; otherwise, cryptographic ambiguity may result when decipherment is attempted.

(4) A large number of sets of enciphering and deciphering [45] keys can be constructed. It is even possible to construct keys which yield reciprocal encipherment, and it is this possibility which makes practicable the construction of a machine or device to accomplish the enciphering and deciphering.

i. Attention is called here to the applications of Table 13 ("Four-square individual frequencies") of Appendix 2; this table has been reproduced here for convenience. If the cryptanalyst has at hand a fairly large volume of cipher digraphs produced by encipherment with a normal four-square, he may use Table 13 as an aid in placing the initial letters and final letters

(TABLE 13, APPENDIX 2)

[Based on a count of 5,000 digraphs]

P_1 C_1

A	B	C	D	E	244	225	375	394	197
F	G	H	I J	K	125	98	193	271	95
L	M	N	O	P	229	199	188	350	251
Q	R	S	T	U	148	162	258	427	295
V	W	X	Y	Z	42	12	34	91	97
212	317	358	308	249	A	B	C	D	E
120	108	216	256	85	F	G	H	I J	K
216	140	152	435	269	L	M	N	O	P
206	121	306	364	284	Q	R	S	T	U
38	29	21	147	43	V	W	X	Y	Z

C_2 P_2

of the cipher digraphs into the appropriate cells of the cipher component sections *on the basis of their uniliteral frequencies*. Thus, if a distribution made of the initial letters of cipher pairs in a particular example shows Q_c, I_c, and C_c to be the letters of *predominantly* high frequency (listed in descending order of frequency), and if the distribution of the final letters shows F_c, Q_c, and P_c as the letters of *predominantly* high frequency (in descending order of frequency), these letters may be tentatively placed into a skeleton four-square matrix as follows (Fig. 70), based on the locations of the highest frequencies as given in Table 13:

```
A B C D E |     C I
F G H I K |
L M N O P |
Q R S T U |        Q
V W X Y Z |
----------+----------
        P | A B C D E
          | F G H I K
        F | L M N O P
        Q | Q R S T U
          | V W X Y Z
```

FIGURE 70.

---

[45] The deciphering keys which apply to the foregoing sample encipherment are (19, 24, 9); (23, 1, 12); (14, 0, 19). The interested student may wish to decipher the cryptogram ZDJXM HHQHY MADOI and establish for himself that it deciphers as NOTHING TO REPORT using these latter keys. In so doing he should remember that, in the final mathematical operation prior to converting the intermediate numbers into plaintext letters, he must subtract 26 (or a sufficient multiple of 26) to arrive at numbers within the range of 0 to 25.

j. In attempting to diagnose the underlying cryptosystem in any particular polygraphic cipher, the student may gain some assistance from the following recapitulation:

(1) In digraphic ciphers the majority of repetitions will be an even number of letters apart and these repetitions should for the most part begin on the first letters of pairs and end on the last letters of pairs. The majority of repetitions in trigraphic ciphers will be some multiple of three letters apart and these repetitions should for the most part begin on the first letters of trigraphs and end on the last letters of trigraphs.

(2) Digraphic ciphers may be revealed as such by the digraphic phi test, with additional support being given by the digraphic blank-expectation test; the presence of a null letter at the beginning of the cipher text might be disclosed by applying the two foregoing tests to a distribution of the digraphs which are formed when the first letter of the text is omitted.

(3) If either the uniliteral frequency distribution for the initial letters or for the final letters of the digraphs in a cryptogram exhibits monoalphabeticity, the cryptogram is probably a pseudo-digraphic cipher involving a large table of the type in Figs. 47*a*, 47*b*, or 48. If both of the foregoing uniliteral frequency distributions reflect monoalphabeticity, the cryptogram may involve the use of a table of the type in Fig. 69.

(4) If the "decipherment" of a cryptogram by means of a four-square matrix containing four normal alphabets yields two monoalphabetic substitutions—one for the initial letters and one for the final letters of the pseudo-decipherment—the cryptogram may be assumed to be an inverse four-square cipher.

(5) If an ocular inspection or statistical evaluation of the cipher text of a cryptogram reveals a large number of "transparencies", the cryptogram probably involves a two-square system.

(6) If a cryptogram contains several cipher doublets, all of which are broken up when the cipher text is divided into digraphs, the cryptogram may well involve normal Playfair encipherment.

(7) If the cipher text of a cryptogram exhibits any invariable affinity of one of the letters J, K, Q, X, or Z for vowels (or, for that matter, for another cluster of 5 or 6 letters), the cryptogram probably is in a small-matrix system employing sections consisting of more than 25 letters.

k. If a particular four-square cryptogram involves the use of a matrix in which either the plain component sections or the cipher component sections are normal alphabets, the matrix will be recovered through cryptanalysis in its *original* form, even when the components which are mixed have been derived by a transposition method or by no method at all. In Playfair cipher solution, the matrix can be recovered in its *original* form as long as the original matrix has been mixed in some systematic manner. However, in the case of two-square solution, there is no guarantee that the matrix can be recovered in its original form unless the original matrix has been keyword-mixed; if the original has been transposition-mixed, for example, the matrix which has been recovered through cryptanalysis—while being cryptographically *equivalent* to the original—will undoubtedly involve a permutation of the rows and columns of the original.

l. When four-square systems are encountered in which the matrix consists of four differently mixed sections, reconstruction of the matrix is accomplished in a manner similar to that used in the analysis of two-square ciphers. If the sections are composed of keyword-mixed sequences, the original matrix may be recovered; this is done by rearranging the rows and columns of each section on the basis of VWXYZ or such similar sequences found in keyword-mixed cases. Otherwise, the reconstructed matrix will in all probability be a permutation of both the rows and the columns of the original matrix, and there may be no way of recovering or of proving the original matrix.

m. In passing, it might be well to mention that any two-square system can be solved as a four-square system in which the matrix is composed of four mixed sections; upon the realization, from phenomena in the matrix reconstruction, that a two-square matrix is involved, the proper conversion can then easily be made.

CHAPTER X

CRYPTOSYSTEMS EMPLOYING IRREGULAR-LENGTH CIPHERTEXT UNITS

	Paragraph
Preliminary observations	74
Monome-dinome alphabets and other alphabets with irregular-length ciphertext units	75
General remarks on analysis	76
Analysis of simple examples	77
Analysis of more complicated examples	78
Further remarks on cryptosystems employing irregular-length ciphertext units	79

74. Preliminary observations.—*a.* The cipher alphabets of nearly all of the various cryptosystems treated thus far in this text have involved cipher units of a constant length.[1] That is, the ciphertext units have been (prior to regrouping into fives for transmission) either single characters, or pairs of characters, or three-character groupings, or, in the case of the Baconian and Baudot alphabets, 5-element ciphertext units; however, within a given cryptosystem the lengths of the ciphertext units have been *consistent*, and it is this consistency that has been of most importance to the cryptanalyst.

b. There is no reason why a cryptographer could not vary the size of the cipher units in a particular cryptosystem, as long as no cryptographic ambiguity in deciphering would result thereby. Furthermore, if the size of the cryptographic units *is* varied within a particular cryptosystem, obstacles are put in the way of cryptanalytic attack on the system—varying the length of the ciphertext groupings complicates the cryptanalyst's preliminary task of dividing the cipher text into the proper units for study. In this connection, the student should refer back to par. 63 and read again the remarks on the use of nulls which *differ in size* from the real cryptographic units. The example contained therein makes it clear that, until such nulls are identified and isolated by the cryptanalyst, he is unable to divide the cipher text properly and make appropriate frequency distributions. However, nulls may sometimes be recognized as such because they do not behave like units which represent actual plaintext elements. For example, in the three almost-identical ciphertext passages below,

(a)	...181Ø5	11343	71129	3219Ø	23231	52937...
(b)	...18151	Ø1343	71129	32192	32Ø31	52937...
(c)	...18151	13437	1Ø129	32192	3Ø231	52937...

the behavior of the digit Ø is characteristic of a null, and when this is recognized and eliminated, the remaining cryptographic text may be broken up into its real units and solved quite readily.

c. Since it has been indicated above that there are weaknesses in a scheme in which all cipher elements do not behave like equivalents for plaintext elements, it would be logical then

---

[1] The only exceptions have been in the digraphic systems using the matrices illustrated in Figs. 57a and 57b in which a plaintext digraph may be represented by a ciphertext digraph, trigraph, or tetragraph, depending upon the identity of the plaintext digraph.

to devise a system in which different-sized ciphertext units all represent actual plaintext elements and thus *do* behave more or less alike. It is easy to draw up cipher alphabets in which, for example, some of the letters are represented by single digits, others by pairs of digits. Such a system, called a *monome-dinome* system,[2] would produce cipher text which is an irregular intermixture of uniliteral and multiliteral equivalents. From the cryptanalytic standpoint, the decomposition of such cipher text could be very difficult for the analyst who does not know which digits to treat separately, which in pairs. Such systems, and similar variations, are given detailed treatment in the following paragraph.

75. **Monome-dinome alphabets and other alphabets with irregular-length ciphertext units.**—*a.* One simple scheme for yielding single-digit equivalents for some letters and two-digit equivalents for others makes use of a rectangular matrix which is similar to some of the biliteral matrices of Chapters VII and VIII, but which differs in that the top row of the matrix has no row coordinate. For examples, see Figs. 71–74, below. Each plaintext character appearing in the

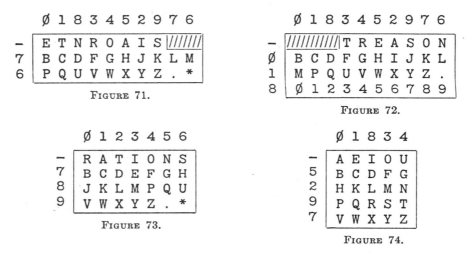

top row in the matrix has as its cipher equivalent merely the *monome* which appears above it, among the column coordinates; thus, in Fig. 71, $E_p=\emptyset$, $T_p=1$, $N_p=8$, etc. Each plaintext character appearing in one of the remaining rows has as its cipher equivalent the *dinome* formed by its row coordinate and column coordinate, respectively; thus in Fig. 71, $G_p=74$, $Q_p=61$, etc.

b. It should be noted that the external construction of all of the foregoing matrices is such that any digit which appears as a row coordinate does *not* occur as the monome equivalent for any letter; this limitation, accomplished by blanking out appropriate cells in the top row or by having the column coordinates distinct from the row coordinates, is necessary in all monome-dinome systems in order that cryptographic ambiguity will not arise. In Fig. 71, the internal composition is such that the plaintext letters which are most frequent in English are the ones which are provided with monome equivalents. This type of arrangement theoretically provides the most economical encryption for any given message—that is, theoretically yields the

---

[2] See in this connection Foote, Alexander, *Handbook for Spies*, New York, 1949, pp. 250–256, wherein is described such a cryptosystem reputedly typical of those used by secret agents in World War II.

shortest possible cipher text for a given plain text—but, of course, greatly limits the number of internal arrangements which may be used. Fig. 75, below, which is split into two separate

```
        5 2 9 7 6
      ┌───────────┐
   5  │ A  B  C  D  F │
   2  │ G  H  I  J  K │          ∅  1  8  3  4
   9  │ L  M  P  Q  S │          E  T  N  R  O
   7  │ U  V  W  X  Y │
   6  │ Z  .  (  )  * │
      └───────────┘
```

FIGURE 75a.   FIGURE 75b.

parts—one providing the monome equivalents and the other providing the dinome equivalents— illustrates another scheme for drawing up a monome-dinome cipher alphabet. In this alphabet, the digits which are used for the initial *and final* elements of dinomes are completely distinct from the digits used as monomes.

c. Most of the foregoing matrices contain a period for punctuation, and the matrix in Fig. 72, containing the single digits ∅–9, provides a means for encrypting numbers without first spelling them out. The matrices in Figs. 71, 73, and 75 contain another character, symbolized by an asterisk, which may be used for punctuation or as a special indicator.[3] The matrix in Fig. 74 uses only nine of the single digits as coordinates, the digit 6 being omitted; this single digit might be employed as a word separator, a stop, or a null. The matrix in Fig. 76, below, illustrates a scheme by which certain high-frequency plaintext digraphs and trigraphs may be represented in the matrix, as well as the single letters and digits. The symbol

```
        ∅  1  8  3  4  5  2  9  7  6
      ┌──────────────────────────────┐
   -  │ R  E  T  A  I  N ////////////// │
   2  │ B  C  D  F  G  H  J  K  L  M │
   9  │ O  P  Q  S  U  V  W  X  Y  Z │
   7  │ .  ,  TH IN ST ED ION ING * # │
   6  │ ∅  1  2  3  4  5  6  7  8  9 │
      └──────────────────────────────┘
```

FIGURE 76.

in this latter matrix could be used as a "repetition indicator" for checking numbers, as in the ciphertext passage 69 65 68 <u>76</u> 69 65 68, meaning the number 752; the symbol * might be used as an indicator meaning "the immediately preceding plaintext letter is repeated" (thus AA patterns would be suppressed in the cipher text). In all of the foregoing matrices the order of inscription of the letters within the matrix, and the particular arrangement of the row- and column-coordinates are both subject to variation.

---

[3] For example, this special character may be put to use as an indicator to show that plaintext numbers begin or end, thus obviating the necessity of including digits within the cipher matrix. In this usage digits in the plain text might be *tripled* and inserted in the cipher text with the appropriate indicator before and after the plaintext digits. Thus, using the matrix in Fig. 71, the plaintext fragment "..HILL 865.." would be encrypted as the cipher sequence 75 2 77 77 66 888 666 555 66 (prior to regrouping into five-character groups).

d. By prearranged convention it is possible to employ ordinary commutative bipartite matrices (such as those already described in Chapters VII and VIII) in a manner which yields monome-dinome encipherment. For example, using the matrix illustrated in Fig. 77, the plaintext word EIGHT could be encrypted as 10 29 7 8 49 (and then, of course, regrouped into five-

```
      6 7 8 9 Ø
   1 │ A B C D E
   2 │ F G H I K
   3 │ L M N O P
   4 │ Q R S T U
   5 │ V W X Y Z
```

FIGURE 77.

character groups). That is, the normal bipartite enciphering conventions would be used, with the exception that the row indicator for the cipher equivalent for a particular plaintext letter would *not* be employed when this row indicator is the same as that for the immediately preceding letter of the plain text.[4] As may be noted, no cryptographic ambiguity in decipherment may arise.

e. Of course, as an extension of the foregoing ideas, there could also be *monome-dinome-trinome* systems, incorporating matrices of the types illustrated in Figs. 78–82, below. In Fig.

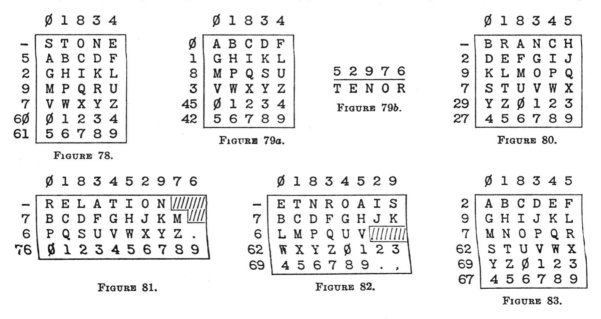

```
       Ø 1 8 3 4
    -│ S T O N E
    5│ A B C D F
    2│ G H I K L
    9│ M P Q R U
    7│ V W X Y Z
   6Ø│ Ø 1 2 3 4
   61│ 5 6 7 8 9
```
FIGURE 78.

```
       Ø 1 8 3 4
   Ø│ A B C D F
   1│ G H I K L
   8│ M P Q S U
   3│ V W X Y Z
  45│ Ø 1 2 3 4
  42│ 5 6 7 8 9
```
FIGURE 79a.

```
   5 2 9 7 6
   T E N O R
```
FIGURE 79b.

```
        Ø 1 8 3 4 5
    -│ B R A N C H
    2│ D E F G I J
    9│ K L M O P Q
    7│ S T U V W X
   29│ Y Z Ø 1 2 3
   27│ 4 5 6 7 8 9
```
FIGURE 80.

```
        Ø 1 8 3 4 5 2 9 7 6
    -│ R E L A T I O N ░░░
    7│ B C D F G H J K M ░
    6│ P Q S U V W X Y Z .
   76│ Ø 1 2 3 4 5 6 7 8 9
```
FIGURE 81.

```
        Ø 1 8 3 4 5 2 9
    -│ E T N R O A I S
    7│ B C D F G H J K
    6│ L M P Q U V ░░░
   62│ W X Y Z Ø 1 2 3
   69│ 4 5 6 7 8 9 . ,
```
FIGURE 82.

```
        Ø 1 8 3 4 5
    2│ A B C D E F
    9│ G H I J K L
    7│ M N O P Q R
   62│ S T U V W X
   69│ Y Z Ø 1 2 3
   67│ 4 5 6 7 8 9
```
FIGURE 83.

83 there is a matrix which may be used for *dinome-trinome* encipherment. Encipherment with this latter matrix is commutative; for example, E_p=24 or 42, and T_p=621 or 162.

---

[4] A variation of this method could make use of a convention by which the *column* indicator is dropped if it is the same as that for the preceding plaintext letter.

f. *Literal* versions of the preceding types of alphabets with irregular-length cipher units are also possible. Several types are illustrated in Figs. 84–88, including among them matrices permitting the use of variants in encryption. Furthermore, any of the commutative variant

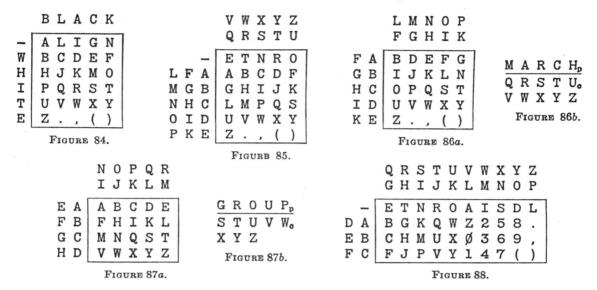

```
    B L A C K                  V W X Y Z                  L M N O P
                               Q R S T U                  F G H I K
  ┌─────────────┐
- │ A L I G N │                    ┌─────────────┐        F A ┌─────────────┐
W │ B C D E F │              -     │ E T N R O │           G B │ B D E F G │
H │ H J K M O │              L F A │ A B C D F │           H C │ I J K L N │
I │ P Q R S T │              M G B │ G H I J K │           I D │ O P Q S T │
T │ U V W X Y │              N H C │ L M P Q S │           K E │ U V W X Y │
E │ Z . , ( ) │              O I D │ U V W X Y │              │ Z . , ( ) │
  └─────────────┘            P K E │ Z . , ( ) │              └─────────────┘
    FIGURE 84.                     └─────────────┘              FIGURE 86a.
                                  FIGURE 85.

                                                                M A R C Hₚ
                                                                Q R S T Uₒ
                                                                V W X Y Z
                                                                FIGURE 86b.
```

```
    N O P Q R
    I J K L M

  E A ┌─────────────┐         G R O U Pₚ           Q R S T U V W X Y Z
  F B │ A B C D E │           S T U V Wₒ           G H I J K L M N O P
  G C │ F H I K L │           X Y Z
  H D │ M N Q S T │           FIGURE 87b.        -   ┌───────────────────────┐
      │ V W X Y Z │                            D A │ E T N R O A I S D L │
      └─────────────┘                          E B │ B G K Q W Z 2 5 8 . │
        FIGURE 87a.                            F C │ C H M U X Ø 3 6 9 , │
                                                    │ F J P V Y 1 4 7 ( ) │
                                                    └───────────────────────┘
                                                        FIGURE 88.
```

matrices treated in par. 58a (i. e., Figs. 27, 28, and 31) may be used in connection with the convention described in subpar. *d*, above, to provide cipher alphabets with irregular-length ciphertext units.

76. General remarks on analysis.—*a.* The first step in the analysis of any cryptogram encrypted in a system with irregular-length cipher units involves dividing the cryptogram into the proper, vari-sized cipher units—that is, reducing the cryptogram to monoalphabetic terms. After this has been done, solution proceeds along the straightforward lines which have been described in earlier chapters of the text. Thus, in this chapter, attention will be focused on this first step of dividing the text into its proper monoalphabetic units. In order to simplify somewhat the general treatment contained in this paragraph, all remarks will be directed at monomedinome systems; most of the principles and methods outlined herein are general enough that they may be modified and applied in the solution of other types of systems with irregular-length ciphertext units.

b. A *cryptographer*, in his process of deciphering a particular monome-dinome cryptogram, would begin by considering whether or not the first digit of the cipher text were among those digits which can start a dinome—that is, whether it were a *row coordinate* or not. If it were, he would treat it along with the next digit of the text as a dinome, and then proceed to consider whether or not the following digit were a row coordinate, etc. If the first digit of the message were not a row coordinate, he would treat it as a monome, and then proceed to consider whether or not the next digit were a row coordinate, etc. One may now see that the cryptographic process of dividing the cipher text into its proper units is based solely on a knowledge of the digits which are the row coordinates of the pertinent matrix. Thus, it may further be seen that the *cryptanalytic* attack on a monome-dinome cipher would first involve an attempt to determine the identity of the row coordinates.

c. If a given cryptogram involves a matrix in which the high-frequency plaintext elements are evenly distributed throughout the various rows, it may be expected that the particular digits occurring with the greatest frequency in a uniliteral frequency distribution made on the cipher text are those which are row coordinates of the pertinent matrix. This may be explained by the fact that the digits used as row coordinates occur in the cipher equivalents for more plaintext letters than do those digits which are used as monomes. However, one must remember that a monome-dinome matrix may involve two, three, four, or more row coordinates and, although in a particular instance it may be that the most frequent cipher digits *are* those digits which have been used as row coordinates, a study of the uniliteral frequency distribution may not make it obvious as to just *how many* coordinates are involved; it may be necessary to make several trials, one considering only the *two* most frequent cipher digits as row coordinates, one considering the *three* most frequent, etc.

d. If trials of the type just mentioned do not yield reduced, monoalphabetic text which will succumb to the principles of plaintext recovery treated in the earlier chapters of this text, it may then be assumed that the cryptogram involves a matrix in which several of the high-frequency letters are arranged together in the top row or in which one or more columns are composed solely of high-frequency letters. Such matrices are likely to produce cipher text in which some of the digits which have been used as monomes occur more frequently than some of those used as row coordinates. Thus, the easy mode of entry via the uniliteral frequency distribution may not be used, and other approaches of a less clear-cut nature must be taken.

e. In an attempt to identify at least one or two probable row coordinates, the analyst should carefully scrutinize the cryptogram itself in order to find passages exhibiting *bipartite characteristics*, such as appear in the sequence 8043818741, wherein the digits 8 and 4 "act" like digits which have been used as row coordinates, being spaced off at intervals of two. A slightly more objective approach involves first making a biliteral [5] distribution of the cipher text, and then considering as a probable row coordinate the initial digit of the particular dinome which the distribution shows to be the most frequent. Of course, this approach is most likely to be valid when the particular dinome occurs with a much greater frequency than the remaining dinomes. While still on the subject of distributions, it is pointed out that the previously-mentioned "bipartite characteristics" manifested in a cryptogram might be disclosed by making a biliteral distribution of *alternate* digits of the cipher text,[6] that is, in the sequence 123456 one would consider the dinomes 13, 24, 35, 46. In such a distribution, one may expect that the most frequent dinomes will be those comprising two digits which were both row coordinates of the pertinent enciphering matrix.

f. If the cipher text of a given monome-dinome cryptogram begins with a doubled digit, this digit is most probably one of the row coordinates of the pertinent matrix; otherwise, the doublet would have to be considered as comprising two monomes and the first word of the underlying plain text would have to begin with a doublet (a very rare contingency in the English language). Similarly, if the cipher text is seen to contain any digit repeated consecutively four

---

[5] The use of the term *"biliteral"* in connection with *digit* cipher text may not be in conformance with the strictest rules of semantics, but the author feels that it is unnecessary to give a new name to an already-familiar type of distribution merely because it is being applied to a different kind of text. However, some who prefer to be purists in this matter term a digraphic distribution which is made on digit text as a "dinome distribution" or "dinomic distribution", and a biliteral distribution made on digit text, a "running dinome distribution".

[6] In the vernacular such a distribution is termed an "A–A" (pronounced "ay-dit-ay") distribution.

or more times, the particular digit may be assumed to be a row coordinate; otherwise, such a sequence of repeated digits would have to represent *at least* a threefold repetition of some one plaintext letter (another rare event in English, although not as rare as that mentioned in the preceding sentence).

g. On occasion it may be found that much time has been spent in the attempt to identify the row coordinates, yet apparently with not all of the coordinates being identified. In such a case, it may be found useful to consider those digits which are *least likely* to be row coordinates, specifically, those which occur least frequently in the cryptogram. The analyst may go through the troublesome cryptogram and place a slant bar (virgule) directly after each such digit as it occurs in the message. These marks may then be taken as an indication of places in the cryptogram where one bona fide cipher unit ends and the next begins. The analyst must then study the digits which directly follow these slant bars with a view to discovering new possibilities for row coordinates—possibilities which, although previously latent, have been made patent by this latest step.

h. In the foregoing subparagraphs, *a* to *g*, the secondary step of testing for the corroboration or invalidation of any particular trial decomposition has been passed over quite briefly. Actually, this step is best described with specific examples of solution, and for this reason is treated in two subsequent paragraphs, 77 and 78, with such examples. However, a few methods which can be applied for the rejection of incorrect hypotheses will be mentioned here, because they are rather basic and simple. If the cryptanalyst finds, after having divided a monome-dinome cipher on the basis of a particular hypothesis, that a long repetition in the cryptogram is not broken up in the same way on each of its occurrences, he may well reject as incorrect the hypothesis on which the division is based. Likewise, the analyst may reject any hypothesis which requires him to make the last digit of a cryptogram a monome when this particular digit has to be considered as a row coordinate as part of the basic assumption.[7] The presence of an inordinate number of *consecutive* monomes may cause one to suspect that a particular decomposition is incorrect; however, probably only continued exposure to traffic of a certain type or involving one kind of enciphering matrix would provide one with a sound basis for knowing *just how many are too many*.

i. There is one practical, straightforward measure for determining the relative goodness of an assumed decomposition which deserves particular mention. It involves considering the ratio of the *number of monomes* produced in a particular decomposition to the *number of remaining cipher units*. In the case of monome-dinome ciphers, for example, in which an assumption of only two row coordinates is made, there can be no more than eight different plaintext letters represented by monomes and the total frequency of those monomes can not exceed the frequency expected of the eight most frequent letters in the language.[8] Since in English the eight most frequent letters occur with a total relative frequency of 66%, any trial decomposition giving rise to a ratio of monomes to dinomes which is considerably more than 66 to 34 (=1.9) may be considered incorrect. Likewise, since an assumption of three row coordinates limits to seven the number of different plaintext letters which may have monome equivalents, and since the seven most frequent letters in English occur with a total relative frequency of 60%, any such assumption giving rise to a ratio of monomes to dinomes which is considerably more than 60 to 40 (=1.5) may be considered invalid. The author does, however, hasten to point out that

---

[7] However, the possibility of a final null or nulls must not be ignored; the presence of nulls at the end of the cipher text would invalidate this reasoning.

[8] The only exception to this statement would be a case wherein a word separator is included as part of the cryptosystem, and that this separator is represented by a monome. This usage, however, seems rather unlikely.

a ratio which is *smaller* in any instance than the pertinent ratio, above, *does not disprove* the particular trial decomposition since the plaintext letters represented by monomes may not necessarily be the letters of highest frequency. The examples in the next two paragraphs will serve to clarify the foregoing considerations.

77. Analysis of simple examples.—a. The following cryptogram, suspected to be a monome-dinome cipher, is available for study:

	5	10	15	20	25	30
A	2 4 0 9 0	1 5 7 0 9	0 8 1 2 1	0 2 0 9 2	9 2 4 0 5	5 6 0 0 1
B	2 7 0 7 2	9 0 4 8 2	4 7 6 0 7	0 9 0 2 2	1 0 2 0 9	2 9 7 2 4
C	0 7 2 9 2	9 1 2 5 7	5 2 9 6 1	0 9 0 4 2	7 2 0 0 2	0 7 2 4 7
D	5 0 5 7 0	9 6 0 8 1	7 2 4 0 9	2 9 0 4 0	4 0 9 7 1	2 4 0 9 7
E	2 9 1 2 8	7 6 0 9 0	4 0 7 5 0	6 5 2 9 7	0 9 0 6 7	2 0 9 0 2
F	0 9 0 4 0	7 4 0 7 6

Cursory examination of the cipher text reveals nothing more significant than the fact that the digit 3 is absent; however, the significance of this escapes us for the moment. A uniliteral frequency distribution of the text is then made, as is illustrated below:

b. The uniliteral frequency distribution shows four marked peaks (2, 7, 9, and ∅) and one pronounced trough (8). A biliteral frequency distribution is made, as shown below, to assist in

	1	2	3	4	5	6	7	8	9	∅
1	–	5	–	–	1	–	1	–	–	3
2	2	1	–	7	1	–	2	1	9	6
3	–	–	–	–	–	–	–	–	–	–
4	–	1	–	–	–	2	1	–	–	10
5	–	2	–	–	1	1	3	–	–	2
6	1	–	–	–	1	–	1	–	–	4
7	1	8	–	1	3	3	–	–	–	5
8	2	1	–	–	–	–	1	–	–	–
9	2	5	–	–	–	2	4	–	–	10
∅	2	5	–	6	2	2	7	2	14	2

196

further evaluation of the properties of the cipher text. It is noted that the 2 and Ø rows, representing the two highest-frequency digits in the cipher text, have the most liberal combinations with the remaining digits; this would indicate that 2 and Ø are likely row coordinates of the cipher matrix. Since the 7 and 9 rows show less affinity of these digits for other digits, 7 and 9 are less likely to represent row coordinates of the matrix; consequently the assumption is made that the matrix involved only two numbered row coordinates, 2 and Ø.

c. The cryptogram is now divided accordingly, and the assumption of 2 and Ø as row coordinates is borne out by the bipartite character of the following passages in the cipher text:

$$(1) \quad .../21/02/09/29/24/05/... \quad \text{(at A14)}$$
$$(2) \quad .../07/09/02/21/02/09/29/... \quad \text{(at B14)}$$
$$(3) \quad .../09/04/27/20/02/07/24/... \quad \text{(at C16)}$$
$$(4) \quad .../24/09/29/04/04/09/... \quad \text{(at D12)}$$

A frequency distribution of the decomposed text is made, as illustrated below:

	1	2	3	4	5	6	7	8	9	Ø
–	7	////	–	1	6	6	12	1	1	////
2	2	–	–	7	1	–	2	1	9	2
Ø	1	5	–	6	2	2	7	2	13	1

The percentage of monomes, 35%, does not exceed the threshold for the sum of the frequencies of the eight highest-frequency plaintext letters; furthermore, since the eight monomes have a much lower frequency than the sum of the eight highest-frequency letters in English, this is an indication that some of the monomes represent plaintext letters of lower frequency.

d. The decomposed text may now be solved, and the message is found to begin with the words "SABOTAGE PLANS..." The original matrix is reconstructed, and is discovered to be based upon the key word VERMOUTH, as follows:

	9	1	6	4	5	8	7	3	Ø	2
–	V	E	R	M	O	U	T	H	/////	
Ø	A	B	C	D	F	G	I	J	K	L
2	N	P	Q	S	W	X	Y	Z	.	,

The reason for the absence of the digit 3 in the cipher text may now be seen: the digit 3 forms a part of only the letters H, J, and Z, and these letters did not occur in the plaintext message.

e. Solution of certain other cases of mixed-length systems progresses as easily as did the solution of the foregoing example.

(1) For instance, in the case of a cryptogram produced by a matrix where the digits used for both the initial and final digits of dinomes are completely distinct from the monome digits (e. g., Fig. 75), it may be seen that "eliminating" from the cipher text those particular digits which were used as monomes in the original enciphering alphabet will leave the remainder of the cryptogram broken up into units all of which contain an even number of digits. (This would not be true in the case of other types of matrices, such as Figs. 71–74, since eliminating the digits which were used as monomes in the pertinent alphabet would remove not only actual cipher monomes but also the final digits of many cipher dinomes.) In view of this fact, if one is confronted with a cryptogram which he assumes to have been produced by a matrix such as that

in Fig. 75, he may use a mechanical method by means of which he will quickly be able to determine which digits are row coordinates and which are not; or, if his basic assumption concerning the type of matrix involved is incorrect, the error will quickly become known to him. He need only make successive trials each of which involves considering a different one of the 10 digits as being one of those which is a monome in the pertinent alphabet; "eliminating" the particular digit from the cryptogram in each trial will inevitably lead to other digits which must also be eliminated throughout the cryptogram in order to maintain the stipulation that all the cipher units which remain must contain an even number of digits. For example, if one assumes that "Ø" is a digit which was a monome, then he must further assume from a sequence of cipher digits such as Ø5Ø35Ø that "5" is also a digit which was a monome; and then likewise "3". Any particular one of the ten trials which is based on an incorrect initial assumption may be expected to end up with all ten digits being considered as digits which were monomes.

(2) In the case of a monome-dinome system in which the row coordinates of the enciphering matrix are distinct from the column coordinates (as in Figs. 73 and 74), solution is expedited by capitalizing on the fact that the digits within the family comprising the row coordinates do not (and cannot) contact themselves or any other digits within the family; using Fig. 73 as an example, it is obvious that the digits 7, 8, and 9 can never be followed by a 7, 8, or 9. (This causal avoidance among certain digits exhibits itself in either a digraphic or a biliteral distribution of the cipher text.) A cryptogram enciphered by such a system may be expected to contain far fewer cipher doublets than would a cryptogram produced by a matrix without the foregoing limitation, and the doublets which do occur will themselves involve but a limited number of the 10 different digits. When solving such a cryptogram, the cryptanalyst need only consider as possible candidates for row coordinates those particular digits which do not appear in cipher doublets. Furthermore, he may with certainty go through the cryptogram placing a slant bar (to indicate the end of a valid cipher unit) after every occurrence of any digit which has appeared in a cipher doublet.

(3) The system described in subpar. 75d and the accompanying Fig. 77 (employing a commutative bipartite matrix) is another system which yields cipher text in which a certain family of digits—namely, the row coordinate digits—cannot contact any other digits in the same family. If the cryptanalyst is confronted by a cryptogram in this system, he knows that the first digit of the cryptogram must be a row coordinate. Then he has only to go through the cryptogram noting the digits which follow this row coordinate digit wherever it occurs in the cryptogram and, in this way, he may be able to identify all the column coordinate digits. Of course, by the process of elimination, he will then know which digits are row coordinates besides the initial digit of the cryptogram, and it will then be possible for him to divide the text into its proper irregular-length ciphertext units.

78. Analysis of more complicated examples.—a. In some cases, the rather simple methods of analysis applied in the preceding paragraph will not bear fruit, either because of the complexity inherent in the *number* of plaintext elements in the cipher matrix, or because of certain unpredictable aberrations caused by the particular *arrangement* of plaintext elements in the matrix. For instance, if a specific matrix contained only the highest-frequency letters in the top row, and if the matrix contained a fairly large number of plaintext elements (and therefore embodied 3 or 4, or more, row coordinates), and if the elements in the dinome rows were balanced from the frequency standpoint, so that the rows would be used with approximately equal frequency, and furthermore if certain of the columns were composed of heavier elements than others (thus producing peaks that might incorrectly be identified as row coordinates)—all these conditions

198

would yield a cryptosystem that might pose considerable difficulties in the way of straight-forward analysis. A case will now be studied that will illustrate typical techniques that would be necessary in more difficult circumstances.

b. The following cryptogram has been intercepted on an enemy net known to be passing monome-dinome traffic:

```
62719   44081   21204   71270   55042   12627

09637   06212   24712   91724   21058   12727

07055   58719   55721   04109   52847   71297

23571   82123   94578   77571   80581   97654

74572   05191   77194   52958   70012   12251

69051   15724   71389   47316   79035   47359

54742   78271   72327   05504   58255   55918
```

The uniliteral frequency distribution for the cryptogram is shown below:

```
  ≡                   ⌐        /
  ⦀⦀⦀       /     ⦀⦀⦀⦀ /
  ⦀⦀⦀ //  ⦀⦀ ⦀⦀⦀ =  ⦀⦀⦀ //  ////
  1 2 3 4 5 6 7 8 9 0
```

c. From the appearance of the uniliteral frequency distribution, it is to be expected that from among the four peaks (1, 2, 5, and 7) some row coordinates must be represented, and since there is not much variance in frequency among these peaks, *perhaps all four* represent row coordinates. In an attempt to obtain as much information as possible from a study of the frequency characteristics of the cipher text, a biliteral distribution is made and is shown below.

	1	2	3	4	5	6	7	8	9	0
1	1	11	1	–	1	2	3	3	5	3
2	7	2	3	3	2	1	9	1	3	2
3	1	1	–	–	3	–	1	1	1	–
4	1	3	–	1	9	–	6	5	2	1
5	3	2	–	3	9	–	6	5	2	2
6	–	3	1	–	1	–	1	–	1	–
7	10	7	2	2	1	1	3	2	1	7
8	3	3	–	1	–	–	3	–	1	1
9	3	–	–	4	4	1	2	–	–	2
0	1	–	1	4	7	1	1	1	2	1

199

Examination of this latter distribution adds support to the impressions gained from the uniliteral frequency distribution, namely, that the row coordinates for the cipher matrix are very likely to be found among the digits 1, 2, 5, and 7. Furthermore the digit 7, because of its high frequency and because of satisfactory combinative qualities in the biliteral distribution, is selected as a definite row coordinate. This will reduce the number of trials that must subsequently be considered.

d. If *all* of the row coordinates of the cipher matrix are found among the various combinations of 7 with 1, 2, and 5, then it is clear that:

(1) if there are but two coordinates of the matrix, these must be either 7 and 1, 7 and 2, or 7 and 5, (three cases);

(2) if there are three coordinates of the matrix, these must be either 7–1–2, 7–1–5, or 7–2–5 (three cases); or

(3) if the matrix has four numbered coordinates, this must entail the combination of 7–1–2–5 (only one case).

e. On the basis of each of the foregoing seven hypotheses, the cipher text is divided and the resulting frequency distributions are shown below:

	1	2	3	4	5	6	7	8	9	Ø
–	////	17	6	16	31	4	////	10	13	9
1	1	8	–	–	–	2	2	1	2	3
7	9	7	2	2	–	1	2	2	1	7

Case I

	1	2	3	4	5	6	7	8	9	Ø
–	18	////	5	16	30	5	////	11	12	15
2	6	2	1	–	1	1	8	1	3	1
7	6	6	2	2	–	1	3	1	1	3

Case II

	1	2	3	4	5	6	7	8	9	Ø
–	21	25	6	13	////	6	////	7	14	12
5	3	2	–	3	6	–	5	5	1	–
7	6	5	2	2	–	1	3	1	1	7

Case III

	1	2	3	4	5	6	7	8	9	Ø
–	//////	4	15	29	3	////	10	10	13
1	1	6	–	–	–	2	3	1	3	2
2	4	1	2	1	2	1	6	1	2	–
7	7	5	2	2	–	1	2	1	1	4

Case IV

	1	2	3	4	5	6	7	8	9	Ø
–	////	16	6	13	////	5	////	4	13	9
1	–	9	–	–	1	1	2	3	1	3
5	3	2	–	3	6	–	4	5	1	–
7	7	5	2	2	–	1	2	1	1	7

Case V

	1	2	3	4	5	6	7	8	9	Ø
–	17	////	5	12	////	5	////	8	11	14
2	6	2	1	1	1	1	8	–	2	2
5	3	2	–	3	5	–	5	5	2	–
7	4	4	2	2	–	1	3	–	1	3

Case VI

	1	2	3	4	5	6	7	8	9	Ø
–	//////	4	12	////	3	////	5	10	12
1	–	7	–	–	1	2	3	3	2	2
2	4	1	2	1	2	1	6	–	1	1
5	2	2	–	3	5	–	4	5	2	–
7	5	4	2	2	–	1	2	–	1	4

Case VII

f. In order to be able to evaluate the relative merits of the seven hypotheses and choose the case which is most likely to be correct, it is possible to resort to a method wherein *group frequencies* of the high-frequency elements from each of the decompositions are studied. In the following table drawn up for this purpose, the column of figures under "x" denotes the cumulative six highest-frequency ciphertext units; under "N", we have the actual frequencies of the first, the first two, the first three . . . , the first six highest-frequency ciphertext units for each hypothesis (compare with the distributions in subpar. *e*); in the adjoining column to the right of each "N" column, the various cumulative frequency values are expressed as percentages of the total number of ciphertext units which remain after the particular trial decomposition. The column labelled "P" gives the cumulative *theoretical* frequencies of the six most frequent letters in English plain text (ETNROA), in cumulative relative order of frequency (i. e., the frequencies of E_p; of E_p and T_p; of E_p, T_p, and N_p; and so on). The following elaboration will serve to clarify the foregoing details.

	I		II		III		IV		V		VI		VII		P
x	N	$\frac{N}{158}$	N	$\frac{N}{161}$	N	$\frac{N}{157}$	N	$\frac{N}{147}$	N	$\frac{N}{138}$	N	$\frac{N}{139}$	N	$\frac{N}{129}$	
1	31	19.6	30	18.6	25	15.9	29	19.7	16	11.6	17	12.2	12	9.3	13.0
2	48	30.4	48	29.8	46	29.3	44	29.9	29	21.0	31	22.3	24	18.6	22.2
3	64	45.0	64	39.8	60	38.2	57	38.8	42	30.4	43	30.9	34	26.6	30.2
4	77	48.7	79	49.1	73	46.5	67	45.6	51	37.0	54	38.8	41	31.8	37.8
5	87	55.1	91	56.5	85	54.1	77	52.4	60	43.5	62	44.6	47	36.4	45.3
6	96	60.8	102	63.4	92	58.6	84	57.1	67	48.6	70	50.4	52	40.3	52.7

g. It is noted that in Case I, the most frequent ciphertext unit has a percentile frequency of 19.6%; the highest two units, a percentile frequency of 30.4%; the highest three, a percentile frequency of 45.0%. When these percentages are compared with the percentile frequency of the highest-frequency letter in English plain text (13.0%), of the highest two letters (22.2%), and of the highest three letters (30.2%), it is clear that Case I does not conform to the characteristics expected of a simple monoalphabetic substitution; therefore Case I is not the correct division of the cipher text. Similarly, Cases II, III, and IV can also be rejected because the cumulative values are *much higher* than the corresponding expectations for plain text. Case VII, on the other hand, demonstrates values *much lower* than the corresponding expectations for plain text; therefore this case too is rejected. This leaves only Cases V and VI, both of which show a close correspondence with plaintext expectations.

h. If there were nothing else in the manifestations of the decomposed cipher text in Case V and Case VI, these two cases would have to be tried in turn, making some tentative plaintext assumptions; of course, only the correct case would consistently yield plain text. However, there is an additional bit of reasoning which may be applied here as a means of deciding which of these two remaining cases is more likely to be correct and ought to be worked on first—namely, it may be reasoned that cipher text which has been decomposed according to an incorrect hypothesis will be likely to contain a larger ratio of monomes to dinomes than would the same text if it had been decomposed according to the correct hypothesis.[9] Case V has a monome-dinome ratio of .916 whereas Case VI has a corresponding ratio of 1.043; thus Case V is indicated as the case which is more likely to be correct.

i. The cipher text is now divided according to the hypothesis of row coordinates of 1, 5, and 7, and the plain text is quickly recovered, facilitated by the pattern of the first word, RECONNAISSANCE. The cipher matrix is reconstructed as follows:

```
    1 7 5 0̸ 2 8 4 9 6 3

-  |////////| A E I N O R T
1  | B F J M S W Z 1 4 7
7  | C G K P U X . 2 5 8
5  | D H L Q V Y 0̸ 3 6 9
```

The reason for the high frequency of the cipher digit 2 is now seen: the combined frequencies of E_p, S_p, and U_p contribute to an inordinate peak for that column coordinate.

j. In retrospect, several important points may be noted in the solution of this particular cryptogram. First of all, the four consecutive 5's in the last two groups of the cryptogram make it a very strong probability that 5 is a row coordinate; otherwise the four 5's would mean a threefold (or even fourfold) repetition of a monome letter, a comparatively rare contingency. Secondly, the digit 1 could have been selected as a row coordinate with considerable certainty, based on the fact that, since the dinome 12 was the highest-frequency element in the biliteral distribution, it may be assumed that at least a number of 12's were causal and therefore 1 must be a row coordinate. In other words, the correct set of coordinates might have been established at the very beginning of the analysis, but for pedagogical reasons it was felt necessary to proceed along the general lines of the solution as given. It is to be noted that, since at the start of solution we did not know exactly how many numbered row coordinates there were in this particular case, we could not apply the ratio of monomes to dinomes at once as the deciding criterion.

k. If mixed-length systems were encountered in actual practice, after the type of matrix became known through solution of several days' traffic, solution of subsequent days' messages would be facilitated because by this time the analyst would be familiar with the general type of matrix used. This knowledge would be of great assistance in making assumptions as to the nature of subsequent matrices. In some cases, the internal arrangement of the matrix might remain fixed, with only the coordinates being changed periodically; in other cases, the internal arrangement and the coordinates of the matrix might change, with only the *size* of the matrix remaining fixed. If it were known, for instance, that the enemy were using a monome-dinome system with

---

[9] This intuitive reasoning has been borne out empirically with reasonable success. 30 monome-dinome ciphers of an average length of 100 digits were decomposed in all possible ways based on the proper hypothesis of two, three, or four row coordinates—whichever correctly applied. In the case of approximately one-half of these ciphers, the correct decomposition yielded a monome-to-dinome ratio which was lower than the monome-to-dinome ratio yielded by any of the other, *incorrect* decompositions. Admittedly, this 50–50 chance is of small note in connection with subpar. *h*, above, where there are only two cases from which to choose anyway, with the concomitant 50–50 chance of either choice being the right one. However, when there are *more* than two from which the analyst must make his choice, the foregoing reasoning should be quite helpful.

only *two* numbered row coordinates, then there would only be $\frac{10 \times 9}{1 \times 2}$ or 45 exhaustive trials (if these had to be made) which would be necessary to guarantee reaching the correct decomposition of the cipher text; if there were *three* numbered coordinates, then there would be a maximum of $\frac{10 \times 9 \times 8}{1 \times 2 \times 3}$ or 120 trials necessary to insure reaching the proper scheme for the decomposition of the cipher text.[10] Such trials, although laborious (and ordinarily unnecessary) when made by manual methods, would be by no means prohibitive if there were available machine processes for assistance.[11] Exhaustive trials would rarely be necessary, except in very difficult cases; in the majority of instances, straightforward methods of cryptanalysis would reduce the large number of theoretical trials to but a few, from which the correct selection could be made.

l. If the exact composition of the internal arrangement of the matrix were known, this knowledge would be useful in determining how the letters of assumed cribs would be enciphered as monomes or dinomes. In any case, if a word of pronounced idiomorphic pattern is assumed, no matter *how* the letters of the word are encrypted as monomes or dinomes, the idiomorphism must be patent in the cipher text; for example, the word ARTILLERY in a monome-dinome system *must* have a consecutively repeated monome or dinome representing L_p, closely flanked on both sides by some particular monome or dinome representing R_p. If unenciphered numbers were to appear in the encrypted text, bracketed by an indicator to signal that numbers begin and end, the recognition of these plaintext numbers would enable the analyst to identify the indicator, and thus, lead to the establishment of one row coordinate.

---

[10] The number of combinations of N different things taken r at a time is given by the form $_NC_r$ $=\frac{N!}{r!(N-r)!}$; thus for the assumption of 3 numbered rows in a monome-dinome matrix, $_{10}C_3$ $=\frac{10 \cdot 9 \cdot 8 \cdot 7 \cdot 6 \cdot 5 \cdot 4 \cdot 3 \cdot 2 \cdot 1}{3 \cdot 2 \cdot 1 \ (7 \cdot 6 \cdot 5 \cdot 4 \cdot 3 \cdot 2 \cdot 1)}=\frac{10 \cdot 9 \cdot 8}{3 \cdot 2 \cdot 1}=120$. The notation N! is read as "N factorial."

[11] If exhaustive trials *were* to be made by machine, an approach via the monome-to-dinome ratio would probably be as successful as any other approach and not as involved as some. As has been briefly mentioned in a preceding footnote, such an exhaustive trial procedure has been applied to 30 cryptograms of an average length of approximately 100 digits, and using the lowest monome-to-dinome ratio as the final selection criterion produced results which were quite satisfactory, *viz.*, in the case of *13* of the cryptograms tested, the procedure yielded the correct row coordinates for the underlying matrices.

Furthermore, when a study was made of those instances wherein this testing procedure failed, it was found that all but four of the unsuccessful instances involved an enciphering matrix which contained the high-frequency letters of English in the top row, that is, which provided monome equivalents for these high-frequency letters. Stated conversely, this testing procedure was quite successful when applied to cryptograms involving matrices in which the high-frequency plaintext elements were evenly distributed throughout the various rows.

The evaluation of the trial testing was carried one step further because, in the case of a cryptogram involving a matrix throughout which the high-frequency elements are *evenly* distributed, one assumes that the correct row coordinates generally can be picked out merely from a study of the uniliteral frequency distribution made on the cryptogram (see subpar. 76c). With this in mind, a further look at the results of the testing brought out that this machine process disclosed the correct row coordinates in five instances where the uniliteral frequency distribution would have led the analyst astray, and "overlooked" only two instances in which the uniliteral frequency distribution would have revealed the correct coordinates.

m. It must be pointed out that mixed-length systems, even more so than other types of systems treated in this text, often present unusual problems for the cryptanalyst. Each case is a distinctly special case,[12] but continued practice in the solution of these types of systems should, as in other situations, cultivate skill and develop abilities in this field.

n. The student may have noted that no mention has been made concerning the possible use of the ϕ test as a means for determining whether or not a particular trial decomposition represents the proper reduction of a cryptogram to monoalphabetic terms. The ϕ test has been ignored throughout this chapter because, when dealing with cipher alphabets which include plaintext elements other than single letters (e. g., such elements as syllables, numbers, indicators, etc.), the value of ϕ_p can only be loosely approximated; furthermore, computation of the value of ϕ_r in a mixed-length cipher is also a rather tenuous matter. For this reason, it has been considered best to describe only methods of solution which do not depend at all on the use of the ϕ test, and thus keep from establishing in the mind of the student any doubt as to the usefulness of this test when applied in other instances, such as those described in earlier chapters of this text.

79. Further remarks on cryptosystems employing irregular-length ciphertext units.—*a.* The subject of the diagnosis or identification of mixed-length cipher systems has not been discussed. This problem can sometimes be extremely difficult in complex cases; however, the general statement can be made that one takes advantage of any phenomena of repetitions that are present in a cryptogram to arrive at the conclusion that a mixed-length system has been encountered. If the repetitions present are separated by numbers of letters without a constant factor, or if the interval between repetitions is a prime number, and if the possibility of a null or nulls (of a different size than the real cryptographic units) has been considered and ruled out, then in all probability the cryptogram involves some sort of mixed-length cipher units. As to exactly *which* kind of mixed-length system is involved, this question can be answered only by detailed analysis, sometimes to the point of actual plaintext recoveries in order to be certain about one's conclusions.[13]

b. It is not imperative that a mixed-length cipher system be produced through the medium of a matrix with row and column coordinates. For example, in one cryptogram that was submitted for solution, the cipher text began as follows:

```
Q K T 2 Q   3 K B 3 K   Q K T Q K   T 3 Q K T   2 K B 3 Q   K T Q R 2
K K T 2 K   K T 2 K B   3 Q K T Q   B Q R K 3   K Q 2 Q K   T 2 Q R 2....
```

The entire cryptogram, containing 490 characters, consisted only of the seven symbols B, K, Q, R, T, 2, and 3. When this cryptogram was solved, the following alphabet was recovered:

A = K3	G = KR2	N = Q2	U = Q
B = KR3	H = Q3	O = QR2	V = QB2
C = QB3	IJ = QKT3	P = QR	W = K
D = KB2	KQ = K2	R = QKT	X = KB
E = KB3	L = KKT3	S = QB	Y = KKT
F = KKT2	M = QR3	T = QKT2	Z = KR

---

[12] And, as one cryptowag has pointed out, some cases are more special than others.

[13] Cf. the discussion of diagnosis in subpar. 69*f.*

To the reader who is a devotee of the royal game, it will be apparent that the foregoing alphabet is based upon chess notation.[14] If however the digits 1–7 had been used in lieu of the symbols above, the cryptogram could still have been correctly divided into its component ciphertext groupings of 1, 2, 3, and 4 digits, based upon an interpretation of the characteristics present in the cipher text, and of the phenomena in a triliteral distribution showing one prefix and one suffix.[15]

c. The concept of irregular-length cryptographic units can be applied to many varieties of systems, both code and cipher. For example, in Fig. 89, below, there is illustrated a four-square matrix in which plaintext digraphs are represented by ciphertext dinomes, trinomes, or tetranomes. The positioning of the monomes in the ciphertext portions of the matrix was governed

A	B	C	D	E	10	12	5	3	13
F	G	H	I	K	14	15	16	8	17
L	M	N	O	P	18	19	40	6	Ø
Q	R	S	T	U	42	43	9	2	7
V	W	X	Y	Z	45	46	47	48	49
10	6	5	7	12	A	B	C	D	E
13	14	15	16	17	F	G	H	I	K
18	19	40	2	Ø	L	M	N	O	P
42	43	8	3	9	Q	R	S	T	U
45	46	47	48	49	V	W	X	Y	Z

FIGURE 89.

by the frequencies of individual components of four-square cipher digraphs,[16] thus permitting optimum compression of the cipher text, i. e., allowing the most liberal use of ciphertext dinomes and trinomes rather than the maximum cipher length of tetranomes; for example, the word REGIMENTAL would be encrypted RE GI ME NT AL.

76 814 06 68 1018

d. The matrix for another mixed-length cipher system, employing dinomes and trinomes for the encryption of plaintext digraphs, is shown in Figs. 90a and b. Using this matrix, the word DIVISION is encrypted as 07 883 32 746. It is noted that consonant-vowel digraphs involving eight high-frequency consonants with five vowels are represented by dinomes, and all other plaintext digraphs are represented by trinomes. In those rare cases where, as in the example MU ZZ LE, an "impossible" digraph appears in the plain text, the insertion of the letter K_p in the plain text at that point in question, similar to the normal Playfair doublet convention, enables the encryption of the word, as MU ZK ZL E. A better variation of the foregoing system

[14] The chess-playing reader might be interested in recovering the key word for this alphabet.

[15] The interested student could make up a cryptogram using seven characters in this fashion, so he could see for himself the methods of attack on such a system.

[16] See Appendix 2, Table 13, "Four-square individual frequencies."

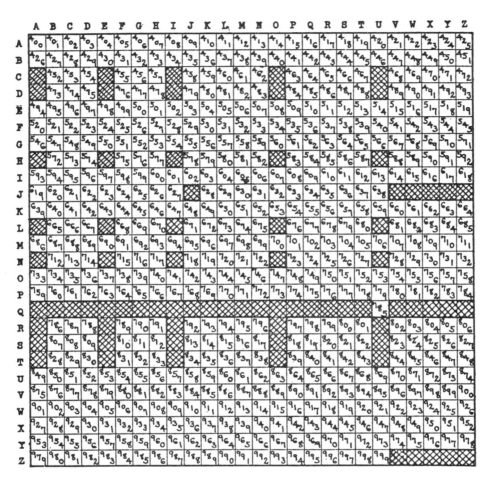

Figure 90a.

	A	E	I	O	U
C	00	01	02	03	04
D	05	06	07	08	09
H	10	11	12	13	14
L	15	16	17	18	19
N	20	21	22	23	24
R	25	26	27	28	29
S	30	31	32	33	34
T	35	36	37	38	39

Figure 90b.

might incorporate a dinome matrix for the 40 highest-frequency digraphs (comprising 42% of English plain text) such as that illustrated in Fig. 91, and a trinome matrix modified in suitable

	0	1	2	3	4	5	6	7	8	9
0	AN	AR	AS	AT	CO	DE	EA	ED	EE	EN
1	ER	ES	ET	FI	FO	HI	IN	IO	IS	LE
2	MA	ND	NE	NT	ON	OR	OU	RA	RE	RT
3	SE	SI	ST	TE	TH	TI	TO	TW	TY	VE

Figure 91.

fashion for the remaining digraphs (with perhaps the matrix coordinates arranged in a mixed sequence). Such a scheme would yield a greater condensing property for the cipher text, but would not be as easy to use as the system described above since the easy mnemonic feature of the matrix in Fig. 90b would be lost.

e. Another idea for a cryptosystem having irregular-length ciphertext groupings employs the diagram in Figs. 92*a* and *b*. This scheme incorporates Playfair digraphic encipherment (with biliteral cipher equivalents) and monographic encipherment (with uniliteral cipher equivalents). In order to disturb the regularity of usual digraphic encipherment (produced by the Playfair-type matrix in Fig. 92*a*), certain selected medium-frequency consonants are enciphered

```
┌─────────────┐
│ A C D E F │        B G M V W
│ H I K L N │        ─────────
│ O P Q R S │        W V M G B
│ T U X Y Z │
└─────────────┘
```

FIGURE 92*a*.   FIGURE 92*b*.

monographically and uniliterally by the reciprocal alphabet shown in Fig. 92*b*. Using Fig. 92, as an example, the phrase "BRIGADE OF ENEMY INFANTRY MOVING ..." would be broken up and enciphered as follows:

```
B RI G AD EO FE NE M YI NF AN TR YX M OX V IN G
W PL V CE AR AF LF M UL SN FH YO ZY M QT G KH V
```

The cipher text, regrouped into fives, WPLVC EARAF LFMUL SNFHY OZYMQ TGKHV, reveals no indication of the uniliteral-biliteral encipherment involved. Since the letters BGMVW represent 8.2% of normal plain text, there is approximately 8% interruption of the regularity of normal digraphic text. Furthermore, since it is expected that about half the time these letters will occur as singles in the plain text, and about half the time an interruptor letter (such as X_p in the example above) will have to be used, this scheme is accomplished by adding only about 4% to the length of the original plain text. Other variations of the basic idea are found in Figs. 93 and 94; in Fig. 93, the Playfair matrix is a 6 x 4 rectangle omitting S and Y, and these two letters

```
┌───────────────┐
│ A B C D E F │      S Y
│ G H I J K L │      ───
│ M N O P Q R │      Y S
│ T U V W X Z │
└───────────────┘
```

```
┌───────────┐
│ A B C D E │       E_p
│ F G H I K │       ───
│ L M N O P │       J_c
│ Q R S T U │
│ V W X Y Z │
└───────────┘
```

FIGURE 93.   FIGURE 94.

form a reciprocal monographic encipherment convention; in Fig. 94, the Playfair matrix is the normal 5 x 5, but with the convention that, unless E_p is the second member of a digraph in the process of encryption, E_p is represented monographically by J_c. In the foregoing two figures, the SY of Fig. 93 could be replaced of course by any other two letters whose combined frequency is in the neighborhood of 6–10%, and the monographic E_p of Fig. 94 could be replaced by any other high- or medium-frequency letter. Instead of Playfair matrices, the digraphic portions of the enciphering schemes of this subparagraph could be accomplished by the use of any other small-matrix digraphic methods.

f. The Morse code, consisting as it does of irregular-length units composed of dots and dashes, lends itself to interesting cryptographic treatment. For example, the dots and dashes (and, of necessity, the *spaces* between Morse characters) might be encrypted by means of the table illustrated in Fig. 95, wherein each of the three elements has approximately the same number of variants. A better idea, however, is to employ variants in the proportions of dots

dot:	A B C D E F G H I
dash:	J K L M N O P Q R
space:	S T U V W X Y Z

FIGURE 95.

dot:	H Y D R A U L I C B E
dash:	F G J K M N O P
space:	Q S T V W X Z

FIGURE 96.

42.4%), dashes (29.1%), and spaces (28.4%) of the letters comprising normal English plain text; such a scheme for variants is shown in Fig. 96. Thus, using the example of Fig. 96, the word ENEMY (which in Morse code is . —. . —— —.——) might be encrypted as RS MDW CQ NFV PIKGZ, which would then be regrouped in fives for transmission. Other ideas for the encryption in digit form of Morse code systems might incorporate alphabets such as those illustrated in Figs. 97 and 98 below:[17]

dot:	1 2 3 4
dash:	5 6 7
space:	8 9 0

FIGURE 97.

dot:	1 3 5 7 9
dash:	2 4 6 8
space:	0

FIGURE 98.

g. Space does not permit detailed examples of analysis of some of the foregoing systems. Admittedly, some of them would pose considerable difficulty in the way of solution; however, if these systems were used in actual practice, then *operational* cryptanalytic methods and entries would make possible successful solution.

---

[17] Further ideas of cryptosystems based on the Morse code will be treated in *Military Cryptanalytics, Part IV.*

Chapter XI

MISCELLANEOUS MONOALPHABETIC SYSTEMS;
CONCLUDING REMARKS

Paragraph

Cryptosystems employing syllabary squares and code charts_____ 80
Cryptosystems employing characters other than letters or figures_____ 81
Special remarks concerning the initial classification of cryptograms_____ 82
Disguised secret communications_____ 83
Concluding remarks_____ 84

80. **Cryptosystems employing syllabary squares and code charts.**—*a.* The various cryptosystems treated in the preceding chapters of this text have in the main fallen into *either* the multi-literal category *or* the polygraphic category. This and the next few subparagraphs will treat of systems which represent a merger of these two categories—namely, biliteral systems which have as plaintext elements not only single letters and digits, but also certain polygraphs selected for the condensation in cipher text that their usage may permit. In addition, treatment will be made of biliteral systems which involve, as plaintext units, a selection of frequent words (that is, which occur frequently in the type of traffic for which the particular cryptosystem is intended) and perhaps some common phrases, such as "reference your message number", "request acknowl-edgement", "nothing to report", etc. Systems which embrace digraphs, trigraphs and other polygraphs as plaintext elements in addition to single letters and digits are called *syllabary systems* because the additional inclusion of these polygraphs permits the encrytion of plain text in a syllabic or quasi-syllabic fashion; most systems of this type involve bipartite matrices in the cryptographic scheme, and these matrices are called *syllabary squares*. When the matrix in this general type of system *also* incorporates words among the plaintext elements, the matrix is termed a *code chart*.

b. The category of systems embodying syllabary squares and code charts as the crypto-graphic vehicle actually constitutes a transition between *cipher* and *code* systems,[1] since a syllabary square or a code chart may be regarded equally properly as either a special type of cipher or a primitive code. However, because syllabary systems follow very closely on the ideas of bipartite matrices, these systems are included in this particular text instead of being reserved for treatment in a subsequent text.

c. A sample syllabary square is illustrated in Fig. 99, below:

	1	2	3	4	5	6	7	8	9	Ø
1	A	1	AL	AN	AND	AR	ARE	AS	AT	ATE
2	ATI	B	2	BE	C	3	CA	CE	CO	COM
3	D	4	DA	DE	E	5	EA	ED	EN	ENT
4	ER	ERE	ERS	ES	EST	F	6	G	7	H
5	8	HAS	HE	I	9	IN	ING	ION	IS	IT
6	IVE	J	Ø	K	L	LA	LE	M	ME	N
7	ND	NE	NT	O	OF	ON	OR	OU	P	Q
8	R	RA	RE	RED	RES	RI	RO	S	SE	SH
9	ST	STO	T	TE	TED	TER	TH	THE	THI	THR
Ø	TI	TO	U	V	VE	W	WE	X	Y	Z

FIGURE 99.

---

[1] See the distinction between the terms *cipher* and *code* as treated in subpar. 11*d*.

It will be noted that the square contains the 26 letters, the 10 digits, and 64 digraphs and trigraphs chosen both on the basis of frequency considerations and the combinative potentialities of the particular polygraphs. The internal arrangement of the square is such as to permit the easy finding of the plaintext elements to be enciphered. Other matrices, of larger dimensions, may contain not only a larger number of different plaintext elements within the matrix, but may also duplicate some of the more frequent plaintext elements and thus incorporate plaintext variants within the matrix. Furthermore, when letters are used as coordinates, variant cipher equivalents may be incorporated into the scheme.

d. Typical of the many ideas that have been employed in the past for code charts is the chart which is shown in Fig. 100, below, and which has been used as a standard tactical cryptosystem

	C,D	E,H	F,I	J,K	T,L	M,O	U,V	Y,G	Z,N	P,Q	X,R	W,S	B,A
M,H	000 Action, ive, ivity, s	02 Addition, al	15 Advance, d, ing, s	45 After	A Aggressor, ive (ly), s	AD Air	Spell/fig. Begins .	AL Airborne	AM Aircraft/ Airplane, s	AN Ammunition	AND Antiaircraft	AR Antitank	ARE Area (of)
T,Q	00 Armor, ed	03 Arrive, al, d, ing, s	16 Artillery	50 Assemble, d, ing, s	AS Attack, ed, ing, s	AT Attempt, ed, ing, s	B Azimuth (in degrees)	BA Battalion, s	BE Battery, ies	BY Begin/start, ed, ings, s	C Bomb, ed, er, ing, s	CA Bridge, d, ing, s	CAN Capture, d, ing, s
K,Z	0 Casualty, ies,	04 Command er, ing, s	17 Communicate, d, ing, ion, s	55 Company, ies	CE Complete, d, ing, ion, s	CH Concentrate, d, ing, ion, s	CO Contact, ed, ing, s	D Coordinate, d, ing, ion, s	DA Corps	DAY Counterattack, ed, ing, s	DE Cross, ed, es, ing	DI Defend/de- fense, s (of)	DO Delay, ed, ing, s
O,L	1 Destroy, ed, ing, s	05 Detach, ed, ment (of), s	18 Dispose, al, d, ition, s	E Division, s	EA Dump, s	ED East (of)	EE Encounter, ed, ing, s	EN Enemy' s	ENT Engineer, s	ER Enlisted Man/Men	ERS Equip, ment, ped, ping	ES Escape, d, ing, s	EST Estimate, d, ing, s (at)
R,X	2 Expect, ed, ing, s (at)	06 Fight, er, ing, s	19 Fire, d, ing, s	F Flank, s	F Force, d, s	FO Forward	FOR Friend, ly	G From	H Front, al, s	HA Fuel, s	HE Gun, s	I Has/have	IL Headquarters
S,P	3 Heavy, ily	07 Hill, s (No.)	20 Hold, ing, s/held	IN Hostile, ity, ities	ING Hour, s	ION How	IS Identify, ied, ies, ing, ication	IT Immediate, ly	IVE Infantry	J Inform, ation, ed, ing, s	K Install, ation, ed, ing, s	L Junction, s (of)	LA Land, ed, ing, s
W,N	4 Large	08 Left (of)	21 Line, s (of)	LE Locate, d, ing, ion, s	LI Machine gun, s (nest)	LO Main	LY Map, ped, ping, s	M Mechanize, d	MA Message, nger, s	ME Mile, s (from), (to)	MENT Mine, d, ing, s	MI Mission, s	MY Morning
A,B	5 Mortar, s	09 Move, d, ing, ment, s	22 Near	N Night	NA No/not/no- thing/negat	ND North (of)	NE Number, s, (of)	NI Objective, s	NO Observe, ation, d, ing, s	NOT Occupy, ied, ies, ing	NT Officer, s	O Operate, d, ing, ion, s	OF Order, ed, ing, s
C,E	6 Over	10 Patrol, led, ling, s	23 Penetrate, d, ing, ion, s	ON Plan, ned, ning, s (to)	OR Platoon, s	OU Point, ed, ing	OUR Position, s	P Post, ed, s	PE Prepare, d, ation, ing, s	Q Prisoner, s	QU Proceed, ed, ing, s, ure	R Radio, ed, s	RA Railway/ Railroad, s
I,G	7 Ready (for) (to)	11 Rear	25 Receive, d, ing, s/receipt	RE Reconnais- sance	RED Refer, ence, red, ring, s (to)	RES Regiment, al, s	RI Reinforce, d, ing, ment, s	RO Replace, d, ing, ment, s	RS Report, ed, ing, s	RT Request, ed, ing, s	S Require, d, isition, s	SA Reserve, d, ing, s	SE Ridge, s
D,J	8 Right (of)	12 River/ Stream	30 Road, s/ Route, s	SH Scout, ing, s	SI Section, s/ Sector, s	SO Send, ing, s/sent (to)	ST Shell, ed, ing, s	T Small/ Small arms	TA South (of)	TE Squad, s	TED Strength, s (of)/strong	TER Stop, ped, ping, s	TH Supply, ies (of)
F,V	9 Support, ed, ing, s	13 Tank, s	35 Target, s	TI Today	TION Tomorrow	TO Tonight	TR Troop, s	U Truck, s/ Vehicle, s	UN Unit, s (of)	US Until	V Urgent, cy, ly	W Vicinity (of)	WE Water
U,Y	01 West (of)	14 What/who	40 When	X Where	Y Will	Z With	Spell/fig. Ends	Period . Withdraw, al, ing, s	Comma , Woods	Colon : Yard, s (from), (:to)	Smcln ; Yesterday	Dash — You, r	Paren ( ) Zone, s (of)

FIGURE 100.

for ground forces by AGGRESSOR, the maneuver enemy in U. S. joint maneuvers and training exercises. This chart provides 2-letter equivalents for letters, numbers, syllables, and a selection of words which occur frequently in low-echelon [2] messages. A particular plaintext value may be designated by a combination of one of the two row coordinates and one of the two column coordinates of the cell containing the plaintext value; thus each plaintext element has four variant equivalents and, for example, the word ARTILLERY contained in the chart may be encrypted *in toto* as TF, TI, QF, or QI. When a complete word contained in the chart is to be encrypted

---

[2] The term *low-echelon* as applied to a cryptographic system means that the system is designed for use at the lower organizational levels such as (in the army) at the regimental level and below. The term *low-grade* as applied to cryptosystems means that the inherent security afforded by the system is low. Cf. the terms *medium-grade*, and *high-echelon* and *-grade*, in the glossary.

in a message, no designator is necessary to indicate this *lower-case* meaning. However, when *upper-case* meanings (i. e., letters, numbers, and syllables) are to be encrypted, it is necessary first to encrypt the designator "Spell/fig. Begins", followed by the cipher equivalents of the particular upper-case meanings; when the spelling is completed, the designator "Spell/fig. *Ends*" is encrypted, to show the return to lower-case meanings. The coordinates of the chart, as used by AGGRESSOR, were random sequences and were changed daily; the inside of the chart remained unchanged.

e. For the most part, the steps used in the recovery of plain text from messages involving syllabary squares differ from those used in the solution of previously-discussed multiliteral systems only in that a larger number of plaintext elements may have to be considered. The cryptanalyst must accordingly modify his interpretation of the frequency characteristics and idiomorphic patterns occurring in such messages. By a careful study of the behavior of frequently recurring cipher units, the analyst is led to conclude that certain units, because of the general characteristics they exhibit, must be representative of numbers, others of punctuation, others of single letters, and so on. This classification is based upon a knowledge of the *general behavior* of the various classes of plaintext elements. For example, cipher units representing digits may be expected to appear in clusters (as in dates and time, and the designations of topographical features, such as hills, road junctions, etc.); whereas those which represent punctuation may be expected to appear at varying intervals throughout the message text (the particular intervals being dependent upon the particular punctuation mark). When this classification has proceeded upon a solid foundation far enough, each set of cipher units is underlined throughout the text in some distinctive manner by means of colored pencils. Subsequent to this, the individual members of each class of cipher units are subjected to closer scrutiny, and based upon a knowledge of the *specific behavior* of the various elements in each class, specific units are identified as having specific plaintext meanings. For example, among those cipher units which the analyst has decided constitute the class which represents plaintext digits, the particular cipher unit representing plaintext "Ø" may be expected to be readily recognizable on the basis that (1) it is one of the three units which appear as the first unit in those clusters which are suspected of representing four-digit time designations *and* (2) it is one of the two cipher units which, with any noteworthy frequency, occur doubled at the end of the same four-unit clusters.

f. When working on messages involving code charts, the cryptanalyst usually starts by attempting to *isolate* sequences of cipher units which represent plaintext letters, syllables, numbers and punctuation. Subsequent to this he proceeds to classify and identify these particular cipher units in the manner described in the foregoing subparagraph; the recovery of *word* meanings is usually accomplished much later. The isolating of the ciphertext units which represent syllabary portions may be readily accomplished in those cases wherein the underlying code chart has only one "Spell/fig. Begins" group and one "Spell/fig. Ends" group, since the recognition of these designators automatically permits one to divide the cipher text into word values and non-word values; the recognition of these designators is made on the basis of their high frequency and their alternating placements throughout the cipher text.

g. As plaintext meanings are recovered in a syllabary square system or code chart system, these meanings should be entered into a skeleton matrix in a manner similar to that used in the solution of the bipartite systems previously described (Chapters VII and VIII). This is done in order to uncover and exploit as early as possible any evidences of systematic construction arising from the arrangement which was used in the underlying matrix. It may be assumed that each syllabary square and code chart *will* normally have had its internal elements arranged in some type of systematic fashion in order to permit the ready finding of plaintext elements during the encryption of a message.

h. Even when only a *single* message encrypted in one of these systems is available, if the internal construction of the underlying matrix is known there may be special approaches to solution, based on the nature of the plaintext elements constituting each row and each column of the particular matrix. For instance, if the words REFERENCE and YOUR and MESSAGE are known to be in the same row of a particular code chart, then it would be quite possible that the ciphertext sequence LA LH LT at the beginning of a message represents the stereotype REFERENCE YOUR MESSAGE; if but a few other similarly identifiable sequences were also available to the cryptanalyst, he could possibly recover the arrangement of the outside coordinates after a relatively few steps.

i. When there are other special circumstances involved, for instance, when isologs or messages with isologous syllabary portions (i. e., spelled-out portions encrypted "off-the-cut", such as IN TER CE P TO R and I NT ER CE P T OR) are present in the cipher text, solution is considerably facilitated. For example, suppose that the enemy is known to be using the code chart of Fig. 100 (the coordinates being as yet unrecovered), and that the following sequences

(1)	... PR	XS	PS	AW	NP	DQ	IZ	...
(2)	... SR	RW	WM	NG	RJ	LP	IX	...
(3)	... PX	XW	NO	WY	XJ	OK	GN	...
(4)	... SX	RB	AW	WP	JS	GX	...	
(5)	... PX	XA	BW	NQ	DY	OX	...	

from certain proforma messages are assumed to represent different encipherments of the word KILOMETERS. First of all, the initial digraph in each sequence must represent K_p, since there are no plaintext polygraphs beginning with K in the chart. Then the $\overline{AW}_c$ in (1) and (4) is noted; this *must* represent O_p, since, from (4), $\overline{AW}_c$ can be seen to represent either L_p, or O_p, and the position of $\overline{AW}_c$ in (1) confirms the identification as O_p. The values for I_p, IL_p, L_p, and LO_p quickly follow, and the variant coordinates for these plaintext values are recorded on the edges of the chart. The endings of the sequences are now examined, and it is noted that $\overline{IZ}_c$ and $\overline{GN}_c$ must represent $\overline{RS}_p$ (since either $\overline{ERS}_p$ or S_p would have digraph equivalents ending in R or X from the already-recovered column coordinates). The recovery of the rest of the text follows easily, with but little experimentation. (The student might continue the solution and profit from the exercise.)

81. Cryptosystems employing characters other than letters or figures.—*a.* In practical cryptography today, the use of characters other than the letters of bona fide alphabets (including recognized Morse and Baudot alphabets) or the 10 digits is comparatively rare. When so-called symbol ciphers, that is, ciphers employing peculiar symbols, signs of punctuation, diacritical marks, figures of "dancing men", and so on are encountered in practical work nowadays, they are almost certain to be simple monoalphabetic ciphers. They are adequately described in romantic tales,[3] in popular books on cryptography, and in the more common types of magazine articles. No further space need be given ciphers of this type in this text, not only because of their simplicity but also because they are encountered in military cryptography only in sporadic

---

[3] The most famous: Edgar Allan Poe's *The Gold Bug;* Sir Arthur Conan Doyle's *The Adventure of the Dancing Men;* Jules Verne's *A Journey to the Center of the Earth.*

instances, principally in censorship activities. Even in the latter cases, it is usually found that such ciphers are employed in "intimate" correspondence for the exchange of sentiments that appear less decorous when set forth in plain language. They are very seldom used by authentic enemy agents. When such a cipher is encountered nowadays it may practically always be regarded as the work of the veriest tyro, when it is not that of a crank or a mentally-deranged person.

b. The usual preliminary procedure in handling such cases, where the symbols may be somewhat confusing to the mind because of their unfamiliar appearance to the eye, is to substitute letters for them consistently throughout the message and then treat the resulting text in the manner in which an ordinary cryptogram composed of letters is treated. This procedure also facilitates the construction of the necessary frequency distributions, which would be tedious to construct by using symbols.

c. A final word must be said on the subject of symbol ciphers by way of caution. When symbols are used to replace letters, syllables, and entire words, then the systems approach code methods in principle, and can become difficult of solution. The logical extension of the use of symbols in such a form of writing is the employment of arbitrary characters for a specially developed "shorthand" system bearing little or no resemblance to well-known and therefore nonsecret, systems of shorthand, such as Gregg, Pitman, etc.[4] Unless a considerable amount of text is available for analysis, a privately-devised shorthand may be very difficult to solve. Fortunately, such systems are rarely encountered in military cryptography. They fall under the heading of cryptographic curiosities, of interest to the cryptanalyst in his leisure moments.[5]

82. Special remarks concerning the initial classification of cryptograms.—*a.* The student should by this time have a good conception of the basic nature of monoalphabetic substitution and of the many variations which may be played upon this simple tune. The first step of all, naturally, is to be able to classify a cryptogram properly and place it in either the transposition or the substitution class. The tests for this classification have been given and as a rule the student will encounter no difficulty in this respect.

b. There are, however, certain kinds of cryptograms whose class cannot be determined in the usual manner, as outlined in par. 25 of this text. First of all there is the type of code message which employs bona fide dictionary words as code groups. Naturally, a frequency distribution of such a message will approximate that for normal plain text. The appearance of the message, however, gives clear indications of what is involved. The study of such cases will be taken up in its proper place. At the moment it is only necessary to point out that these are *code* messages and not *cipher*, and it is for this reason that in pars. 24 and 25 the words "cipher" and "cipher messages" are used, the word "cryptogram" being used only where technically correct.

c. Secondly, there come the unusual and borderline cases, including cryptograms whose nature and type can *not* be ascertained from frequency distributions. Here, the cryptograms are technically not ciphers but special forms of disguised secret writings which are rarely sus-

---

[4] The use of symbols for abbreviation and speed in writing goes back to the days of antiquity. Cicero's freedman and amanuensis, Tiro, is reported to have drawn up "a book like a dictionary, in which he placed before each word the notation (symbol) which should represent it, and so great was the number of notations and words that whatever could be written in Latin could be expressed in his notation." The designation "Tironian notes" is applied to this type of shorthand.

[5] An example is found in the famous Pepys Diary, which was written in shorthand, purely for his own eyes by Samuel Pepys (1633–1703). "He wrote it in Shelton's system of tachygraphy (1641), which he complicated by using foreign languages or by varieties of his own invention whenever he had to record passages least fit to be seen by his servants, or by 'all the world.' "

ceptible of being classed as transposition or substitution. These include a large share of the cases wherein the cryptographic messages are disguised and carried under an external, innocuous text which is innocent and seemingly without cryptographic content—for instance, in a message wherein specific letters are indicated in a way not open to suspicion under censorship, these letters being intended to constitute the letters of the cryptographic messages and the other letters constituting "dummies." Obviously, no amount of frequency tabulations will avail a competent, expert cryptanalyst in demonstrating or disclosing the presence of a cryptographic message, written and secreted within the "open" message, which serves but as an envelop and disguise for its authentic or real import. Certainly, such frequency tabulations can disclose the existence *neither* of substitution *nor* transposition in these cases, since both forms are absent. The next paragraph contains more about these latter cases.[6]

83. **Disguised secret communications.**—*a.* As was mentioned above, there is a general class of methods of secret writing in which a secret message is concealed within the text of an apparently innocuous plaintext message; also, by extension, a secret message may be concealed within otherwise bona fide media such as maps, drawings, charts, music manuscripts, bridge hands, chess problems, shopping lists, stock quotations, and so on. The addressee of such a communication, knowing where to look for the secret elements, does so and from them is able to read the message contained within its covering disguise. When the plaintext elements of the secret message are concealed by surrounding them with the plaintext elements of an innocent cover text, such a system is known as a *concealment system*. When, however, the plaintext elements of the secret message are not themselves concealed within a cover text, but instead have *code* equivalents which are actual plaintext words or phrases and which are used to form an apparently innocent message, such a system is called an *open code system*.

b. An example of a concealment system message is the communication "HAVE ESTABLISHED LOW PRIORITY", in which the secret message "help" has been concealed as the first letter of each word of the covering text. As an example of an open code, in the message "AUNT MARY LEFT FOR DETROIT ON FRIDAY", the words AUNT MARY might stand for "five troop ships", DETROIT might mean "Southampton", and FRIDAY might stand for "Monday." An often-cited case of open code is the message "A SON IS BORN", which allegedly was sent out by German-controlled radio stations all over the world in August, 1914, meaning that war was about to be declared.

c. The solution of *concealment systems* may pose considerable difficulties for the cryptanalyst, who is placed in the rather odd situation where he might have before him a simple system, *if* he can but find the system. Most of the statistical and other tools at the disposal of the cryptanalyst are of no avail to him in the attack on concealment systems. First of all, he might not even know whether or not a given piece of correspondence *does* contain a secret message; often the only reason for an examination of a particular message, other than a random sampling case, is that the originator or the addressee is on a suspect list and therefore the communication is considered for possible secret writing. The difficulty in analysis is usually not brought about by the complexity of the system, for concealment systems are almost always cryptographically simple. The difficulty of the problem arises from the lack, at the outset, of tangible cryptographic elements into which the cryptanalyst can "get his teeth". There is primarily the

---

[6] The subparagraph which the student has just read (82c) contains a hidden cryptographic message. With the hints given in par. 83 let the student see if he can uncover it.

question of determining whether or not a secret text actually exists,[7] and if it does, locating the elements which constitute it.

d. Clearly objective methods for recognizing a concealment system message as such prior to recovering the secret text itself are not available. However, the reader may find useful a list of various situations which a censorship cryptanalyst should regard with suspicion and which may be indications of concealment system messages. Such a list of situations is given below:

(1) A letter is sent airmail or special delivery, when the contents do not warrant such speed and expense; (2) there is a discrepancy between the dating and the postmark of a letter; (3) the contents of a letter do not seem to warrant the time taken to write it, yet it appears to be composed with care and exceptional neatness; (4) the subject matter is out of accord with known facts and circumstances; (5) there are undue spacings between words, or there appear to be some "carefully placed" words in the text; (6) a writer is known to use colons habitually after the salutation, and a letter is intercepted which has a dash or a semicolon after the salutation; (7) there is a pronounced irregularity in the manner of the dotting of i's or the crossing of t's, or there is undue shading or other abberations in the formation of letters; (8) there is a pronouncedly stilted style or forced terminology; (9) there are inconsistencies in the style of the writer, involving misspellings or other errors incompatible with the apparent education of the writer; (10) there are peculiar or excessive underlinings which are not rational with the apparent stress intended; (11) the writer purports to be a child, writing in a childish scrawl, yet he uses words which are unlikely for a child or he forces misspellings which somehow do not ring true; (12) in a map or sketch, there are unnecessary breaks in border outlines, routes, etc.; (13) in a music manuscript, there is an excruciatingly bad (even for an "amateur composer") melodic or harmonic progression, or there are implausible accents or marks of expression; (14) in a diagram of a chess problem, there is an "impossible situation"; (15) there are entirely too many references to names of people, places, objects, or items, in what purports to be a friendly letter; (16) in short, *anything* that appears "just not quite right."

e. Locating the elements constituting the secret text of a concealment system message and deriving the meaning of the secret text are practically synonymous. This phase in the solution of a concealment system message can involve a tremendous amount of time and labor, simply

---

[7] Success in this type of analytic work requires extraordinary patience and perseverance, keen powers of observation nurtured by unrelenting suspicion, a lively imagination, exceptional ingenuity, and organized methods of analysis—plus a firm foundation and considerable experience in the methods and practices of concealment systems.

In this connection, it is worthwhile to cite an extract from an official report prepared in 1946 by the wartime Office of Censorship:

"Detection of concealed messages is based on the principle that there is no absolutely safe disguise for duplicity. Espionage letters have weaknesses and identifying characteristics, which modern techniques can minimize but never completely eliminate. Seasoned examiners develop an ability to relate facts and think clearly about possibilities. They develop a keen perception of, or alertness to, certain peculiarities, an attitude of suspicion toward certain indicators, and experience or training in handling certain types of materials.

"The texts of letters containing concealed messages do not ring true; they lack spontaneity, and the normal emphasis which people give to certain thoughts or ideas is absent. Something comparable in social life is the stilted behavior and speech of a person who is obliged to entertain a stranger with whom he feels nothing in common; he behaves unnaturally; he desires to be polite, but in order to do so he must hide his boredom and pretend an interest he does not feel. Exactly the same is true in the writing of cover texts or open code letters—the attempt to pursue two aims simultaneously results in strain. Skill and experience may overcome the strained-text hazard to a high degree, but they can never completely dispel the distortion and dislocation of a normal emphasis inevitable in a cover letter."

because it generally requires considerable experimentation with possible systems—and the number possible is enormous. Appendix 6, "Classification guide to concealment systems", presents an extensive list, but at this point it will suffice to indicate a few such systems. The letters of the secret message might be concealed as the first, second, or third letters of the cover text; or they might be concealed as the final, penultimate, or antepenultimate letters of the words; or they might be concealed by means of a specific key into prearranged variable place-ments within the words of the innocent text. The secret text might be read by considering the letters which follow or precede all unnecessary breaks in cursive handwriting; or the secret text might be indicated by shaded letters or by pin pricks over significant letters, or even by elongated tails on words pointing to significant letters in the line above. In the analysis of concealed-letter systems, it is advisable to write the successive words of the cover text one below the other, in a column, aligned by their beginnings and subsequently to rewrite them columnwise aligned by their endings; this will assist in disclosing a secret text hidden in a fixed position relative to the beginnings or endings, or in diagonal routes near those locations (see Fig. 101a). It is also advisable to write out the cover text in rectangular arrangements of various widths, in order to disclose secret text which might have been concealed in every nth letter of the entire cover text (see Fig. 101b). In cases where physical indicators are employed, such as breaks in handwriting or as shaded letters, an examination of the letters in the immediate vicinity of such indicators would disclose the secret text.

Cover text:

UNCLE EZRA SEEMS DESPONDENT.
HAVE YOU HEARD THE LAST REPORT?

```
        U N C L E
        E Z R A
      S E E M S
D E S P O N D E N T
        H A V E
        Y O U
    H E A R D
        T H E
      L A S T
    R E P O R T
```

Secret text: NEED HELP

FIGURE 101a.

Cover text:

WHEN YOU SEE CHESTER AT
MADISON'S HOUSE TELL HIM
LOIS DEPARTED.

```
W H E N Y O
U S E E C H
E S T E R A
T M A D I S
O N S H O U
S E T E L L
H I M L O I
S D E P A R
T E D
```

Secret text: NEED HELP

FIGURE 101b.

f. Some systems involve the concealment of entire words, instead of just individual letters. Thus, for example, the secret text might consist of (1) every nth word of the cover text; (2) the first and last words of every line; (3) words preceding or following punctuation marks; (4) words bisected by an imaginary line running diagonally from the upper left to the lower right of the sheet of paper; or countless varieties of similar schemes. Grilles have also been used, the secret text being written through the apertures of the grille on placed positions on the sheet of paper, and then a covering letter written to surround and camouflage the secret text. In the solution of concealed-word systems, examining the text produced by counting off every *n*th word may bear fruit; if the secret text is long enough, the validity of the assumed secret text may be proved by the consistency of the decimation. In cases wherein a variable key has been used to indicate which words constitute the secret text, proof of the assumed secret text may be impossible, unless the key is short compared to the message lengths, or unless additional messages in *exactly the same key* are available for comparison to test an assumed key.

g. There have been many cases in which a secret text has first been converted into the dots, dashes, and spaces of the Morse code, or encrypted in a Baconian or a Trithemius cipher; then this converted text was concealed within an innocent text in any one of the almost infinite number of possible ways. Some of these ways in which the multiliteral elements of the preliminary conversion may be represented are by (1) the lengths of words; (2) the number of vowels or consonants in the words; (3) the number of syllables in the words; or (4) by the ways in which *t*'s are crossed or *i*'s are dotted. The solution of such systems involves experimentation with basic hypotheses concerning the manner in which multiliteral elements are denoted, followed by a recombination into monoalphabetic terms (under the assumption of a Morse, Trithemian, or Baconian system) and solving the reduced monoalphabetic text. Another method for a concealment system involves the use of a bipartite matrix employing coordinates consisting of vowels (or, for that matter, any other set of five or six letters); the secret text is first enciphered in this biliteral system, and then the vowels are surrounded by consonants to form the plain text of an innocent cover message. As in most concealment systems, *once such a subterfuge is suspected or assumed*, then and only then is solution possible.[8]

h. In addition to literal vehicles to conceal secret text, pictorial or physical vehicles have often been used for this purpose. Sketches, drawings, graphs, etc., have been used as the surrounding medium for actual letters of the secret plain text, or the secret text has been incorporated in such sketches and drawings by means of a shorthand or the multiliteral equivalents in a Morse, Baconian, or Trithemius alphabet. In Fig. 102*a* there is an actual example from World War II censorship activities, while in Fig. 102*b* there is a problem submitted to one of the authors by a World War II class of officers undergoing instruction in cryptanalysis. Solution of these examples is left to the student who is inclined to pursue such matters. As a matter of analysis, the student should be able to see why the second example was at once diagnosed as containing a plain text written backwards, enciphered with an *arbitrary* alphabet. If the student has not yet consulted the guide to concealment systems in Appendix 6, he should do so now.

i. The detailed discussion thus far has been limited to concealment systems. In cases of *open code*, unfortunately there are neither clear-cut methods of analysis nor of recognition; there is simply *no* rational way of proving that a message such as "AUNT MARY LEFT FOR DETROIT TODAY" contains a secret meaning, unless it is known for a fact that the sender has no aunt named Mary; and even then there still might exist a friend of the sender's who is affectionately called "Aunt Mary"—or, for that matter, she might be someone *else's* aunt.[9] And once having suspected or even proved that there *is* something rotten in Denmark, proof of the content of the hidden meaning is simply out of the question unless the sender is somehow convinced to mend his

---

[8] At this point the student might like to try his hand on the secret text hidden in subpar. 82*c*.

[9] In one instance, it has been related that a censor reviewed a telegram transmitted by a person on a suspect list. The telegram read "FATHER IS DECEASED." The censor, smelling a rat, changed the text to read "FATHER IS DEAD" and waited. Sure enough, several hours later came a query: "IS FATHER DEAD OR DECEASED?"

Und hier ist ein Traum den
ich gestern Nacht träumte
Was soll es bedeuten? ....

FIGURE 102a.

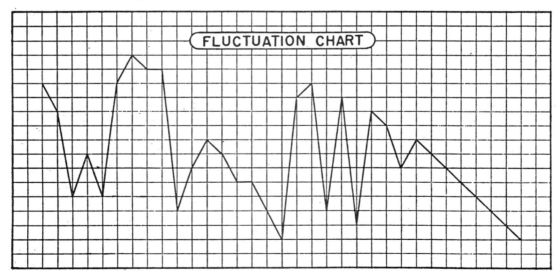

FLUCTUATION CHART

FIGURE 102b.

ways and thereupon volunteers the information. In many wartime instances where open codes have been used, a legal case could not be proved against a suspect without his cooperation.[10]

j. A prominent case of the use of open code in espionage communications was that of an Axis spy, Mrs. Velvalee Dickinson, who in August, 1944, was sentenced in New York to ten years' imprisonment and was fined $10,000 after pleading guilty to the charge that a series of letters she had written to an agent in Buenos Aires in the early part of 1942 contained secret messages hidden in the plain text. These messages gave information regarding the location and condition of Allied warships in Pacific ports. The two agents professed to be dealers in antique dolls and used a prearranged code giving secondary meanings to words pertaining to the sale of dolls. Mrs. Dickinson would send out letters advertising or offering to sell certain of her antique dolls to the addressee. She would write the doll's name and after the name a brief description; then she would write, as in an ordinary business letter, the price of each doll. The original cause for suspicion was the extreme variation in prices over a range of three or four letters of what was apparently the same doll or the same type of doll. A great many letters were necessary in order to build up a case sufficient to prove the use of open code. It is doubtful even then that the use of open code could have been legally proven except for the fact that, faced with so much evidence against her, she chose to confess this use.

k. In addition to concealment systems and open codes, there are still other methods for hiding the existence of secret text. The majority of these methods embrace the following:

    (1) secret inks;

    (2) microscopic writing, involving use of micropantographs; and

    (3) photographic methods, including "microdots" (i. e., the reduction of a page of copy to a negative the size of a miniature dot, which is then affixed on a period or on the dot of an "i"), double printing, double exposure, or concealment within photographs.

The *modus operandi* and analysis of these latter methods are, however, beyond the scope of this text.

84. Concluding remarks.—*a.* The student will have by this time appreciated that monoalphabetic substitution ciphers are for the most part quite easy to solve, once the underlying principles are thoroughly understood. As in other arts, continued practice with many examples leads to facility and skill in solution, especially where the student concentrates his attention upon traffic all of the same general nature, so that the type of text which he is continually encountering becomes familiar to him and its peculiarities or characteristics of construction give clues for short cuts to solution. It is true that a knowledge of the general phraseology of messages, the kind of words used, their sequences, and so on, is of very great assistance in practical work in all fields of cryptanalysis. In operational cryptanalysis, it is of vital importance to gain a knowledge of the language habits of a particular group of correspondents, to permit the rapid exploitation of the cryptosystem involved. Thus, at least initially, all possible traffic is cryptanalyzed, even that in simple systems and that of comparatively little intelligence value. Word lists obtained empirically are of more value than "intuitive" or academic compilations; however, at the outset, reference may of course be made to these latter compilations.[11]

---

[10] Almost any element of a communication can have a code meaning; e. g., a reference to a particular kind of a flower might mean "two transports leaving tomorrow." Among the elements that have been used are the following: (1) proper nouns, place names, person's names, relatives, flowers, etc.; (2) description of bidding in a game of bridge; (3) references to particular novels or other books (4) advertisements; (5) military 24-hour clock system (permitting 1440 different prearranged meanings); (6) references to musical compositions.

[11] See in this connection the word and idiomorph lists comprising Appendix 3.

b. Some of the simpler subterfuges which the student should be on the lookout for in mono-alphabetic substitution are the following:

(1) As a simple departure from monoalphabetic substitution, a message might be broken up into sections, and each section enciphered monoalphabetically with a different mixed cipher alphabet. Obviously, a single, composite frequency distribution for the whole message will not show the characteristic crest and trough appearance of a simple monoalphabetic cipher, since a given cipher unit will represent different plaintext letters in different parts of the message. But if the cryptanalyst will carefully observe the distribution *as it is being compiled*, he will note that at first it presents the characteristic crest and trough appearance of monoalphabeticity, and that after a time it begins to lose this appearance. If possible he should be on the lookout for some peculiarity of grouping of letters which serves as an indicator for the shift from one cipher alphabet to the next. If he finds such an indicator he should begin a second distribution from that point on, and proceed until another shift is encountered. By thus isolating the different portions of the text, and restricting the frequency distributions to the separate monoalphabets, the problem may be treated then as an ordinary simple monoalphabetic substitution.[12] Consideration of these remarks in connection with instances of this kind leads to the comment that it is often more advisable for the cryptanalyst to compile his own data, than to have the latter prepared by clerks, especially when studying a system *ab initio*. For observations which will certainly escape an untrained clerk can be most useful and may indeed facilitate solution. For example, in the case under consideration, if a clerk should merely hand the completed over-all uniliteral distribution to the cryptanalyst, the latter may be led astray; the appearance of the composite distribution might convince him that the cryptogram is much more complicated than it really is. While still on the subject of frequency distributions, it is pointed out that, although earlier (par. 43) the *triliteral frequency distribution* was cited primarily for its usefulness in extracting frequency data relative to the digraphs and trigraphs occurring in a simple substitution cipher, this particular type of distribution is used extensively in the manual attack on many other types of cryptograms because it provides one of the best means for systematically locating all of the repetitions which appear in a message.

(2) There have been cases where direct and reversed standard alphabets have been used alternately in a single cryptogram, the change of alphabets being made at irregular intervals, or changed at the end of every word or with each group of five letters. If the interruption takes place at too short an interval, not only will a frequency distribution be of no avail, but also it would be almost impossible for the cryptanalyst to determine when and how the change of alphabets occurs from a mere examination of the cipher text. However, if the cryptanalyst is on the alert *to try the simplest thing first*, completing the plain-component sequence on the assumption of standard alphabets will yield a solution where otherwise a solution might be out of the question.

(3) Another subterfuge that has been encountered is the encryption by means of a mono-alphabetic uniliteral substitution of a message whose plain text has first been written *backwards* (or for that matter, an ordinary simple substitution cipher *sent* backwards). Ciphers of this type may successfully resist the unsystematic attempts of solution which a tyro might make;

---

[12] The cryptanalyst should be on the alert for the possibility of *related* alphabets in such a system; if related alphabets *have* been used, the reconstruction of the primary components from the solution of one portion of the message would enable the reading of the other portions of the message by means of the generatrix method treated in par. 50.

however, the experienced analyst would probably quickly recognize the weak subterfuge if he were to examine the frequencies of cipher digraphs, trigraphs, and tetragraphs, in relation to the uniliteral frequencies of their component letters.

c. Monoalphabetic substitution with variants represents an extension of the basic principle, with the intention of masking the characteristic frequencies resulting from a strict monoalphabeticity, by means of which solutions are rather readily obtained. Some of the subterfuges applied in the establishment of variant or multiple values are simple and more or less fail to serve the purpose for which they are intended; others, on the contrary, may interpose serious difficulties to a straightforward solution. But in no case may the problem be considered of more than ordinary difficulty. Furthermore, it should be recognized that where these subterfuges are really adequate to the purpose, the complications introduced are such that the practical manipulation of the system becomes as difficult for the cryptographer as for the cryptanalyst.

(1) A few words may be added here in regard to a method which often suggests itself to laymen, but which is very old indeed in the art. This consists in using a book possessed by all the correspondents and indicating the letters of the message by means of numbers referring to specific letters in the book. One way consists in selecting a certain page and then giving the line number and position of the letter in the line, the page number being shown by a single initial indicator. Another way is to use the entire book, giving the cipher equivalents in groups of three numbers representing page, line, and number of letter (for example, 75–8–10 means page 75, 8th line, 10th letter in the line). Such systems are, however, extremely cumbersome to use and, when the enciphering is done carelessly, can be solved. The basis for solution in such cases rests upon the use of adjacent letters on the same line, the accidental repetitions of certain letters, and the occurrence of unenciphered words in the messages, when laziness or fatigue intervenes in the enciphering.[13]

(2) It may also be indicated that human nature and the fallibility of cipher clerks is such that it is rather rare for an encipherer to make full use of the complement of variants placed at his disposal. The result is that in most cases certain of the equivalents will be used so much more often than others that diversities in frequencies will soon manifest themselves, affording important data for attack by the cryptanalyst.

d. There is one additional aspect of cryptography within the realm of monoalphabetic substitution ciphers that should be discussed at this point—the aspect involving *repetitive* monoalphabetic substitution.

(1) Suppose a message undergoes a primary encipherment by means of a single mixed, non-reciprocal cipher alphabet, and this primary cipher text then undergoes a secondary encipherment by means of the same or a *different* mixed alphabet. The resulting cryptogram is still monoalphabetic in character, and presents very little, if any, augmentation in the degree of security (depending upon the type of alphabet employed).[14] Here an entirely illusory increase in

---

[13] In 1915 the German Government conspired with a group of Hindu revolutionaries to stir up a rebellion in India, the purpose being to cause the withdrawal of British troops from the Western Front. Hindu conspirators in the United States were given money to purchase arms, and ammunition and to transport them to India. For communication with their superiors in Berlin the conspirators used, among others, the system described in this subparagraph. A 7-page typewritten letter, built up from page, line, and letter-number references to a book known only to the communicants, was intercepted by the British and turned over to the United States Government for use in connection with the prosecution of the Hindus for violating our neutrality. The author [W. F. F.] solved this message without the book in question, by taking full advantage of the clues referred to.

[14] The only possible slight increase in security lies in the fact that the key words for the primary and secondary encipherments might be made more difficult to recover or even impossible to recover.

security is involved and an ineffectual complexity is introduced; the process may indeed be repeated indefinitely without producing the desirable result of added security. Similarly, the same illusory increase in security is present in the case of repetitive multiliteral encipherments involving regular-length ciphertext units, *as long as the repetitive encipherments are made "on the cut".*

(2) In the case of repetitive polygraphic encipherment made on the cut, a moderate increase in security is achieved over the degree of security normally provided by a single polygraphic encipherment. For instance, in the case of repetitive digraphic encipherment using, let us say, a four-square system for the first encipherment and a modified Playfair system for the second step, the final encipherment is still monoalphabetic digraphic in character, except that the cryptosystem might have to be resolved as involving a more-or-less random square table, instead of being recovered in its primary and secondary steps; all the repetitive encipherment has accomplished is that it has added to the difficulty of reconstruction of the matrices used—but this, in the case of a digraphic system, is a reasonably fair increase in security, since we expect solution to be expedited through an early recovery of the matrix.

(3) When, however, successive multiliteral or polygraphic encipherments are made "off the cut" for the second step, the increase in security can be considerable, since the end result no longer exhibits the phenomena of monoalphabeticity and the *cryptanalytic* complexity of the system has been thereby materially enhanced.[15] For example, using the two-square matrix illustrated in Fig. 55 on p. 138, the message REENFORCEMENTS NEEDED undergoes the following encipherments:

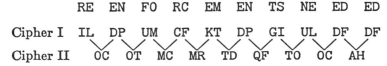

```
          RE   EN   FO   RC   EM   EN   TS   NE   ED   ED
Cipher I  IL   DP   UM   CF   KT   DP   GI   UL   DF   DF
            \/   \/   \/   \/   \/   \/   \/   \/   \/
Cipher II   OC   OT   MC   MR   TD   QF   TO   OC   AH
```

The first encipherment, IL DP UM. . . . , is subjected to a second encipherment by considering the digraphs "off the cut", resulting in the encryptment OC OT MC. . . . In the final cryptogram, the first and last letters of the primary encipherment may be retained as is, or they may be combined

[15] A rather ingenious idea proposed by Charles Eyraud in his excellent work, *Précis de Cryptographie Moderne,* Paris, 1953, pp. 224–225, involves a repetitive encipherment using two different monome-dinome matrices. In Eyraud's example, using the two matrices illustrated, the plain text "ECRITURES SECRETES" is first enciphered

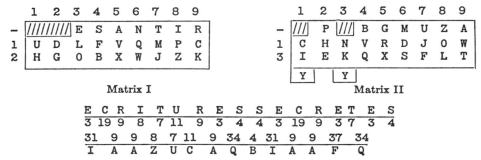

with Matrix I, then the digits are recombined into letters using Matrix II with the resulting cipher text IAAZU . . . . (It is interesting to note that the 17 letters of the plain text are encrypted by only *14* letters in the final cipher!) The letter Y_p is eliminated from Matrix I, and is included in Matrix II to take care of a final 1 or 3 in the first encipherment which otherwise could not have been encrypted as a single element.

for the second encryption, for added security; thus the final cryptogram may read either IOCOT .....OCAHF, or ROCOT.....OCAHG.   When this sort of secondary encipherment is applied in a repetitive multiliteral cipher, the system is called a *fractionating system*.   The cryptanalysis of these systems, which is often quite complex, will be treated in subsequent texts.

e. If the cryptanalyst is fortunate enough to have a pair of isologs, one message of which is in a monoalphabetic substitution system and the other in a transposition system, it may be possible for him to make exact identifications of the elements in the substitution cipher based on the plaintext letter frequencies present in the transposition cipher.   Then, having the plain text, the solution of the transposition is greatly facilitated.

f. As has already been stated in subpar. 2c, mathematics and mathematical methods have an important place in the art of cryptanalysis.   This text has included only those introductory statistical and mathematical applications which apply to monoalphabetic systems.   If it appears to the student that there has been a rather extensive treatment of too-specialized techniques, let him be reassured that these have been included as being in the nature of collateral information, rather than being an absolute necessity in the solution of the particular problems to which they were applied.   As a final word of caution to the student the following extract from a report by C. H. O'D. Alexander is included:

"There is a considerable danger that a learner, when he realizes that statistical methods can be of some use, will attempt to use them where they are quite inappropriate.   If he does this a few times and finds it gets him nowhere, he then gives the whole thing up as a waste of time and does not use such methods where he might.   There is also the worse danger of doing statistical tests for their own sake so that they are used as a method of passing the time and avoiding real thought about the problem to be solved."

g. The general problem of cryptanalytic diagnosis has been discussed briefly in various chapters of this text.   The problem is far from simple, since many variations and conventions may be encountered in the various systems treated in this text; furthermore, the problem is made even harder by the fact that certain systems, themselves quite simple, may be combined to produce a system much more difficult to diagnose.   The lack of *precise* diagnostic tests, such as those available in the natural sciences,[16] is brought about by the fact that variations and conventions introduced into otherwise conventional systems may change radically the

---

[16] The author feels that it is of value to pursue further a discussion of how the science of cryptanalytics compares with some branch of one of the natural sciences, when the diagnostic procedures involved in each are considered.   In that branch of biology called taxonomic botany, for example, the first steps in the classificatory process are based upon observation of externally quite marked differences; as the process continues, the observational details become finer and finer, involving more and more difficulties as the work progresses.   Towards the end of the work the botanical taxonomist may have to dissect the specimen and study internal characteristics.   The whole process is largely a matter of painstaking, accurate observation of data and drawing proper conclusions therefrom.   Except for the fact that the botanical taxonomist depends almost entirely upon ocular observation of characteristics while the cryptanalyst in addition to observation must use some statistics, the steps taken by the former are quite similar to those taken by the latter.   It is only at the very end of the work that a significant dissimilarity between the two sciences arises.   If the botanist makes a mistake in observation or deduction, he merely fails to identify the specimen correctly; he has an "answer"—but the answer is wrong.   He may not be cognizant of the error; however, other more skillful botanists will find him out.   But if the cryptanalyst makes a mistake in observation or deduction, he fails to get any "answer" at all; he needs nobody to tell him he has failed.   Further, there is one additional important point of difference.   The botanist is studying a bit of Nature—and she does not consciously interpose obstacles, pitfalls, and dissimulations in the path of those trying to solve her mysteries.   The cryptanalyst, on the other hand, is studying a piece of writing prepared with the express purpose of preventing its being read by any persons for whom it is not intended.   The obstacles, pitfalls, and dissimulations are here consciously interposed by the one who encrypted the message.   These, of course, are what make cryptanalytics different and difficult.

appearance and manifestations expected in the cipher text produced by the known systems, yielding "hitherto-unencountered phenomena." Each cryptosystem is then actually an individual and unique case in diagnosis.[17]

(1) For example, encrypted text which is made up of four-letter groups having the pattern consonant-vowel-consonant-consonant does not *necessarily* involve a code system, even, though this grouping is a frequent one in four-letter code systems; the basic system might still be a cipher system, with the apparent characteristics of a code system. Upon closer examination, it might be possible to disprove a code system, based on the nonappearance of certain other characteristics that should be present in a code system.

(2) If a cryptogram or a set of cryptograms contain only the letters A through O in the cipher text, all that can be said initially is that only 15 letters are present in the encrypted text, and that the system must be one of substitution, either cipher or code. If a cipher, then the system must of course be a multiliteral system (including perhaps a mixed-length system), not excluding, for example, a digraphic system or a code chart. For instance, in the biliteral matrix of Fig. 103, below, the ciphertext units consist only of pairs of consonants, and the plaintext elements include the 26 letters and the 374 most frequent digraphs; thus the system is essentially a digraphic system. Such a system would not be at once recognized as a digraphic system; and if the vowels were used as nulls, the diagnosis of the cryptosystem would be considerably impeded.[18]

	B	C	D	F	G	H	J	K	L	M	N	P	Q	R	S	T	V	W	X	Z
B	A	AA	AB	AC	AD	AE	AF	AG	AH	AI	AK	AL	AM	AN	AO	AP	AR	AS	AT	AU
C	AV	AW	AY	B	BA	BE	BI	BL	BO	BR	BT	BU	BY	C	CA	CC	CE	CH	CI	CK
D	CL	CO	CR	CT	CU	CY	D	DA	DB	DC	DD	DE	DF	DG	DH	DI	DL	DM	DN	DO
F	DP	DQ	DR	DS	DT	DU	DV	DW	DY	E	EA	EB	EC	ED	EE	EF	EG	EH	EI	EJ
G	EL	EM	EN	EO	EP	EQ	ER	ES	ET	EU	EV	EW	EX	EY	EZ	F	FA	FC	FE	FF
H	FI	FL	FO	FR	FS	FT	FU	FY	G	GA	GC	GE	GF	GG	GH	GI	GL	GN	GO	GP
J	GR	GS	GT	GU	GW	H	HA	HB	HC	HD	HE	HF	HI	HL	HM	HN	HO	HR	HS	HT
K	HU	HY	I	IA	IB	IC	ID	IE	IF	IG	IK	IL	IM	IN	IO	IP	IR	IS	IT	IV
L	IX	IZ	J	JA	JE	JO	JU	K	KA	KE	KI	KS	L	LA	LB	LC	LD	LE	LF	LG
M	LI	LL	LM	LN	LO	LP	LR	LS	LT	LU	LV	LW	LY	M	MA	MB	MC	ME	MI	MM
N	MO	MP	MR	MS	MT	MU	MY	N	NA	NB	NC	ND	NE	NF	NG	NH	NI	NK	NL	NM
P	NN	NO	NP	NR	NS	NT	NU	NV	NW	NY	O	OA	OB	OC	OD	OE	OF	OG	OH	OI
Q	OK	OL	OM	ON	OO	OP	OR	OS	OT	OU	OV	OW	OX	OY	P	PA	PE	PF	PH	PI
R	PL	PM	PN	PO	PP	PR	PS	PT	PU	PY	Q	QU	R	RA	RB	RC	RD	RE	RF	RG
S	RH	RI	RL	RM	RN	RO	RP	RR	RS	RT	RU	RV	RW	RY	S	SA	SB	SC	SD	SE
T	SF	SG	SH	SI	SK	SL	SM	SN	SO	SP	SR	SS	ST	SU	SW	SY	T	TA	TB	TC
V	TD	TE	TF	TG	TH	TI	TL	TM	TN	TO	TP	TR	TS	TT	TU	TW	TY	TZ	U	UA
W	UB	UC	UD	UE	UG	UI	UL	UM	UN	UP	UR	US	UT	V	VA	VE	VI	VO	W	WA
X	WE	WH	WI	WL	WN	WO	WR	WY	X	XA	XC	XE	XF	XI	XN	XP	XT	Y	YA	YB
Z	YC	YD	YE	YF	YG	YH	YI	YL	YM	YN	YO	YP	YR	YS	YT	YW	Z	ZA	ZE	ZI

FIGURE 103.

[17] Baudouin (*op. cit.*, Chapter XIV) drew up a sort of check list of the classificatory procedures which an analyst might follow when attempting to diagnose the cryptosystem underlying a particular cryptogram or cryptograms. However, the science of cryptanalytics, being what it is, does not lend itself to successful completion of such diagnostic "check lists." Thus, the one compiled by Baudouin is far from satisfactory and is of no more than academic interest to the present-day practicing cryptanalyst.

[18] For a discussion of how such a system would be attacked from scratch, see par. 10 of Appendix 7.

h. The often extensive and elaborate treatment of the many varieties of cryptosystems within the scope of this text has not been given solely for the sake of the analysis of the particular systems involved, but rather to illustrate the general cryptanalytic techniques which are applied to various problems. In being guided along the lines of "thinking cryptanalytically", the student has been put in a position to analyze successfully many possible variations and modifications of the cryptosystems treated in this text and in the accompanying course of problems. The cryptosystems in this text and accompanying course have been solved for the most part from one or two messages. Naturally, there is a certain amount of artificiality in the examples and messages employed herein. The texts of messages have been manipulated, especially in connection with the accompanying problems, in order to illustrate pedagogical principles and the application of cryptanalytic techniques. In actual practice, instead of the one or two messages, five might be required; or for that matter, fifty or more might be necessary in order to effect a solution. In operational practice, there is frequently a high incidence of garbles which would have a pronounced impact on not only a facile identification of the cryptosystem but also on its subsequent solution. *Speed* is an essential criterion in operational practice; a cryptosystem must be broken and messages read as soon as possible, to be of maximum use to a field commander—messages read six or twelve months after they were sent are hardly of more than historical interest. Nevertheless, when a system is cryptanalyzed for the first time, no matter *when* it is broken it helps maintain cryptologic continuity which is of extreme importance in successful operational practice.[19]

i. The student should now study, if he has not already done so, the various appendices to this text. Through them, he may gain an insight into further aspects of cryptology and topics related to the art of cryptanalysis. Practice on many different ciphers of the types covered in this text will tend to sharpen the wits and give to the student confidence and facility in the cryptanalysis of unknown examples. It is for this reason that a course of problems (Appendix 9) is a necessary adjunct to the study of this text; as was previously mentioned, one month's actual practice in solution is worth a whole year's mere reading of theoretical principles.

j. It may be of assistance to indicate, by means of a graphic outline, the relationship existing among the various cryptographic systems thus far considered. The outline will be augmented with each succeeding text as the different cryptosystems are encountered, and will constitute what is termed a "synoptic chart of cryptography". The synoptic chart for this text (Chart 9) is appended at the end of this chapter. Looking at this chart the student may see that, although it is essentially dichotomous in form, at several levels there appears a sort of cryptographic *tertium quid*—some category (or categories) of cryptosystems which properly belongs at the particular level shown, but which does not directly fit into either of the two *primary* subdivisions already appearing at that level. However, if the student will study the synoptic chart attentively, it will assist him in fixing in mind the manner in which the various systems covered thus far are related to one another, and this will be of benefit in clearing away some of the mental fog or haziness from which he is at first apt to suffer.

k. There remain five more volumes to this series of basic texts on the art of cryptanalysis. *Military Cryptanalytics, Part II,* will deal mainly with periodic polyalphabetic substitution ciphers, including periodic numerical systems, together with an introduction to transposition solution; *Part III* will deal with varieties of aperiodic substitution systems, elementary cipher devices and cryptomechanisms, and will embrace a detailed treatment of cryptomathematics and diagnostic tests in cryptanalysis; *Part IV* will treat transposition and fractionating systems,

---

[19] See also in this connection the remarks in Appendix 7, par. 8.

and combined substitution-transposition systems; *Part V* will treat the reconstruction of codes, and the solution of enciphered code systems; and *Part VI* will treat the solution of representative machine cipher systems. In addition, throughout the five remaining texts there will be interpolated statistical techniques applicable to the systems treated, and information on the application of analytical machines in cryptanalytic problems. The security classification of each succeeding text will vary according to the information contained therein. It is not intended that the student study all six texts; life is too short to become an expert cryptanalyst in all fields of the art. *Parts I* and *II* embrace most of the necessary fundamentals of cryptanalysis; the succeeding four volumes will impart knowledge on more specific advanced categories of systems with which the cryptanalyst may be faced.

VUIFH HAFWN JMVDJ JWHIZ JWNRJ M

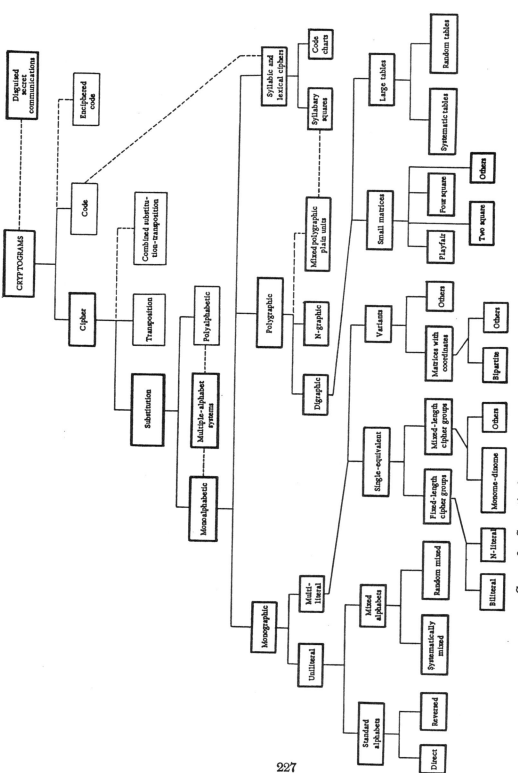

CHART 9. Synoptic chart of cryptography for *Military Cryptanalytics, Part I.*

227